THIRD EDITION

A History of Cambodia

THIRD EDITION

A History of Cambodia

David Chandler

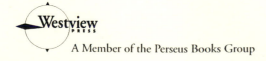

Westview
PRESS

A Member of the Perseus Books Group

Copyright © 2000 by Westview Press, A Member of the Perseus Books Group

Published in 2000 in the United States of America by Westview Press, 5500 Central Avenue, Boulder, Colorado 80301-2877, and in the United Kingdom by Westview Press, 12 Hid's Copse Road, Cumnor Hill, Oxford OX2 9JJ

Find us on the World Wide Web at www.westviewpress.com

Library of Congress Cataloging-in-Publication Data
Chandler, David P.
  A history of Cambodia / David Chandler.—3rd ed.
    p.   cm.
  Includes bibliographical references and index.
  ISBN 0-8133-3511-6 (pb)
  1. Cambodia—History.   I. Title.
DS554.5.C46   2000
959.6—dc21   99-058181

The paper used in this publication meets the requirements of the American National Standard for Permanence of Paper for Printed Library Materials Z39.48-1984.

For Liz, Maggie, and Tom

Contents

12 Revolution in Cambodia   **209**

13 Cambodia Since 1979   **227**

Illustrations

Preface

I began studying Cambodia forty years ago when I was enrolled as a student of Khmer at the Foreign Service Institute in Washington, D.C. Over the years that followed I contracted a multitude of intellectual debts, which it's a pleasure to acknowledge here. Since I began my research for the first edition of this book in 1977, many people have helped me to maneuver what I have written into print. I am grateful to them all.

Chapters 6–13 are based in part on my research with primary sources. Chapters 6 and 7 are drawn largely from my doctoral dissertation, *Cambodia Before the French: Politics in a Tributary Kingdom, 1794–1847* (Ann Arbor, 1974). Chapters 8 and 9 reflect archival work I carried out in Aix-en-Provence and Paris in 1977, 1983, and 1986. Much of the material in Chapter 10 can also be traced to these archival forays. Of the chapters written for the second edition, Chapters 11 and 12 benefited from interviews I carried out between 1986 and 1998, from unpublished materials, and from documents released by the U.S. State Department under the provisions of the Freedom of Information Act. Chapter 13, expanded for the third edition, draws on documentary material from several sources and on information collected during several visits to Cambodia between 1990 and 1999.

The first five chapters, on the other hand, rely heavily on secondary materials. My debt to the writings of L. P. Briggs, George Coedes, Claude Jacques, Michael Vickery, and my colleague Ian Mabbett should be evident from the notes. The material in Chapters 2 and 5 owes much to Vickery's pioneering work. Chapter 5 was further enriched by the insights of Ashley Thompson and Claude Jacques as well as by the invaluable recent research of Saveros Pou, Khin Sok, and Mak Phoeun.

Ben Kiernan and Ian Mabbett read the first edition in draft and suggested several improvements. Kate Frieson made helpful comments on the chapters written for the second edition, and the suggestions for improvement made by my wife, Susan, on all three versions of the text were always persuasive. For the third edition, I'm especially grateful for help from Steve Heder, Claude Jacques, Judy Ledgerwood, Miriam Stark, and Youk Chhang. This new edition, like the earlier ones, is dedicated to our children. I'm grateful, finally, to my successive editors at Westview— Mervyn Adams Seldon, Susan McEachern, Deborah Lynes, Carol Jones,

Michelle Trader, and Christine Arden—for their comments, encourage-ment, and support. Nguyen van Hung made the translations from Viet-namese in Chapters 6 and 7; translations from French, Khmer, and Thai, unless otherwise noted, are my own.

A major intellectual influence that may be perceptible in the book is that of the late Paul Mus, whose insights into Southeast Asian society and culture illuminated my first two years of graduate study. Other teachers, students, and friends have also made important contributions along the way. These include the late Harry Benda, May Ebihara, Robert Elson, Kate Frieson, Steve Heder, Charles F. Keyes, Ben Kiernan, J. D. Legge, David Marr, David Joel Steinberg, John Tully, Alexander Wood-side, and David Wyatt. The portions of the book dealing with the Khmer Rouge also gained from my discussions over the years with Richard Arant, David Ashley, Youk Chhang, Alexander Hinton, Christophe Peschoux, Nate Thayer, and Serge Thion.

I'm grateful for access to the facilities of Harvard University, where I began my research for the book in 1977, and to those of Cornell Univer-sity, which I visited on several occasions between 1977 and 1999. Staff members of the French colonial archives in Aix-en-Provence were ex-tremely helpful when I worked there in 1977 and 1986. For many years I was assisted ably and often by the interlibrary loan personnel of the Monash University Library. And in 1998–1999, while preparing the third edition, I drew on the ample library holdings of Georgetown University, the University of Wisconsin, and the University of Oregon.

In other publications, I have recorded my gratitude to Cambodian friends in 1960–1962, 1970, and 1971. Few of them survived the holocaust of the 1970s, and it's appropriate to record my gratitude to them once again, singling out Long Anar, Chhea Ton, the villagers of Krol Ko ham-let, Kompong Speu, and the late Dik Keam, formerly librarian of the In-stitut Bouddhique, who was murdered near Kratie as a "class enemy" in 1977.

Photographs were supplied by Claude Jacques (one photo), Walter Veit (four photos), Jacques Nepote (one photo), Christine Drummond (one photo), Roger Smith (one photo), Serge Thion (one photo), Brian L. Stevens (one photo), Kelvin Rowley (one photo), Stephen Randall (one photo), Nate Thayer (one photo), and James Gerrand (one photo). The re-maining photographs are my own.

Any mistakes that have slipped past so many skilled and helpful peo-ple are obviously mine.

David Chandler
Washington, D.C., November 1999

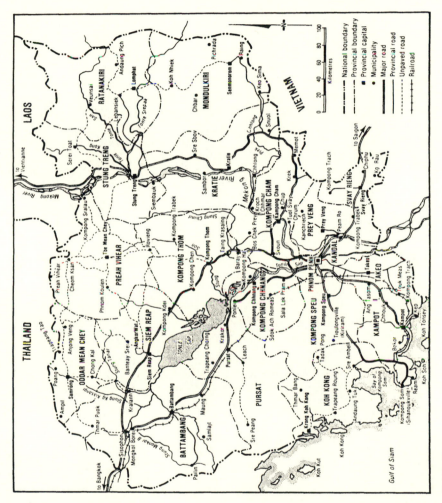

Cambodia

CHAPTER 1

Introduction

This book will examine roughly two thousand years of Cambodian history. Chapters 2 through 5 carry the story up to the end of the eighteenth century; the remaining chapters deal with the period between 1800 and 1999. One reason for writing the book has been to close a gap in the historiography of Southeast Asia. No lengthy history of Cambodia has appeared since the publication of Adhémard Leclère's *Histoire du Cambodge* in 1914.[1] Subsequent surveys, in French and English, have limited themselves to the study of particular eras or have relied primarily on secondary sources.[2] Over the last sixty years or so, moreover, many of Leclère's hypotheses and much of his periodization—to say nothing of his style of approach—have been revised by other scholars, weakened by new documents, or altered by archaeological findings. The colonial era has ended and needs examination in terms of preceding history; moreover, the post-Angkorean era, discussed in Chapters 5 through 7, has often been ignored even though it clearly forms a bridge between Angkor and the present. The time has come, in other words, to reexamine the primary sources, to synthesize other people's scholarly work, and to place my own research, concerned mainly with the nineteenth and twentieth centuries, into the framework of a general history, with a nonspecialist audience, as well as undergraduates, in mind.

As it stands, the book examines several themes. One of these has to do with the effects on Cambodian politics and society of the country's location between Thailand and Vietnam. This theme, which is discussed in detail in Chapters 6 and 7, has been crucial only since the second half of the eighteenth century. For nearly two hundred years, the presence of two powerful, antagonistic neighbors forced the Cambodian elite to prefer one or the other or to attempt to neutralize them by appealing to an outside power. Cambodian kings tried both alternatives in the nineteenth century. Sihanouk, Lon Nol, and Pol Pot all attempted only one—the second; the regime of the State of Cambodia (SOC), formerly the People's Republic of Kampuchea, which lasted from 1979 until 1991, committed itself to the patronage of Vietnam. The problem became less crucial in the late 1990s, when Cambodia and Vietnam joined Thailand in the Association of Southeast Asian Nations (ASEAN).

Another theme, really a twentieth-century one, has to do with the relationship of present-day Cambodians to the past. The history of Angkor, after all, was deciphered, restored, and bequeathed to them by their colonial masters. Why had so many forgotten it? What did it mean to have the memories and the grandeur brought back to life, in times of terror and dependence? And in what ways are the post-Angkorean years and the colonial era connected to these earlier periods?

A third theme arises from the pervasiveness of patronage and hierarchical terminology in Cambodian thinking, politics, and social relations. For most of Cambodian history, it seems, people in power were thought (by themselves and nearly everyone else) to be more meritorious than other people. Despite some alterations, this belief remained essentially unchanged between Cambodia's Indianized phase and the onset of Theravada Buddhism.[3] The widespread acceptance of the status quo meant that in Marxist terms, Cambodians went through centuries of mystification. If this is so, and one's identity was so frequently related to subordination, what did "independence" mean?

A final theme, related to the third, springs from the inertia that seems to be characteristic of rural society. Until very recently, alternatives to subsistence agriculture and incremental social improvements of any kind were rarely available to most Cambodians and were in any case rarely sought, as the outcome could be punishment or starvation. In the meantime, crops had to be harvested and families raised as they had been harvested and raised before. The way things had always been done, in the village and the palace, was also seen as the way things should be done. Clearly, this attitude suited elite interests and kept the rest of society "in line"; but perhaps because mystification was so widespread, the process may well have been less cynical than we might wish to think. Throughout Cambodian history, in any case, government (or *rajakar*, literally "royal work") was the privilege enjoyed by people freed in some way from the obligation of growing their own food. The governed grew food for them in exchange for their protection.

This conservative cast of mind, perceptible at so many stages of Cambodian history, has led some writers to suggest that Cambodia and its people were "unchanging" and "asleep." This myth of changelessness, on occasion, suited the French administration, as it implied docility; for later observers, there has been something "un-Cambodian" about revolutionary efforts, however misguided and inept, to break into a new kind of life.

The notion of changelessness is a myth or at least an oversimplification of events, but it has persisted for too long among students of Cambodian history and among Cambodians who make a virtue of a conservative point of view. It must be used with caution, especially in this book, for each of the chapters that follow records a major transformation in Cambodian life. The first perceptible one came with the mobilization of population and resources to form an Indianized polity at the start of the Christian era, discussed in Chapter 2. Another followed the concentration of power at Angkor in the ninth and tenth centuries, which is described in Chapter 3. A state emerged that some scholars would see as a classic example of Wittfogel's notion of oriental despotism or of Marx's concept of an Asiatic mode of production.[4] Still another transformation, discussed in Chapter 4, overtook the Khmer when their capital was destroyed by Cham invaders in 1177 and was rebuilt into a Buddhist city by Jayavarman VII, who was a Mahayana Buddhist. Soon after his death, around 1220, still another transformation occurred: the conversion of most Cambodians from a loose-fitting form of Shaivistic Hinduism, with perhaps some Mahayana overtones, to Theravada Buddhism. The implications of these changes are treated in Chapter 5. The abandonment of Angkor two centuries later and the southward drift of Cambodia's demographic center of gravity probably had even more profound effects.

Because the sources are so thin and unreliable, the post-Angkorean period is difficult to study; but it is clear that this era was very different in many ways from its Angkorean forebear. For one thing, the spread of Theravada Buddhism (and its corollary, Thai cultural influence) diminished the importance of brahmanical advisers to the king and broke down the influence of brahmanical families who had crowded around the throne looking for preferment. In Angkorean times, these families had controlled much of the land and manpower around Angkor through their connections with royally sponsored religious foundations. As these foundations were replaced by *wats* (Buddhist temples), the forms of social mobilization that had been in effect at Angkor diminished in importance; so did extensive irrigation. The two or three annual harvests of rice that had been reported at Angkor came to a halt. The elite undoubtedly grew less numerous as a result; at the same time, foreign influences, particularly from the Islamicized regions of Southeast Asia, became apparent at the Cambodian court.

Unfortunately for us, these transformations occurred in a poorly documented era. Through documents, we can examine Cambodian society before and after them, but not while they were taking place. We have no clear idea, for example, why so many people changed religions when they did. Similarly, although there were clearly some economic incentives involved, it is hard to say why (and when) a landholding priestly elite transformed itself into, or was replaced by, an elite more interested in patronage and trade.

In the seventeenth and eighteenth centuries, Cambodia became a victim of its location. Its capital region (Phnom Penh/Udong/Lovek) lay at the eastern edge of the Theravada cultural zone that included Burma and Siam and very close to the expanding frontier of Sinicized Vietnam. The region, in other words, lay along a cultural fault line. This fact affected the thinking and behavior of Cambodia's leaders, drawn into games of realpolitik that they could never expect to win. By the end of the eighteenth century, Cambodia had been devastated by civil wars and invasions from both sides; it was even without a monarch for fifteen years. The early 1800s, discussed in Chapters 6 and 7, formed perhaps the darkest portion of the post-Angkorean era. After a brief taste of independence under King Duang (r. 1848–1860), the kingdom succumbed to French protection. Its rulers may have preferred this state of affairs to Thai hegemony, but French rule soon came to resemble the "civilizing mission" imposed upon them earlier in the century by the Vietnamese.

The economic, social, and cultural changes of the colonial period in Cambodia resembled those that occurred elsewhere in Southeast Asia, but they were less intense than those that affected Java, Burma, and the Philippines over somewhat longer periods of systematic colonial rule. As in these other colonies, however, the changes that swept Cambodia helped to put together the framework for the Cambodian nation-state that emerged very briefly in 1945 and again in 1953.[5]

The three most obvious transformations in this period, discussed in Chapters 8 and 9, were in foreign trade, communications, and demography. Rice and corn, grown for the first time in large quantities for export, and rubber, grown for the first time altogether, now linked Cambodia with a world outside Southeast Asia. Its economy, never especially strong, became dependent. Nothing altered with political independence; most of Cambodia's foreign exchange throughout the 1950s and 1960s came from earnings on the export of rice, rubber, and corn.

Perhaps the most visible difference between colonial and precolonial Cambodia, however, had to do with communications. By the 1920s, one could travel across Cambodia by car in a couple of days—a journey that had taken months in the nineteenth century. Cambodians began moving around the country by road and rail and found markets for their products opening up. The social changes that accompanied this new freedom of movement were obviously important, although they are hard to document precisely.

Finally, for every Cambodian who had greeted the French (if the image is appropriate) in 1863, there were four to say good-bye. Cambodia's population, estimated at slightly less than a million when the protectorate was declared, had risen to more than four million by 1950. By keeping the kingdom at peace and by introducing some improvements in hygiene the French presided over a demographic revolution that, when it intensified in the 1960s, soon put serious pressures on Cambodian resources.[6]

It is difficult to say how decisive the Japanese occupation of Cambodia was, particularly as the French remained in nominal control until early 1945. With hindsight, however, it is clear that the summer of 1945, when Cambodia was granted independence, had a profound effect on many Cambodian nationalists, both conservative and radical. In the late 1940s, a new political ideology based on resistance rather than cooperation and on independence rather than subordination also took hold among many rural Cambodians, as well as in sectors of the Buddhist clergy and among the educated elite. Some of these people opted very early for a revolutionary alternative to the status quo, occasionally with disastrous effects. These developments in the 1940s and early 1950s, discussed in Chapter 10, have continued as an undertone to Cambodian political ideology ever since.

In March 1970, Cambodia's National Assembly, dominated since 1955 by Cambodia's chief of state, Prince Norodom Sihanouk, decided to remove the prince from power, and several months later, the new government declared that Cambodia had become a republic. This move, which brought to an end over a thousand years of Cambodian kingship, occurred in the context of a Vietnamese Communist invasion, U.S. involvement in the Vietnam War, and a burgeoning civil war inside Cambodia between the government and forces allegedly loyal to Sihanouk. The latter were controlled by the clandestine Communist party of Kampuchea (CPK), led by Saloth Sar, who was known to the world after 1976 as Pol Pot.

The Communists were victorious in 1975, and during the next three years, many of Cambodia's institutions were destroyed or overturned, and the urban population, forcibly exiled from towns and cities, was put to work alongside everybody else (except for soldiers and CPK cadres) as agricultural laborers. The new regime abolished money, markets, formal schooling, Buddhist practices, and private property. In the headlong rush toward a socialist Utopia, over a million Cambodians, or one in seven, died of overwork, malnutrition, and misdiagnosed diseases or were executed.

The regime of Democratic Kampuchea (DK) effectively destroyed itself when its leaders decided in 1977, with Chinese encouragement, to wage war on the Socialist Republic of Vietnam. By that time, economic disaster in the countryside and uncertainty about the loyalty of high-ranking CPK members had led Pol Pot and his colleagues to set in motion purges of the CPK, during which at least fifteen thousand people were executed at the regime's secret prison after interrogation and after providing detailed, but often spurious, confessions of guilt.[7] Tens of thousands of others, especially in the eastern part of the country, were later killed for "supporting" the Vietnamese incursions of 1978. These men and women were said to have "Cambodian bodies and Vietnamese minds." Such actions hastened the collapse of DK and paved the way for yet another transformation, and in 1979, Cambodia, known as the People's Republic of Kampuchea (PRK) and later as the State of Cambodia (SOC), struggled to its feet under Vietnamese protection. For several years, the regime submitted to Vietnamese guidance and control, particularly in the realms of defense, internal security, and foreign relations.

The process of rediscovering and reshaping Cambodia's identity, which is not the same as reconstructing its prerevolutionary appearance, continued into the 1990s and so did yet another transformation, whereby Cambodia today is edging into the wider community of Southeast Asian nations. This process was stalled in the 1980s by repeated United Nations votes that condemned Vietnam's invasion of Cambodia and allowed DK representatives to occupy Cambodia's UN seat. Lacking diplomatic recognition (aside from allies of Vietnam), the PRK was unable to obtain development assistance so the country's economic recovery was slow. Resistance forces, claiming loyalty to Sihanouk, the CPK, and an amorphous middle-class grouping, found sanctuary in Thailand and received political support from the United Nations, spearheaded, ironically, by the United States and China. Throughout the 1980s, Pol Pot's forces, estimated at between twenty thousand and forty thousand armed men and women, also benefited from extensive Chinese military aid.

Given the importance of these successive transformations, and because coherent economic data about Cambodia are so scarce, this book says very little about Cambodia's resources or its economy, except in passing. These have been remarkably consistent over the two millennia to be examined. In early times, discussed in Chapter 2, the cultivation of grain, probably wet rice, supported the people of the Mekong Delta, in the region known to the Chinese as Funan. Chinese accounts tell us that farmers stored water in small, man-made ponds, which they used for bathing and perhaps for irrigation, much as they were to do until the upheavals of the 1970s, when Cambodia's rural economy expanded rapidly and to a large extent broke down. The hydraulic works at Angkor, discussed in Chapter 3, amplified this earlier technology. The relationships between the seasons, water, rice, and subsistence agriculture have remained the same throughout Cambodian history. Supplements to the diet, however, may have changed somewhat. The amount of wild game has undoubtedly decreased, and in the colonial and postcolonial eras, imported and processed items became available. The mainstay supplements, however—fish, roots, locally grown spices—appear to have changed very little from one century to the next.

Until very recently, the same could be said for much of Cambodia's rural technology. Pots, sickles, ox-carts, and cotton cloth—to name only four—appear to have changed little between the twelfth century, when they appeared on bas-reliefs at Angkor, and the 1980s.

A third consistency in the Cambodian economy lies in the field of exports. Until the colonial era, when plantation crops that were grown for export (primarily rubber, pepper, and rice) transformed Cambodia's national economy, the goods Cambodia exported were, for the most part, ones that grew wild in the woods. These included such things as rhinoceros horns, hides, ivory, cardamom, lacquer, and perfumed wood. Because these exports paid for the luxuries imported by the Cambodian elite, it is important to note the symbiosis that existed between woodland populations responsible for gathering these products and the people who had settled in the agricultural plains. This relationship is examined in a nineteenth-century context in Chapter 6.

Another theme of the Cambodian economy is the country's victimization by monsoons. Like many other countries of Southeast Asia, Cambodia has two distinct seasons rather than four. The rainy season, dominated by the southeasterly monsoon, lasts from May to November. The rest of the year is dry. Over the years, rice farmers and administrators have calibrated their activities to the ebb and flow of these conditions. In the wet season, much of Cambodia is under water. As a result, in precolonial times at least, military campaigns almost never began in wet weather; at the same time, because there was little to do in the fields once the rains had started, these months came to be favored by young men who wanted to spend short periods in monasteries as Buddhist monks.

Unlike the other countries of mainland Southeast Asia, Cambodia has no mountain ranges running north to south, providing barriers for east-west penetration. Low ranges of hills mark off its northern frontier and parts of its frontier with Vietnam, but these have never posed serious problems for invaders. Cambodia's vulnerability to attack, especially after the decline of Angkor, is a recurrent feature of its history and a theme of its foreign relations. Conversely, in its periods of greatness, Cambodia expanded easily into the plains of southeastern and central Thailand.

On the other hand, because Cambodia had no deep-water port of its own until the 1950s, overseas commerce reached the Cambodian capital by coming upriver from the China Sea. For this reason, foreign influences, like foreign armies, tended to come overland. The conversion of the kingdom to Theravada Buddhism in the thirteenth and fourteenth centuries, discussed in Chapter 4, is an example of this process of infiltration and osmosis.

The transformations and continuities I have listed came under attack in 1975, when Cambodia's entire historical experience was challenged and discredited by Democratic Kampuchea and the regime worked hard to dissolve continuities, real and imagined, between revolutionary Cambodia and anything that had happened in earlier times.[8] We also have little idea how severe the damage was to rural Cambodian society during the U.S. bombing of 1973, when for six months B-52 bombers from Guam and Thailand dropped nearly twice as many tons of bombs on rural Cambodia as they had dropped on Japan in World War II. To put it mildly, however, the damage to the countryside and the repudiation of history have had important effects on people's memories and behavior.

The complexity of these events should encourage historians to be cautious. It may be too soon and it is certainly very difficult to speak with assurance about Cambodian society in its postrevolutionary phase. But the times that DK spokesmen were accustomed to call "two thousand years of history" remain relevant to recent events and deserve discussion.

CHAPTER 2

The Beginnings of Cambodian History

No one knows for certain how long people have lived in what is now Cambodia, where they came from, or what languages they spoke before writing was introduced, using an Indian-style alphabet, around the third century A.D. Carbon-14 dates from a cave at Laang Spean in northwestern Cambodia, however, suggest that people who knew how to make pots lived in the cave as early as 4200 B.C. Another cave, near the ocean, was inhabited about a thousand years later. Presumably the first Cambodians arrived long before either of these dates; evidence of a more primitive, pebble-working culture has been found in the eastern parts of the country. Skulls and human bones found at Samrong Sen, inhabited since around 1500 B.C., suggest that these prehistoric Cambodians resembled Cambodians today, after account is made for recent infusions of Chinese and Vietnamese blood.[1]

Whether the early people came originally from China, India, or island Southeast Asia is still debated by scholars, and so are theories about waves of different peoples moving through the region in prehistoric times. But recent finds suggest that mainland Southeast Asia had a comparatively sophisticated culture in the prehistoric era; some scholars even attribute the first cultivation of rice and the first bronze-casting to the region. In any case, it is likely that by the beginning of the Christian era the inhabitants of what is now Cambodia spoke languages related to present-day Cambodian, or Khmer. Languages belonging to the Mon-Khmer family are found widely scattered over mainland Southeast Asia, as well as in some of the islands and in parts of India. Modern Vietnamese, although heavily influenced by Chinese, is a distant cousin. It is impossible to say when these languages split off from one another; some linguists believe that the split took place several thou-

9

sand years ago. Unlike the other national languages of mainland South-east Asia, then—aside from Vietnamese—Khmer is not a newcomer to the area. This continuity is one of many that strike students of Cambodia's past. What is interesting about the cave at Laang Spean is not merely that it was inhabited, on and off, for so long—the most recent carbon-14 date from the cave is from the ninth century A.D.—but that the methods used to make pottery found at the earliest level, and the patterns incised on them, have remained unchanged for perhaps six thousand years.

The "changelessness" of Cambodian history was often singled out by the French, who in the nineteenth and twentieth centuries saw themselves as introducing change and civilization to the region. Ironically, this theme was picked up by Pol Pot's revolutionary regime, which claimed that Cambodians were asleep or enslaved for two thousand years. Both points of view ignore a great deal of evidence; arguably, the revolution of the 1970s was the fifth major one that Cambodia has undergone since prehistoric times. But prerevolutionary Cambodians were less contemptuous of tradition than Pol Pot was. "Don't choose a straight path," a Cambodian proverb tells us. "And don't reject a winding one. Choose the path your ancestors have trod." Part of this conservatism, perhaps, is characteristic of a subsistence-oriented society, in which experimentation can lead to famine and in which techniques of getting enough to eat are passed from one generation to the next.

Very little is known about the daily lives of Cambodians in prehistoric times; but we do know that their diet, like the diet of Cambodians today, included a good deal of fish. It seems likely that their houses, from an early date, were raised above the ground and made accessible by means of ladders. Clothing was not especially important; early Chinese accounts refer to the Cambodians as "naked." After about 1000 B.C., perhaps, they lived in fortified villages, often circular in form, similar to those inhabited nowadays by some tribal peoples in Cambodia, Laos, and Vietnam.[2] The Cambodians, like other early inhabitants of the region, had domesticated pigs and water buffalo fairly early, and they grew varieties of rice and root-crops by the so-called slash-and-burn method, common throughout the tropics as well as in medieval Europe. These early people probably passed on many of their customs and beliefs to later inhabitants of the region, although we cannot be sure of this, for there are dangers of reading back into prehistoric and early Cambodia what we can see among so-called primitive tribes or twentieth-century peasants. We cannot be sure that these modern customs have not changed over time. Hairstyles, for example, changed dramatically in Cambodia as recently as the early eighteenth century, and in the 1970s they were changed again by the revolutionary regime.

All the same, it is unlikely that certain elements of Cambodian life and thinking, especially in the countryside, have changed a great deal since Angkorean times (ninth to mid-fifteenth centuries) or even over the last few thousand years. These elements might include the village games played at the lunar new year; the association of ancestor spirits (*nak ta*) with stones, the calendar, and the soil; the belief in waterspirits, or dragons; the idea that tattoos protect the wearer; and the custom of chewing betel, to name a few.

INDIANIZATION

The notion of changelessness dissolves, however, when we discuss the set of revolutionary changes that suffused Cambodia at the beginning of the Christian era. This was the centuries-long phenomenon known as Indianization, whereby elements of Indian culture were absorbed or chosen by the Cambodian people in a process that lasted more than a thousand years.[3] No one knows precisely when the process began or how it worked at different times. All-inclusive theories about it advanced by French and Dutch scholars usually put too little emphasis on the element of local choice; a few writers, on the other hand, have tended to exaggerate its importance. Generally, as George Coedes has remarked, scholars with training in Indian culture emphasize India's "civilizing mission"; those trained in the social sciences stress the indigenous response.[4]

Historians must deal with both sides of the exchange. The process by which a culture changes is complex. When and why did Indian cultural elements come to be preferred to local ones? Which ones were absorbed, revised, or rejected? In discussing Indianization, we encounter the categories that some anthropologists have called "Great" and "Little" Traditions, the first connected with India, Sanskrit, the courts, and Hinduism, and the other with "Cambodia," Khmer, villages, and folk-religion. In the Cambodian case, these categories are not especially useful. We cannot play down the Great Tradition in Cambodian village life; where do the customs of monastic Buddhism fit in, for example, or Little Tradition activities, like ancestor worship and folk stories, at the court? Village wisdom always penetrated the court, and princely values, enshrined in Hindu epics and Buddhist legends, or *jataka* tales, penetrated village life. The two aspects of society were complementary and antagonistic at different times.

Nevertheless, the process of Indianization made Cambodia an Indian-seeming place. In the nineteenth century, for example, many Cambodian peasants still wore recognizably Indian costumes and behaved more like Indians than they did like their closest neighbors, the Vietnamese. Cambodians ate with spoons and fingers, for example, and carried goods on their heads; they wore turbans rather than straw hats and skirts rather than trousers. Musical instruments, jewelry, and manuscripts were also Indian in style. It is possible also that cattleraising in Cambodia had been introduced by Indians at a relatively early date; it is unknown, to a great extent, in the rest of mainland Southeast Asia.

Trade between prehistoric India and Cambodia probably began long before India itself was Sanskritized. In fact, as Paul Mus has suggested, Cambodia and southern India, as well as what is now Bengal, probably shared the culture of "monsoon Asia," which emphasized the role played by ancestral, tutelary deities in the agricultural cycle.[5] These were often located for ritual purposes in stones that naturally resembled phalluses or were carved to look like them. Sacrifices to the stones, it was thought, ensured the fertility of the soil. Cults like this were not confined to Asia, but it is useful to see, as Mus has, that an Indian traveler coming across them in Cambodia would "recognize" them as Indian cults honoring the god Siva or one of his consorts. Similarly, a Cambodian visiting India, or hearing about it, would see some of his own cults in those that honored the Indian god.

During the first five hundred years or so of the Christian era, India provided Cambodia with a writing system, a pantheon, meters for poetry, a language (Sanskrit) to write it in, a vocabulary of social hierarchies (not the same as a caste system), Buddhism, the idea of universal kingship, and new ways of looking at politics, sociology, architecture, iconography, astronomy, and aesthetics. Without India, Angkor would never have been built; yet Angkor was never an Indian city, any more than medieval Paris was a Roman one.

Indian influence in Cambodia was not imposed by colonization or by force. Indian troops never invaded Cambodia, and if individual Indians enjoyed high status, as they often did, it was partly by convincing local people that they deserved it. When Indians came, at first as adventurers perhaps, they were absorbed into the local population. Indianization never produced the identity crisis among Cambodians that Chinese colonization and cultural imperialism produced among the Vietnamese. Cambodia never resisted India, which was not, in any case, a unified state; moreover, unlike Vietnam vis-à-vis Han China, Cambodia never looked to India—after the fourteenth century or so—for ideas, approval, or advice. Indianization gave a format and a language to elite Cambodian life, but it was not narrowly political. Moreover, the hierarchical arrangements that came to characterize the language and behavior of the Cambodian elite, although owing something to Indian models, never sprang from a recognizable caste system affecting Cambodian society as a whole. At the village level, caste considerations never took root; what resembled a caste "system" at the medieval Cambodian court, moreover, probably was little more than a set of ritual procedures that showed respect for Indian traditions.[6] Another by-product of Indianization in Cambodia is that Cambodian nationalism, unlike its Vietnamese counterpart, has not generally pictured itself as the product of a struggle against foreign invaders and advice. Instead, national identity, until recent times, was seen as the sum of social arrangements in effect inside Cambodia. Indianization and elements of life that may be traceable to India were merely components of the sum. The fact that they came from India (just as our polysyllables so often came from Greece and Rome) was not considered a reason for alarm.

Like many Southeast Asian countries, Cambodia has a legend that traces its origin back to the marriage of a foreigner and a dragon-princess, or *nagi*, whose father was the king of a waterlogged country. According to one version of the myth, a brahman named Kaundinya, armed with a magical bow, appeared one day off the shore of Cambodia; a dragon-princess paddled out to meet him. Kaundinya shot an arrow into her boat; this action frightened the princess into marrying him. Before the marriage, Kaundinya gave her clothes to wear, and in exchange, her father, the dragon-king, "enlarged the possessions of his son-in-law by drinking up the water that covered the country. He later built them a capital, and changed the name of the country to 'Kambuja.'"[7]

This myth is of Indian origin, as is the name "Kambuja," and perhaps it describes some obscure confrontation that had occurred in the Aryanization of southern India rather than an event in Southeast Asia. But even if it is useless as a "fact," it offers us an interesting starting point for Cambodian history. In the myth, Cambodians see themselves as the offspring of a marriage between "culture" and "nature." Kaundinya's acceptance by his father-in-law, who drains the kingdom for him, is crucial to his success. This idea would have been familiar to Cambodians, for a prospective bridegroom often had to gain his in-laws' approval by living with them before his marriage. In the myth, the local people (i.e., the dragons) respect the brahman and in his honor give the kingdom an Indian name (which first appears in a Cambodian inscription in the ninth century A.D.).[8] Later on, monarchs would trace their ancestry to this mythical pair, who represented, among other things, a "marriage" between the sun and the moon. To be a legitimate king, it seems, one had to be a Cambodian and an Indian at the same time.

"FUNAN"

The Kaundinya myth was recorded by Chinese officials, and indeed, for the first few centuries of the Christian era, written sources for Cambodian history are almost entirely Chinese. These are supplemented by archaeological findings, especially from the remains of an ancient trading city located near the modern Vietnamese village of Oc-Eo in the Mekong Delta, excavated during World War II by an archaeological team supervised by Louis Malleret.[9]

Roman coins found at the site date from the second and third centuries A.D., and some Indian artifacts, including seals and jewelry, can be dated to the same period. Malleret believed that the port declined in importance in the fourth century. No contemporary records about it have survived, however, and we do not know what it was called by its inhabitants.[10] Because of its location, and some of the artifacts found at the site, Malleret concluded that the port was used by pilgrims and traders moving between India and China in the first centuries of the Christian era. Its extent suggests that it played an important part in this trade, and its location was ideal for ships hugging the coast and "turning the corner" from or into the South China Sea.[11] The city probably provided warehousing for goods in transit between India and China and was an outlet for products collected from the forested interior of Cambodia and Vietnam.

Until the twentieth century, forest products and precious metals made up the bulk of Cambodia's export trade. These included gold, elephants, ivory, rhinoceros horn, kingfisher feathers, wild spices such as cardamom, and other products such as lacquer, hides, and aromatic wood. Plantation exports such as rubber and pepper were developed in the colonial era; and rice exports, which have made up the bulk of twentieth-century Cambodian foreign trade, were of little use in early times, when nearly everyone in the region produced enough to feed themselves. The point to make about these high-value, low-bulk goods is that they were cultivated or caught by forest people rather than by inhabitants of cities. Many of them probably traveled considerable distances before they reached Oc-Eo, and so did the goods or coins that traders used to pay for them. Oc-Eo, then, may well have been the principal gateway through which Indianization extended into the heartland of Cambodia. There were other gateways, such as the Indianized kingdom of Champa, which developed in the early Christian era along the south-central coast of Vietnam.

Until very recently, many scholars believed that Oc-Eo was the seaport for an important kingdom, identified by Chinese sources as "Funan" and located by George Coedes (using linguistic evidence rather than archaeological findings) near the small hillock known as Ba Phnom, in southeastern Cambodia, east of the Mekong. According to Coedes, "Funan" derives from the old Khmer word for mountain (*bnam*), and he located the ritual center of the kingdom at Ba Phnom. A cult to Siva as a mountain deity existed in Cambodia as early as the fifth century A.D. and may well have been enacted on Ba Phnom. An Indian traveler to China reported: "It is the custom of the country to worship the celestial god Mahesvara [Siva]. This deity regularly descends on Mt. Mo-Tam so that the climate is constantly mild and herbs and trees do not wither."[12]

Paul Wheatley has suggested that the cult originated in southern India and that the mountain was not Ba Phnom but another hillock not far away, in what is now Vietnam.[13] The evidence that either mountain was a cult site is stronger than the evidence that Funan was a major, unified kingdom[14] or that its political center was associated with either hill. What made the place important to the Chinese was that a principality dubbed Funan by the Chinese offered tribute to the Chinese emperor, on an irregular basis, between A.D. 253 and 519. Sanskrit and Khmer inscriptions from a century later are available for study, but these do not provide evidence for a major kingdom. It is possible, nonetheless, that small chiefdoms in Cambodia occasionally banded together and called themselves a kingdom for the purposes of sending tributary goods to China (an ideal occasion for encouraging trade) or of seeking Chinese help against their neighbors. It is also possible that Funan was thought to be a major kingdom because the Chinese wanted it to be one and, later, because French scholars were eager to find a predecessor for the more centralized kingdom of Angkor, which developed in northwestern Cambodia in the ninth century A.D.

Despite their usefulness in many ways, Chinese sources present peculiar problems to the historian, as many of them uncritically repeat data from previous compilations as if they were still true. Nonetheless, Chinese descriptions are often as vivid as this one about Funan:

> The King's dwelling has a double terrace on it. Palisades take the place of walls in fortified places. The houses are covered with leaves of a plant which grows on the edge of the sea. These leaves are six to seven feet long, and take the form of a fish. The king rides mounted on an elephant. His subjects are ugly and black; their hair is frizzy; they wear neither clothing nor shoes. For living, they cultivate the soil; they sow one year, and reap for three. . . . These barbarians are not without their own history books; they even have archives for their texts.[15]

There is evidence that the major step during the Funan period toward the integration of the small, dry-rice-growing and root-cultivating principalities, whose people worshiped Siva, with hunting and gathering societies inland from Oc-Eo was the introduction, perhaps as late as A.D. 500, of systematic irrigation; drainage probably came earlier. We have seen in the Kaundinya myth that drainage was attributed to the good offices of a dragon-king. But the most important passage related to this innovation,

and to Indianization, is a Chinese one, which appears at first to be a gar-
bled version of the original myth:

> Then the kingdom was ruled by a brahman named Kaundinya. A spirit an-
> nounced to him that he would be called upon to govern Funan, so he trav-
> elled there . . . and the people of Funan came out to meet him, and pro-
> claimed him king. He changed the institutions to follow Indian models. He
> wanted his subjects to stop digging wells, and to dig reservoirs in the future;
> several dozen families could then unite and use one of these in common.[16]

Seventh- and eighth-century inscriptions speak of rice fields adjacent to
religious foundations, suggestive of irrigated rice, and aerial photographs
of the Mekong Delta show silted-over canals, which may have been used
for drainage as well as transport.[17] If irrigation was widely used before
the ninth century A.D., it was not on an especially large scale and, with the
exception of the seventh-century agglomeration of Isanapura (now
known as Sambor Prei Kuk, near Kompong Thom), the village was the
most characteristic unit of pre-Angkorean Cambodia. Indeed, Isanapura
probably consisted of villages grouped around a common ritual center,
whose stone buildings have survived. Even after the introduction of wet-
rice technology, perhaps in the fourth or fifth century A.D., the area under
irrigation—that is, under control of supravillage organizations—was
never very great. Moreover, it seems likely that most villagers in the hinterland continued to grow dry rice and to cultivate roots, supplementing
their diet by hunting and gathering, long after irrigation and wet-rice cultivation had taken hold in comparatively Hinduized communities.

People, rather than land per se, are needed to cultivate wet rice. With
this fact in mind, as well as the low density of the population in the entire area (always excepting Java, Bali, and the Red River Delta in Vietnam), it is easy to see why throughout Southeast Asian history overlord-
ship and power were so often thought of and pursued in terms of
controlling people rather than land. There were periods of Cambodian
history, under Jayavarman VII in the twelfth century, for example, when
far-flung territorial control was an important part of a king's prestige.
Nonetheless, territory per se (mere forest in most cases) was never as important as people.

Indeed, the notion of alienable ownership of land, as distinct from land
use, does not seem to have developed in pre-Angkorean Cambodia.
Land left fallow for three years reverted to state control. The king, theoretically at least, was the lord of all the land in the kingdom, which meant
that he could reward people with the right to use it. Many of the Cambodian-language inscriptions from the Angkorean period, as we shall see,
dealt with complicated disputes about access to land and labor resources.

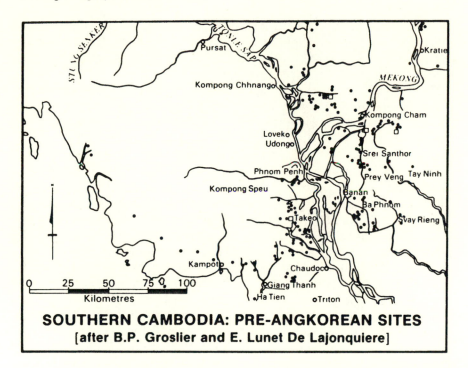

SOUTHERN CAMBODIA: PRE-ANGKOREAN SITES
[after B.P. Groslier and E. Lunet De Lajonquiere]

The record of inscriptions and, by inference, of architectural remains from the first eight centuries A.D. fails to provide evidence of large-scale unified kingdoms on Cambodian soil and—aside from Angkor Borei and, to a lesser extent, Isanapura—very little evidence of the development of urban centers. There seems to have been some continuity among members of the elite, traceable in part to their tendency to marry among themselves. At the same time, it seems likely that Cambodia, like much of the rest of early Southeast Asia, contained a collection of small states, each equipped with a court and an elite, and that these segments had entourages, or "strengths" of people, growing food for them who could also be called upon to fight. Presumably, these states traded among themselves and raided each other, particularly for slaves. It seems likely also that each "king," when undisturbed (or when disturbing others), thought of himself as a universal monarch, benefiting from Indian teachers, as well as a local chieftain, performing identifiable Cambodian tasks.

Leadership was measured to a large extent by skills in rival performance and perhaps by prowess, which in turn was measured by success in battle, by the ability to attract a following, and by the provision of protection. As J.D.M. Derrett has pointed out, protection, along with rainfall, is the sine qua non of peasant society: protection from enemies, from

rival overlords, from the forces of nature.[18] In recognition of this necessity, overlords in the time of Funan and throughout Cambodian history
often included in their reign-names the suffix *varman* (originally "armor";
hence, "protection").

The overlords themselves thought that they could not live without supernatural protection, and most of them sought this, in part, through
their devotion to Siva. Here they were assisted, for a time at least, by a
group of Indian brahmans, the so-called *pasuputa*, who enjoyed a vogue
in India and elsewhere in Southeast Asia around the fifth and sixth centuries A.D.[19] These wandering ascetics preached that personal devotions
to Siva were more rewarding than meticulous attention to brahmanical
rituals or to the law of destiny, or *karma*. Technically, an overlord's devotion did not require the intercession of the *pasuputa*, and some of them
presumably did without it. In any case, these self-made Hindus were
perceived, and saw themselves, as superior men, vehicles of Siva, the god
who "ceaselessly descended" onto the holy mountain. The transmission
of Siva's potency via the overlord and his ritual acts to the people and the
soil was an important source of cohesiveness in Cambodian society.[20] It
has also been a source of continuity. As late as 1877, human sacrifices to
a consort of Siva were conducted at Ba Phnom at the beginning of the
agricultural year. Like those described in fifth-century Chinese sources,
these had the objective of transmitting fertility to the region, and like the
Chinese rituals, they were sponsored by local officials.[21]

In the Funan era, Buddhism also flourished in Cambodia, and the Buddhist concept of merit, which until very recently suffused Cambodian
thinking about society, resembles, in some ways, the notions of prowess
and salvation just discussed. In both schemes of thought, power and ability were seen—especially by those who did not have them—as rewards
for virtuous behavior in previous lives. The loss, diminution, or absence
of power, moreover, revealed to people that a previous existence had
been in some way flawed. A person's status in society, therefore, was pro-
grammed by performance in the past, and one's behavior here and now
determined where one would stand when one returned to life. To improve personal status, then, one could accumulate merit by performing
virtuous acts, such as subsidizing a temple or being generous to monks,
donating a gilded image of a god, or financing religious festivals. Acts
like these were thought to redeem the person sponsoring them. As we
shall see, the great temples at Angkor were also thought of as redemptive
gestures of this kind, a bargain struck by kings with their immediate ancestors and, through them, with the gods. No one at the time, or later,
could see if the bargains were a success, but the thought of neglecting to
make them, especially when the afterlife meant a return to earth, occurred seldom, if at all.

The notions of "patron," "client," and "entourage" become important during later stages of Cambodian history—they are useful keys to nineteenth-century Cambodian life—but it would be dangerous to assume that precisely similar arrangements were in effect in Cambodia in the sixth and seventh centuries A.D. We do not know how overlords came to power, for example, or how they recruited followers. We do not know what made followers linger in their service, or what the services entailed. But the evidence suggests that we can describe pre-Angkorean society in Cambodia as an aggregation of leaders and followers, occupying spaces of territory and spaces in society that were thought about in terms of centers and peripheries, corresponding to the Indian concept of mandalas. With such a multiplicity of centers, Cambodia was decentralized; segments of what we would call "society" (i.e., the total of the aggregations) acted independently of each other or were related in sporadic ways.

Things were not quite so simple, however. Localized religious cults, like the ones Evéline Porée-Maspero and others examined in Cambodia in the 1940s and 1950s,[22] generally stressed the welfare of the community rather than that of the individual, for without communities to perform the work, irrigated rice cannot be grown. Rural life requires alliances. The human sacrifices at Ba Phnom were one example of this communal orientation. Others included the complex of rituals still ushering in the agricultural year in the 1990s (the sacred furrow, the towers of sand, and so forth); the royal cults that in effect negotiate with the dead for the welfare of the kingdom; and the boat races that take place in flooded rivers at the end of planting. Although these cults at first appear to be antagonistic to each other (the Great and Little Traditions once again), in fact they were complementary.

Because genealogies were not maintained in Cambodia, except among the elite, the *nak ta,* or ancestor people, had no family names. They thus became the symbolic ancestors of people in a particular place, or by dying in a place they came to patronize its soil. *Nak ta* in inhabited sites could be spoken to and tamed; those in the forest or in abandoned places were thought to be more powerful and more malignant. As a place was inhabited, over the years ancestral traditions gathered around it, although seldom to the same extent as in China or Vietnam.[23] The pre-Angkorean record is almost silent about *nak ta,* but we can assert, by reading back from modern data, that a confrontation between Hindu and local beliefs was rarer than a blending of the two.

The tendency to syncretize, in fact, was noted by early Chinese visitors. The passage that refers to Siva's continuous descent onto Mt. Mo-Tam, for example, also mentions a *bodhisattva,* or Buddha-to-be, that was held in reverence at the time. Occasionally, two Indian gods were blended with each other, as Siva did with Vishnu to form Harihara, a composite deity much favored by Angkorean kings. By combining the attributes of Siva, the creator and destroyer of worlds, with those of Vishnu, the preserver, Harihara provided a range of inspiration and displayed an ideal monarch's ability to hold contradictory forces in balance.

The process of blending different religions meant that here and there local spirits received the names of Indian gods, just as localized Greek and Roman deities were renamed in the early years of Christianity. Hindu temples also were often built near sites favored by pre-Indian celebrations; there are Neolithic remains underneath the palace at Angkor.[24] What was being stressed at times like this was the continuity of habitation and the continuity of sacredness—ideas in themselves with deep roots in Cambodian culture. If ancestors became Indian gods in times of centralization and prosperity, the gods became ancestors again when the rationale for Hinduism and its priestly supporters diminished or disappeared. Thus at Angkor, and in Cham sites in Vietnam studied in the 1930s by Paul Mus, Indian images and temples were worshiped in quite recent times—not as emanations from "India" but as mysterious products of the *nak ta*.[25] This is partly because the literature of the Cham and Cambodian elites, which was used to explain and justify the images and temples, had disappeared or could no longer be deciphered, while the language that village people used in their religious lives remained to a large extent unchanged from the pre-Indian era to colonial times.

The most enduring cult, as Mus has shown, was the cult of the lingam, or stone phallus. This widely diffused motif, and the cults associated with it, exemplified links between ancestor spirits, the soil where they and the lingam "grew," and the fertility of nearby soil for agricultural use. Because of the territorial aspect of the cult (a lingam could be moved from place to place, ceremoniously, but was potent in only one place at a time) and the notion that the lingam was a patron of a community, it was closely supervised by local overlords and, in the Angkorean era, by the king. As early as the fifth century A.D., a cult honoring a mountain god at the hill of Lingaparvata in southern Laos—nowadays known as Wat Ph'u—involved human sacrifices; the site was notable because it contained an enormous natural lingam, some 18 meters (59 feet) high.[26] Lingaparvata, like Ba Phnom, was patronized as an "ancestral" site by several Angkorean kings.

The period of Funan, then, which lasted until the sixth century A.D., was one in which Cambodia's political center of gravity was located south and east of present-day Phnom Penh. During this period, trade between India and China was intense, and one of the principal components of this trade was Buddhist religious objects. Local religious practices emphasized devotion to Siva, Vishnu, and the Buddha, as well as to minor Hindu deities. Politics centered on villages and groups of villages, rather than on a tightly organized kingdom; irrigated rice allowed for surpluses and for some social differentiation, but not as much as developed later on. The main point to stress about the period, from the historian's point of view, is that we know about it from Chinese sources, which tell about local customs, centralization, and commodities for trade. We hear no Cambodian voices, as we do from the seventh century onward in the form of stone inscriptions. After the waning of "Funan," in fact, our sources become richer and harder to use.

GOVERNMENT AND SOCIETY IN EARLY CAMBODIA

The first dated Khmer-language inscription from Cambodia was incised in A.D. 611, with the earliest Sanskrit inscription being carved two years later.[27] There are over a hundred datable inscriptions, in both languages, from the seventh century, and these give us a picture of the way Cambodian society was put together. According to the inscriptions, Cambodian society was divided, informally at least, into those who understood Sanskrit and those who understood only Khmer. For several hundred years, Sanskrit was used in inscriptions that supposedly spoke directly to the gods. Khmer, on the other hand, has always been the language of Cambodian men and women, those who were protected by the gods and descended, as gods did not, from the highly localized *nak ta*. Sanskrit inscriptions, in verse, praise the meritorious actions of kings and the elite, such as building temples, financing monasteries, and offering gifts to brahmans. Some of the speakers trace or doctor their genealogies, as if to cash in on or invent ancestral merit; many praise brahmans at the expense of other segments of the society; and all are fulsome in praise of those in power. Much of the verse, according to Indianists, is highly polished, subtly worded, and well composed, comparing favorably with Sanskrit poetry composed in India at the time.

Khmer inscriptions, on the other hand, are all in prose. They record the founding of temples and the details of temple administration, such as the numbers and names of people attached to a particular foundation. They also give inventories of temple treasures and list the dimensions of rice fields, orchards, and ponds in a temple's jurisdiction. Many of them outline the duties of slaves and set the amount of taxes—payable in labor or in kind—levied to support the temple priests. Usually they close with a curse—always in Khmer—threatening people who neglect, rob, or disrupt the temple in question with punishment over many generations.

A little too neatly, perhaps, the line between Sanskrit and Khmer separates the so-called Great and Little Traditions. On the one hand, there are wealth, poetry, intricacy, wordplay, priests, direct access to the gods—i.e., a language that protects. On the other, there are poverty, prose, straightforward catalogs, slaves, and the world of ordinary people—i.e., a language about what receives protection. Both sets of inscriptions used the same sort of alphabet derived from India and, as a rule, were carved by the same masons. Presumably poets and priests, if they wanted to do so, could read them both. But were they intended to be read? In general, they are accessible enough, carved on temple door posts or on independent steles; probably the texts were also kept on perishable material in archives somewhere else. The reason they were carved at all may be that writing on stone, the medium of the gods, served a special purpose. Stone was not used in secular sites; these, including palaces and ordinary dwellings, were built of wood, bamboo, and other perishable materials. Sanskrit, moreover, was said by the elite to be the language favored by the gods; stone was associated with permanence, which is to say the dead. In incising the stones, Cambodians were speaking, collectively, to their ancestors; the inscriptions themselves, if in Sanskrit, spoke directly to the gods. A curse, or an oath of allegiance, inscribed on stone was thought to be stronger as a result.

Moreover, the juridical aspect of the inscriptions should not be overlooked. Through the recording of land grants on stone, for example, it was thought that beneficiaries would be recognized and protected; similarly, curses (in Khmer) might serve as burglar alarms and preserve the sites from depredations.

The division between Sanskrit and Khmer was also the division between those who grew rice and those who did not. It was everyone's ambition to be "rescued from the mud," but very few succeeded; most of those who did were placed, in Angkorean times, into various *varna*, or caste groupings, which made up perhaps a tenth of the society as a whole. These people included clerks, artisans, concubines, artists, high officials and priests, as well as royal servants, relatives, and soldiers. Because they seldom served as slaves, and only a few of them were important enough to patronize a temple, they appear rarely in Cambodian inscriptions. This gap means, among other things, that we never know the names of the people who designed and carved the magnificent statuary and temples of Angkor. By the seventh century, in fact, the city of Isanapura was already the most extensive complex of brick and stone buildings in all Southeast Asia, built a century ahead of similar constructions in Java. More than a hundred religious constructions have been found. All the same, the presence of these free people somewhere between the summit of society, symbolized by the king's palace and his sacrificial mountain, and the rice fields that surrounded them should not encourage us to call them a "bourgeoisie" or even a "middle class," because the terms are not transferable and our information about them is too sparse.

The connotations of Western-oriented social terms like these bedevil us when we look to other Cambodian social groups. We have already noted that the term "king," or *raja*, probably meant less in Funan than it did in medieval Europe. Another important term, *knjom*—which can be translated as "slave"—seems to have meant something more ambiguous to the Khmer than our word "slave." For one thing, as Judith Jacob has shown, *knjom* was only one of some fourteen categories of slaves in pre-Angkorean Cambodia.[28] They had many levels of social status, different origins, and many kinds of duties. Those toiling in the fields resembled black slaves in the antebellum American South. Others, especially those attached to temples, may have seen themselves as enjoying clerical status. And yet, as all of these groups of people apparently could be bought, sold, and given away and had no freedom to escape, they were not servants either. Many of them were probably bondsmen working off debts contracted by themselves or by their parents. Were they serfs? The question should make us wary of the interchangeability of terms, and recent Communist statements that early Cambodia was "feudal" are inaccurate even when it is clear that the society was exploitative and divided sharply between haves and have-nots. The evidence that connects slaves to *places* is incomplete, although some of them appear to have been attached to certain places for several generations. This suggests hereditary servitude, or a liability to be called on, attached to a place rather than to a particular lord. Some villagers were free to grow their own rice but were not free to move; others appear to have been owned by temples; still others, by members of the elite. Practice and theory seem to have varied from time to time and from place to place; generalizations about Cambodian society in this period are difficult to make.

Evidence from Khmer-language inscriptions suggests that slaves of various kinds made up the majority of the Cambodian population at any given time. Free peasants were liable to calls on their time and energy to perform public works, favors for an overlord, or service to a temple or to serve in wars. Many of them, in fact, were prisoners of war or their descendants.

The slaves themselves pass in and out of Cambodian history as mere names. These are a mélange of Sanskrit and Khmer words. From one inscription to another, they range from respectful references (some *knjom* are referred to by the equivalent of "Mr." or "Ms.," for example) to derogatory ones, in which slaves have names like "dog," "imperfect," "red in the face," and "bad-smelling." By and large, slaves with recognizably Sanskrit names (such as "loves justice," "slave of Siva," or merely "Dharma") tended to have slightly higher status than the others, and many of them may have served as musicians and dancers. Many of their

A ninth-century statue buried in the forest near Kompong Cham. Author's photo, 1962.

names would be recognizable in Cambodia today; the names of flowers, for instance, are still widely used for girls.

Another difference between pre-Angkorean slaves and those of the antebellum United States is that the villages they lived in, the food they ate, and the beliefs they shared were not very different from those found in times of "freedom" (whatever the term meant to a rice farmer at this time) or from those of the masters whom they served. If the *knjom* had been uprooted, they usually came from fairly similar cultures; the gap between the city and the countryside was not yet meaningful or wide. As servants of temples, moreover, many *knjom* participated in rituals that punctuated the year, such as the times when gilded images were washed, clothed, and paraded round a temple, or later on when the eyes of a

Eighth-century statues abandoned in the forest near Kompong Cham. Author's photo, 1962.

Buddha-image were ceremonially "opened." They crowded around royal processions and made decorations for palanquins as these passed through. The *knjom* lived in the vicinity of grandeur. Among themselves, they explained grandeur, in turn, in terms of merit and merit in terms of protection. They saw themselves as engaged, like others in the society, in plotting their own redemption; what better way to do this than to serve the priests who served the temple gods?

We can come to these tentative conclusions by reading back from recent Cambodian life or by studying bas-reliefs, statues, artifacts, and inscriptions. But as almost always in Cambodian history, we write the peasants' words, as it were, without having access to their voices. What would they have said? It is difficult to imagine without asking a second question: To whom would they be talking? Among themselves, of course, most Cambodian peasants are relatively frank and egalitarian, but they take few risks in the presence of outsiders. The peasants' apparent acceptance of superiors has led some scholars to argue for an essential harmoniousness in traditional Cambodian society. But Cambodian history is filled with rebellions and civil wars, and events since 1970 should make us wary of views that insist on Cambodian peasants' natural passivity. In the absence of peasant voices it is almost as hard, all the same, to make a case for persistent tumult as for harmony. Most of the time, there was plenty of cause for both.

Yet pre-Angkorean Cambodia, and perhaps even Angkor itself, was not an integrated despotic state. Instead, it was a collection and a sequence of principalities sharing a despotic language of politics and control. Because the rulers of these principalities all saw themselves as absolute, they were rivals of each other and thus independent. And yet throughout the eighth century (a period about which Chinese sources are silent, for no tribute arrived in China), Cambodia was gradually becoming more politically coherent—in a process masterfully described, using Khmer-language inscriptions, by Michael Vickery. Integration involved increased population, increased wet-rice technology, alterations in patterns of local authority, and apparently random inputs such as victories in war or protracted periods of peace. As Cambodia's center of gravity continued to shift northward, the area of Aninditapura, in the vicinity of present-day Angkor, grew in importance in relation to the principalities along the upper Mekong, at Sambor and elsewhere. The distribution of pre-Angkorean inscriptions indicates that the more populated sections of Cambodia—as in the twentieth century, but not in the Angkorean era— were along the banks of the Mekong and lower Tonle Sap, particularly to the south of present-day Phnom Penh, with other settlements along the upper Mekong near present-day Kratie.

Until quite recently, scholars sought to consolidate this assortment of small kingdoms under the name "Chenla," given to one of them by the Chinese and preserved in nineteenth-century Vietnamese as a name for Cambodia. The Chinese, in fact, distinguished between two "Chenlas," one associated with the Mekong Delta (and known as "water Chenla"), the other ("land Chenla") apparently located somewhere on the upper reaches of the Mekong, perhaps near present-day Wat Ph'u in southern Laos. The Chinese were not averse to exaggerating the importance of the "barbarian" states from which they received tribute. European scholars in the nineteenth and twentieth centuries, perhaps forgetting the multiplicity of kingdoms that had characterized medieval Europe or precolonial Africa, also chose to see Chenla as a centralized successor state to Funan, thus making a neat progression from the earliest of these "mighty" kingdoms to the one concentrated at Angkor.[29]

In a brief and persuasive essay, however, Claude Jacques has crippled the usefulness of this interpretation. In Jacques's words,

Inscriptions give evidence in the Khmer country of a multitude of little realms and princedoms; those which the Chinese called Funan and Zhenla, on grounds unknown so far, were among them and may have been the most important. It seems that some princes managed, sometimes, to take the leadership of a more or less large group of realms; but this situation was to all appearances only temporary.[30]

It is clear nonetheless that by the seventh and eighth centuries A.D., coastal trading states in Cambodia such as Funan (and others like it elsewhere in Southeast Asia) had faded or changed into polities further inland, known in the Cambodian case by the collective term "Chenla." The wealth of these new kingdoms derived primarily from wet-rice agriculture and from the mobilization of manpower rather than from subsistence agriculture and trade. Ideologies from India, which survive today in architecture, sculpture, and inscriptions, seem to have played a prominent role in molding and directing these societies, perhaps because ideas of this hierarchical kind were useful in legitimizing the extraction of surpluses more or less by force. Rituals may have become associated with wealth as time went on, and wealth may have become tied to supernatural skills, in a process of state formation discussed by Michael Vickery and Jonathan Friedman among others.[31] It is impossible, however, to recapture the process from the documents that have survived. What is important in terms of the sweep of Cambodian history is that the geographical and economic shifts of the seventh and eighth centuries reversed themselves in the fourteenth and fifteenth centuries, and just as the first set of changes can be associated with the formation of Angkor in the ninth and tenth centuries, the second set can be associated with the establishment of a less monumental, less ambitious, and somewhat more outward-looking state.

CHAPTER 3

Kingship and Society at Angkor

Scholars usually place the Angkorean period of Cambodian history between A.D. 802 and 1431. In fact, these years mark neither a beginning nor an end. The northwestern part of Cambodia, where the state we know as Angkor (the name derives from the Sanskrit word *nagara*, meaning "city") sprang up in the ninth century, had been inhabited by Khmer-speaking peoples for several hundred years. Moreover, although the city was partially abandoned in the fifteenth century, it was restored as a royal city in the 1570s. More important, one of its major temples, Angkor Wat (i.e., the city-temple), was probably never abandoned by the Khmer, for it still contains Buddhist statuary from every century between the fifteenth and the nineteenth and inscriptions on its walls from as late as 1747.[1] When the Angkor complex was "discovered" by French missionaries and explorers in the 1850s, Angkor Wat contained a prosperous Buddhist monastery inside its walls, tended by more than a thousand hereditary slaves.

The conventional dates are useful all the same, for they mark off Cambodia's period of greatness. At various times in these six hundred years, and only then, Cambodia—known in its own inscriptions as Kambuja-desa—was the mightiest kingdom in Southeast Asia, drawing visitors and tribute from as far away as present-day Burma and Malaysia as well as from what were later to be Thai kingdoms to the west.

SOURCES FOR ANGKOREAN HISTORY

At the same time, these periods of systematic domination were infrequent and relatively short. We know too little about social conditions at this time, moreover, to classify all Cambodian kings as "oriental

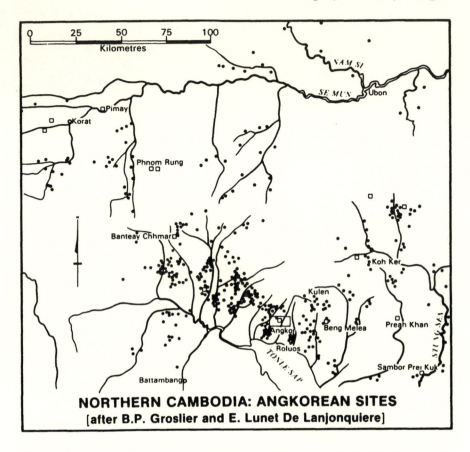

NORTHERN CAMBODIA: ANGKOREAN SITES
[after B.P. Groslier and E. Lunet De Lanjonquiere]

despots." Some of them, as far as we can tell, accomplished little or nothing; others left scores of inscriptions, temples, statues, and public works. Some kings ruled over a centralized, many-layered administration; others seem to have controlled only a few hundred followers. One fact that emerges from studying the kings in order—as L. P. Briggs and George Coedes have done—is the variety of people and regions they were able to command.[2] Seen from the top, where written records emerge, the Angkorean period is easy to generalize about but hard to penetrate. Seen in terms of artistic styles, media, and motifs—including the facility of Cambodian poets in Sanskrit—it is possible to talk about "progress," "development," and "decline" without being able to say why some periods were "progressive" and others "decadent." Seen from the bottom, it is easy to generalize again about continuity between the era and recent times, but we are handicapped by the poverty of our sources.

Sources, indeed, pose major problems. Those connected with Sanskrit inscriptions on the one hand and Khmer-language ones on the other have been discussed in Chapter 2, but it is important to see how the biases of these documents produce a skewed picture of Cambodian society at Angkor. The Sanskrit poems proclaim the grandeur of kings; the Khmer inscriptions exhibit the precision with which jurisdictional squabbles were prosecuted and slaves registered. Here and there, we can use inscriptions to cross-reference official careers; here and there—especially when they provide inventories of temple treasures and personnel—they give us a glimpse of material culture. But it is as if U.S. history had to be reconstructed from obituary notices, wills, deeds, and Fourth of July orations and little else.

These kinds of documents, of course, are meticulously dated. This means that, with some exceptions, the chronological framework of Angkor—particularly for the monarchs who reigned there—has been reconstructed after having been forgotten by the Cambodians themselves. The job of chronological reconstruction was never easy; it occupied much of the career of perhaps the greatest scholar associated with early Southeast Asian history, the French savant George Coedes (1886–1968). Coedes was unwilling to speculate about matters not dealt with by inscriptions and left his successors with a variety of tasks concerning the corpus of Cambodian inscriptions he established.[3]

The inscriptions themselves, being dated, are rooted in time; being parts of permanent buildings, they are rooted in the landscape too. In spite of this, with rare exceptions, the inscriptions are not the place to look for details of life among Cambodia's rural poor, or for clear statements of the political process as it operated at Angkor. Instead, they usually refer to extraordinary events—contracts entered into by people and gods—observed from "above" in poetry or from "below" in prose. The *history* they give us is comparable, in a way, to the lighting and extinction of hundreds of torches, here and there, now and then, over the landscape of eastern mainland Southeast Asia. As each is lighted, we can look around and discern a few details of historical fact: Temple X was dedicated to such and such an Indian god, by so and so, on such and such a date. It had a particular number of slaves attached to it, identified by name and sex, and with children identified in terms of whether they could walk or not. The temple lands stretched east to a stream, south to a small hill, west and north to other landmarks—and then the light goes out. We know little about the way this temple fitted into the context of its time, whether its patrons enjoyed official status, or whether the temple remained in use for months or centuries. In some inscriptions, descendants return to the site to restore it in honor of their ancestors; other temples seem to have lasted only as long as individual patrons did.

The other sources we have for the study of Cambodian history are the temples themselves, and the statues and bas-reliefs they contain, as well as artifacts dating from Angkorean times that have been unearthed throughout Cambodia. These tell us a good deal about the sequence and

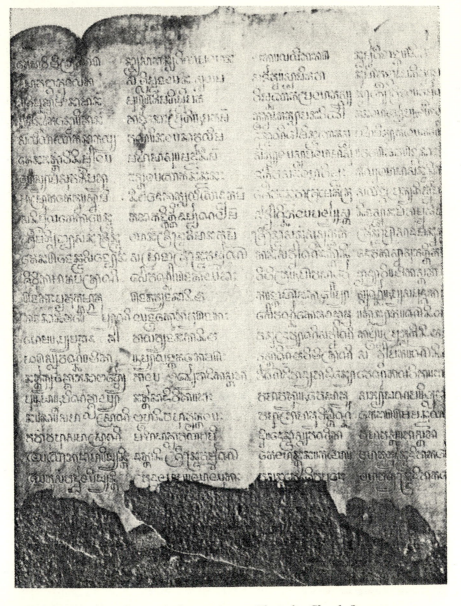

A Cambodian inscription, ninth century A.D. Photo by Claude Jacques.

Guardian spirit, Preah Ko, ninth century. Photo by Walter Veit.

priorities of Cambodian elite religion, about the popularity of certain Indian myths, and about ways in which they reflect the preoccupations of
the elite. They also tell us about fashions in hemlines, hairstyles, and jewelry; these have been used to arrange a chronology of artistic styles. The
bas-reliefs are informative about weapons, armor, and battle tactics, and
those from the thirteenth-century temple-mountain, the Bayon, are a rich
source for details about everyday Cambodian life.[4]

So in addition to deeds, obituary notices, and orations, we can work
with tableaux showing the people of Angkor, for the most part disguised
as mythical figures and with bas-reliefs showing them going about their
daily business. What is missing from our sources are documents that
stand above the others, giving an overall view of the society, or those that
in a sense come from "underneath" it, providing details about such
things as taxes, landownership, life-stories, and folk beliefs.

JAYAVARMAN II AND THE FOUNDING OF ANGKOR

What happened in 802? From the Sdok Kak Thom inscription, incised in
A.D. 1050 in northwestern Cambodia—a major source for Cambodian
chronology and religious history—we learn that in this year the monarch
we call Jayavarman II, residing in the Kulen hills to the north of what
was to become the Angkor complex, participated in a ritual whereby he
became a "universal monarch."[5] The ceremonies also celebrated a cult
with which the inscription is particularly concerned, that of the *devaraja*,
a Sanskrit term that translates as "god king" or "king of the gods," un-
questionably a cult linking the monarch with Siva. The ceremony had apparently been preceded some years earlier by an "auspicious magic rite"
celebrated at the cult site of Ba Phnom in the southeast.[6]

Jayavarman II and his son, Jayavarman III, left no inscriptions of their
own, and this has encouraged scholars until recently to suggest that the
importance granted to these kings as "founders of Angkor" has been ex-
aggerated. The Sdok Kak Thom inscription is primarily concerned with
the sacerdotal family that, for more than two hundred years, officiated at
the *devaraja* celebrations. And yet the biographical details that the inscription provides are very useful. Jayavarman II apparently resided in
five parts of Cambodia at different times in his career. He appears to have
moved from the southeast, near Ba Phnom, to the upper Mekong Basin,
near Sambor, before moving west to occupy Aninditapura, to the north
and east of the Tonle Sap, or Great Lake.

What was Jayavarman doing in these places? Despite all the facts we
know about him—more extensive than for many later kings—there is
still something mysterious about him. Who was he? Where did he come

from? In a persuasive essay, Claude Jacques has argued that he arrived (or returned) from a place called "Java" (perhaps the island of that name, perhaps a kingdom in Sumatra) around A.D. 770, when he was about twenty years old.[7] One of his first actions, according to a tenth-century inscription found in the area of Ba Phnom, was to perform a ceremony that "made it impossible for Java to control holy Cambodia." We do not know what the ceremony involved or why Jayavarman II was impelled to declare his independence at this time and in this way. Coedes has pointed out that although the ceremony clearly preceded the one performed on Mt. Kulen, it could easily have been one of several, in many parts of the kingdom, as Jayavarman moved through them over the next thirty years.

The references are tantalizing and incomplete. Was the ceremony performed at Ba Phnom imported from "Java"? Or was it one that linked Jayavarman II with ancestral spirits at Funan? The ceremony was important enough to be noted in an inscription concerned primarily with other things two centuries later. Given Ba Phnom's enduring importance as a cult site, as recently as the 1940s, the second explanation is tempting, but evidence is lacking to support it.

The rest of Jayavarman's early career has been traced by Jacques and Oliver Wolters.[8] Primarily, it involved a series of military campaigns and the formation of alliances, through marriages and grants of land, with locally powerful people willing to transfer some of their allegiance to a newcomer claiming to be a universal monarch. An undated inscription gives the borders of Jayavarman II's kingdom as being "China, Champa, the ocean, and the land of cardamoms and mangoes"—perhaps located to the west.[9]

The assimilation of the Angkorean region into "Kambuja-desa" occupied more than twenty years. No inscriptions have survived from this period, and temples appear to have been small or made of perishable materials. These undocumented years are crucial all the same, for at this time the related notions of nationhood and kingship, remolded to fit the Cambodian scene, appear to have been gathering force. Both terms should be used with caution. "Nationhood" may have meant little more than having a name (Kambuja-desa) with which to contrast one's fellows with outsiders. Cambodians were insiders, owing their allegiance to a particular "universal" king, whose relation to them resembled Siva's relationship with the other gods. Perhaps both these ideas came in from Java, but they were probably already known from the Indian literature of statecraft, familiar to brahmans known to have been in Cambodia at this time.

The evidence for these suggestions springs from inscriptions carved long after Jayavarman's death. But Wolters and Jacques have argued convincingly that in his progress through Cambodia, the future king welded together an assortment of disparate regions into some sort of self-aware community. Whether or not Jayavarman II succeeded in this task (or even if the task was what he had in mind) is open to question because of the obscurity that surrounds his reign. But it is clear that the kings who came after him honored him as the founder of a kingdom and as the instigator of a particular way of looking at Cambodia that was different from what their own, more provincial ancestors had been able to achieve. Jayavarman II also served a more practical purpose. Cambodian folk thinking has always placed great emphasis on the veneration of ancestors, or *nak ta*, associated with particular places. Once the royal capital of Cambodia came to be at Hariharalaya (present-day Roluos), where Jayavarman II finally settled, subsequent kings came to honor him as a kind of ancestral "founder-spirit" of the sort that every Cambodian village possessed until recently.

Although it is no longer tenable to say that the cult of the *devaraja* was in some way a ritual process by which a king *became* a god, or a "god-king," the evidence of ritual and ideological connections between Cambodian kings and the god Siva is extensive, even if the *devaraja* cult as such may not have played as large a part in the sacralization of Cambodian kingship as the authors of the Sdok Kak Thom inscription would like us to believe. The cult, in other words, was *a* royal cult, rather than *the* definitive one; Hermann Kulke has argued persuasively that the cult involved a statue of Siva, himself *devaraja*, or king of the gods, that was paraded through the streets of Angkor—and other royal capitals at festivals—in remembrance, perhaps, of the role the cult had played at the beginning of the Angkorean period, when Jayavarman II freed Cambodia from Java.[10]

YASOVARMAN AND HIS SUCCESSORS

His son, Jayavarman III, came to the throne young, was an elephant hunter, and died after ruling "wisely," in A.D. 877.[11] The writer who provided this information had a special interest in continuity, after all, with regard to the *devaraja* cult, for the Sdok Kak Thom inscription presumes, perhaps mistakenly, that the ruler who patronized the *devaraja* cult was the legitimate and unique ruler of Cambodia. This may have become the case, especially after the middle of the tenth century, but it is interesting that Jayavarman III's successor, the first to embark on a systematic program of temples and inscriptions at Hariharalaya, made only one muted reference to this predecessor, tracing his own legitimacy to relatives of a wife of Jayavarman II (not Jayavarman III's mother) and to a pair of "kings" about whom nothing else has come to light. Presumably, this was a way of casting his genealogy back beyond Jayavarman's usurpation, thus connecting himself with the pre-Angkorean rulers to enhance his own legitimacy.

In fact, this very king, Indravarman (r. A.D. 877–889), was himself a usurper, which may account for his muddled genealogy. His reign is important because it was the first of many to be marked by a triadic pattern of royal behavior described in the 1930s by the art historian Philippe Stern.[12]

The first phase was to sponsor irrigation works in honor of his subjects and the watery divinities of the soil. During Indravarman's reign, a large reservoir was constructed at Hariharalaya to trap rainwater. It was known as the Indratataka and covered 300 hectares (650 acres). An inscription tells us that as soon as Indravarman became king, he made this promise: "In five days, I will begin to dig."[13] Another purpose of such reservoirs was to indicate the extent of a king's power, and of his alliances with the gods, by re-creating on earth geographical features associated in people's minds with the mythical home of the gods, Mt. Meru, where lakes surround the central mountain. This north Indian fantasy, translated to waterlogged Cambodia, is not devoid of irony; but neither are the Gothic towers in U.S. college towns.

The second phase was for a monarch to honor his parents and his other ancestors by installing statues of these people, usually in the guise of gods. Indravarman sponsored statues of his parents (as well as of others, including his mother's parents and Jayavarman II and his wife, depicted as embodiments of Siva and his consort) in the stuccoed brick temple complex known today as Preah Ko (Sacred Cow).

This charming temple, completed in 879, inaugurated what is now called the Roluos style of Cambodian architecture.[14] In this style, several features that were to become important later—including the custom of enclosing temples in a series of concentric moats and walls—appeared for the first time. The sophistication of carving and the predominance of floral motifs suggest that these skills had been developed earlier by carving wood. Although of modest size in comparison with later temples, Indravarman's monuments of Preah Ko and Bakong—his "temple-mountain"—were far more grandiose, in conception and appearance, than anything that had preceded them and hint at developments in religious ideology and social mobilization for which other evidence is lacking.

An inscription from Preah Ko indicates that Indravarman had become a universal monarch by subduing unspecified contenders: "In battle, which is like a difficult ocean to cross, he raised a pathway, made up of the heads of his arrogant enemies; his own troops passed over on it." The inscription also tells us: "It seems that the creator [Indra] tired of making so many kings, had fashioned this king named Indravarman [literally 'protected by Indra'] to form the joy of the three worlds, uniquely."[15]

Inscriptions far from Roluos suggest that Indravarman commanded, at least briefly, loyalties in northeastern Thailand and the Mekong Delta that confirm his seemingly inflated rhetoric. One of these, carved in honor of one of his teachers (himself a cousin of Jayavarman II), goes even further:

> Ruler of the entire world which he had conquered, established on the slopes of Mt. Meru, he was even steadier than the sun, which occasionally was distant.
>
> Atop the lordly heads of the kings of China, Champa and Yavadvipa [Java?] his reign was like a flawless crown, made from a garland of jasmine flowers.[16]

Statements like this about kings, which may strike us as excessive, were circumscribed by the traditional characteristics of the gods the kings were being made to resemble. A poet's skill was thought to consist of piling up these characteristics and half-concealing some of them behind metaphors, similes, and puns. Just as the verses enumerated ways in which a king was like the god, the temples were catalogs and pictures of the world of the gods—a sort of mirror image. In this sense, the temples can be seen as puns, or plays on words, and mirror images of another world.

The final phase of Indravarman's program, as detected by Philippe Stern, was to erect a temple-mountain. This is now known as the Bakong and took the form of a stepped pyramid. Unlike the reservoir, or the Preah Ko, the Bakong was dedicated to the king himself and was to serve, after his death, as his sarcophagus. Coedes estimated that thirteen Angkorean kings, beginning with Jayavarman II, built such temple-mountains.[17] Not all of them have survived, and those that have can be read in different ways. First, they were planned as duplicates of the mythical mountain, Mt. Meru, which stood north of the Himalayas at the center of the universe. Like Mt. Meru, they were homes for the gods and for deceased worthies—not only kings—who had been assimilated into heaven. They were also tombs, housing the ashes of the king. In some cases—particularly Angkor Wat—they were astronomical observatories as well.[18] In sum, the temples were cities of and for the dead.

Bakong was the first Cambodian temple to be built primarily of stone rather than brick; it was also the first to assume a precisely pyramidal shape. The temple was reconstructed by French archaeologists in the 1930s, but by then, nearly all of its bas-reliefs had disappeared.

Indravarman's son, Yasovarman, who reigned from 889 to about 910, was an important king. His inscriptions and his buildings suggest that he wanted to do more than his father and to focus Cambodia around a royal *city*. Yasodharapura, the "city" of Angkor, bore his name until the fourteenth century.

Yasovarman's first official action appears to have been to endow "a hundred" religious hermitages, equipping each with a royal rest-house and a set of regulations.[19] Twelve nearly identical inscriptions related to these hermitages have been discovered. Two are near Roluos; six of the others are from southeastern Cambodia, where Yasovarman, through his mother, claimed family connections from pre-Angkorean times. The spread of the inscriptions suggests that "Kambuja-desa" was becoming a recognized concept as well as an ideal.

Soon after this, Yasovarman honored his parents by building the four brick temples, now known as Lolei, on an island he built in the middle of his father's reservoir. At the northeast corner of the reservoir—often an honored direction in Cambodian religious thinking[20]—he built a raised highway running northwestward toward the area 16 kilometers (10 miles) away where he planned to establish his capital city. This area now houses the Angkor complex.

Yasovarman's choice of Angkor was probably influenced by his plan to build his own temple-mountain there on the summit of a natural hill. His choices included a hill (Phnom Krom) that was too close to the Tonle Sap and another (Phnom Bok) that was too far away.[21] He constructed small temples on these two hills, however, and built his main temple on the hill known today as Phnom Bakheng (literally, "Mount Mighty Ancestor") and then as *phnom kandal* ("central mountain"), which still lies close to the center of the Angkor complex.

The Sdok Kak Thom inscription tells us that Yasovarman "established the royal city of Sri Yasodharapura and brought the *devaraja* from Hariharalaya to this city. Then he erected a central mountain (*phnom kandal*)."[22] Yasovarman's mountain was not identified as Phnom Bakheng until the 1930s. In conception and execution, it is far more grandiose than any of his father's monuments. Its symbolism has been studied in detail by Jean Filliozat, who has shown that the number of levels, statues, towers, and stairways, when "read" separately and together, correspond to various numbers—particularly 33 and 108—endowed by Indian religion with metaphysical significance; in some cases, pilgrims approaching the monument would be able to catch this allusion by counting the number of towers they could see.[23]

To the east of Phnom Bakheng, Yasovarman built a reservoir, the Yasodharatataka, roughly 6.5 kilometers (4 miles) long and 3 kilometers (2 miles) wide. Along its southern shore he had monasteries built for sects that honored Siva, Vishnu, and the Buddha. Elsewhere throughout his kingdom, he ordered temples built on natural hills, the most notable being Preah Vihear, on the edge of the precipice that nowadays forms part of the frontier between Cambodia and Thailand.[24]

These activities suggest that Yasovarman was able to command a far larger pool of manpower than his predecessors had done. It is likely that many of these were unwilling workers, captured in raids or battles or forced to immigrate from elsewhere in the kingdom. Yasovarman's inscriptions show him to have been a cosmopolitan monarch, aware of the grandeur of Indian civilization and tolerant of different religious beliefs. As usual, however, the sources reveal very little about his political activities, his alliances, or his idiosyncratic ideology. We have tantalizing glimpses of administrative reforms, including evidence that in Yasovarman's legal code, fines were levied in relation to one's ability to pay and a suggestion that taxes were efficiently collected, in kind, throughout the kingdom. But for the most part we must settle for proclamations of his greatness: "He was a lion-man; he tore the enemy with the claws of his grandeur; his teeth were his policies; his eyes were the Veda. His glory was like a roar in all directions; his virtues made up his name."[25] Here as so often in Sanskrit versification, many of the words are deliberate double entendres; the phrase "his eyes were the Veda," for example, plays on the similarity between the verb "to see" and the noun "sacred teachings." These double meanings, as we have seen, appear at many points in Angkorean verse, as well as in the architecture of the temples.

Yasovarman died around 910. He was succeeded by two of his sons in turn. Little is known about them, and by 921 a brother of one of Yasovarman's wives had set up a rival city at Koh Ker, in what is now an inhospitable area about 85 kilometers (60 miles) north of Angkor. The rival began at once to perform kingly actions, such as building a reservoir and beginning work on a temple-mountain. In 928, when the reigning king died at Yasodharapura, the usurper proclaimed himself king with the title Jayavarman IV. Work continued on his temple-mountain, known today as Prasat Thom, until about 930. The temple itself, housing a lingam estimated to have been 18 meters (59 feet) high and about 5 meters (16 feet) in diameter (and probably made of metal, or encased in metal, for it has disappeared), was in fact the highest of the temples erected in Cambodia, with the exception of Angkor Wat.[26] Jayavarman IV's inscriptions boasted that the construction surpassed those of previous kings.

We do not know the roots of his colossal self-esteem, the basis of his following, or what prompted him to shift the capital so far from Yasodharapura. Kulke has argued that Jayavarman's declaring himself king

while the *devaraja* image was still at Yasodharapura weakened the legitimacy of the cult.[27] Jayavarman, in fact, extended it by proclaiming himself and his kingship to be a *portion of the god* housed in his temple-
mountain. In this way, he claimed to draw his legitimacy directly from
Siva, a notion adopted by several later kings after the capital had returned to Yasodharapura.

Although Jayavarman's claims may seem hollow or pompous to us, it
is clear that by force or persuasion he was able to rule at Koh Ker over
large numbers of people, and in considerable splendor, for twenty years.
His influence may well have extended into what is now northeastern
Thailand, where several temples in the Koh Ker style have survived.
After his death in 942, one of his sons reigned briefly, and in 944 one of
his nephews (on his mother's side, a nephew of Yasovarman as well) returned to Yasodharapura as King Rajendravarman II. In the words of a
later inscription, this king "restored the holy city of Yasodharapura, long
deserted, and rendered it superb and charming by erecting houses there
that were ornamented with shining gold, palaces glittering with precious
stones, like the palace of [Indra] on earth."[28]

Although little is known about Rajendravarman's reign, his imitation
of procedures enacted by Yasovarman, such as building a temple honoring his ancestors in the middle of a lake, indicates that he wished to restore Angkorean kingship rather than to start a dynasty of his own or to
connect himself with Jayavarman's dynasty at Koh Ker. Under Rajendravarman, two temple-mountains were built—the Mebon and Pre
Rup—as well as numerous other temples, especially in the north. His
reign appears to have been peaceful, except for a successful campaign
against Champa, and it ushered in a period of prosperity at Angkor that
lasted for almost a hundred years. One aspect of this prosperity is the literary polish of Rajendravarman's Sanskrit inscriptions. One of these, the
Pre Rup stele, runs to almost three hundred stanzas, glorifying Rajendravarman's genealogy, his learning, and his performance as king.[29] Another aspect of his reign was the commercial expansion of the Khmer
kingdom westward into what is now northeastern Thailand; a third was
his public tolerance of Buddhism. Rajendravarman appears to have studied Buddhism himself, and the minister in charge of public works
throughout his reign was a prominent Buddhist.

Rajendravarman died in 968 and was succeeded by his son Jayavarman V, who was still a boy and appears to have spent several years
under the close supervision of relatives and high officials. These men and
their families figure largely in the highly polished inscriptions from his
reign. Perhaps the loveliest of the temples at Angkor, now known as Banteai Srei ("Fortress of Women"), was dedicated at the beginning of the
reign by an official who was later Jayavarman's guru, or tutor.[30] There is

evidence that this delicate, small-scale temple, carved of pinkish sandstone, once served an important urban area. Today it lies half-concealed in light forest about 16 kilometers (10 miles) north of the main Angkor complex; it was discovered by a French surveying party only in 1916.

Although Shaivite like his father and many of the brahmans at the court, Jayavarman V was tolerant of Buddhism, and Buddhist scholarship flourished during his reign. An elegantly written inscription from Wat Sithor in Kompong Cham dating from this period shows how syncretic Buddhist thinking inside Cambodia had already become, fusing elements of Buddhism and Shaivism in a way that led the nineteenth-century Sanskritist Emile Senart to note: "Everywhere one senses a manifest preoccupation to disturb people's habits as little as possible, and to submerge deep differences inside surface similarities."[31] Inscriptions play down Jayavarman V's role as a builder of temple-mountains. His own, the Takeo temple, appears to be unfinished.

Jayavarman V's death in 1001 ushered in a turbulent and destructive period, but by 1003, another king, whose origins are unknown, was reigning at Angkor although the rest of the kingdom was not under his control. In the north, a prince calling himself Suryavarman—later to be king as Suryavarman I—was mentioned in several inscriptions.[32]

Some scholars have argued that neither of these kings was Cambodian by blood. As Michael Vickery has shown, however, Suryavarman was almost certainly a Cambodian member of an elite family with links to the northeastern part of the kingdom.[33] It is intriguing that the blueprint used by Suryavarman to take power in the first decade of the eleventh century so closely resembles the one chosen two centuries before by Jayavarman II. The process involved sporadic warfare as well as the formation of coalitions—by force, marriage, and cajolery—that enabled the pretender to reduce or buy off the power of local chiefs. Vickery suggested that Suryavarman had powerful allies among the priestly families that dominated the government at Angkor, and inscriptions of the time show him moving slowly westward, toward a partly depopulated capital, over a period of years—an indication in itself about the intricacy of his alliances.

Suryavarman won his final battle, an inscription tells us, "from a king surrounded by other kings." One new element in his rise to power is his patronage of Buddhism. There is evidence from hostile inscriptions that as he rose to power he destroyed *vrah*, or religious images,[34] but the meaning of this charge is unclear. Had Suryavarman been a Buddhist, perhaps the destruction would represent iconoclasm pure and simple. It is more likely that it was connected with the delegitimation of certain religious foundations whose patrons had been slow or unwilling to cooperate with him. Another inscription, in fact, suggests that during his reign the king deliberately impoverished members of the elite who had amassed great fortunes and thus represented distinct political threats.

One of Suryavarman's first actions in reaching Yasodharapura was to arrange that an oath of loyalty be sworn to him publicly, by as many as four thousand officials, known as *tamvrac*, at the newly constructed royal palace. The oath has survived in an inscription, the only one of its kind. It states that the officials will be loyal to the king, and adds:

> If all of us who are here in person do not keep this oath with regard to His Majesty, may he still reign long, we ask that he inflict on us royal punishment of all sorts. If we hide ourselves in order not to keep this oath . . . may we be reborn in the thirty-second hell as long as the sun and moon shall last.[35]

The oath closes by asking that those who keep it be awarded religious foundations to administer as well as food for their families—as "recompense due to people who are devoted to their master." Loyalty, in other words, was to be rewarded by the right to extract surpluses from regions under some sort of control by *tamvracs*, who were linked by allegiance to the king. The oath marks an intensification of royal power and also the imposition of a newly constituted, or reconstituted, elite connected to the control of land.

Suryavarman's reign, in fact, was characterized by the intensification of several aspects of kingship, coming at a time when bureaucratic power rivaled or even surpassed the power of the king. Suryavarman expanded the territory under Angkorean control, colonizing the western end of the Tonle Sap with new religious foundations. Further away, in the same direction, he annexed the Theravada Buddhist kingdom of Louvo, centered on present-day Lopburi in central Thailand. He also expanded the irrigation works at Angkor, in a move that suggests that his other policies had increased the population of the city. Because this hydraulic program was linked to increased bureaucratic centralization, it is possible to refer to Suryavarman's reign as one that employed the so-called Asiatic mode of production referred to by Marx and others.

Under Suryavarman, priestly and bureaucratic functions, seldom separate in practice, were institutionalized. Government-sponsored religious foundations became conduits for government revenue and largesse in ways that remain obscure but that probably were connected with the power of priestly-bureaucratic families around the king.

His administration was an urbanizing one. A French scholar, Henri Mestrier du Bourg, has shown that whereas for the preceding three reigns roughly twenty toponyms contained in inscriptions end with the suffix *pura*, or "city" (cf. Singapore, the "lion city"), under Suryavarman the number jumped to forty-seven, further evidence that his rise to power involved herding people into conglomerations from less tightly administered rural areas. Perhaps some of these *pura* were cities in name only, to enhance the prestige of locally based elites, but the evidence for urbanization coincides with other things we know about Suryavarman's reign.[36]

There is also evidence that merchants engaged in local and overseas trade became more active while Suryavarman was king. Throughout Cambodian history, the majority of such people appear to have been, in ethnic terms, outsiders—Chams, Chinese, or Vietnamese—but references to merchants as a group are more frequent in inscriptions dating from Suryavarman's reign. As usual, foreign trade involved the exchange of "wild" goods from forested areas for "civilized" ones, such as cloth or porcelain, but as Kenneth Hall has shown, commodities such as land, rice, buffalo, and slaves were also traded by Cambodians at this time for manufactured or exotic goods from other countries.[37]

The extent to which Suryavarman's reign mobilized bureaucratic and coercive talents to concentrate people at Yasodharapura marked a departure from the past, and the success of his tactics showed subsequent kings that the kingdom could be organized and expanded by forcing its cultivators to work throughout the year. The food needed to support the coercive apparatus (priests, kings, bureaucrats, and armies) could not be supplied by the single annual harvests that previously had sufficed for ordinary people to survive.

In extending his power in this way, Suryavarman enjoyed the advantages of a usurper. He was free to choose and reward his trusted followers, rather than finding himself hemmed in at the beginning of his reign by hangers-on from other courts. At first, governing the country with new officials probably meant that more attention was paid to local issues, for the new officials would still have debts to their clients in the countryside that their successors could ignore.

Suryavarman's successor, Utyadityavarman II (r. 1050–1068), was a devotee of Siva. Guided by a powerful guru, he revived interest in the *devaraja* cult and also revived the custom of building a massive temple-mountain—in his case, the Baphuon—to house the lingam associated with his reign. As an inscription carved under his successor tells us:

> Seeing that in the middle of Jambudvipa, the home of the gods, there rose up a golden mountain, he made a golden mountain in the center of his city, out of emulation. On the summit of this mountain, in a golden temple, shining with celestial brilliance, he set up a Sivalinga made of gold.[38]

A heavenly angel (*thevoda*) from an eleventh-century temple, Thommanon. Author's photo.

ANGKOREAN KINGSHIP

There are three ways of looking at Cambodian kingship in its heyday at
Angkor. One is to study the king's relationship with Siva. Paul Mus, in a
brilliant essay written in 1933,[39] has argued that Siva's popularity in classical Southeast Asia may be traced in large part to his role as an ancestral
spirit, emerging from the earth (and thus from the ancestors) at first "ac-
cidentally," in the form of an outcrop of stone, later purposefully, carved
into the shape of a lingam representing the ancestors, and later still, as
representing the rulers *and* ancestors of a particular place. Siva in this
sense was a literary form of an ancestor spirit, held responsible for fertil-
izing the soil by inducing rain to fall on the region under his jurisdiction.
This aspect of Cambodian kingship (found elsewhere in Southeast Asia,
particularly in Vietnam) endured into the 1960s in the countryside. Siva
and his consort, Uma, were gods to whom sacrifices—buffaloes or
human beings—were addressed because they were thought of as di-
vinizations of what lay under the earth. Intriguingly, when looked at in
this way, the Cambodian king, as a patron of agriculture, resembles a
Chinese emperor far more than a *raja* of traditional India.

The role of a Cambodian king was not merely to bring rain or to keep
everyone's ancestors contentedly at bay. A second way of looking at
Cambodian kingship, through the eyes of the people, is to see it in terms
of the king's repeated and ritual enactment of lordliness and superiority
in battle, sexuality, poetry, possessions, ceremony, and so forth. Seen in
this way, the king was not an earth spirit or a priest but the hero of an Indian epic. This is the view taken in most of the Sanskrit-language inscriptions of Cambodia that praised kings as embodiments of virtue, actors *above* society, associated in many cases with the sky, the sun, Indra,
Vishnu, and Rama rather than with earthly or ancestral forces. As living
superlatives (for each king was seen as "the greatest" rather than as one
of many), kings provided the poets with a point of comparison, a kind of
polestar from which society, flowing outward and downward, metaphorically organized itself, first through the *varnas* near the king and from
then on to free people, villagers, and slaves. The king was superhuman
without being helpful in any practical sense. He was a hero, occupying
the top of society because of his merit and his power.

To members of the Angkorean elite, this reenactment of lordliness had
at least two purposes. The first was to present godlike behavior (e.g.,
building a temple-mountain in imitation of Mt. Meru or defeating
"hordes" of enemies) in order to obtain blessings for the king and the
kingdom. The correct performance of rituals—especially exacting with
regard to timing—was crucial to their efficacy. In this context, the word
"symbol," in a twentieth-century sense, is rather empty. The king be-

lieved in the rituals. So did his advisers. Ceremonies were the vehicles through which his lordliness—in which he also believed—was acted out.

A third way of looking at kingship is in terms of everyday Cambodian life. Sanskrit inscriptions are far less useful here than the Cambodian ones. Although society at Angkor, at first glance, appears to have been almost mechanically organized into strata, the inscriptions point to webs of relationships, responsibilities, and expectations within which everyone appears to have been entangled. Seen in this way, the king, as a polygamist, a patron, and a giver of names, was perhaps the most entangled of them all. Ian Mabbett's thoughtful study of Angkorean kingship shows the range of things a king was expected to do, approve, and know about.[40] These included bestowing titles and emblems on his high officials; granting land and slaves to numerous religious foundations; constructing and maintaining irrigation works; constructing, decorating, and staffing temples; and conducting foreign relations, particularly, in this era, with Champa to the east of the capital and with various tributary states to the north and west. The king was also the court of last appeal, and the inscriptions tell us how obscure squabbles involving landholdings often floated up through the judicial system to reach him—a feature of kingship that endured into the twentieth century.

At the same time (although the inscriptions tell us little about it), to survive, a king had to be a political operator. As Mabbett has pointed out, many Sanskrit inscriptions praise the acumen of kings in terms of their resemblances to Rama or their knowledge of Indian political texts. As political manuals, these learned writings certainly gave Cambodian kings plenty of room for maneuver, but it is in just this area—the day-to-day preferments, quarrels, and decisions—that the inscriptions are of so little help. The *flavor* of life at court in Angkorean times is inaccessible.

The inscriptions are of more assistance in telling us about the other levels of Cambodian society—free people and slaves—but again only at the moments described, recalled, or honored by an inscription. Mabbett's study of slavery at Angkor, which builds on earlier ones by Y. Bongert and A. Chakravarti, shows the bewildering complexity of categories in use for what we would call "slaves" and the bewildering number of tasks that were assigned to them.[41] As suggested in Chapter 2, it is still impossible to sort the terms out either diachronically or across the corpus of inscriptions. There are cases, for example, of "slaves" who owned slaves; "slaves" who married members of the royal family; and "free" people who were disposed of by others, just like slaves. Working back from later periods, one gets the impression that most of the people at Angkor were subjects (*reas*) rather than objects, or free people. They were at the disposition of patrons, who had the right to sell them to other people, and, in many cases, they disposed of "lower" people themselves. In the inscriptions, slaves are listed as commodities.

These people were certainly the "giants" who were once thought to have built Angkor. What can be gleaned about their everyday lives, especially from bas-reliefs, shows us that their tools, clothing, and houses changed little between Angkorean times and the period of the French protectorate. The bas-reliefs also depict their domestic animals, games, and marketing, as well as clowns, shamans, ascetics, and peddlers. We are on less firm ground, however, when we seek to reconstitute their beliefs or the stories they told each other. No popular literature can be traced back to Angkor, and post-Angkorean Cambodia was radically altered by its close association with Thai society and Thai ideas. This absence of written sources makes it difficult to bring the ordinary people of Angkor to life, except through the things they made—reservoirs, temples, statues of stone and bronze, unglazed pottery, and so on. What did a slave at Angkor think about his master? Was a master to be imitated, hated, or revered? How far "down" into the society—or into a person's mind—did Indian ideas, gods, and vocabulary penetrate? There is evidence that the population was more literate in Khmer than it was in Sanskrit, but nothing is known about the way literacy was taught. The picture that emerges is one of familiarity with Indian culture (and perhaps knowledge of occasional Indian visitors as well) among the elite, thinning out in the rest of the society, until in the villages, as in the nineteenth century, we find ancestral spirits given Hindu names and Hindu statues treated as ancestral gods.

As we have seen, Cambodia's imitation of India stopped short of importing the Indian caste system, although, as Mabbett has shown in another penetrating essay,[42] a set of ritual orders using *varna* nomenclature formed part of the king's repertoire of patronage, for caste standing was occasionally bestowed by the monarch on his own clients or on the clients of his associates. Except at the beginning of a dynasty, a Cambodian king, like most Chinese emperors, could rule only by extending networks of patronage and mutual obligations outward from his palace, at first through close associates and family members but becoming diffuse—and more dependent on local power-holders—at the edges of the kingdom. Villagers far from Angkor would probably seldom have known the king's name any more than they did in the early twentieth century, when the following passage was recorded by French ethnographers working among the Cambodian population of southern Vietnam:

> In former times . . . there were no canals, and no paths; there were only forests, with tigers, elephants, and wild buffaloes; no people dared to leave their villages.

For this reason, hardly anyone ever went to the royal city. If anyone ever reached it, by poling his canoe, the others would ask him about it. "What is the king's appearance like? Is he like an ordinary man?" And the traveler, seeing all these ignorant people asking questions, would reply: "The king has an elegant, beautiful appearance, unstained by dust or sweat; he has no scars . . ." but of course often he had never seen the king at all.[43]

ANGKOR WAT

The last years of the eleventh century were ones of turmoil and fragmentation. At different times, two or even three "monarchs" contended for the title of absolute ruler. At the end of the century, however, a new dynasty, which was to last for more than a hundred years, began to rule at Angkor. Little is known about the first two of its kings, Jayavarman VI and his brother, Dharanindravarman I, but their great-nephew, Suryavarman II, under whom Angkor Wat was built, was, like Yasovarman II and Suryavarman I, another unifying monarch. If his inscriptions are to be believed, he gained power while still young after winning a battle against a rival prince: "Leaving the ocean of his army on the field of combat . . . he bounded to the head of the elephant of the enemy king, and killed [him] as a *garuda* on the slope of a mountain might kill a snake."[44]

Suryavarman II was the first king to rule over a unified Cambodian kingdom since Utyadityavarman II's death in the 1060s. The parallels with Suryavarman I, who was probably no relation, are numerous and instructive. Both kings came to power following periods of fragmentation and disorder. They responded to this, once Yasodharapura was in their hands, with vigorous administrative policies, with a pragmatic style of kingship, and by expanding the territory and manpower under their control. Suryavarman II campaigned in the east, against Vietnam and Champa, using mercenaries drawn primarily from tributary areas to the west. He established diplomatic relations with China—the first Angkorean king to do so. Like Suryavarman I, he also sought to separate himself in religious terms from his immediate predecessors. Suryavarman I had done this by his patronage to Buddhism, whereas his namesake chose to exhibit a devotion—unusual for a Cambodian king—to Vishnu. In both cases, innovative or personal policies went along with a legitimizing cluster of actions, which linked the kings with pre-Angkorean pilgrimage sites like Wat Ph'u, with Hindu gurus associated with previous kings, and with artistic styles extending back into the reigns of the people they had managed to overthrow.

Suryavarman II's devotion to Vishnu led him to commission the largest, perhaps the most beautiful, and one of the most mysterious of all the monuments of Angkor—the temple, tomb, and observatory now known as Angkor Wat.[45] The temple was begun at the start of his reign, and it was not completed until after his death, about 1150. There is striking evidence, recently uncovered, that its central statue of Vishnu, long since vanished, was dedicated in July 1131, which was probably Suryavarman's thirty-third birthday—a number with important cosmic significance in Indian religion.

What is so mysterious about the temple? First, it opens to the west, the only major building at Yasodharapura to do so. In addition, its bas-reliefs—more than a mile of them around the outer galleries of the temple—are to be followed by moving in a counterclockwise direction, starting from the northwest quarter. Now the customary way of reading a bas-relief or of walking around a temple was to keep it all on one's right by moving in a clockwise direction, known by the Sanskrit term *pradaksina*. The reverse direction was usually associated with the dead; so was the west, for obvious meteorological reasons. (The word for "west" in modern Khmer also means "sink" or "drown.") Some French scholars argued, therefore, that Angkor Wat, unlike the other temples at Angkor, was primarily a tomb.[46]

The arguments raged in learned journals until 1940, when Coedes proposed that Angkor Wat, like fifteen other royally sponsored Cambodian monuments, be thought of as a temple *and* a tomb. He cited stone receptacles, perhaps sarcophagi, that held part of the "treasure" of these other temples. As for the unusual orientation of Angkor Wat, Coedes suggested that this may have been in honor of Vishnu, Suryavarman's patron-deity, often associated with the west; Angkor Wat is the only temple at Angkor that we know to have been dedicated to him. The twelfth century, in fact, saw a vigorous revival of Vaisnavism, associated with popular religion, on the Indian subcontinent; this revival, it seems, like earlier ones in Indian religion, had repercussions at Angkor.

Between 1940 and the 1970s, little scholarly work was done on Angkor Wat. Scholars and tourists were content to marvel at the artistry of its bas-reliefs (many of them concerned with the prowess of Rama), the delicate and yet overwhelming proportions of the temple, and its continued hold on the imagination of ordinary Cambodians. In the mid-1970s, however, Eleanor Mannika (then Moron) began studying the dimensions of the temple in detail, convinced that these might contain the key to the way the temple had been encoded by the savants who designed it.[47] After determining that the Cambodian measurement used at Angkor, the *hat*, was equivalent to approximately 0.4 meter (1.3 feet), Mannika went on to ask how many *hat* were involved in significant dimensions of the temple, such as the distance between the western entrance (the only one equipped with its own causeway) and the central tower. The distance came to 1,728 *hat*, and three other components of

Angkor Wat, twelfth-century temple dedicated to Vishnu. The largest religious building in the world, its image has appeared on several successive Cambodian flags since 1953. Photo by Walter Veit.

this axis measured, respectively, 1,296, 867, and 439 *hat*. Mannika then argued that these figures correlated to the four "ages," or *yuga*, of Indian thought. The first of these, the Krita Yuga, was a supposedly golden age, lasting 1,728,000 years. The next three ages lasted for 1,296,000, 864,000, and 432,000 years, respectively. The earliest age, therefore, was four times longer than the latest; the second earliest, three times longer; and the third earliest, twice as long. The last age is the Kali Yuga, in which we are living today. At the end of this era, it is believed, the universe will be destroyed, to be rebuilt by Brahma along similar lines, beginning with another golden age.

The fact that the length of these four eras correlates exactly with particular distances along the east-west axis of Angkor Wat suggests that the "code" for the temple is in fact a kind of pun that can be read in terms of time and space. The distances that a person entering the temple will traverse coincide with the eras that the visitor is metaphorically living through en route to the statue of Vishnu in the central tower. Walking forward and away from the west, which is the direction of death, the visitor moves backward into time, approaching the moment when the Indians proposed that time began.

In her research, Mannika also discovered astronomical correlations for ten of the most frequently recurring distances at Angkor Wat. Astronomers working with her found that the siting of the temple was related to the fact that its western gate aligned at sunrise with a small hill to the northeast, Phnom Bok. Moreover, at the summer solstice "an observer . . . standing just in front of the western entrance can see the sunrise directly over the central tower of Angkor Wat."⁴⁸ This day, June 21, marked the beginning of the solar year for Indian astronomers and was sacred to a king whose name, Suryavarman, means "protected by the sun" and who was a devotee of Vishnu.

The close fit of these spatial relationships to notions of cosmic time, and the extraordinary accuracy and symmetry of all the measurements at Angkor, combine to confirm the notion that the temple was in fact a coded religious text that could be read by experts moving along its walkways from one dimension to the next. The learned *pandits* who determined the dimensions of Angkor Wat would have been aware of and would have reveled in its multiplicity of meanings. To those lower down in the society, perhaps, fewer and fewer meanings would be clear. We can assume, however, that even the poorest slaves were astounded to see this enormous temple, probably with gilded towers rising 60 meters (200 feet) above the ground and above the thatched huts of the people who had built it.

Two implications of Mannika's research are that other temples at Angkor might well be studied and decoded and that this decoding can provide insights into religious and astronomical texts that have disappeared but on which the architecture of temples was based.

Suryavarman II probably led a campaign against Vietnam as late as 1150, but the date of his death is unknown. In fact, the period 1145–1180 produced almost no inscriptions, and its history must be re-created from later sources. Suryavarman's successor, perhaps a cousin, reached the throne under mysterious circumstances, probably in a coup d'état. This new king, Dharanindravarman II, appears to have been a fervent Buddhist, although there is a possibility that he never reigned as king at Yasodharapura. Around 1160, he was succeeded by Yasovarman II, whose reign is recalled in one of Jayavarman VII's inscriptions. There Yasovarman is given credit for putting down a mysterious revolt in the northwest. The people who led this revolt, according to the inscription, were neither foreigners nor members of the elite; in bas-reliefs at the temple of Banteai Chhmar, they are depicted as people with animal heads.⁴⁹ Perhaps the revolt, like the Communist rebellion in the 1970s, was a supposedly unthinkable one, organized by the downtrodden segments of the society and by "forest people" against an allegedly unassailable elite.⁵⁰

Instability continued in the 1160s; Yasovarman was assassinated by one of his subordinates, who then declared himself to be king. At this time also, the tributary state of Louvo sent tributary missions to China, suggesting at least partial independence from Angkor. The absence of inscriptions and the questionable legitimacy of rulers reinforce the impression of rapid change.

Perhaps, as B. P. Groslier has suggested, the hydraulic organization of the kingdom had already begun to falter during the reign of Suryavarman II.[51] This system of reservoirs and canals, which guaranteed one harvest a year in dry times and two with adequate rainfall, was the basis of Angkor's rice-oriented agricultural economy and allowed the concentration of large populations in the area. Groslier has suggested that the system reached peak efficiency in the mid-eleventh century, as the hydraulic components of Angkor Wat a hundred years later were much smaller than those around earlier temple-mountains. Indeed, Groslier goes on, under Suryavarman II, for the first time in Cambodian history, hydraulically based cities were built at considerable distances from Angkor—at Beng Melea and Kompong Svay. Perhaps this was done because the water resources in the Angkor region, which had lasted so long, had now been tapped to the limit. Water came from a network of small streams, running south from the hills to the north along the slight slope that extended to the shores of the Tonle Sap. As demands for water increased, these streams were diverted closer and closer to their sources. This process reduced the nutrients that the streams brought to fertilize the Angkorean plain.

Because the slope of the plain is so slight, in dry periods the canals would probably have been nearly stagnant, especially if unstable political conditions, warfare, or epidemics had drawn off the labor normally used to maintain them. Groslier suggested, as other scholars have done, that this increasing stagnation may well have coincided with the appearance of malaria on the Southeast Asian mainland, accelerating the process.[52] Here, as so often, we lack generalized statements about conditions at Angkor or any overall statistics that might tell us about the size and composition of the population, the condition of the hydraulic network at particular times, and the relationship—or lack of it—between particular kings and productive agricultural life.

The close relationship between water management, priesthood, and temple foundations that characterized Angkor somewhat resembles the social organization of ancient Egypt and is similar also to the Maya civilization of medieval Guatemala.[53] In all three cases, grain surpluses (of wheat, rice, or maize) were collected for the benefit of the state and its prevailing ideologues, the priests, who served as patrons of temples and advisers to the kings. In various ways, all three cultures—like the regime of Democratic Kampuchea in the 1970s—were engrossed in what Marx described as the Asiatic mode of production, although, as we have seen, some kings at Angkor, like Suryavarman, were more "Asiatic" than others.[54]

CHAPTER 4

Jayavarman VII and the Crisis of the Thirteenth Century

Between Suryavarman II's death around 1150 and Jayavarman VII's coronation in 1181, only one dated Cambodian inscription has survived. What we know about this period must be filtered through inscriptions carved at Jayavarman's behest, reflecting his view of the world as well as what he wanted people to believe about his early life. Because he was not, apparently, an entirely legitimate contender for the throne, his early years, like those of so many Cambodian founder-kings, are poorly documented.

Jayavarman's biography was pieced together by George Coedes, who saw him as a pinnacle of Cambodian history rather than an aberration.[1] Jayavarman's inscriptions and what they tell us about his point of view make radical departures, in many ways, from what had gone before. Because of this radicalism and grandeur, Jayavarman VII has tended to dominate the historiography of Cambodia, particularly since Coedes's work in the 1930s. His reign, as we shall see, contained several mysteries and contradictions.

Jayavarman appears to have been a first cousin of Suryavarman II and the son of a royal prince, Dharanindravarman, who may have reigned briefly as king and who was certainly a fervent Buddhist. B. P. Groslier has cast doubts on the first of these assertions[2] because it is so poorly documented and because it places Jayavarman in the direct line of succession in a way that makes the facts we know about his life even more difficult to understand.

It seems likely, all the same, that Jayavarman as a young man served in some capacity at Yasovarman's court. From 1166 to 1177, Jayavarman appears to have lived away from Angkor, perhaps in the vicinity of the temple now known as the Preah Khan in Kompong Svay. A portrait statue of him, manifestly younger than others produced later in his reign, has been found at this location.³ The dimensions of the temple and its carvings provide evidence of the evolution of Cambodian artistic styles and also suggest that even in semiexile, Jayavarman was able to exercise systematic control over a sizable pool of labor. Was the city of Preah Khan subservient to Angkor or a rival to it? How did Jayavarman relate to the usurper-king who followed Yasovarman to the throne? Even more important, what were his relationships with Champa to the east? It is important to ask these unanswerable questions in order to place Jayavarman's reign, following his accession in 1178, in the context of his early life and in the framework of Cambodian foreign relations.

JAYAVARMAN VII AND BUDDHIST KINGSHIP

Throughout his time of waiting to be king, Jayavarman immersed himself in the teachings of Mahayana Buddhism—the variant still followed in much of northern Asia. More than any other king, he labored to integrate Buddhist notions with Cambodian ideas of kingship. Buddhist kingship, as he practiced it, differed in several ways from the more eclectic Hindu model that had been followed for centuries at Angkor and was to form the basis, ceremonially, of Cambodian kingship until it was overturned in the 1970s. In the traditional version, a king, alive or dead, was thought to enjoy a special relationship with a particular deity—usually Siva, more rarely Vishnu, occasionally the composite of them both known as Harihara—to whom his temple-mountain was eventually dedicated. The kings used this special relationship to explain their grandeur while their subjects assumed that the relationship had something to do with the provision of adequate rainfall.

Because Cambodian society was hierarchically organized, and because the king was thought to centralize the kingdom, most Cambodians—like their contemporaries in medieval Europe—probably recognized the necessity for a king. Rare inscriptions—and perhaps the act of constructing reservoirs—indicated that an individual king occasionally had his subjects' welfare on his mind. In human terms, however, the king was nearly always a distant, mysterious figure concealed inside an awesome palace. The notion that he was accountable to his people—expressed, for example, in royal audiences—does not seem to have caught hold. Inside his palace, and within the network of kinship and preferment relationships extending from it, the king was the master and the victim of a system whereby people clamored for his favors, for titles, for the right to own slaves or sumptuous possessions.

Buddhist kingship, of course, grew out of this Indian tradition (the Buddha had been an Indian prince), but in Jayavarman's reign these no-

A tower at the Bayon, Jayavarman VII's temple-mountain, twelfth century
A.D. Photo by Walter Veit.

tions were modified in several ways. Jayavarman was no longer seen as the devotee of a divinity or as drawn up to the divinity in death. Instead, Jayavarman sought to redeem himself and his kingdom by his devotion to Buddhist teachings and by the performance of meritorious acts.[4]

Before examining how these ideas of kingship acted themselves out during the reign of Jayavarman, it is important to stress that his program was not aimed at reforming Cambodian society or at dismantling such "Hinduized" institutions as Brahmanism, slavery, and kingship. Far from it; in his conservatism and his elitist frame of reference, Jayavarman VII was a recognizably twelfth-century king, although in Cambodian terms he was also a revolutionary one. Put very starkly, the difference between a Hindu king and a Buddhist one is akin to the difference between a monologue that no one overhears and a soliloquy addressed to an audience of paid or invited guests. A "Hindu" king's rule was an aggregation of statements—rituals, temples, poems, marriages, inscriptions, and the like—and his grandeur and godliness. A Buddhist king made similar statements, but he addressed them, specifically, to an audience consisting of his people. This made the people less an ingredient of the king's magnificence (as his thousands of followers had always been) than objects of his overwhelming compassion, an audience for his merit-making and participants in *his* redemption. This is, at least, what many of Jayavarman VII's inscriptions and temples appear to have been saying.

Why did Jayavarman VII choose to break so sharply with the past? Scholars have given several explanations. These include his apparent estrangement from the court at Angkor, combined with his resentment toward the usurper who had proclaimed himself king in 1167; a "master plan" of buildings, ideology, and kingship that had been maturing in his mind, after years of study; and very possibly, the influence of a scholarly, ambitious wife. These proposals are helpful, but they do not identify the real key to Jayavarman's reign—the Cham invasion of Angkor in 1177. As Paul Mus and Jean Boisselier have shown, we can see Jayavarman's entire reign as a response to this traumatic event.[5]

Jayavarman's own links with Champa appear to have been close, and in the 1160s, he apparently spent several years there. Was he a hostage, or an exile, or was he leading a military campaign? It seems likely that he became exposed to Mahayana Buddhism while he was in Champa; the religion was very popular there. Perhaps his absence was connected in some way with being out of favor at the Cambodian court, for he returned home only after Yasovarman II had been deposed. As the sources of our uncertainty are Jayavarman's own inscriptions, all that is clear about the prelude to the Cham invasion of 1177—and indeed about Jayavarman's early career—is that later on he found little to boast about in these obviously formative years.

Because inscriptions tend to trace the causes of war to royal ambition, treachery, and revenge—that is, to the world of the *Ramayana*—it is difficult for us to determine exactly why Champa invaded Cambodia, by land in 1177 and then by water in 1178.[6] The prospects of booty and prisoners were certainly part of the Cham rationale; so were memories of earlier defeats. Two Chinese, shipwrecked off the coast of Champa, apparently helped the Chams in both campaigns. One taught them to fire crossbows while mounted on horseback,[7] and the Cham king's enthusiasm for this tactic led him to raid the Chinese mainland and the island of Hainan in search of horses. Not finding enough of them, Chinese sources assert, he decided on a second attack on Cambodia by water—this time, with the aid of a Chinese navigator, who piloted the expedition up the Mekong, the Great Lake, and the Siem Reap River, taking the city of Yasodharapura by surprise: "With a powerful fleet, [he] pillaged it and put the king to death, without listening to any proposal of peace."[8]

Jayavarman's whereabouts in 1177 are unknown, but he appears to have done nothing about the invasion. In 1178, however, he gathered arms and supporters for a new campaign against the Chams, defeating them in another naval battle, although an inscription suggests that a Cambodian prince—not Jayavarman himself—killed the Cham king "with a hundred million arrows." When Jayavarman went to Angkor after the invasion, he found the city "plunged into a sea of misfortune" and "heavy with crimes." Some of these troubles could be traced to the unmeritorious reigns of predecessors; others to the fractionalization of power inside the kingdom, referred to in an inscription later written by his wife: "In the previous reign, the land, though shaded by many parasols, suffered from extremes of heat; under [Jayavarman] there remained but one parasol, and yet the land, remarkably, was delivered from suffering."[9]

Jayavarman VII was crowned in 1181, therefore, owing little to his predecessors and much, as his inscriptions tell us, to his acumen, his Buddhist faith, and his victories in battle. Over the next thirty years or so (the precise date of his death is unknown) he stamped the kingdom with his personality and his ideas as no other ruler was able to do before Norodom Sihanouk in the 1960s and Pol Pot later on. Like these two figures, Jayavarman may have wanted to transform Cambodia and perceived himself as the instrument of the transformation.

Much of the interest in his reign, moreover, springs from the tension inherent in the words "Buddha" and "king." Using the Hinduized apparatus of kingship and the material grandeur associated with it, Jayavarman also sought in all humility—if his inscriptions are to be believed—to deliver himself and all his people from suffering. As a king, he had roads built throughout his kingdom, perhaps to accelerate his military response to uprisings or invasions; as a Buddhist, he made his beneficence known through these roads. His program of public works, indeed, was probably more extensive than that of any other Cambodian king. This nationalization of kingship by a man who was arguably the most otherworldly of Cambodia's kings has given Jayavarman's reign a contradictory appearance. Sentences about the man soon fall into the pattern of "on the one hand" and "on the other."

For example, many of the bas-reliefs on the Bayon, depicting battles against the Chams, contain vivid scenes of cruelty. Similarly, some of Jayavarman's inscriptions praise his vengefulness and his skill at political infighting vis-à-vis the Chams. On the one hand, the portrait statues of him that have come down to us depict him as an ascetic deep in meditation.[10] From his inscriptions, we learn that "he suffered from the illnesses of his subjects more than from his own; the pain that afflicted men's bodies was for him a spiritual pain, and thus more piercing."[11] Yet, on the other hand, his roads, temples, rest-houses, reservoirs, and hospitals were thrown up with extraordinary haste between his coronation in 1181 and the second decade of the thirteenth century; some were completed after his death. There were so many of these projects, in fact, that workmanship was often sloppy, and by the end of his reign local supplies of sandstone and limestone for use at Angkor seem to have run out.[12] Hundreds of thousands of ordinary people, inscriptions tell us, labored to erect and maintain these constructions built, at the ideological level, to deliver them from pain. To a twentieth-century eye, this seems ironic to say the least, but we should remember that suffering in Buddhist terms should not be taken merely in a physical sense; it must also be related to the purposes of life and to the ways that suffering of certain kinds can serve the teachings of the Buddha. Suffering to praise the Buddha by building Jayavarman's city, for example, assured the workers of less suffering and greater happiness—in another life.

Why was Jayavarman's building program carried out with so much haste? He was perhaps as old as sixty when he reached the throne; the buildings may have been part of his race against time. A more speculative answer is that in his years away from Angkor he had conceived a Buddhist-oriented construction program that could only be completed, and *had* to be completed, at Angkor while he was still alive. The program may have been part of a process of personal redemption, although the sins for which he was atoning are not clarified by his inscriptions. What we know about the first years of his reign comes from inscriptions written at a later stage. It seems that these years were probably spent in deflecting yet another Cham attack (depicted as a naval battle in the bas-reliefs of the Bayon), in quelling a rebellion in the northwest, and in rebuilding the city of Angkor. Major shifts in population, as usual, followed these military campaigns, as the Preah Khan inscription of 1191 suggests: "To the multitude of his warriors, he gave the capitals of enemy kings, with their shining palaces; to the beasts roaming his forests, he gave the forests of the enemy; to prisoners of war, he gave his own forests, thus manifesting generosity and justice."

As with other Cambodian kings, it would be wrong to make a sharp distinction between Jayavarman's politics and his religion, between temporal and spiritual powers, and between his ideas about himself and his ideas about his kingdom. Before we dismiss him as a mindless megalomaniac, however, it is worth recalling that had no one shared his vision or believed in his merit, he would never have become king, especially starting out from such a weak position, and certainly would not have been able to remain in power. High officials, brahmans, evangelical Buddhists, and military men probably saw advantages, and probably worldly ones, in the physical expansion of the kingdom, partly by means of royally subsidized religious foundations and partly through bringing previously indifferent populations under some form of Angkorean control. By the beginning of the thirteenth century, in fact, Angkor was extracting tribute from much of what is now Thailand and southern Laos as well as from Champa, occupying the coastal areas of central Vietnam. To these corners of the known world—and to China, to which the king sent tributary missions—the multiple half-smiling faces of Jayavarman's temple-mountain and his portrait statues addressed their benignly powerful glance.

The art historian Philippe Stern, who studied Jayavarman's reign in detail, perceived three stages in the development of his iconography and architecture.[13] These coincide with the three phases of construction noted by Stern for earlier Cambodian kings—namely, public works, temples in honor of parents, and the king's own temple-mountain.

The public works of earlier kings, as we have seen, usually took the form of reservoirs (*baray*). Other projects, such as roads and bridges, may also have been built, but they are seldom noted in inscriptions. Jayavarman's program departed from the past. His hospitals, probably established early in his reign, were built to the west of Angkor and as far north as central Laos. The Ta Prohm inscription says that these hospitals could call on the services of 838 villages, with adult populations totaling roughly eighty thousand people. The services demanded appear to have been to provide labor and rice for the staffs attached to each hospital, or approximately a hundred people, including dependents.[14] The so-called hospital inscriptions give details about the administration of the hospitals and about the provisions and staff allocated to them.

A second set of Jayavarman VII's public works consisted of rest-houses placed at approximately 16-kilometer (10-mile) intervals along Cambo-

dia's major roads.[15] There were fifty-seven of these between Angkor and
the Cham capital and seventeen more between Angkor and a Buddhist
temple-site at P'imai in northeastern Thailand. Finally, there was Jayavarman's own reservoir, known now as the northern Baray and during his
reign as the Jayatataka, located to the northeast of Yasodharapura.

These innovations stemmed from what Jayavarman saw as his mission
to *rescue* his subjects, as the hospital inscription says:

> Filled with a deep sympathy for the good of the world, the king swore this
> oath: "All the beings who are plunged in the ocean of existence, may I draw
> them out by virtue of this good work. And may the kings of Cambodia who
> come after me, attached to goodness . . . attain with their wives, dignitaries,
> and friends the place of deliverance where there is no more illness."[16]

THE TEMPLES OF JAYAVARMAN VII

In the second stage of Jayavarman's reign he erected temples in honor of
his parents. The first of these, now known as Ta Prohm ("Ancestor
Brahma"), was dedicated in 1186; it honored Jayavarman's mother in the
guise of Prajnaparamita, the goddess of wisdom, conceived metaphorically as the mother of all Buddhas. The temple also housed a portrait
statue of Jayavarman's Buddhist teacher, or guru (the word *kru* means
"teacher" in modern Khmer), surrounded in the temple by statues of
more than six hundred dependent gods and *bodhisattvas*. The syncretism
of Cambodian religion is shown by the fact that Shaivite and Vaisnavite
ascetics were given cells on the temple grounds alongside Buddhist
monks and learned men. The appearance of Ta Prohm today gives a poor
idea of its original appearance, for unlike the other major temples at
Angkor, it has never been restored; instead, it has been left to the mercy
of the forest.

The next temple complex to be built by Jayavarman VII is known
nowadays as the Preah Khan ("Sacred Sword"). Its inscription says that
it was built on the site of an important Cambodian victory over the
Chams, and its twelfth-century name, Jayasri ("Victory and Throne"),
may echo this event. No other inscription mentions this battle, fought so
close to Yasodharapura as to suggest a second Cham invasion of the city.
Groslier, however, has argued that it took place and has proposed that it
is depicted in bas-reliefs at the Bayon.[17]

Preah Khan was dedicated in 1191 and houses a portrait statue of
Jayavarman's father, Dharanindravarman, with the traits of Lokesvara,
the deity expressive of the compassionate aspects of the Buddha. The
symbolism is relentlessly appropriate, for in Mahayana Buddhist thinking the marriage of wisdom (*prajna*) and compassion (*karuna*) gave birth

A twelfth-century bas-relief at the Bayon depicting warfare between Chams and Khmers. Photo by Walter Veit.

to enlightenment, which is to say, to the Buddha himself, the Enlightened One.[18] In this stage of Jayavarman's artistic development, Lokesvara appears more and more frequently, and throughout his reign, the triad of Prajnaparamita (wisdom), the Buddha (enlightenment), and Lokesvara (compassion) was central to the king's religious thinking. The placement of the two temples southeast and northeast of the new center of Yasodharapura (later occupied by the Bayon) suggests that the three temples can be "read" together, with the dialectic of compassion and wisdom giving birth to enlightenment represented by the Buddha image that stood at the center of the Bayon, and thus at the heart of Jayavarman's temple-mountain.

The inscriptions from these two "parent temples" show us how highly developed the Cambodian bureaucracy had become, particularly in terms of its control over the placement and duties of the population, but also in terms of the sheer number of people in positions of authority who were entitled to deposit and endow images of deities inside the temple. Ta Prohm housed several thousand people, as its inscription attests:

> There are here 400 men, 18 high priests, 2,740 other priests, 2,232 assistants, including 615 female dancers, a grand total of 12,640 people, including those entitled to stay. [In addition, there are] 66,625 men and women who perform services for the gods, making a grand total of 79,265 people, including the Burmese, Chams, etc.[19]

Similarly, the people dependent on Preah Khan—that is, those obliged to provide rice and other services—totaled nearly 100,000, drawn from more than 5,300 villages. The inscription goes on to enumerate the men and women who had been dependent on previous temple endowments. Drawn from 13,500 villages, they numbered more than 300,000. The infrastructure needed to provide food and clothing, for the temples—to name only two types of provision—must have been efficient and sophisticated.

Three interesting points emerge from the inscriptions. One is that outsiders—"Burmese, Chams, etc."—were accounted for in different ways than local people were, perhaps because they were prisoners of war without enduring ties to individual noblemen, priests, or religious foundations. Another is that the average size of the villages referred to in the inscriptions appears to have been about 200 people, including dependents—still the median size of rice-growing villages in Cambodia in the 1960s. Finally, the inscriptions indicate that the temples, although dedicated to the Buddha and serving as residences for thousands of Buddhist monks, also housed statues and holy men associated with different Hindu sects. Jayavarman VII obviously approved of this arrangement, for we know that he also retained Hindu thinkers and bureaucrats at his court. Indeed, it is probably more useful to speak of the coexistence of Hinduism and Buddhism in Jayavarman VII's temples, and perhaps in his mind as well, than to propose a systematic process of syncretization.

The jewel-like temple known as Neak Po'n ("Twining Serpents") forms an island in the Jayatataka and was probably completed by 1191, for it is mentioned in the inscription of Preah Khan:

> The king has placed the Jayatataka like a lucky mirror, colored by stones, gold, and garlands. In the middle, there is an island, drawing its charm from separate basins, washing the mud of sin from those coming in contact with it, serving as a boat in which they can cross the ocean of existences.[20]

The island with its enclosing wall, constructed in a lotus pattern, was intended to represent a mythical lake in the Himalayas, sacred to Buddhist thinking. Around the temple, as at the lake, four gargoyles spew water from the larger lake into the smaller ones. The temple itself, raised above the water by a series of steps, was probably dedicated, like

Preah Khan, to Lokesvara, whose image appears repeatedly in high relief on its walls.

Groups of statues were also placed at the four sides of the temple. Unfortunately, only one of these, representing the horse Balaha, an aspect of Lokesvara, can be identified with certainty; two others are probably representations of Siva and Vishnu. Jean Boisselier has argued that the presence of these gods inside the enclosure can be read as a political statement, showing that the former gods of Angkor were now submitting to the Buddha. But why should they do so? Boisselier, following Mus, has suggested that Shaivism and Vaisnavism were seen to have failed the Cambodians when the Chams were able to destroy so much of Angkor in 1177. Lake Anavatapta, moreover, was sacred not only to all Buddhists but particularly to Buddhist rulers, or *chakravartin*, beginning, legend asserts, with the Emperor Asoka, who was able magically to draw water from the lake to enhance his own purity and power.[21]

Boisselier has argued that the political significance of the temple goes even further, as it was known in the Preah Khan inscription as the Rajasri, translatable as "the regalia," and Neak Po'n probably housed palladia of the kingdom. Boisselier believed that it was torn down by the Thai when they captured Angkor in 1431 and, according to their chronicles, carried off Cambodia's regalia to their own capital city of Ayudhya. In the Thai view, the destruction of Neak Po'n delegitimized the universal kingship of Jayavarman VII and his successors. In the sixteenth century, when Ayudhya was invaded by the Burmese, these very regalia were carried off to Burma, where two Cambodian statues, perhaps from Neak Po'n, can now be seen in Mandalay.[22]

In this second phase of his iconography Jayavarman VII also sponsored additions to many earlier structures—notably the temples of P'imai in northeastern Thailand and Preah Khan in Kompong Svay. New constructions at this time included the massive ruin known today as Banteai Chhmar in northwestern Cambodia.[23]

The sheer size of these foundations suggests a trend toward urbanization under Jayavarman VII, or at least a tendency to herd and collect large numbers of people from peripheral areas into the service of the state. It seems likely that Jayavarman VII, like Suryavarman II before him, was attracted to the idea of increasing centralization and the related idea of bureaucratic state control. Perhaps these ideas formed part of what he perceived as a mission to convert his subjects to Buddhism or were connected with organizing people to respond swiftly to foreign threats.

The second phase was marked by several stylistic innovations. These included the motif of multifaced towers, inaugurated at the small temple of Prasat Preah Stung and carried to its apex in the entrance gates to the city of Angkor Thom and, ultimately, in the hundreds of faces that look down from the Bayon; the stone walls surrounding the entire city, apparently for the first time in Angkorean history; and the causeways of giants outside the gates of the city.

These constructions can be read in terms of both politics and religion. Boisselier, following Mus, has compared the wall-building at Angkor Thom to a fortified Maginot Line, supposedly offering an impenetrable defense against any Cham invasion. At the same time, the walls can be said to represent the ring of mountains that surround Mt. Meru or Jayavarman's temple-mountain, the Bayon.

After capturing the Cham capital in 1191, Jayavarman probably spent the rest of his reign at Yasodharapura. At this point, his buildings began to show signs of hasty construction and poor workmanship, as well as of a shifting ideology; the temple that was to become the Bayon, for example, was radically altered at several points in the 1190s[24] and probably in the thirteenth century as well, after Jayavarman's death. It is tempting to seek an explanation for the haste and quantity of Jayavarman's monuments in his personality or in otherwise unknown aspects of his life. Did the temples represent an attempt to impose his legitimacy and point of view on his successors? Was he attempting to purify Angkor after it had been desecrated by the Chams? Did he have personal shortcomings to atone for? Evidence to answer these questions is thin, but it is certainly true that Jayavarman, for whatever reason, tried to stamp Cambodia with an ideology drawn from Mahayana Buddhism and with his own personality as well. These two aspects of his reign overlap in his portrait statues and perhaps most dramatically in the symbolism of his temple-mountain and of the city that surrounded it.

An inscription from the end of Jayavarman's reign describes the city as his bride: "The town of Yasodharapura, decorated with powder and jewels, burning with desire, the daughter of a good family . . . was married by the king in the course of a festival that lacked nothing, under the spreading dais of his protection."[25] The object of the marriage, the inscription goes on to say, was "the procreation of happiness throughout the universe."

At the center of the city was the Bayon (literally, "ancestor *yantra*," *yantra* being a magical geometric shape), with its hundreds of gigantic faces, carved in sets of four, and its captivating bas-reliefs, depicting everyday life, wars with Champa, and the behavior of Indian gods. The temple at one time housed thousands of images. Its central image, discovered in the 1930s, was a statue of the Buddha sheltered by an enormous hooded snake, or *naga*.

There has been considerable controversy about the symbolism of the temple and about what was meant by the causeways leading up to it, with giants (*asura*) and angels (*devata*) engaged in what looks like a tug of war, grasping the bodies of two gigantic snakes. Some have argued that the causeways represented the well-known Indian myth of the churning of the sea of milk. Others have agreed with Mus, who saw them as rainbows, leading people out of their world into the world of the gods. At another level, the *asuras* represented the Chams and the *devatas*, Cambodians. In this respect, it is tempting to perceive the city, and most of Jayavarman's works, in dialectical terms. For example, as we have seen, the pair Lokesvara (compassion/father) and Prajnaparamita (intelligence/mother) give birth to the Buddha (enlightenment, thought to be the child of wisdom and compassion)—i.e., Jayavarman VII himself. We have encountered this turn of mind before, in the cult of Harihara and in the opposition and synthesis in Cambodian popular thought of divinities associated respectively with water/moon/darkness and earth/sun/brightness. Similarly, the struggle between the Cambodians and the Chams, acted out along the causeways and in the bas-reliefs at the Bayon and at Banteai Chhmar, can be seen as bringing to birth the new, converted nation of Cambodia, in which the Buddha has won over the Hindu gods of Champa. This dialectic may well be the "message" of the Bayon, which Boisselier has called the "assembly hall of the city of the gods."[26] Once again, the message can be read in terms of the civil polity as well, and so can the half-smiling faces with their half-closed eyes that dominate the temple. As so often in Angkorean art, it would be narrow and inaccurate to interpret these haunting faces as representing only one kind of deity, performing one kind of task. In a way, for example, they serve as guardians of the Buddha and his teachings; in another, glancing out in the four directions, they oversee the kingdom and perhaps represent civil and military officials of the time. Boisselier, who has argued that they are princely manifestations of Brahma, has noticed also that their tiaras resemble those worn by the Cham *asuras* along the entrance causeways. Perhaps, as Hiram W. Woodward has suggested, this signifies the conversion of the Chams to Buddhism.[27]

Another extraordinary feature of the Bayon, found also at Banteai Chhmar, is that its bas-reliefs depict historical Cambodian events rather than, say, incidents in the *Ramayana* or some other literary work that coincide with or resemble historical events. The battles depicted on the Bayon are fought with recognizable weapons, and other panels depict ordinary people buying and selling, eating, gambling, raising children, picking fruit, curing the sick, and traveling on foot or in ox-carts. Nearly all the customs, artifacts, and costumes depicted in the bas-reliefs could still be found in the Cambodian countryside at the end of the colonial era. Although the voices of these people are missing from Jayavarman's inscriptions, they move across his bas-reliefs with unaccustomed freedom, citizens at last of the country they inhabit, adorning a king's temple as they never had before. Perhaps the bas-reliefs are intended to show that the people have been converted and saved—which is to say, revolutionized—by Jayavarman's example. They also exhibit the "lowest" of the worlds one traverses on the way to enlightenment; in this sense, they resemble their counterparts carved on the eighth-century Javanese Buddhist monument, the Borobudur.

Unless more inscriptions come to light from Jayavarman's reign, he will remain mysterious to us, because there are so many ambiguities about his personality and his ideas. The mystery springs in part from the wide-ranging social and ideological changes that characterized thirteenth- and fourteenth-century Cambodia and may have been due in part to forces that Jayavarman or people near him set in motion.

Another source of ambiguity can be traced to the uneasy coexistence in Jayavarman's temples and inscriptions of an overwhelming compassion and an overwhelming will, of a detachment from things of the world—symbolized by the horse Balaha at the Neak Po'n—and a detailed program aimed at transforming the physical world of Angkor, which had been so badly damaged by the Cham invasion. A third mystery is the silence—both in terms of buildings and inscriptions—that followed Jayavarman's reign and appears to have begun in his declining years. We have no way of telling if Jayavarman was in some sense to blame for this inaction, as in subsequent inscriptions he is hardly ever mentioned. The patterns of continuity, stressed so often in earlier inscriptions, seem to have been broken or damaged severely by his reign.

THERAVADA BUDDHISM AND THE CRISIS OF THE THIRTEENTH CENTURY

The largest change affecting Cambodia in the thirteenth century was the conversion of most of its people to the Theravada variant of Buddhism, discussed below.[28] What role Jayavarman VII played in this conversion is impossible to judge. The history of his reign is the story of the imposition of one man's will on a population, a landscape, and a part of Asia, ostensibly in the service of an ideal, Mahayana Buddhism, which in its allegedly "liberating" fashion bears an ominous resemblance to the ideology of Democratic Kampuchea, which was also imposed from above. It is very doubtful that Jayavarman VII saw the Cambodian elite as his enemies, as Pol Pot did, or preferred "forest people" to those living at Angkor, but his break with the past, his obsession with punitive expeditions, the impetuous grandeur of his building program, and his imposition of a national religion rather than his patronage of a royal cult all have parallels with events in the 1970s. Interestingly, the only feature of

Angkorean life singled out for praise by Democratic Kampuchea was precisely the full-scale mobilization of the people that Jayavarman VII, but very few other kings, managed to carry out.

Some writers have connected Cambodia's conversion to Theravada Buddhism to the upheaval that affected Southeast Asia in the wake of the Mongol invasions of China; others have seen it as evidence of the growing influence of Mon- and Thai-speaking peoples, who were already Theravada Buddhists, on the people of Angkor. We know that wandering missionaries from the Mon-language parts of Siam, from Burma, and from Ceylon played an important part in the process and that Cambodian pilgrims visited Ceylon to learn about Theravada Buddhism and to obtain clerical credentials. We also know some of the agents of the change, but it is difficult to say why conversion was so rapid and so widespread. Some scholars argue that the Theravada variant, unlike Brahmanism or Mahayana Buddhism, was oriented toward ordinary people. Others have seen the conversion as a rejection of the personalized megalomania of Jayavarman VII. Perhaps the most likely explanation, advanced by L. P. Briggs,[29] is that the increasing interaction between Khmer- and Mon-speaking residents of the Thai central plain, with the Mons being devotees of Theravada Buddhism, led gradually, over half a century or so, to the conversion of Khmer-speakers further east. We have no way of telling what aspects of the sect were more attractive than others, or which segments of society were drawn most rapidly to it. The conversion in any case was by no means total, for the Chinese envoy Zhou Daguan, at the end of the thirteenth century, noted that Brahmanism and Shaivism, as well as Theravada Buddhism, still enjoyed the status of approved religions at Angkor.[30] Nor was it entirely peaceful, for it seems to have come soon after King Jayavarman VIII (r. 1243–1295), a usurper, rejected Jayavarman VII's brand of Buddhism, ordered the defacement of hundreds of Buddha images at the Bayon and elsewhere, and attempted to alter some of these images, iconographically, into Hindu ones, by changing their postures, adding beards, and so on. He also tried to turn the Bayon into a Hindu temple, and embellished the two largest Hindu temples at Angkor—namely, Angkor Wat and the Baphuon. The latter temple made a strong impression on Zhou Daguan, who visited Angkor soon after Jayavarman VIII's death.

In other words, it is likely that the thirteenth century—the least recorded of the Angkorean centuries in terms of datable inscriptions—was marked at Angkor by a serious religious upheaval or by a succession of upheavals, which had political causes and effects as well.

The end of Jayavarman's reign and the reign of his successor, Indravarman II, are both obscure. Inscriptions found at the Bayon have little to say about the last phase of Jayavarman's life. Those at the four corners of his city, apparently all inscribed at the time of his death, however, provide helpful references to Jayavarman's wars against the Chams and the Vietnamese. These inscriptions are written, Coedes contended, in execrable Sanskrit. Several of them (like some of the bas-reliefs at the Bayon) are unfinished, almost as if the workmen had dropped their chisels on receiving news of the king's death.[31] This hypothetical scene is brought to life by the Swedish author Jan Myrdal, writing about Angkor:

> The craftsmen were at work while the old masters sat in the shade talking. Now and then they came over, to keep an eye on the work. Then one of the apprentices comes running. He shouts: "Now he's dead!" At this the craftsmen stopped hacking at the stone wall and put down their tools . . . and went off home.[32]

Surveying the art of the post-Angkorean era from another perspective, Ashley Thompson has written:

> The wild iconographic mingling of the vegetable, animal and human that announces the divine above each sanctuary threshold is gone. Images of fantastic creatures and powerful gods no longer populate the landscape. . . . The sensuality and majesty of the divine virtually disappear.[33]

Because of the grandeur of the beginning of Jayavarman's reign and the obscurity of its closing years, some authors have argued that he died of leprosy after many years of isolation. Evidence to support this argument springs from Cambodian oral tradition, already active by the end of the thirteenth century, that a leper king had reigned at Angkor.

Although the contention that Jayavarman VII was a leper fits some of the evidence, it is possible that the "leper king" was his successor, Indravarman II (r. 1220–1243), who continued his father's building program, expanding and embellishing the Bayon and adding stone walls to several of Jayavarman VII's temples. A likelier candidate, however, might be Indravarman's successor, Jayavarman VIII (r. 1243–1295), an iconoclastic Hindu. Whether the king's leprosy was real or invented by his enemies to describe serious failures of kingship (connected, perhaps, with his iconoclasm or with defeats at the hands of Thai armies in the mid-thirteenth century) is impossible to determine.[34]

This dearth of written information coincides with a critical period of Cambodian history. The thirteenth century as a whole was a period of crisis throughout mainland and insular Southeast Asia—a time of rapid change, significant movements of population, foreign invasions, altered patterns of trade, the appearance of new religions, and shifts in the balance of power.[35] In Burma, Siam, Laos, and Cambodia, the major change was the growth of Theravada Buddhism at the expense of state-sponsored and caste-enhancing Hindu cults. In the long run, this change had several ramifications. Brahmans retained their positions at court for ceremonial purposes but otherwise diminished in importance. The rich mythical and literary bases of Indian literature and iconography, reflected up to now in bas-reliefs, sculpture, architecture, and inscriptions, narrowed perceptibly to satisfy the more austere requirements of Theravada aesthetics. And Cambodian literature, like the local version of the *Ramayana,* came to be suffused with Buddhist values.

In terms of foreign relations, the most important development affecting Cambodia at this time was the weakening of its control over the people to the northwest of Angkor, in present-day Thailand. Although Cambodian cultural influence remained strong in the central plain (where the Thai capital of Ayudhya was to be founded in the fourteenth century), Cambodian political control diminished. Principalities that formerly sent tribute to Angkor, such as Sukot'ai and Louvo, now declared their independence. So did principalities in Laos and others to the south. Angkor was once again vulnerable to invasion from every direction but the east, as Champa was no longer a power to be reckoned with. A major Thai invasion, in fact, occurred toward the end of the thirteenth century.

ZHOU DAGUAN'S ACCOUNT
OF ANGKOR, 1296–1297

The record by Chinese envoy Zhou Daguan of his stay in Cambodia in 1296–1297 is the most detailed account we have about everyday life and the appearance of Angkor.[36] Zhou's memoir is rich in circumstantial detail as he was not constrained by the Indian traditions that remove ordinary people from literary consideration. In his account, for example, we see Cambodians bathing, selling goods, and marching in processions. From our point of view, it is a shame that Zhou devoted so much of his short manuscript to exotic revelations of "barbarian" life. In fact, although he provided us with a newsreel—or perhaps a home video—of his stay at Angkor, our appetites are whetted for the feature film he might have made had he known (or cared) about the gaps that have persisted ever since in the historical record.

The account, in translation, runs to fewer than forty pages, divided into forty sections. These range from a short paragraph to several pages and, topically, from religion, justice, kingship, and agriculture (to name only four) to birds, vegetables, bathing customs, and slaves. Many features of thirteenth-century Cambodian life that Zhou described—including clothing, tools, draft animals, and aspects of rural commerce—are still observable today, and others—such as slavery, sumptuary laws, and trial by ordeal—endured in modified form until the nineteenth century at least.

Five of Zhou's sections deal with religion, slaves, festivals, agriculture, and the king's excursions. Zhou found three religions enjoying official status at Angkor; they appear to have been Brahmanism, Theravada Buddhism, and Shaivism. The brahmans, Zhou noted, often attained high positions as officials, but he could find little else to say about them: "I do not know what models they follow, and they have nothing which one could call a school or a place of teaching. It is difficult, also, to know what books they read." The Theravada monks, known colloquially by a Thai phrase (*chao ku*), closely resembled their counterparts in Theravada Southeast Asia today: "They shave their heads, and wear yellow robes, leaving the right shoulder bare. For the lower half of the body, they wear a yellow skirt. They are barefoot."

Like the palace and the houses of high officials, Zhou tells us, Buddhist monasteries could have tile roofs, but those of ordinary people had to be made of thatch. Zhou was impressed by the simplicity of the Theravada Buddhist *wats*, noting that (unlike Mahayana temples in China) they contained "no bells, cymbals, flags, or platforms," housing only an image of the Buddha made of gilded plaster. Finally, Zhou described the method used to inscribe palm leaf manuscripts, which persisted well into the twentieth century, particularly in the case of religious and historical texts.

The Shaivites, whom Zhou called "Taoists," inhabited monasteries that were less prosperous than Buddhist ones, in which "the only image which they revere is a block of stone analogous to the stone found in shrines of the god of the soil in China." Although monastic Shaivism declined in importance after the abandonment of Angkor and eventually disappeared altogether, Indianized cults, including the use of linga, continued into modern times, and officials calling themselves brahmans continued to work at the Cambodian court, where they were entrusted with the performance of royal rituals and with maintaining astronomical tables. When monastic Theravada Buddhism is added to these two "religions," we note that the three categories for religious activity singled out by Zhou Daguan survived, in modified form, into very recent times.

Zhou's account makes it clear that many of the people living at Angkor were in some sense slaves, for he tells us that "those who have many [slaves] have more than a hundred; those who have only a few have from ten to twenty; only the very poor have none at all." He went on to say that slaves are generally taken as captives from mountain tribes, a practice that persisted into the colonial era. It seems likely, in fact, that this is the way Cambodian society built itself up, over time, gradually absorbing and socializing "barbarians," who figure in such large numbers in the inscriptions in Angkorean times. In Zhou's account, slaves were set apart from other people by several prohibitions: "They can sit or lie down only underneath a house. For their work, they can ascend into the house, but then they must kneel down, join their hands together, and prostrate themselves. After that they can move forward." Slaves enjoyed no civil privileges; their marriages were not even recognized by the state. Forced to call their masters "father" and their mistresses "mother," they tried frequently to escape and, when caught, were tattooed, mutilated, or chained.[37]

Although Zhou is informative about people at court and about slaves, he is vague about the proportion of society in the 1290s that was neither in bondage nor part of the elite. Clearly, the people with "a few" slaves would fall into this category; so would the private landowners, discussed in an earlier context by Merle C. Ricklefs;[38] and so would the Sino-Cambodians who were active in local and international trade. Special privileges were extended to the elite and to religious sects, and special prohibitions applied to slaves, but about those in between—the people, in fact, who probably made the kingdom prosper—we know far less than we would like.

When Zhou goes into detail, however, his account is often illuminating. His description of what he called a new year's festival, which occurred toward the end of November, is a good example of his narrative skill:

> In front of the royal palace, a great platform is built, capable of holding a thousand people, and decorated with lanterns and flowers. In front of it, at a distance of one hundred and twenty feet, another platform is built, one hundred and twenty feet high by laying pieces of wood end to end. This is done in the same way as a scaffolding for Buddhist *stupas*. Each night, three, four, five or six of these are built. On top of them, rockets and firecrackers are attached. The cost of these is met by the provinces and by the noble families. When night has fallen, the king is asked to watch the spectacle. The rockets are released and the firecrackers lighted. The rockets can be seen [about a mile] away. . . . The festival goes on like this for fifteen days. Every month there is a festival.

This ceremony, probably observed by Zhou himself, appears to have been celebrated at the end of the rainy season, when the waters of the Tonle Sap begin to subside, setting in motion the first stages of the agricultural year. After the move to Phnom Penh in the fifteenth century, the ceremony became known as the water festival and was similarly marked by fireworks, floats, and royal patronage until the monarchy was overthrown in 1970. The festival was revived, along with the monarchy, in 1993.

As for agriculture, Zhou noted that three or even four rice harvests a
year were possible—a statistic singled out by Democratic Kampuchea in
its efforts to revolutionize production. It is unlikely that this abundance
applied throughout the country, for at Angkor, several harvests were possible only because of the concentration of manpower there, the rich allu-
vial soil, and the water storage system perfected in the region over several hundred years. Another factor was the peculiarly helpful conduct of
the Tonle Sap. According to Zhou's comments on the agricultural cycle's
relationship to this beneficent body of water:

> In this country it rains for half of the year; in the other half, it hardly rains at
> all. From the fourth to the ninth month, it rains every afternoon, and the
> water level of the Great Lake can reach seven or eight fathoms [approxi-
> mately 50 feet]. The big trees are drowned; only their tops can be seen. Peo-
> ple who live on the shores all go away to the mountains. Later, from the
> tenth month to the third [of the following year], not a drop of rain falls, and
> the Great Lake can be navigated only by small boats. . . . The people come
> back down at this point and plant their rice.

The "miracle" of the Tonle Sap amazed many subsequent travelers to
Angkor. As long as the region supported a large population, the deposits
left by receding water provided useful nutrients for the soil. Even after
Angkor was abandoned, the lake remained the most densely populated
natural fishbowl in the world, providing generations of Cambodians
with much of the protein for their diet.

We would welcome the chance to interrogate Zhou Daguan about the
working of agriculture at this time. For example, how was the rice surplus handled? Were cultivators for the most part free people or some
kind of slaves? Did agriculture differ markedly at Angkor from that in
other parts of the kingdom? How much land was in the hands of members of the royal family and how much was controlled by Buddhist *wats*?
What did this control imply?

As we have no answers to these questions, we must be grateful to
Zhou for what he gives us. His description of rural marketing, for example, could easily have been written about the Cambodia of today:

> In this country, it is the women who are concerned with commerce. . . .
> Every day, a market takes place which begins at six in the morning and ends
> at noon. There is no market made up of shops where people live. Instead,
> people use a piece of matting, which they spread out onto the earth. Each of
> them has her own location, and I believe that fees are charged for these lo-
> cations.

It seems likely, in view of Cambodia's trade with China, that many Chinese had by this time settled in Cambodia to engage in commerce. According to Zhou, the products exported by Cambodia in the thirteenth century were those that had been exported since the time of "Funan"; they were to form the bulk of Cambodian exports until the twentieth century. These were such high-value, low-bulk items as rhinoceros horns, ivory, beeswax, lacquer, pepper, feathers, and cardamom. Imported products included paper and metal goods, porcelain, silk, and wicker. It is unclear from Zhou's account how products were paid for, but it seems likely that some form of barter took place at the rural level, with Chinese coins and credit in circulation at Angkor and at the ports.

Zhou was fascinated by the king reigning at Angkor during his visit (Indravarman III, r. 1296–1308), but he seems to have been nonplused by the king's accessibility during his stay. Zhou observed the king five times.

> Every day the king holds two audiences to deal with government affairs. There is no set agenda. Functionaries or common people who want to see him sit on the ground and wait for him to appear.

The king had reached the throne, Zhou remarked, in a curious manner:

> The new king was the son-in-law of the former one [Jayavarman VIII]. Before assuming the throne, he was a general. Now the father loved his daughter, but she robbed him of his golden sword, and took it to her husband. Thus the king's true son was deprived of the succession. . . . [Indravarman] had this prince's toes cut off and hid him in a cell.

These events, which had taken place just before the Chinese embassy's arrival, are alluded to discreetly by some inscriptions that date from Indravarman's reign. One of them refers to the "old age" of Jayavarman VIII and a "host of enemies" inside the kingdom; another mentions that Indravarman shaded the country with his single umbrella, whereas no shade had existed before, under "a crowd of [such] umbrellas."[39]

The transition between the reigns of Jayavarman VIII and Indravarman III, in fact, probably marked a sharp transition in Cambodian history, although we do not learn of it from Zhou Daguan. Under Jayavarman VIII in 1285, the last stone temple, the Mangalartha, was erected in the Angkor region. It was built by a high-ranking official and dedicated to Siva; the "single umbrella" to which its inscription refers may well have been Jayavarman's intolerant Hinduism. We know that Indravarman III was careful to sponsor Theravada Buddhists as well as brahmans, and it is tempting to speculate about a religious ingredient in his apparently nonviolent coup d'état.

The king's procession, like so much else in Zhou's account, gains in interest when compared with similar processions recorded in the colonial era.[40] It becomes clear in comparing the procession with the one marking Sihanouk's coronation, or other twentieth-century processions for which records have survived, that ceremonial Cambodian life and the hierarchical arrangement of such events changed little between Angkorean times and our own era. In Zhou's words,

> When the king goes out, troops are at the head of the escort; then come flags, banners, and music. Palace women, numbering from three to five hundred, wearing flowered cloth, with flowers in their hair, hold candles in their hands, and form a troupe. Even in broad daylight, the candles are lighted. Then come other palace women, bearing royal paraphernalia made of gold and silver. . . . Then come the palace women carrying lances and shields, [and] the king's private guards. . . . Carts drawn by goats and horses, all in gold, come next. Ministers and princes are mounted on elephants, and in front of them one can see, from afar, their innumerable red umbrellas. After them come the wives and concubines of the king, in palanquins, carriages, on horseback, and on elephants. They have more than a hundred parasols, flecked with gold. Behind them comes the sovereign, standing on an elephant, holding his sacred sword in his hand. The elephant's tusks are encased in gold.

Zhou then described a royal audience of the sort that Indravarman conducted on a daily basis and closed his account by remarking superciliously, "One can see by all this that even though it is a kingdom of barbarians these people certainly know what a ruler is."

CHAPTER 5

Cambodia After Angkor

Probably the least-recorded period of Cambodian history falls between Zhou Daguan's visit to Angkor and the restoration of some of the temples there by a Cambodian king named Chan in the 1550s and 1560s. The two intervening centuries witnessed major, permanent shifts in Cambodia's economy, its foreign relations, its language, and probably—although this is harder to verify—the structure, values, and performance of Cambodian society. Evidence about these shifts that can be traced to the period itself, however, is very thin. When the amount of evidence increases and becomes reliable around 1550 or so, many of the shifts had already taken place.

Evidence from the period consists largely of Chinese references to Cambodia, for almost no inscriptions appear to have been carved, on stone at least, inside the kingdom between the middle of the fourteenth century and the beginning of the sixteenth. Indeed, whereas over a thousand inscriptions have been catalogued for the years prior to 1300, less than a hundred more were carved in later centuries. Other sources include a Cham inscription and some from Thailand; two Thai chronicles from the seventeenth century, one of them very fragmentary, probably contain some accurate information about events in these two hundred years. The Cambodian chronicles that purportedly deal with this period appear to have been drawn for the most part from folklore and from Thai chronicle traditions, and unlike those dealing with events after 1550, they are very difficult to corroborate from other sources.

THE SHIFT FROM ANGKOR TO PHNOM PENH

The Chinese evidence is important, for as Michael Vickery has convincingly argued, the shifts in Cambodia's geographical center of gravity in the fourteenth century were probably connected with the rapid expansion of Chinese maritime trade with Southeast Asia, and particularly with the mainland, under the Mongols and the early Ming. Twenty-one tributary missions were sent from Cambodia to the Ming court in China between 1371 and 1432—more, it seems, than throughout the entire Angkorean period—and although some of these missions may have been purely ceremonial, it seems likely that they came primarily to trade and to arrange for trade, and perhaps also to request Chinese support against the frequent depredations of the Thai. The number of missions, and the respect accorded them by the Chinese, indicate not only that Cambodia remained active and powerful during this period but also that the Cambodian elite, perhaps now less rigidly tied to Hindu religious foundations and the ceremonial duties of brahmanical bureaucracy, were eager to exploit the possibility of commercial relations with China. How and why this shift in their thinking and behavior occurred are impossible to ascertain, but Michael Vickery, Claude Jacques, and Oliver Wolters have held that the shift should not necessarily be connected with the notion of "decline," for, as Wolters has remarked, "perhaps we have become too ready to regard the decline of Angkor in the fourteenth and fifteenth centuries as being on a catastrophic scale."[1] Indeed, throughout this period, rulers inside the present-day frontiers of Cambodia were able to compete for resources and trade with their new and prosperous neighbors in Ayudhya to the west. The region of Angkor itself, as recent studies have revealed, was quite heavily populated, and several buildings at Angkor were restored in these years. The Cambodians were also able to convince the Chinese of their own continuing importance and were occasionally able, well into the seventeenth century, to defeat the Thai in war.

Because this shift of emphasis was accompanied by so few "Angkorean" activities (such as stone temple construction, inscriptions, and expanded irrigation works), authors have often spoken of "decline" where "change" would be more appropriate. "Decline," for one thing, fails to explain Cambodia's enduring strength; for another, the word suggests that Jayavarman VII, for example, was in some ways a more authentically Cambodian king than the Theravada one observed in 1296 by Zhou Daguan. Some authors have connected the abandonment of Angkor—a historical event that may not even have taken place before the 1560s—with a national failure of nerve and certainly with major losses of population. Such losses, the argument runs, would have made it impossible to maintain irrigation works at Angkor, and the water, becoming stagnant, could have become a breeding place for malarial mosquitoes, further depleting the population in a spiraling process. Still other scholars have argued that Theravada Buddhism was in some ways subversive of Angkorean cohesion while it invigorated the politics of Ayudhya and Pagan in Burma; the "peaceable" nature of this variant of the religion has been used to explain Cambodian defeats, but not its victories or those of the Thai, who shared the same beliefs.

What emerges from the evidence is that Cambodia was entering what Ashley Thompson has called its "middle" period well before the abandonment of Angkor. Angkorean institutions—inscriptions, stone temples, a Hindu-oriented royal family, and extensive hydraulic works, to name only four traditions—seem to have stopped, faded, or been redirected soon after the conversion of the Cambodian elite to Theravada Buddhism, an event that probably took place not long after Jayavarman VII's death. It would be premature to see these changes as springing uniquely or even primarily from the ideology or content of the new religion. It is more likely that they were related to the rise of the Theravada kingdom of Ayudhya to the west and to the entanglement, which was to last until the 1860s, between the Thai and Cambodian courts. People, ideas, texts, and institutions migrated west from Angkor to Ayudhya, where they were modified and eventually re-exported into Cambodia to survive its genuine decline from the eighteenth century onward. Much of this migration would have consisted of prisoners of war, including entire families swept off to the west after successive Thai invasions of Angkor, the most important occurring in 1431. As this process was going on, other people and institutions were also migrating southward to the vicinity of Phnom Penh, where the capital of Cambodia was to remain for the next six hundred years.[2]

The suitability of Phnom Penh as a site for a Cambodian capital sprang in large part from its location at the confluence of the Mekong and the Tonle Sap. A fortified city at this point—the "four faces"—could control the riverine trade from Laos as well as trade in rough pottery, dried fish, and fish sauce from the Tonle Sap, to say nothing of incoming goods— primarily Chinese in origin—approaching Cambodia from the Mekong Delta, still largely inhabited by Khmer. Once the choice had been made to become a trading kingdom—and it is impossible to say when, how, or why this happened—locating the Cambodian capital at Phnom Penh no longer made economic sense. At the same time, it seems likely that Angkor itself remained an urban complex throughout the fifteenth century, as Claude Jacques's recent research has shown.[3]

It also seems likely that the shift of the capital to the south represented a momentary triumph, later legitimized and prolonged, of regional interests, and perhaps those of an individual overlord, at the expense of people lingering near Angkor or gathering strength in the Menam Basin to the west. These members of a southeastern Cambodian elite—for these interests were those of chiefs and their followings, rather than rice farmers singly or en masse—probably took advantage of their distance from Ayudhya to trade with China on their own account. It seems likely as well that they could rely on support from overlords long entrenched in the region, which was the heartland of "Funan," an area where Angkorean writ may often have been ignored.

But these are suppositions. It is more certain that the myth connected with the founding of Phnom Penh, which tells of an old woman's discovery of a Buddha image floating miraculously downstream, was concocted after the city had come to life, under a name suggestive of its location at the crossroads of two rivers, a name that has survived into modern Khmer as Chatomuk, or "four faces"—an interesting echo of the iconography of the Bayon.[4]

The role played by foreigners adept at trade in this new city is difficult to assess, but influential figures probably included speakers of Malay, from Champa or the Indonesian islands, who left such words behind in the Cambodian language as *kompong*, or "landing place," and *psaar*, or "market," as well as several bureaucratic titles and administrative terms. The Malay legacy may indeed have been deeper than this and needs to be explored, for seventeenth-century European descriptions of riverine Cambodia, and the way its politics were organized, strongly resemble descriptions from this era and, later, of riverine Malaya.[5] Other foreigners active in Phnom Penh were the Chinese, already busily trading at Angkor in the thirteenth century; there were three thousand of them in Phnom Penh in the 1540s. It seems likely that Chinese and Malay traders and their descendants married into the Cambodian elite, just as the Chinese continued to do later on, tightening the relationships among the king, his entourage, and commercial profits.

By the late fifteenth century, it seems, the social organization, bureaucracy, and economic priorities of Angkor—based on the importance of forced labor and the primacy of a priestly caste—were no longer either strong or relevant. New forms of organization, new settlement patterns, and new priorities based in part on foreign trade became feasible and attractive.

Some of the reasons for the changes that Cambodia underwent in this period have already been suggested. Another element conducive to change might be called the emulation factor, affecting both Phnom Penh (and other capitals nearby) and Ayudhya. These were newly established trading kingdoms, respectful—but perhaps a little wary—of the idea of Angkor. By the 1400s, Ayudhya and these Cambodian cities looked to each other rather than to a brahmanical past for exemplary behavior. Until the end of the sixteenth century, moreover, "Phnom Penh" (or "Lovek" or "Udong") and "Ayudhya" considered themselves not separate polities, but participants in a hybrid culture. The mixture contained elements of Hinduized kingship, traceable to Angkor, and Theravada monarchic accessibility, traceable perhaps to the Mon kingdom of Davaravati, which had practiced Theravada Buddhism for almost a thousand years, as well as remnants of paternalistic, village-oriented leadership traceable to the ethnic forerunners of the Thai, tribal peoples from the mountains of southern China. Throughout the fourteenth century and much of the fifteenth, the language common to both kingdoms was probably Khmer. In both societies the Buddhist *sangha,* or monastic order, was accessible, in its lower reaches at least, to ordinary people. Brought into contact through wars, immigration, and a shared religion, the Thai and the Khmer blended with each other and developed differently from their separate forebears.

This blending was rarely peaceful. Both kingdoms estimated political strength in terms of controlling manpower rather than territory and interpreted such strength (and tributary payments) as evidence of royal merit and prestige. The Thai would have learned from the Khmer, and vice versa, to a large extent via defectors and prisoners of war. Between the fourteenth century and the nineteenth century there were frequent wars, generally west of the Mekong, between the Cambodians and the Thai. These laid waste the regions through which invading and retreating armies marched. The invasions usually coincided with periods of weakness in the areas that were invaded. In the 1570s, for example, after Ayudhya had been sacked by a Burmese army, several Cambodian expeditions were mounted against Siam.

CAMBODIA IN THE FIFTEENTH AND SIXTEENTH CENTURIES

The narrative history of the fifteenth and sixteenth centuries, about which we know so little, can be disposed of fairly quickly. The Thai-oriented administration of the Angkor region, it seems, was overthrown by forces loyal to Phnom Penh toward the middle of the fifteenth century—that is, about twenty years after the last Thai attack on the old capital. Once the Thai were removed from the scene at Angkor, however, neither they nor the Cambodians sought to administer the area for more than a hundred years. During this period, a succession of kings, whose names and dates as reported in the chronicles are probably fictional, held power in Phnom Penh.

By the end of the fifteenth century, the chronicles suggest, conflict had developed between these new rulers, as they renewed and formalized their relations with Ayudhya and with officials or chieftains with followings rooted in the southeastern *sruk,* or districts. Some of these forces, the chronicles state, were led by a former slave; Europeans writing somewhat later stated that this new king was in fact a relative of the monarch whom he had deposed.[6] What is important for later events is that the deposed king, Chan, took temporary refuge in Ayudhya before returning with an army to depose the usurper. His restoration under Thai patronage set a precedent that many Cambodian kings were to follow. So did the fact that he was deposed by forces coming from the eastern portions of the kingdom.

From the 1620s onward, these regions of dissidence could often rely on Vietnamese support. A Cambodian king married a Vietnamese princess in the 1630s and, as a bride-price, allowed Vietnamese authorities to set up customs posts in the Mekong Delta, then inhabited largely by Khmer but beyond the reach of Cambodian administrative control. Over the next two hundred years, Vietnamese immigrants poured into the region, still known to many Khmer today as "lower Cambodia" or Kampuchea Krom. By the end of the twentieth century, over five hundred thousand Cambodians were living in Vietnam, surrounded by more than ten times as many Vietnamese. They retained their distinctive culture, and many twentieth-century Cambodian political leaders—including Son Sen, Son Sann, Ieng Sary, and Son Ngoc Thanh—were born and raised as members of this minority.

In Cambodia itself, the presence of rival patrons to the west and east set in motion a whipsaw between Thai and Vietnamese influence over Cambodia, and between pro-Thai and pro-Vietnamese Cambodian factions at the court. This conflict lasted until the 1860s and revived in different form after the Communist victory in Vietnam in 1975.

The first European to write about Cambodia was probably Tome Pires, whose *Suma Oriental* was written between 1512 and 1515. The kingdom is described as a warlike one, whose ruler "obeys no one," and Pires hinted at the richness of the products that could be obtained from it.[7] He was relying, however, on hearsay; the first eyewitness account comes to us from the Portuguese missionary Gaspar da Cruz, who visited Lovek toward the end of King Chan's reign in 1556. He left after about a year, disappointed by his inability to make converts, and chose to blame his failure on the superstitions of the people and their loyalty to Buddhist monks. Da Cruz was impressed, indeed, by the solidarity of the Cambodians, and in an interesting passage he remarked that they

> dare do nothing of themselves, nor accept anything new without leave of the king, which is why Christians cannot be made without the king's approval. And if some of my readers should say that they could be converted without the king knowing it, to this I answer that the people of the country is of such a nature, that nothing is done that the king knoweth not; and anybody, be he never so simple may speak with the King, wherefore everyone seeketh news to carry unto him, to have an occasion for to speak with him; whereby without the king's good will nothing can be done.

He suggested that the *sangha* contained more than a third of the able-bodied men in Cambodia or, by his estimate, some hundred thousand—a fact with clear implications for politics and the economy. These monks commanded great loyalty from the population, and da Cruz found them to be

> exceedingly proud and vain . . . alive they are worshipped for gods, in sort that the inferior among them do worship the superior like gods, praying unto them and prostrating themselves before them: and so the common people have great confidence in them, with a great reverence and worship: so that there is no person that dare contradict them in anything. . . . [It] happened sometimes that while I was preaching, many round me hearing me very well, and being very satisfied with what I told them, that if there come along any of these priests and said, "This is good, but ours is better," they would all depart and leave me alone.[8]

The absence of inherited riches cited by da Cruz is a vivid example of royal interference in everyday life. When the owner of a house died, da Cruz remarked, "[a]ll that is in it returneth to the king, and the wife and children hide what they can, and begin to seek a new life." Possessions, in other words, were held by people at the king's pleasure, as were ranks, land, and positions in society. This residual absolute power, it seems, gave the otherwise rickety institution of the monarchy great strength vis-à-vis the elite. One consequence of the arrangements cited by da Cruz was that rich families could not, in theory at least, consolidate themselves into lasting antimonarchical alliances; the king's response to them (dispossessing a generation at a time) suggests that kings distrusted the elite.

Da Cruz said nothing about Angkor, although a later Portuguese writer, Diego do Couto, reported in 1599 that some forty years beforehand (in 1550 or 1551) a king of Cambodia had stumbled across the ruins while on an elephant hunt. The story is not confirmed by other sources, but dated inscriptions at Angkor reappear in the 1560s, suggesting that the date of the rediscovery may be accurate, although it may have taken place during a military campaign instead of during a hunt, for the Angkor region was a logical staging area for Cambodian armies poised to invade Siam.

Do Couto wrote that when the king had been informed of the existence of ruins,

> He went to the place, and seeing the extent and the height of the exterior walls, and wanting to examine the interior as well, he ordered people then and there to cut and burn the undergrowth. And he remained there, beside a pretty river while this work was accomplished, by five or six thousand

men, working for a few days. . . . And when everything had been carefully cleaned up, the king went inside, and . . . was filled with admiration for the extent of these constructions.[9]

He added that the king then decided to transfer his court to Angkor; if he ever did so, in fact, it was probably for only a brief period. Two inscriptions from Angkor Wat, moreover, indicate that the temple was partially restored under royal patronage in 1577–1578. Both of these, and two more incised at Phnom Bakheng in 1583, honored the king's young son, in whose favor he was to abdicate in 1584, possibly to delay a coup by his own ambitious and more popular brother.[10] The identically worded Phnom Bakheng inscriptions may refer to this infighting by expressing the hope that the king would no longer be tormented by "royal enemies." It is equally possible, however, that the phrase refers to the Thai royal family, with whom the Cambodian elite had been quarreling throughout the 1570s.

Indeed, in spite of the apparent ideological solidarity noted by da Cruz and the florescence of Buddhism reflected in several inscriptions, the period 1560–1590 was a turbulent one in which Cambodian troops took advantage of Thai weakness (brought on in part by the Burmese sacking of Ayudhya in 1569) to attack Thai territory several times. According to European sources, the Cambodian king, worried by internal and external threats, changed his attitude toward Catholic missionaries, allowing them to preach and sending gifts of rice to the recently colonized centers of Malacca and Manila in exchange for promises of military help (which never in fact arrived). Earlier, the king had apparently attempted to seek an alliance, or at least a nonaggression pact, with the Thai.

The flurry of contradictory activities in the field of foreign relations suggests an instability at the court that is reflected in the frequent moves the king made, his premature abdication, and his unwillingness or inability to remain at peace with the Thai, who unsuccessfully laid siege to Lovek in 1587, a date confirmed by an inscription from southeastern Cambodia.[11] If subsequent Cambodian diplomatic maneuvering is a guide, it seems likely that these sixteenth-century moves were attempts by the king to remain in power despite the existence of heavily armed, more popular relatives and in the face of threats from Ayudhya and the surprisingly powerful Lao states to the north.

By 1593, Thai preparations for a new campaign against Lovek forced the Cambodian king to look overseas for help. He appealed to the Spanish governor-general of the Philippines, even promising to convert to Christianity if sufficient aid were forthcoming. Before his letter had been acted on, however, the king and his young son fled north to southern Laos, and another son was placed in charge of the defense of Lovek; the city fell in 1594.

Although Cambodian military forces were often as strong as those of the Thai throughout most of the seventeenth century, and although, as we shall see, European traders were often attracted to Cambodia almost as strongly as they were to Ayudhya, Thai and Cambodian historiography and Cambodian legend interpret the capture of Lovek as a turning point in Cambodian history, ushering in centuries of Cambodian weakness and Thai hegemony. The facts of the case as they appear in European sources are more nuanced than this, but the belief is strong on both sides of the poorly demarcated border that a traumatic event (for the Cambodians) had taken place.

The popular legend of *preah ko preah kaev,* first published in fragmentary form by a French scholar in the 1860s, is helpful on this point and worth examining in detail.[12] According to the legend, the citadel of Lovek was so large that no horse could gallop around it. Inside were two statues, *preah ko* ("sacred cow") and *preah kaev* ("sacred precious stone"); inside the bellies of these statues, "there were sacred books, in gold, where one could learn formulae, and books where one could learn about anything in the world. . . . Now the king of Siam wanted to have the statues, so he raised an army and came to fight the Cambodian king."

The legend then relates an incident contained in the chronicles as well. Thai cannon fired silver coins, rather than shells, into the bamboo hedges that served as Lovek's fortifications. When the Thai retreated, the Cambodians cut down the hedges to get at the coins and thus had no defenses when the Thai returned in the following year to assault the city. When they had won, the Thai carried off the two statues to Siam. After opening up their bellies, the legend tells us,

> they were able to take the books which were hidden there and study their contents. *For this reason* [emphasis added] they have become superior in knowledge to the Cambodians, and for this reason the Cambodians are ignorant, and lack people to do what is necessary, unlike other countries.

Although keyed to the capture of Lovek, the legend may in fact be related to the long-term collapse of Angkor (insofar as this could be "remembered") and perhaps to the relationships that had developed between Siam and Cambodia by the nineteenth century, when the legend emerged in the historical record. The temptation to prefer the earlier collapse as the source for the legend may spring from the fit between the legend's metaphors and what we know to have happened—i.e., the slow transferal of Cambodia's regalia, documents, customs, and learned men from Angkor to Ayudhya in the period between Jayavarman VII's death and the Thai invasion of 1431. The statue of *preah ko* is a metaphor for Cambodia's Indian heritage and probably represents Nandin, the mount of Siva. The less precisely described *preah kaev* is a metaphor for Buddhist legitimacy, embodied by a Buddha image like the one taken from Vientiane by the Thai in the 1820s (and known as a *preah kaev*) to be enshrined in the temple of that name in Bangkok; a replica is housed in the so-called Silver Pagoda in Phnom Penh. The seepage of literary skills from Cambodia to Siam, and the increasing power of the Thai from the seventeenth century onward, are ingredients in the legend, which, like that of the leper king discussed in Chapter 4, may contain a collective memory of real occurrences half-hidden by a metaphorical frame of reference. The Cambodian scholar Ang Choulean, in his discussion of this legend, has called it "partially historic, mostly legend, but above all totally coherent."[13]

The myth, in other words, may have been used by many Cambodians to explain Cambodia's weakness vis-à-vis the Thai in terms of its unmeritorious behavior (chasing after the coins) and its former strength in terms of palladia that could be taken away.

The last five years of the sixteenth century, when the capture of Lovek took place, are well documented in European sources. These years were marked by Spanish imperialism in Cambodia, directed from the Philippines and orchestrated largely by two adventurers named Blas Ruiz and Diego de Veloso.[14] Their exploits illuminate three themes that were to remain important in Cambodian history later on. The first was the king's susceptibility to blandishments and promises on the part of visitors who came, as it were, from "outer space." Both Spaniards were honored with bureaucratic titles and given *sruk* to govern and princesses for wives. The second theme was the revolution in warfare brought on by the introduction of firearms, particularly naval cannon, which played a major part in all subsequent Cambodian wars. Because they were masters of a new technology, Ruiz and de Veloso were able to terrorize local people—just as their contemporaries could in Spanish America, while accompanied by fewer than a hundred men.

The third theme was that by the end of the sixteenth century, the Cambodian king and his courtiers had become entangled in the outside world, symbolized at the time by the multitude of foreign traders resident in Lovek and Phnom Penh. European writers emphasized the importance of these people and the foreign residential quarters at Lovek. These included separate quarters for Chinese, Japanese, Arabs, Spanish, and Portuguese as well as traders from the Indonesian archipelago; they were joined briefly in the seventeenth century by traders from Holland and Great Britain.[15] The traders worked through officials close to the king and members of the royal family, as well as through their compatriots. In the seventeenth century, according to Dutch sources, foreign traders were required to live in specific areas of the new capital, Udong, reserved for them and to deal with the Cambodian government only through appointed representatives, or *shabandar*. This pattern may have originated in China and also applied in Siam; its presence at Lovek in the depths of Cambodia's "decline," like other bits of data, suggests that the kingdom was by no means dead.

The Spanish missionary San Antonio also left an account of the closing years of the sixteenth century that includes the adventures of Ruiz and de Veloso. His account is often illuminating and occasionally comic, as when he attributed the construction of the temples at Angkor to the Jews, echoing local disbelief in Cambodian technology.[16] In addition, he was convinced that Spain should colonize the kingdom for religious and commercial reasons, and this may have led him, like many early explorers, to exaggerate the value of its resources, as French visitors were to do in the 1860s. His impressions of prosperity may have sprung from the fact that visitors were forced by the absence of overland communication to limit their observations of Cambodia to the relatively rich and populated areas along the Mekong north of Phnom Penh—an area that was still one of the most prosperous in Cambodia when it was studied four hundred years later by Jean Delvert.[17] The goods that San Antonio saw included gold, silver, precious stones, silk and cotton cloth, incense, lacquer, ivory, rice, fruit, elephants, buffalo, and rhinoceros. The last was valued for its horns, skin, blood, and teeth as a "subtle antidote for a number of illnesses, particularly those of the heart"—a reference to the Chinese belief that rhinoceros by-products were effective as aphrodisiacs. Like Frenchmen of the 1860s, San Antonio stressed that Cambodia was prosperous because it was a gateway to Laos, which, almost unknown to Europeans, was assumed to be some sort of El Dorado. He closed his discussion of Cambodia's prosperity with a passage that might seem to have been lifted from "Hansel and Gretel": "There are so many precious things in Cambodia that when the king [recently] fled to Laos, he scattered gold and silver coins, for a number of days, along the road so that the Siamese would be too busy gathering them up to capture him."[18]

San Antonio also remarked that the country contained only two classes of people, the rich and the poor:

> The Cambodians recognize only one king. Among them there are nobles and commoners. . . . All the nobles have several wives, the number depending on how rich they are. High ranking women are white and beautiful; those of the common people are brown. These women work the soil while their husbands make war. . . . The nobles dress in silk and fine cotton and gauze. Nobles travel in litters, which people carry on their shoulders, while the people travel by cart, on buffalo, and on horseback. They pay to the principal officials, and to the king, one-tenth of the value of all goods taken from the sea and land.

The slave-owning, nonmercantile "middle" class noted by Zhou Daguan in the thirteenth century seems by now to have diminished in importance, although there is evidence from legal codes and at least one chronicle that it continued to exist.[19] It is possible that its place was taken in Cambodian society by foreign traders and semi-urban hangers-on, while ethnic Khmer remained primarily rice farmers, officials, monks, and gatherers of primary produce. Another mediating "class" in Cambodian society, of course, consisted of the *sangha*, about whom San Antonio's contempt exceeded his curiosity. What emerges from his account, and from others by European visitors, is a picture of a Cambodian social structure that remained essentially unchanged from the sixteenth century to the nineteenth.

As so often in Cambodian history, the rice farmers are omitted from the record. We see the people the visitors saw—the king, the elite, the foreign traders, and their slaves. Inland from the *kompong*, villages were linked to the trading capitals by economic relationships, by taxation, and by the social mobility provided by the *sangha*; the villagers were leading their own lives. At least, this is what we must suppose, for without these people, kingship and other institutions in Cambodia would have withered on the vine. But like the particles of subatomic physics, in terms of which atomic behavior makes sense, these major actors are invisible to the eye.

In the first half of the seventeenth century, Cambodia became for the first time since the "Funan" era a maritime kingdom, with the prosperity of its elite dependent on seaborne overseas trade, conducted in large part by the European traders, Chinese, and ethnic Malays operating out of Sumatra and Sulawesi. Japanese and European visitors—Dutch, English, and Portuguese—left records of this period that are useful as they corroborate and supplement the Cambodian chronicles. These people were also involved in factionalism at the court and in plotting among themselves.

The period came to a climax of sorts in the early 1640s when a Cambodian king married a Malay woman and converted to Islam. He is known in chronicles as the "king who chose [a different] religion." In 1642, a Dutch naval force attacked Phnom Penh, to avenge the murder of Dutch residents of the capital, but it was driven off. In the 1650s, rival princes sought military help from Vietnam to overthrow the Moslem monarch, and when the troops came, they were reinforced by local ones recruited in eastern Cambodia—a pattern followed in Vietnamese incursions in the nineteenth century and the 1970s. After a long campaign, the Cambodian king was captured and taken off in a cage to Vietnam, where some sources assert that he was killed and others that he died soon afterward of disease.

The remainder of the seventeenth century saw a decline in international trade as Cambodia's access to the sea was choked off by the Vietnamese and by coastal settlements controlled by Chinese merchants who had fled southern China with the advent of the Qing dynasty. The newcomers turned Saigon into an important, accessible trading center. Phnom Penh became a backwater, and by the eighteenth century, Cambodia was a largely blank area on European maps.

VALUES IN SEVENTEENTH-CENTURY CAMBODIA

It would be wrong to suggest that seventeenth-century Cambodian society can be best understood in terms of timelessness. In many ways, it differed from its nineteenth-century counterpart. For example, nineteenth-century Cambodia had been brought to its knees by foreign powers; seventeenth-century Cambodia was still reasonably independent. Nineteenth-century Cambodia was isolated from the outside world by the same two powers—Siam and Vietnam—that dominated its internal politics; seventeenth-century Cambodia, on the other hand, traded freely with many countries. Also, the elite Cambodian literary tradition, enshrined in the local version of the *Ramayana*, the *Reamker* ("the Glory of Rama"), as well as in the inscriptions at Angkor Wat and other works, was, as we shall see, far more vigorous in the seventeenth century than in the nineteenth.

Saveros Pou has attributed these changes in part to Thai influence but more profoundly to what she referred to as a "slow degradation of values from the seventeenth century on."[20] It is easy to share her impression after reading the *Reamker* alongside some of the fatuous verse-novels composed in the 1880s or after comparing the seventeenth-century legal codes, translated by Adhémard Leclère, with the scattered and timorous documents left behind by nineteenth-century kings. Although the values she referred to emanated from the elite, Pou saw the decline as one that altered the collective acceptance of traditional values. She saw these values, in turn, as linked with Buddhist notions of the cosmos (enshrined in the didactic poem known as the "Trai Phum," or "Three Worlds"), especially as these filtered into Buddhist teaching in oral form, enshrined in the aphoristic collection of "laws," or *chbab*, memorized by Cambodian schoolchildren until very recently.[21] In other words, she viewed seventeenth-century Cambodia as a nation abiding by rules that were later watered down, abused, or forgotten.

These values—seldom in fact acted out by a particular monarch—are those that delineate proper conduct for the people. This conduct has to do in large part with one's position in society and governs the way one relates to others. Everyone, of course, comes equipped with several positions, being at the same time older than some and younger than others, richer and poorer, wiser and more foolish, and so on. An elderly "inferior" is to be addressed with respect, for example; so is a younger monk, and a monk of peasant origin, in theory at least, is to be paid homage by a king. In many cases, moreover, one person's patron is someone else's client.

The *chbab* stress several normative relationships of this kind, the most important of which are probably those with parents and teachers. According to the *chbab*, these authority figures convey material to be memorized. There is nothing to discuss. The teacher's relation to his student, like so many relationships in Cambodian society, is lopsided. The teacher, like a parent, bestows, transmits, and commands. The student, like the child, receives, accepts, and obeys. Nothing changes in the transmission process, except perhaps the ignorance of the student; knowledge is passed on from student to student over generations, and if this involves little or no "progress," we should recall that the idea of progress is not especially widespread and was not well known in precolonial Southeast Asia. What kept society coherent, Cambodians thought, was the proper observance of relationships among people as well as the shared acceptance of Buddhist ideology. The first of these involved proper language and appropriate behavior. The Khmer language, like many others in Southeast Asia (Javanese is perhaps the best example), displays differences between people in the pronouns they use in speaking to each other and, in exalted speech (used to describe royalty or monks, for example), in many verbs and nouns as well. Except among close friends not otherwise related (for relatives, family-oriented pronouns would normally be used), no word in traditional Khmer translated readily as "you" or "I." Instead, words emphasized the status of the speaker in relation to the person addressed. Thus, "you" could be directed "up," or "down," as could "I" and the other personal pronouns.[22]

Cambodian thinkers also saw the universe in graded terms, with people inhabiting "middle earth." This is a familiar concept in many cultures, and so is its corollary, that behavior on earth has been prescribed by heroes who have passed "above" or "below" us. To those of us accustomed to expanded (or fragmented) frames of reference, this picture of the world entails enslavement or mystification. To scholars like Saveros Pou, however, and, it would seem, to the poets who composed the *Reamker*, the picture offered little to complain about in moral or aesthetic terms.[23] Perhaps there is a relationship between the day-to-day dangers of a society and the energy of belief that its thinkers invest in otherworldly or exceptionally beautiful alternatives. But to say this is to suggest that the *Reamker* is essentially a vehicle by which to escape society; its authors and many of its listeners, on the other hand, might say that the poem was an excellent vehicle for understanding it.

Egalitarian ideals and the related notion of class warfare have perhaps eroded our sympathies for hierarchical societies, which in contemporary terms—themselves ephemeral, of course—appear to make no sense. We think of society as being at war with itself, or at peace, brushing up against other societies with different interests, and so on. Seventeenth-century Cambodians had no word for "society" at all; the word *sangkhum* appears to have entered the language via Pali, and Thailand, in the 1930s. They preferred to think of themselves in terms of a king and his subjects; in terms of a spectrum of relative merit; or as people, scattered over time and space, sharing recognizable ideals that sprang, in turn, from being farmers, being lowly, being Buddhists, and speaking Khmer.

Perhaps the best way to enter the thought-world of seventeenth-century Cambodia is to look at the *Reamker* itself. The version that has survived contains only some of the events related in the Indian original, and many of these have been altered to fit into a Theravada Buddhist frame of reference and into Khmer. Although its characters inhabit a recognizably Indian, brahmanical world (as well as half-mythical kingdoms far away, it seems, from Southeast Asia), their behavior, language, and ideals are very much those of the Cambodian people who assembled to listen to the poem or to watch it enacted by dancers, poets, and musicians. These additional dimensions resemble the way in which medieval and Renaissance painters in Europe depicted Greek and biblical figures wearing European clothes.

The plot of the *Reamker* can be easily summarized. Sent out in disgrace from the kingdom he was about to inherit, Prince Ream (Rama), accompanied by his wife, Sita, and his younger brother, Leak (Laksmana), travels in the forest and has many adventures until Sita is taken away by the wicked Prince Reab (Ravana), who rules the city of Langka. Aided by the prince of the monkeys, Hanuman, Ream attacks Langka, hoping to regain his wife, and wins a series of battles. Here the narrative breaks off. In terms of plot alone, it is difficult to understand the hold the *Reamker* has had for so long on the Cambodian imagination. Its language is often terse, and the development of the action is occasionally obscure. This is partly because the poem has come down to us as a series of fairly brief episodes, each suitable for mime (with the verse to be recited) and geared to a performance by dancers or leather shadow puppets.

In modern times, episodes from the poem were often enacted by the palace dancers; in the countryside, events from the poem were acted out as part of village festivals.[24] A complete oral version, somewhat different from the printed text, was recorded in Siem Reap in 1969.[25] The relation of these Cambodian poems to other versions elsewhere in Southeast Asia is an important issue that remains to be explored.

Reenactment of the *Ramayana*, Battambang, 1966. Photo by Jacques Nepote.

What probably captivated so many Cambodians about the *Reamker* was its combination of elegance and familiarity. Its subject—the conflict of good and evil—is the theme of much epic literature. On one level, the poem is a statement of Theravada Buddhist values; on another, a defense of hierarchy and the status quo; and on a third, it is about the contrast between what is wild (*prey*) and what is civilized. The poem, in a sense, is itself a civilizing act, just as the Javanese word for "chronicle" (*babad*) is derived from one that means to "clear the forest."[26] Goodness in the poem and its three heroes is linked to meritorious action and elegance. Evil characters are unpredictable, passionate, in disarray.[27] The contrast is by no means mechanical, however, and is worked out in the course of the poem with considerable subtlety. The savage ruler of the forest,

Kukham, for example, is filthy and spontaneous but is redeemed by his meritorious deference to Ream. On the other hand, Reab, the prince of Langka, consumed with passion and a slave to it, is almost as royal and at times nearly as elegant as Ream and Sita.

The role played by the *Reamker* in prerevolutionary Cambodia resembles the one enjoyed by the *wayang,* or shadow-puppet theater, in Java and Bali. Many Cambodians, in their occasional encounters with the poem, found in it a completeness and balance probably missing from their everyday lives. Good and evil, as we all can see, are at war, and evil is often victorious. In the poem, however, the two are perpetually in balance, held in place, as it were, by almost equal quantities of ornamental verse. In the strophes that have survived, the major actors are never destroyed, perhaps because evil and good must survive in order to define each other. In the *Reamker,* as in many of the poems enacted in *wayang,* "nothing happens"[28] in the sense that nothing important is different from one end of the poem to the other. Certainly nothing changes or turns around. The poem is useless as a revolutionary text, and it is also useless, in a narrow sense, as a historical document, because we cannot locate it in a particular time and place. Its verbal elegance and its austerity, however, allow us a glimpse of the seventeenth-century Cambodian elite's range of values and of a high artistic polish that would be difficult to associate with a period of intellectual decline.

Placed against what we know of events in the seventeenth century, the gap between ideals and reality, as expressed in the poem, is wide and deep. Chronicles and European sources reveal a country whose capital was isolated from its hinterland; whose royal family was murderous, intriguing, and unstable; and which was at the mercy, much of the time, of elite factions, national catastrophes, and invaders. The persistence of Cambodian elites, however, and the continuity of overseas trade suggest that these crises, real enough at the time, were periodic rather than perpetual and affected the parts of the country that armies moved across rather than those outside their paths.

A revealing social document from this period is a collection of fifty anecdotes, allegedly provided by an elderly female member of the royal family when a new set of Cambodian law codes was promulgated in the 1690s.[29] These deal with the notion of *lèse majesté* and thus concern the position of royalty in Cambodian society; they also reveal the strengths and weaknesses of Cambodian kingship at this time. The king's greatest strength, it seems, sprang from his capacity to assign and revoke titles, which were permissions to exploit people less fortunately endowed. Offenders against the king could be stripped of their possessions, and crimes of *lèse majesté,* even at several removes, were severely dealt with. One anecdote, for example, relates how a princess ordered her advisers to find her some fish. The officials encountered a fisherman, who muttered that they had no right to take his fish without paying for them. The officials took the fish and informed the princess about him, and he was fined for disrespect. Another anecdote relates that a king, out hunting, wandered from his entourage and encountered a buffalo tender, who addressed him in ordinary language. Instead of punishing the man, the king returned to his followers to declare that he had increased his fund of merit, as he had obeyed the law that did not allow a king to punish subjects for disrespect outside the palace. "If I had shot the man when I was alone," he said, "I would have done a prohibited thing, and after my death I would have fallen into hell, because, after all, the man didn't know that I was the king." Other anecdotes reveal that the monarch was often used by ordinary citizens as the court of last resort, as Zhou Daguan had suggested in the thirteenth century.

These anecdotes differ from the chronicles and from the *Reamker* by providing day-to-day information about the king. They provide a picture of a variegated, conservative, and hierarchically organized society, consisting of a few thousand privileged men and women, propped up by an almost invisible wall of rice farmers, in which great emphasis was placed on rank and privilege and on behavior thought to be appropriate to one's status. The texts also reveal how perilous it was to enjoy power in seventeenth-century Cambodia. The king ruled through changeable networks of favorites and relations, and he governed in many cases, it would seem, by pique. Officials rose into favor and fell from one day to the next. A chronicle from this period, for example, relates that a royal elephant trainer was named minister of war (*chakri*) after saving the king's life while hunting. A European minister, on the other hand, fell from office for having struck a monk who had inadvertently splashed water on his cloak.[30] Although the society was permanently ranked, change was possible and could rarely be predicted.

VIETNAMESE AND THAI
INTERFERENCE IN CAMBODIA

The impression of instability was exacerbated by increasing foreign interference, particularly from the Vietnamese, whose "march to the south" (*nam tien*) had carried colonists into the Mekong Delta by the 1620s. In 1626, the Nguyen overlords of the south[31] broke off their ties with the northern Le dynasty and began governing the southern region on their own. Although the area was lightly populated, Nguyen control soon had the effect of sealing off Cambodia's southeastern frontier. The Vietnamese intrusion also had three long-term effects. First, the takeover of Saigon (known to Cambodians even today as Prey Nokor), first by customs agents in the 1620s and seventy years later by Nguyen administrators, meant that Cambodia was now cut off from maritime access to the outside world, especially after other, smaller ports along the Gulf of Siam were occupied in the early eighteenth century by Chinese and Sino-Vietnamese entrepreneurs and Vietnamese troops.[32] Cambodian isolation, which lasted nearly two hundred years, was unique in precolonial Southeast Asia, with the exception of Laos. Second, the Nguyen institutionalization of control, a process that took more than two hundred years, eventually removed large portions of territory and tens of thousands of ethnic Khmer from Cambodian jurisdiction. This process produced a legacy of resentment and anti-Vietnamese feeling among Cambodians inside Cambodia that fueled the collapse of Democratic Kampuchea and has persisted among many Cambodians up to the present. Finally, by taking over the delta and extending de facto control over the Gulf of Siam (a state of affairs that lasted through the eighteenth century), the Nguyen placed Cambodia in a vise between two powerful neighbors; its capital region, moreover, was more accessible to Saigon than to Ayudhya or Bangkok.

A side effect of the advent of Vietnamese power was that the Cambodian royal family was now able to split along pro-Thai and pro-Vietnamese lines. Depending on which power supported an incumbent, his rivals would seek support from the other to overthrow him. The history of Cambodia in the eighteenth and nineteenth centuries, therefore, is one of repeated invasions from Vietnam and Siam, preceded and followed by ruinous civil wars. Instability at the center extended into the *sruk*. Because loyalty to the throne was costly, perilous, and easy to avoid, by the end of the eighteenth century large areas of the kingdom were under only nominal control from Udong, and this state of affairs, in turn, decreased the king's ability to respond to foreign invasions. The king's power to reward his friends and punish dissidents had been weakened by the rapid succession of monarchs, communication difficulties, and the need to withstand repeated foreign attacks.

At the same time, it seems likely that a certain continuity persisted at the capital among the bureaucratic elite. Several inscriptions at Angkor from the late seventeenth and early eighteenth centuries record the careers of important officials whose graceful rise to increasing responsibility contrasts sharply with the jagged sequence of events related by the chronicles.[33] Moreover, Vietnamese and Thai accounts agree that at several points in the eighteenth century (when it would be tempting to assert that Cambodia had already been bled white), Cambodian forces managed to repel their invading armies. This suggests, at the very least, that some regional leaders, nominally officials of the crown, were able in a crisis to mobilize enough supporters to harass and defeat a foreign expeditionary force, especially when skilled in guerrilla warfare.

Evidence from the chronicles suggests, however, that one of the darkest periods of Cambodian history came in the last few decades of the eighteenth century. The ingredients—dynastic instability, foreign invasions, civil wars—were familiar ones, but this time they were on a large scale.

The 1750s and 1760s were relatively calm as far as invasions from Siam and Vietnam were concerned, but they also saw a series of coups and countercoups by rivals in the royal family that involved assassinations and reprisals. In 1767, Ayudhya fell to a Burmese army, and when a Thai prince and his entourage sought asylum in Cambodia and threatened to set up a legitimate kingdom there, a Thai regional overlord, Taksin, who had assumed royal power in Siam, launched a series of expeditions against Cambodia beginning in 1768.[34] His aims were to reestablish Thai hegemony over the region and thus to backdate what he interpreted as his own enormous fund of merit. He also sought to avenge himself against the Cambodian king who, according to the chronicles, refused to send gifts to him because he was the "son of a Chinese merchant and a commoner," charges that appear to have been true. There is some evidence also that he wanted to put his own son on the Cambodian throne.

Thai pressure on the kingdom persisted into the 1770s, when the Nguyen were distracted by a populist rebellion, led by the so-called Tay Son brothers, which threatened to overturn institutions throughout Vietnam. Sensing weaknesses in northern Vietnam, Thai armies attacked overland via Angkor, and their naval expeditions laid waste several small ports along the Gulf of Siam, partly in order to divert Chinese traders from this region to the vicinity of Bangkok and partly to avenge an earlier expedition financed by Chinese merchants from these coastal enclaves that had almost succeeded in capturing the new Thai capital, Thonburi. In 1772, the Thai burned down Phnom Penh. Seven years later, a Thai protégé, Prince Eng, then only seven years old, was placed on the Cambodian throne at Udong under the regency of a pro-Thai official. In 1782, Taksin himself was deposed, to be replaced by his minister of war, then campaigning in Cambodia. The personal involvement of these two men in Cambodian affairs set a pattern for Thai interference there throughout the nineteenth century, although publicly, and perhaps privately as well, their motives for intervention included the more noble one of protecting Cambodian Buddhism and related institutions against persistent and heretical Vietnamese incursions.

By the 1780s, the heir to the Nguyen throne, fleeing the Tay Son, had taken refuge in Bangkok, providing the basis for a rapprochement between the two nations when and if the prince assumed control of all Vietnam, as he did in 1802.

Prince Eng was taken off to Bangkok in 1790 and was anointed there by the Thai before being sent back to Cambodia four years later. His reign, which opened up a cycle of nineteenth-century history, is discussed in Chapter 6; the fact that he was crowned in Bangkok is symbolic of his dependence on the Thai.

CONCLUSIONS

The two main features of Cambodia's "middle" period were a shift of the capital from the rice-growing hinterlands of northwestern Cambodia to the trade-oriented riverbanks in the vicinity of Phnom Penh on the one hand and the increasing importance of foreign powers in Cambodian internal affairs on the other. It seems clear that the apparent self-sufficiency of Angkor was as much related to the absence of military rivals as to the inherent strength or flexibility of Angkorean institutions. Many of these institutions, in fact, persisted into the middle period, both in Cambodia and in Thailand, and got in the way of rapid bureaucratic responses (supposing that this was psychologically possible or culturally rewarding) in the face of foreign and domestic pressure.

Because of the shortage of data, it is impossible to trace the ideological history of Cambodian villagers or to compare their responses to experiences in the Angkorean era to those in subsequent times. How much difference did it make for them to become Theravada Buddhists, for example? What were the effects on daily life of the commercialization of the elite after 1500—to say nothing of the other changes noted in this chapter? Did the Europeans they saw have any effect on them? And what differences did they perceive, aside from linguistic ones, in being "Cambodian" instead of "Thai"?

There were several important changes between the fourteenth century and the beginning of the nineteenth, and the most important of these, perhaps, was the decline in importance of a brahmanical priestly class that had effectively linked landholdings, control of slaves, religious practices, education, and the throne. Perhaps equally important, but harder to pin down, was the widespread and apparently increasing influence of the Thai on Cambodian life. Frank Huffman has shown that the transformation that occurred in the Khmer language in the post-Angkorean period, which reached its climax in the nineteenth century, amounted to the replacement of Angkorean syntax by its Thai counterpart.[35] Saveros Pou regarded this process as inimical to Cambodian identity, especially in terms of its effects on literary style, but recognized its importance in the history of the period.

Another important change—the intrusion of the Vietnamese into Cambodian life—came later on, reaching peaks in the nineteenth and twentieth centuries. Even in the eighteenth century, however, Vietnamese activities had the effect of sealing off Cambodia from the outside world at exactly the moment when other Southeast Asian countries, especially Siam, were opening up.

A final change was the decline in the popularity of kingship. Of all the post-Angkorean kings of Cambodia, only Duang (r. 1848–1860) and Norodom Sihanouk seem to have struck a sustained chord of popular approval. The discontinuity between the palace and the people that is noticeable in the legal anecdotes of the 1690s probably widened in the chaos that affected the entire country in the following century. But this "decline," like many notions put forward about Cambodian history, is impossible to verify. After all, during the heyday of Angkor, we have only the kings' own words to support the notion that they were popular. Like the *Ramayana*, the king and his entourage had roles to play in people's thinking, but they played *central* roles only in their own. Although Clifford Geertz's phrase "theater state"—originally applied to precolonial Java and more recently to nineteenth-century Bali[36]—can be used with caution to describe Cambodian court life, most Cambodian people probably knew and cared less about it than some scholars, entranced perhaps by the exoticism of the "theatrical" arrangements, might prefer. In periods of stability, of course, Cambodians probably had more time for ceremony, and more surplus to pay for ceremonies, than in periods of warfare, famine, or distress. Between 1750 and 1850, however, the failure of successive kings to deliver protection and stability may well have undermined the relevance of the monarchy in the eyes of the rural poor. But the texts that have survived are ambiguous and inconclusive, and, as we shall see, when popular monarchs like Duang or Norodom Sihanouk came onto the scene, they were revered more than ever. In any case, the rural poor could imagine no alternative set of political or patronage arrangements, outside of easily snuffed-out millenarian rebellions, that could grant them the protection they needed to plant, harvest, and survive.

CHAPTER 6

State, Society, and Foreign Relations, 1794–1848

In the half century or so before the arrival of the French, who established a protectorate over Cambodia in 1863, Cambodian ideas about political geography did not include the notion that "Cambodia" was defined primarily by the lines enclosing it on a map.[1] Maps were rarely used, and no locally drawn map of Cambodia in the early nineteenth century appears to have survived.[2] Instead, to the people who lived there, "Cambodia" probably meant the *sruk* where Cambodian was spoken and, more narrowly, those whose leaders (*chaovay sruk*) had received their official titles and seals of office from a Cambodian king.

Cambodians also thought of their country, metaphorically, as a walled city with several imaginary gates. One chronicle places these at Sambor on the upper Mekong, Kompong Svay north of the Tonle Sap, Pursat in the northwest, Kampot on the coast, and Chaudoc, technically across the frontier in Vietnam in the Mekong Delta.[3] Fittingly, these gates were the places where invading armies traditionally swept into Cambodia. The territory they enclosed, in the form of a gigantic letter "C" (there was no eastern gate, for armies did not cross the Annamite cordillera), covered roughly half the area of Cambodia today.

Inside this imaginary wall, *sruk* varied in size and importance. Although boundaries were generally vague, some, like Pursat and Kompong Svay, extended over several hundred square miles; others, like Koh Chan or Lovea Em, were islands in the Mekong or short stretches along the river.

SOCIETY AND ECONOMY

Little information about the size and composition of Cambodia's population in this period has survived. During the period of Vietnamese suzerainty in the 1830s, a census was taken, but the Vietnamese dismissed its figures as deflated.[4] French administrators in the 1860s, working from roughly compiled tax rolls, estimated Cambodia's population at slightly less than a million.[5] The area between Cambodia's imaginary gates, therefore, may have supported about three-quarters of a million people in the 1840s, but probably fewer, for the records are filled with accounts of regions being depopulated by famine, flight, and invading armies.

This population was overwhelmingly rural. The largest town, Phnom Penh, probably never held more than twenty-five thousand people.[6] The royal capital at Udong and the villages around it supported a population of ten thousand or so in the late 1850s; and the Khmer-speaking city of Battambang, rebuilt by the Thai in the late 1830s, had three thousand inhabitants in 1839.[7] The only parts of the kingdom that were relatively densely settled before the 1860s were those to the south and east of Phnom Penh, like Ba Phnom and Bati, and to the north along the Mekong River south of Chhlong. Significantly, these relatively wealthy *sruk* were often located outside the routes of invasion and retreat chosen by the Thai and the Vietnamese.

Nearly all the people were ethnic Khmer, who occupied themselves with rice farming and with monastic and official life. Commercial and industrial tasks were handled by minority groups. Marketing, garden farming, and foreign trade, for example, were handled by Chinese or by people of Chinese descent.[8] Cattle trading, weaving, and commercial fisheries were controlled by a Moslem minority composed partly of immigrants from the Malay archipelago—known as *chvea*, or Javanese, in Khmer—and partly of immigrants from Champa. The Kui people in the northern part of the country smelted Cambodia's small deposits of iron ore. In the capital, a handful of descendants of Portuguese settlers who had arrived in the sixteenth and seventeenth centuries served as translators for the king and were in charge of his artillery pieces.[9] Before the 1830s there seem to have been few Vietnamese residents. Indeed, even without accurate statistics, it seems likely that there were proportionately fewer of these various groups in the kingdom until the arrival of the French, when the numbers of Chinese and Vietnamese residents in Cambodia increased enormously.[10]

Near the imaginary gates, in thinly populated *sruk* like Kratie, Pursat, and Kompong Svay, tribal groups, such as the Porr, Stieng, and Samre, lived in isolated villages and collected the forest products that formed the main source of a monarch's income and the bulk of the goods that Cambodia sent abroad.

By the standards of other states in Southeast Asia, Cambodia was poor. Unlike Burma and Laos, its soil contained few gems or precious metals. Unlike Siam, its manufacturing, trade, and commerce were underdeveloped, and finished goods, like brassware, porcelain, and firearms, came from abroad. Unlike Vietnam, its communications were poor and its internal markets undeveloped. Agricultural surpluses were rare, savings were low, and money was used only at the palace and by minority groups. Cambodia had a subsistence economy; most of its people spent most of their time growing rice. Landholdings tended to be small (even high officials seldom had access to more than a few hectares), yields were low, and irrigation works, which might have increased production, were rare.

To the Vietnamese emperor, Minh Mang, writing in 1834, Cambodia was truly a "barbarian" country because "the people do not know the proper way to grow food. They use mattocks and hoes, but no oxen. They grow enough rice to have two meals a day, but they do not know how to store rice for an emergency."[11] Villagers often maintained a common pond, or *trapeang*, to water their rice, as they had done at least since "Chenla"; but there were no longer any of the dams and canals that had characterized Angkorean civilization. This was partly because there were now so few mouths to feed. There were no incentives and little technology for farmers to vary their crops, market their surpluses, or increase their holdings. Communications between the *sruk* were poor; there were no roads to speak of until the 1830s, and bandits, invading armies, and the followers of local officials carried off what surpluses they could find.

Foreign trade was restricted because the potentially important entrepôt of Phnom Penh was cut off from the outside world for most of this period by the authorities in southern Vietnam. After 1808, in fact, visitors to Phnom Penh needed Vietnamese permission to go there. Ports on the Gulf of Siam, like Kampot, engaged in some coastal and peninsular trade, but they were more closely integrated into the Vietnamese and Thai economies than into the Cambodian one.[12]

A few ships traded with central Cambodia every year. Cargo lists from two of these, bound for China and Japan respectively in about 1810, have survived.[13] Their cargoes consisted of relatively small amounts of several different products—300 pounds of ivory and 200 pounds of pepper, for example, were among the goods exported to Japan; those going to China included small consignments of cardamom, hides, feathers, tortoise shells, and aromatic wood. Exports to Vietnam in the 1820s—trade with Vietnam was conducted partly in a tributary framework—included such goods as ivory, gutta percha, cardamom, dried fish, and elephant hides.

These were traditional exports. The lists are like others that have come down from the seventeenth century and, via Chinese sources, from the Angkorean period.[14] External trade—including tribute, as we shall see—was an important source of the king's revenues and probably was important to the Chinese community in Phnom Penh and to privileged

A rice-growing village in Kompong Speu, 1961. Author's photo.

members of the king's entourage. But it was insignificant as far as the rest of the country was concerned.

Most Cambodians lived in villages. These can be divided, for the early nineteenth century at least, into three broad types. The first can be called *kompong* after the Malay word meaning "landing-place," which often formed part of their names—as in Kompong Svay and Kompong Som.[15] These were located along navigable bodies of water and could support populations of several hundred people. Often they would include a *chao-vay sruk* and his assistants; the *kompong* was usually enclosed in a stockade. Some of the inhabitants were likely to be Chinese or Sino-Khmer, Malay, and Cham, although minorities tended to keep to themselves in separate hamlets that formed elements of the *kompong*. *Kompong* were in touch with others on the same body of water, with rice-growing villages around them, and indirectly with the capital and the court. Through trading, travel, hearsay, and invasions, people in the *kompong* had some awareness of events elsewhere.

Rice-growing villages, the second category, enclosed the *kompong*—ideally, in a broken arc. Poorer and smaller than *kompong*, rice-growing villages were numerous and more likely to be populated by ethnic Khmer. Houses were scattered around in no special order near a Buddhist monastery, or *wat*, and also near the pond or stream that provided water for the village. Rice-growing villages were linked to the *kompong* and the world beyond in irregular ways—through incursions of officials looking for recruits or rice; through the *wat*, whose monks were encouraged to travel about in the dry season; through festivals at the new year and at other points in the calendar; and through trade with the *kompong*, exchanging rice and forest products for metal, cloth, and salt.

Rice-growing villages were unstable because they lacked means of defense and because, unlike in Vietnam, no institutionalized ancestor cult anchored people to one place rather than another. The chronicles are filled with references to villagers running off into the forest in times of crisis. In times of peace, their lives were shaped by the contours of the agricultural year and the ceremonies—Buddhist, animist, and, vestigially, Hindu—that marked off one stage of the rice-growing cycle from another.[16]

The opposition between "wild" and "civilized," noted in the discussion of the *Reamker* in Chapter 5, persisted in the literature of the nineteenth century. A verse chronicle from Wat Baray, in the north-central part of the kingdom, deals with this theme repeatedly while offering a chronological treatment of nineteenth-century events. The chronicle relates the fortunes of a bureaucratic family caught up in the turmoil of Vietnamese occupation and civil war. Driven into the forest, they lose their identity, regaining it only when new titles are bestowed on male members, first by a Thai monarch and later by a Cambodian one. The chronicle was composed to celebrate the restoration of Wat Baray in 1856, and the audience to whom it was recited would for the most part have recognized the events related in it as true. What gives the chronicle its literary resonance is the way in which the lives of the characters follow patterns laid down for them by the *Reamker* and Buddhist ideology. The restoration of their status accompanied the restoration of the king; demerit was seen, in some way, as associated with the forest, a lack of official titles, and misbehavior impossible to trace.

Similarly, in a poignant Cambodian folktale, probably well known in the 1800s, three girls who are abandoned by their mother become wild and turn into birds, happily crossing the border between forest and field where, as it turns out, the birds they have become are most frequently to be found.[17] Because people's grip on the things we take for granted was so precarious in nineteenth-century Cambodia—dependent on the goodwill of foreigners and overlords, on rainfall, and on health in a tropical climate—it is understandable that "civilization," or the art of remaining outside the forest, was taken so seriously by poets and audience alike.[18]

The third type of village lay hidden in the *prei*, or wilderness, that made up most of Cambodia at this time. Here the people were illiterate and usually non-Buddhist; they spoke languages related to Khmer but owed no loyalties to the *kompong* or the capital unless these had been forced from them. The villages were frequently raided for slaves, and they were economically important because they were able to exploit forest resources that were valued in the capital and abroad. Their political loyalties, however, were to other villages in the *prei* where people spoke the same dialect and performed similar religious rites.

PATRONAGE AND GOVERNMENT

Little information has survived about the way Cambodian villages were governed in the early nineteenth century. Some French writers have asserted that Cambodian villages had no government at all,[19] and in most of them, indeed, relations with outsiders and with the state were sporadic and unfriendly. Quarrels within a village or among neighbors were settled by conciliation rather than by law, and they often smoldered on for years. Villages were usually "ruled," for ceremonial purposes and for the purposes of relations with higher authorities, by elderly men chosen for their agricultural skill, literacy, and fair-mindedness. Taxes in rice and labor seem to have been paid, irregularly, on demand. Village government was perhaps more noticeable in the *kompong*, where there were more officials and hangers-on, but there is no evidence that any villages in Cambodia were governed by formally constituted councils of elders, as was the case in nineteenth-century Vietnam.[20]

Rice-growing villages and those in the *prei* could be days apart from each other and from the nearest representative of authority. In their isolation, the villagers faced inward to the lives and traditions they shared with one another. They identified themselves and saw their history in terms of localized religious traditions passed on from one generation to the next. Outside the villages, just past the fields in most cases, lay the *prei*, crowded with wild animals, malarial mosquitoes, and the spirits of the dead. Beyond the *prei*, where villagers seldom ventured, lay the world of the *kompong*, the capital, and the court.

French writers in the nineteenth century often denigrated Cambodian society (one of them referred to its institutions as "worm-eaten débris")[21] and compared it unfavorably with their own "rational," centralized one or with that of the Vietnamese. The trend has continued among some anthropologists concerned with Thailand, who refer to Thai peasant society as "loosely structured."[22] The phrase is helpful—whether or not one attaches values to "tight structure"—in the sense that in Thai and Cambodian villages in the nineteenth century, there were no "durable, functionally important groups" or voluntary associations aside from the family and the Buddhist monastic order, or *sangha*. When a village organized itself—for defense, for instance, or for a festival—it did so for a short time in response to a specific need.

Despite the apparent informality of these arrangements, there was considerable structural consistency in each Cambodian village and family. This arose from the fact that Cambodians always identified themselves in terms of their status relative to the person being addressed. This identification located them for the moment at a particular, but by no means fixed, point in a flexible set of dyadic relationships extending downward from the king and the *sangha* through the graded bureaucracy of the capital and *kompong* to the villages and past them to the landless debt-slaves and minority peoples living literally at the edges of the state. As with most systematic social arrangements, what mattered to the people who used the system was the place they occupied inside it. If a person's place was relatively secure, people in weaker positions sought him out and offered homage in exchange for protection. The society, in a sense, was fueled by the exchange of protection and service implied in these "lopsided friendships," as they have been called.[23] In a village context, these links might be with older or more fortunate members of one's family, monks in the local *wat*, bandit leaders, government officials, or holy men (*nak sel*) who appeared from time to time, promising their followers invulnerability and riches.

In the *kompong* and the capital, where people no longer grew their own food, patronage and clientship became more important and more complex. Having a patron and having clients were connected with one's chances to survive. People with access to power accepted as many followers or slaves as they could. In many cases, these men and women had contracted debts to their patrons, which they then spent their lifetimes working off. The widespread presence of slavery in nineteenth-century Cambodia should cloud over, to an extent, the sunny notion that clients entered their "lopsided friendships" as volunteers with a variety of choices. But it is true that many people enslaved themselves to a patron, or *me* (the word can also mean "mother"), to protect themselves against the rapacity of others.

The rectitude and permanence of these relationships had been drummed into everyone from birth. Cambodian proverbs and didactic literature are filled with references to the helplessness of the individual and to the importance of accepting power relationships as they are. Both sides of the patron-client equation, in theory at least, saw their relationships as natural, even obligatory ones. "The rich must protect the poor," a Cambodian proverb runs, "just as clothing protects the body."[24]

The relationships were seldom that genteel. Throughout Southeast Asia, patrons, like kings, spoke of "consuming" the territory and people they controlled, and there are few just officials in Cambodian folklore, in which officials are compared to tigers, crocodiles, and venomous snakes. Rural government was seen as an adversary proceeding. In one *sruk* at least, when a new *chaovay sruk* took office, a cockfight was held. One bird represented the newly arrived official; the other, the people of the *sruk*. The outcome of the fight supposedly gave both sponsors a hint about the balance of power that was expected to ensue.[25]

Why did the people accept these demeaning arrangements? Partly it was a case of *force majeure.* The alternatives of individual flight or organized resistance were often impossible. Moreover, a man without a patron was fair game, and an unknown patron, like a foreigner, was more of a threat than one who lived nearby. Although the *chaovay sruk* often "ate" what little material wealth he could get his hands on, the social distance between him and the rest of the *kompong* was not especially great. His wives, for example, were local women. He lived in a simple house, chewed betel, and sponsored festivals at the *wat* and ceremonies to propitiate the *nak ta.* These officials shared their clients' food, their belief in magic, their vigorous sense of the absurd, and their distrust of other officials and all outsiders. Probably because they lived among the people they supposedly controlled, *chaovay sruk* were more responsive to local issues than were authorities in the capital. The fact that all these "lopsided friendships" could be renegotiated in times of stress added to the instability of the system and perhaps to its attractiveness in the eyes of villagers and slaves.

For most Cambodians, these shifting networks of subordination and control, chosen or imposed, benevolent or otherwise, marked the limits of their experience and of their social expectations. Their ideas about the king, on the other hand, and about the Buddhist *sangha* took a different form and were expressed in a different language. Although it is useful to place the king and the *sangha* at the end of imaginary chains of local and spiritual authority extending down through the officials to the people, the people saw them as operating on a different plane and on a different set of assumptions. Little is known about the *sangha* in nineteenth-century Cambodia, and it could be misleading to assert that conditions were the same as those in Siam or Burma. There is no evidence, for example, that the *sangha* played a political role vis-à-vis the royal family, although monks and ex-monks were active in the anti-Vietnamese rebellion of 1821.[26] By and large, monks were widely respected as repositories of merit, as sources of spiritual patronage, and as curators of Cambodia's literary culture. They occupied a unique and thus mysterious place in Cambodian life because they had abandoned—temporarily at least—agriculture, politics, and marriage.

People's ideas about the king tended to be grounded in mythology rather than their own experience. The relationship of the king to most of

Casting a net on the Mekong, 1988, a technique that has remained unchanged for several hundred years. Photo by Christine Drummond.

his subjects was not negotiated, rarely enforced, and seldom face-to-face. For most of the early nineteenth century, by choice or by circumstance, the monarch was confined to his palace or lived in exile in Siam or Vietnam. Because they never saw him and given the weight of traditional and popular literature about him, villagers' views of the king tended to be vaguer and more approving than their views of each other, their patrons, or even the *nak ta*. The king was at once as real and as unreal as the Lord Buddha. People would have accepted the *Ramayana*'s description of royal duties; they were "to be consecrated, to sacrifice, and to protect the people."[27] Many of them believed that the king could influence the weather; unlike the *sauphea*, or judges, he could dispense true justice; he was often the only political source of hope among peasants. This does not mean that he was always or even often in their thoughts; but when he appeared in his capital after years of exile, like Eng in 1794 and Duang nearly half a century later, the event ignited widespread rejoicing.

There were several other segments of Cambodian society that affected people's lives in the villages and the outcome of Cambodian politics as a whole. These included minor *sruk* officials and hangers-on, who were appointed in some cases from the capital and in others by the *chaovay sruk*; ex-monks, or *achar*, who acted as religious spokesmen and millenarian leaders, often in opposition to the *chaovay sruk;* itinerant traders, actors, and musicians; and poor relations of the rich, who were able to act as go-betweens. Unfortunately, the elite-centered chronicles usually devote little space to these categories of people, so it is difficult to assess their power, except directly: A rice-growing village going into revolt against the Vietnamese—as many did in 1820 and 1841, for example—was unlikely to have done so merely through the exhortations of a high official.

THE *OKYA*

Historical records, on the other hand, have left a good picture of Cambodia's high-ranking officials, or *okya*.[28] Included in their number were the *chaovay sruk* and the officials surrounding the king. It is impossible to say how many *okya* there were at any given time. Lists of officials assembled in the 1860s and 1870s for the French are full of gaps and contradictions. Many of the titles in these lists do not appear to have been used, and titles occur in other sources that do not appear in the lists. Roughly, however, there seem to have been about two hundred *okya* in the capital and the countryside throughout most of the nineteenth century. The number was probably smaller after defections to the Thai in the 1830s and larger after Duang's accession. For these two hundred men, about seven hundred titles were available for use. Some of these, like those carried by the king's highest advisers and by most of the *chaovay sruk*, were always used. Others seem to have lapsed, for a while at least, after having been used by one or several incumbents.

Everything about the titles and the work associated with them, except the fact that they were conferred on the incumbent by the king, was subject to adjustment. Sometimes a title carried a rank, and sometimes it was associated with a job, such as maintaining the king's elephants, guarding his regalia, or collecting taxes. Certain titles were reserved for certain *sruk*, and the word *sauphea* when it occurred in a title often implied judicial functions. But none of these rules was rigorously applied. Favorites or people out of favor were given jobs to do or removed from them on an ad hoc basis. People went up the ladder (or fell off) quickly. For example, one official whose function was to be in charge of the throne room of the second king (hardly an arduous calling) was named to head a diplomatic mission to Bangkok in 1819. Another, whose duties were to survey the levels of rice in the royal storehouses, led an army against the Thai in Battambang in 1818; and the list could be extended.

The titles that *okya* carried usually consisted of two or three honorific words, like *ratna* ("jewel") or *verocana* ("splendor"), drawn from Pali or Sanskrit. The *okya* received them along with the seals of office and insignia of rank (which included tiered umbrellas, betel containers, court costumes, and the like) from the king's hands, in an intentionally awesome ceremony built around an oath of allegiance that had been in effect in more or less the same form for at least eight hundred years.[29] At that time, and at regular intervals, the *okya* were expected to give presents to the king. French writers equated this exchange of titles and gifts with the notion that Cambodian government was corrupt, because jobs were available only to the highest bidder. At one level of thinking this was true, but little ethical weight was given to the transaction—high bidders, after all, were people whose power had to be reckoned with. Twice a year, the *okya* assembled at the royal *wat* near the palace, where they drank the "water of allegiance"—water brought to the capital, in theory, from streams throughout the kingdom—and renewed their oaths of allegiance to the king. Failure to attend this ceremony was tantamount to treason.

Once in office, an *okya* became part of the *komlang*, or strength (i.e., entourage) of some higher-ranking person. This might be one of the king's advisers, a member of the royal family, or the king himself. A similar system was in effect in Siam. It is not clear whether these alliances were meant to check or to enhance the power of the *okya* in question—probably they served both purposes at once. The interconnections between certain regions, official posts, family ties, and particular jobs in this period remain obscure. One manuscript chronicle, dating from the early nineteenth century, suggests that the landholdings of *okya* in certain regions persisted from one generation to the next, even when the titles of one *okya* were not passed along to his son.[30] Titles among *okya* were not hereditary. Even the successor to the throne was chosen, after a monarch's death, from among several eligible candidates. A similar fluidity affected *okya* families, although high status seems to have run in particular families.

Despite these continuities, there were few certainties in Cambodian political life. Theoretically, the survival of an *okya* depended on the king, and Akin Rabibhadana cited a 1740 Thai decree that "a king can turn a superior person into a subordinate person, and vice-versa. When he gives an order, it is like an axe from heaven."[31] In reality, however, a king's power depended on how recently he had attained it and how many outstanding debts he had; it was hampered in any case by poor communications between the capital and the *sruk*.

A new king at the start of a dynasty, or after a period of exile, could often act like an "axe from heaven" and fill *okya* positions with men who had been loyal to him in his climb to power. King Duang rewarded his followers in this way in the 1840s, as we shall see, just as the first kings of the Chakri dynasty in Thailand (1782–) and Nguyen dynasty in Vietnam (1802–1945) rewarded theirs. Under a weak king, on the other hand, or one entangled in long-standing obligations, perhaps to older people, *okya* tended to root themselves in the *sruk* and to become more or less independent. In at least one *sruk* in the late nineteenth century, the *chaovay* was selected by other officials there and given seals of office by the regional governor, or *chaomuang*, who was Thai.

Uncertainty was an occupational hazard of Cambodian life. Everyone was on the lookout against everyone else. An *okya*'s obligations toward his king, his family, and his patrons sometimes overlapped and sometimes were in conflict. The other *okya* were potential allies and potential enemies; alliances and betrayals that took advantage of existing power balances occupied a good deal of an *okya*'s time.

Cambodia in the 1800s was not a bureaucratic society, like China or Vietnam, and in times of peace an *okya*'s official duties were light. He had to wait upon his patron; there was little paperwork to do; and many tasks, like requisitioning supplies for the palace or raising armies for defense (there was no standing army), were farmed out among several *okya*, perhaps to keep a single official from becoming too powerful and perhaps because there were no institutional mechanisms to prevent ambitious *okya* from shouldering each other aside in search of profit.

The judgment implied in these remarks may be too strong. Some *okya* were accomplished poets and musicians, and others were generous patrons of Buddhism and the arts. A few emerge from the chronicles as competent, innovative, or brave, but the uncertainty of favor, the ubiquity of rivals, and the unreliability of followers militated against an *okya*'s being active or even attracting official notice. The *okya* and the people, then, were tied to each other with bonds of terror, affection, duty, and contempt within the framework of a shared culture. In Cambodian terms, the system worked, but when the Vietnamese tried to use the *okya* as their spokesmen in Cambodia in the 1830s and 1840s, they found the *okya* incapable of governing the country in a Vietnamese way—which is to say, of *administering* regions, conducting cadastral surveys, collecting taxes, and making detailed reports.

Aside from the king's five closest advisers, who formed a kind of cabinet, the most active and visible *okya* were the *chaovay sruk*, whose role as patrons in the countryside has been discussed. These men enjoyed considerable freedom and considerable power. They were authorized to collect taxes from their *sruk*, which meant that they had access to any surplus crops they could lay their hands on, and they were authorized to mobilize manpower for warfare or public works. In practice they maintained small private armies—rather like their counterparts, the riverine chieftains of nineteenth-century Malaya. In populous *sruk*, these armies sometimes contained several thousand men; in others, they seem to have acted as bodyguards for the *chaovay sruk*. Access to manpower and rice meant that, in effect, the *chaovay sruk* controlled the balance of power in the kingdom. In fact, they more often acted individually than collectively, responding to local interests and dyadic arrangements. This meant that a king could count on some *chaovay sruk* but not on others and that invading armies might find some *chaovay* friendly and others opposed to them.

Some *chaovay sruk* were more important than others. Five of them, called *stac tran*, or kings of the field, were the highest-ranking *okya* and were responsible, in an unspecified way, for the governance of several *sruk* at once.[32] Each grouping was known as a *dei*, or earth. Unfortunately, nineteenth-century references to the phrase *stac tran* occur only in French texts, and the meaning of *tran* itself is not clear. The officials seem to have acted as viceroys, or stand-ins for the king, in the performance of annual ceremonies in the five *dei* honoring the *nak ta*. They had the power to order executions, which the other *chaovay sruk* did not. In a functional sense, they echoed the five high ministers around the king.

These five ministers in the capital were led by a first minister, sometimes referred to as the *ta-la-ha*, and included ministers of justice (*yomraj*), of the army (*chakrei*), of the navy and foreign trade (*kralahom*), and of the palace (*veang*). Each of these officials maintained his own *komlang* and probably had economic and patrimonial links with certain *sruk*. Loosely defined territorial responsibilities of these men overlapped or extended those of the *stac tran* and the *chaovay sruk*, as well as those of certain members of the royal family, who were also entitled to "consume" particular regions. In times of stress, as several chronicles reveal, *okya* retreated to their villages, where they had relatives and land. Despite these regional links, however, the high-ranking *okya* spent their time close to the king, except in war, when some of them were called on to recruit troops and act as generals in the field. Their careers were tied to the fortunes of the king. Their effect on life in the countryside is not so clear. The palace-oriented chronicles probably exaggerate the importance of these men, and so did the Vietnamese when they looked for people to help them centralize and tidy up Cambodian government in the 1830s.

The last segment of Cambodian society that came between the villagers and their king consisted of other members of the royal family. In theory, there could be hundreds of these, for kings were traditionally polygamous, but in the nineteenth century a series of deaths and coincidences sharply reduced their number. King Eng, who died in his twenties, had no surviving brothers and only five children. The oldest of these, Prince Chan, came to the throne when he was only six. When he died more than thirty years later, he left four daughters but no sons. His three brothers (the fourth had died as a child) went to Bangkok in 1812 and stayed there, with brief exceptions, until Chan's death in 1835. This meant that for most of his reign Chan was the only male member of the

royal family living in Cambodia. The factionalism and jockeying for position, a conventional feature of Cambodian court life before and since,
took place offstage, in Siam, and in the late 1830s, in the Cambodian *sruk*
under Thai control.

The Cambodian king, at the pinnacle of society, was remote from his
subjects. Scholars have argued that this remoteness was expected of an
Asian king; he was to rule by his largely invisible example, just as the sun
shone, and he was to act as the custodian of a fund of merit and power—
viewed perhaps as an interlocking, expendable commodity—that he had
accumulated in previous existences en route to the throne. What has
sometimes been called the "purely" religious or symbolic importance of
kingship in Southeast Asia, as transmitted in Indianized texts, has been
overstressed. The frontiers between political and religious actions and institutions were neither sharply delimited nor especially important; in
their daily lives, kings were as concerned with mere survival as with their
religious roles. Nonetheless, it would be incorrect to blot out the religious
importance of kingship with evidence—however easy to assemble—of a
given king's fallibility. Having a king was indispensable. According to the
Ramayana, a country without a king enjoys "neither rain nor seed, neither
wealth nor wife, neither sacrifices nor festivals,"[33] and the alarm of the
okya in 1840–1841 when Cambodia was briefly without a monarch shows
how deeply ingrained these notions were. Only a king was empowered to
hand out the official titles, seals of office, and insignia of rank that held the
Cambodian official class together; one Cambodian law even stated that an
official without a seal did not need to be obeyed.[34]

In addition to setting Cambodia's official class in motion—an action
that had no consistent effect on village life—the Cambodian monarch,
like his counterparts elsewhere in Southeast Asia, presided over a series
of partly brahmanical, partly Buddhist, and partly animistic ceremonies
that, from the villagers' point of view, defined the boundaries of his merit
and the limits of the agricultural year; these were closely related to the
success of their harvests. The ceremonies included ones that honored the
king's ancestors and the *nak ta*, ones that inaugurated and closed the rice-
growing cycle, and ones that marked off stages of the Buddhist and solar
calendars. In many of them the king was assisted by court "brahmans"
called *baku* who also acted as guardians of his regalia—the sacred sword,
arrows, and other objects that he handled once in his lifetime, at his coronation. It is impossible to decide if the regalia were "political" or "religious." Without them, a monarch could rule—handing out titles, raising
armies, and so forth—but he could not reign; he had not been consecrated, as Prince Duang discovered in the 1840s when the Vietnamese
withheld the regalia from him until they could extract favorable peace
terms from the Thai.

The monarch's powers, then, although perhaps overstressed in the written record, remained considerable in the eyes of the *okya* and among the common people. The absence of a monarch was felt, at many points in the society, perhaps more acutely than his presence on the throne.

CAMBODIA'S RELATIONS WITH VIETNAM AND SIAM

As we have seen, the two most important characteristics of post-Angkorean Cambodia were the shift in the country's center of gravity from Angkor to Phnom Penh, with the commercial and demographic ramifications that the move implied, and the roles played by the Thai and Vietnamese. Nineteenth-century Cambodia, therefore, must be seen in part against the background of its foreign relations.

These relations were carried out with two countries, Vietnam and Siam, and occurred within a framework of rivalry between the two larger kingdoms. Rivalry sprang from the unwillingness of either court to accept the other as equal or superior; this unwillingness, in turn, can be traced in part to the traditional language of tributary diplomacy, which stressed the inequality between the sender and the recipient of tribute.

A major objective of Southeast Asian diplomacy in the nineteenth century, indeed, was the ritualized expression of differential status through the ceremonial exchange of gifts. The rules for these tributary exchanges grew out of the particular system in which they occurred. The Thai and the Vietnamese, for example, had separate ones, which overlapped inside Cambodia.

Both systems owed a good deal to their counterpart in China,[35] which had been in effect since the third century B.C. and was still in operation in the 1800s. From a Cambodian point of view, the Thai variant was looser and more idiosyncratic, for the Thai made allowances for local customs and local products; the Vietnamese did not. The latter were rigid in copying the Chinese model. In 1806, for example, Vietnamese Emperor Gia Long, in choosing gifts to send to the Cambodian king, transmitted facsimiles of the ones he had received, at the beginning of his own reign, from the Chinese emperor. Some of these, such as "golden dragon paper for imperial decrees" and Chinese bureaucratic costumes, were meaningless to the Khmer. The seals of investiture sent from Hué to Udong were irrelevant to Cambodians because they had camels carved on them, like the seals that the Chinese court sent to tributary states in central Asia and, incidentally, to Vietnam. One puzzled Cambodian chronicler referred to the animal as a "Chinese lion."[36]

From Vietnam's point of view, Vietnam was "above" Cambodia, just as China was "above" Vietnam. At the same time, of course, Cambodia was "below" Vietnam and Vietnam was "below" China. In other words, Vietnam was the master in one relationship and the servant in the other. As a by-product of this duality, the "civilized" goods sent from Hué to Udong were facsimiles of those sent from Beijing to Hué, while the "barbarian" goods transmitted from Udong were the same sorts of products that Vietnam transmitted to China.[37]

In the matter of tributary gifts, the Thai were more flexible than the Vietnamese. The Chakri kings sent gifts to nineteenth-century Cambodian kings that the recipients could recognize and use. In exchange, the Thai seem to have settled for whatever products they could get. Sometimes Cambodia sent pepper, at other times lacquer and *kravanh* cardamom. There is no evidence, however, that the Cambodians ever transmitted the gold and silver ornamental trees (*banga mas*) that were a feature of tribute to Bangkok from other dependent states.[38]

Similarly, the embassies that King Chan (r. 1797–1835) sent to Bangkok and Hué obeyed different sets of rules, as embassies to Bangkok were larger, more frequent, and more informal. The differences between the two diplomatic systems paralleled differences in Thai and Vietnamese official attitudes toward themselves, each other, and the Khmer. These differences became crucial and painful for the Khmer in the 1830s, when the Vietnamese emperor sought to administer Cambodia directly, in a Vietnamese way. From a Cambodian point of view, however, what mattered about the Thai and Vietnamese tributary systems and attitudes toward Cambodia was not that they were different and made different sorts of demands but, rather, that they were condescending, overlapping, and expensive.

Thai and Vietnamese official relations with each other, until they soured in the 1820s, were marked by considerable informality.[39] This arose in part from a mutual unwillingness on the part of the Thai and the Vietnamese to accept or impose authority, because they enjoyed roughly similar power and prestige. The problem of hegemony did not yet arise in their relations with the Khmer, and notions about the roles both states should play in Cambodia were quite consistent. The barbarity of the Cambodian people and the subservience of their king, for example, were taken for granted, and so was the corollary that each superior state had a sort of civilizing mission to carry out inside Cambodia. The rulers saw themselves, in their official correspondence, as destined to supervise the Khmer. As one Thai diplomatic letter put it, "It is fitting for large countries to take care of smaller ones"; others referred to Chan as an "unruly child" and to the confluence of Thai and Vietnamese policies in Cambodia as "fruit and seeds forming a single unit."

Some of this language was a mask for realpolitik, but these images are nonetheless suggestive. The language of diplomatic correspondence, like the languages in everyday use in Southeast Asia, used pronouns that were hierarchical and family-oriented, and relationships between states were often described by using images of child-rearing. In these, the Thai and the Vietnamese became the "father" and the "mother" of the Khmer, whose king was referred to as their "child" or their "servant." In the 1860s, a French official mused perceptively that Siam was Cambodia's father because its king gave names to the monarch, whereas Vietnam was seen to be the mother because its rulers provided the Khmer with seals of office.[40] Whatever the reasons, Thai and Vietnamese statements, like those made later by the French, amounted to unilateral declarations of dependence. The family-oriented images were unjustified and far-fetched, but they give us a useful way of looking at the period—that is, as the continuing struggle between increasingly incompatible parents for the custody of a weak but disobedient child.

Although Thai political ideas were often couched in Buddhist terminology and Vietnamese ones in terms of a Sino-Vietnamese Confucian tradition, Thai and Vietnamese objectives in Cambodia, seldom voiced explicitly, were similar. Like the Nguyen, they were eager to extend their prestige along their frontiers and to amplify their self-images as universally accepted kings. The Thai rulers also wanted to link themselves as patrons of Buddhism to the *chakravartin*, or wheel-turning monarchs, who had reigned for so many centuries at Ayudhya. These ambitions led the rulers of both states to expand the land and people under their control.

After 1810, King Chan and his advisers were swept up into a game of power politics that they had little chance to change and no opportunity to win. They had no choice. In Vietnamese terms, Cambodia was a "fence," a buffer state, and a dumping-ground for colonists. To the Thai, the Cambodians were fellow-Buddhist "children" basking in a fund of Chakri merit, who could provide cardamom for the court and manpower for Chakri wars. The Thai wanted the Cambodians to be loyal; the Vietnamese wanted access to Cambodia's land and, incidentally, the king's recognition of their superiority. The Thai demanded service and friendship, but they were usually unable—given the way they organized their armies and the distance between Bangkok and Phnom Penh—to provide protection. The Vietnamese, on the other hand, provided protection of a sort, but their actions led to the disappearance of Cambodia as an independent state. By different routes, then, the Thai and the Vietnamese often came to do the same things: taking over certain *sruk*, making hostages of the ruler and his relations, and curtailing the independence of the *okya*.

To Chan and his advisers, the outcome of this game was not obvious at first. In the early part of his reign, his alliance with Vietnam was probably meant only to deflect some of the pressures on him from the Thai. Letters took so long between Bangkok, Udong, and Hué that Chan was able to buy time on several occasions by saying one thing to the Thai and another to the Vietnamese. Moreover, for most of his reign, he kept his communications open with both capitals by means of the embassies he sent them. In fact, Chan may well have been under the impression that the equilibrium that prevailed in the early years of his reign was his own creation and that he had more bargaining power with his patrons than he really did. In this way, he resembled his younger brother's great grandson, Norodom Sihanouk, who ruled Cambodia in the 1960s.

Even if the balance of forces and the inactivity of the Thai and the Vietnamese reflected Thai and Vietnamese choices dictated by their own perceptions of national interest and even if Cambodia's independence reflected what were for the moment limited Thai and Vietnamese ambitions rather than Cambodian skill, there were still advantages to Chan in blurring the lines of his allegiance. One of the chronicles, allegedly quoting Emperor Gia Long, makes this point quite clear:

> "Cambodia is a small country," the Emperor said. "And we should maintain it as a child. We will be its mother; its father will be Siam. When a child has trouble with its father, it can get rid of suffering by embracing its mother. When the child is unhappy with its mother, it can run to its father for support."[41]

Chan was not alone in playing this game. He was joined by his rivals in the Cambodian royal family, whose alternating loyalties led King Rama III of Siam, writing in the early 1840s, to say: "The Cambodians always fight among themselves in the matter of succession. The losers in these fights go off to ask for help from a neighboring state; the winner must then ask for forces from the other."[42]

Chan's freedom of action was illusory. He survived as king only so long as one of his patrons and all of his rivals were inactive and so long as the relatively active patron provided him with military help. When either patron turned his attention fully to Cambodia, there was nothing Chan could do to deflect the destruction that ensued. Like Prince Sihanouk in the 1960s, or Pol Pot a decade later, Chan remained "neutral" as long as stronger powers allowed him to do so. Chan suffered an additional disadvantage in having no world leaders or world forums to turn to—no Mao Zedong, no Association of Southeast Asian Nations (ASEAN), and no United Nations.

CHAPTER 7

The Crisis of the Nineteenth Century

The first sixty years of the nineteenth century form the darkest portion of Cambodia's recorded history before the Armageddon of the 1970s. Invaded and occupied repeatedly by Thai and Vietnamese forces, the kingdom also endured dynastic crises and demographic dislocations. For a time in the 1840s, it ceased to exist as a recognizable state. Just as Jayavarman VII's ideology can be compared in some ways to the ideology of Democratic Kampuchea, the first half of the nineteenth century bears some resemblance to the 1970s in terms of foreign intervention, chaos, and the sufferings of the Cambodian people.

Fortunately for historians, there is a wide range of sources to consult in Thai, Cambodian, and Vietnamese. The record that the sources reveal, however, is incomplete. For example, the ruler of Cambodia for much of this period, King Chan, is rarely quoted in surviving sources, and none of his own writings has survived; a crucial actor has no lines. Similarly, Thai-language sources often thin out just when we might wish to have more information about the politics of Thai foreign policy in the period.

The period opens and closes with Thai-sponsored coronations. Between these two events and particularly after 1810, invasions from Vietnam and Siam alternated with internal rebellions and court-sponsored resistance to invaders while the court, especially under Chan, pursued a dangerous policy apparently aimed at preserving independence (or merely staying alive) by playing the Thai and the Vietnamese off against each other. Although the political history of the period is reasonably clear, the politics leading up to the events, and people's motivations, are often difficult to discern. The pattern that emerges is one in which Cambodia drifted first away from Thai control, then into the hands of the Vietnamese, and finally back to Thai protection. By the early 1840s, much of its territory, the capital region in particular, was administered as a component of Vietnam. Three events in the drift can be singled out for study. These are the Thai absorption of northwestern Cambodia in exchange for putting Eng on the throne, the anti-Vietnamese millenarian rebellion that broke out in southeastern Cambodia in 1820, and the succession crisis of 1835 following a disastrous Thai military expedition. Each of these events marked a stage in the process of Cambodia's diminishing ability to control its own affairs.

THE IMPOSITION OF VIETNAMESE CONTROL

Eng's restoration in 1794 is treated in the Cambodian chronicles as an event of miraculous significance. When he left Bangkok, they assert, "the sky did not grow dark, nor did rain fall, but thunder boomed in the noon sky, making a noise like a mighty storm."[1] The restoration was indeed dramatic, for in the preceding fifteen years Cambodia had not been governed at all. A former official named Baen had been installed in Udong by the Thai, had been given the title of *ta-la-ha*, or first minister, and had busied himself with recruiting troops to fight the Tay Son inside Cambodia and in Vietnam. In 1794, after so many years of service, Rama I seems to have felt obliged to reward him in some way.

The reward he chose to bestow, however, was hardly his to give, as it consisted of the large and prosperous *sruk* of Battambang and Mahanokor (or "great city," containing the ruins of Angkor). Baen had held power in this region for part of the 1780s and probably retained a personal following there, but in awarding the two *sruk* to him, Rama I removed them from Eng's jurisdiction without absorbing them into Siam. In the 1790s and for most of the nineteenth century, Thai suzerainty seems to have meant only that Baen and his successors were not obligated to provide laborers for Eng and had to transmit gifts—generally wild cardamom—to Bangkok from time to time.

Details about the transfer are impossible to uncover, and perhaps documents were never drawn up. In the 1860s, in fact, a French official in Cambodia, seeking information about the Thai claims, reported to his superiors that "[Siam] is unable to present any documentation about the cession. The present king of Cambodia [Eng's grandson Norodom], his officials, old men who have been consulted, and Eng's widow, who is still alive, are all of the opinion that none exists."[2]

In the twentieth century, however, the "loss" of the two *sruk* poisoned Thai-Cambodian relations. Siam gave them up under pressure from France in 1907 but resumed control over most of their territory from 1941 to 1946. In the context of the 1790s, however, it is unlikely that Rama I was pursuing a long-range plan, and his grandson, Rama IV, put the matter succinctly when he wrote that "the Thai kingdom was able to enlarge itself [at this time] because it had the greater power."³

After building himself a palace in Udong and visiting Bangkok with a tributary mission in 1796, Eng died at the beginning of 1797. His reign had been uneventful, and his contributions to Cambodian history were almost inadvertent. By returning to Udong, which had been without a king for so long, he brought Cambodia back to life; by fathering four sons, he founded a dynasty that was to reign in Udong and Phnom Penh until 1970. These two contributions, rather than specific actions on his part, probably account for the reverence with which he is treated in Cambodian chronicles compiled for his descendants.

The next ten years, until his son Chan's coronation in 1806, are poorly documented; but for reasons that remain unclear, the young prince became alienated from the Thai court at some point and seems to have begun to formulate a pro-Vietnamese foreign policy. Whatever its causes—Thai sources hint at a feud between the young prince and Rama I—Chan's anti-Thai orientation is a persistent theme of his long reign.⁴

As soon as he had been crowned, for example, he hastened to strengthen Cambodia's tributary connections with Vietnam while maintaining his subservience to Bangkok, becoming, in the words of the Vietnamese emperor, "an independent country that is the slave of two."⁵ The process was even more complicated, for Chan's increasing animosity toward the Thai alienated some of his own *chaovay sruk*, especially in the northwest, and his personal insecurity is indicated by his request to the Vietnamese emperor at about this time that he be allowed to recruit Vietnamese residents of Cambodia to form his personal bodyguard. The pace of his alienation from Bangkok accelerated after Rama I's death in 1809. Chan refused to attend the cremation, and when two officials who had attended the ceremony showed signs of being pro-Thai, Chan had them executed without trial.

In 1811–1812 conflict broke out inside Cambodia between Thai and Vietnamese expeditionary forces. The Thai supported one of Chan's dissident brothers; the Vietnamese responded to Chan's requests for help. All three of Chan's brothers fled to Bangkok at this time, leaving him free for the rest of his reign to pursue a pro-Vietnamese policy, even though the campaigns of 1811–1812 were indecisive. Their net effect was to reduce Chan's freedom of action, as his growing dependence on the Vietnamese was greater than his former allegiance, so reluctantly given, to Bangkok. Twice a month, wearing Vietnamese bureaucratic costumes supplied by Hué, the king and his entourage had to visit a Vietnamese temple near Phnom Penh—where the capital had been moved in 1812—and bow before a tablet bearing the Vietnamese emperor's name. Over the next twenty years, Chan fought with decreasing success to achieve a measure of independence.

Three events stand out from these early years of relatively loose Vietnamese control. These are the unsuccessful Cambodian attack on the northwestern *sruk* in 1816; the excavation of the Vinh Te Canal in southern Vietnam, using Cambodian labor, around 1820; and the anti-Vietnamese uprising that broke out soon afterward in southeastern Cambodia and in Khmer-populated portions of Vietnam.

The military expedition of 1816 was the last attempt before the 1960s by a formally constituted Cambodian army to take the offensive against foreign troops, and it was a failure. Perhaps to placate the Thai, or merely because the campaign had failed, Vietnamese authorities in Phnom Penh asked Chan to discipline the *okya* who had led the expedition. Taken to Saigon afterward, the official was reprimanded and fined. The sequence of events, insignificant in itself, epitomizes Chan's helplessness in the face of Vietnamese pressure.

The Vinh Te Canal, in turn, became a symbol of Vietnamese mistreatment of the Khmer, and the rebellion that followed its excavation revealed the depth of anti-Vietnamese feeling in the *sruk*, the persistence of millenarianism, and perhaps the ambiguities in Chan's subservience to the Vietnamese.[6] In 1817, Vietnamese officials in Saigon recruited several thousand Vietnamese and a thousand Cambodian workers to excavate—or perhaps merely to restore—the Vinh Te Canal, running between the Gulf of Siam and the fortified citadel of Chaudoc, a distance of perhaps 40 kilometers (25 miles). According to a Cambodian chronicle, work on the canal was arduous in the extreme: "Workers were divided into groups. One Vietnamese marched at the head of each group, another at the back, and a third in the middle. The Vietnamese would beat the Cambodians on the back, to make them hurry. . . . Everyone was exhausted, and covered with mud."[7]

This account of the excavations is followed immediately by an account of an anti-Vietnamese rebellion, placed by other sources in 1820–1821. This suggests a causal relationship between the two events, which is reinforced by the fact that the revolt broke out fairly close to the site of the canal. This site was Ba Phnom, the small mountain in southeastern Cambodia that has been identified with Jayavarman II's arrival in Cambodia from "Java." In the nineteenth century it was an important population center and also a religious site.[8] The Ba Phnom revolt was led by a former monk named Kai, who claimed to be a holy man capable of making predictions. As he gathered allegedly invulnerable supporters around him, he forged a political movement. Moving north and west from the vicinity of Ba Phnom, his followers attacked Vietnamese military posts. A mixed Khmer-Vietnamese force sent against him by Chan failed, one source asserts, because the *okya* in charge of it deserted with their troops and turned on the Vietnamese. A purely Vietnamese force sent from Saigon, however, eventually defeated the rebels near Kompong Cham. The leaders were executed in Saigon, and some of their followers were beheaded in Phnom Penh.

The differences between Cambodian and Vietnamese accounts of the rebellion pose interesting questions, such as where Chan's loyalties lay. Chan may have known Kai as a monk in Phnom Penh, and in any case the king, whom the Vietnamese were to find "extremely superstitious" toward the end of his reign, would probably not have moved vigorously against a Khmer believed to have supernatural powers. Whatever Chan's views might have been, his response to the rebellion had to be restricted and discreet. There are parallels here with the situation that faced his nephew, King Norodom, in 1884, when an anti-French rebellion led by *okya* broke out in the countryside while Norodom was under French protection in Phnom Penh. Similar problems confronted his great-grandson, Norodom Sihanouk, in turn, in the 1950s and again in 1970–1975.[9]

It is unclear how large the rebellion was or how much of a threat it posed in military and territorial terms; we know little about its goals beyond the assassination of Vietnamese. Vietnamese records understandably play down its importance; the locally oriented *bangsavatar* probably exaggerates its extent, momentum, and success. All the sources agree, however, that it was directed against the Vietnamese rather than against Chan and his *okya*, and that monks, former monks, and local officials were active in its ranks.

The chronicle version composed in the 1850s tended to confirm its audience's ideas about themselves, the Vietnamese, and history. "All" Vietnamese were cruel, "people of merit" (*nak sel*) were powerful, and Khmer could not (or at least should not) be made to fight against Khmer. The Buddhist orientation of the text can be seen when we learn that the *nak sel*'s followers were rendered invincible by prayers and amulets but lost this invincibility when they acted contrary to Buddhist law by killing people themselves. Without the special powers connected with nonviolence, the rebels—including former monks—were all slaughtered, and when they died, "Rain fell for seven days. It fell without stopping, night and day. The unimportant and the mighty were forced to run for shelter. In the cold air, everybody shook. There was no way of knowing when the sun set or when it rose. The nation was unhappy."[10]

It would be difficult to exaggerate the atmosphere of threat, physical danger, and random violence that pervades primary sources like this one and perhaps much of everyday life in nineteenth-century Cambodia. The sources are filled with references to torture, executions, ambushes, massacres, village burnings, and the forced movement of populations. The wars of the time were localized rather than national in scope, and expeditionary forces, which usually numbered only a few thousand men, were small by twentieth-century standards; at the same time, invaders and defenders destroyed the villages they came to, killed or uprooted anyone they met, and ruined the landscape they moved across. Very few prisoners of war were taken or kept alive. A seventeenth-century Cambodian law, translated by Adhémard Leclère, stated that an expeditionary force needed only three days' supply of food, because unfriendly populations that could be robbed were thought to be never more than three days' march away.[11] Parallels to the civil war that devastated Cambodia in the 1970s, and to the behavior of both sides, are obvious.

One enigma of this period is Chan himself. We know very little about him except that he was timid. A Vietnamese text from 1822 states that he was ill much of the time and kept inside his palace;[12] the Vietnamese emperor wrote of him in 1834, just before his death, that a "fresh wind or the cry of a bird could make him flee."[13] At the same time, Chan retained considerable freedom of maneuver. All through the 1820s he kept his lines of communication with Bangkok open. Tributary missions went to Bangkok every year, and Chan may have used them to provide intelligence to Thai officials, to sound out Thai policies, and to remain in contact with his brothers.

Relations between the two kingdoms broke down in the late 1820s as a result of Vietnamese support for an anti-Thai rebellion that erupted in 1824–1825 around Vientiane. The breakdown also sprang from the fact that the rulers in Hué and Bangkok in the 1830s, Rama III and Minh Mang, unlike their fathers, owed nothing to each other and were free to pursue vigorous foreign policies, one of which was to increase influence, and therefore to court conflict, over Cambodia. Minh Mang was also suspicious of the Vietnamese viceroy in Cambodia, Le Van Duyet, whom he believed—correctly, as things turned out—to be associated with breakaway sentiment in southern Vietnam.

The Thai made some tentative military probes into western Cambodia in 1830–1831, but Rama III saw no chance of success until Duyet's death in 1832. When Minh Mang attempted to replace the viceroy's entourage with officials loyal to Hué, his move ignited a full-scale rebellion that was centered around Saigon and led by Duyet's adopted son.

News of the revolt quickly reached Rama III, who decided to assemble an expeditionary force. He saw several advantages in doing so. First, he could humiliate Minh Mang, whose forces had been tangentially involved in the Vientiane rebellion and elsewhere in the Thai tributary states of Laos. By seeking to establish a new tributary state in southern Vietnam, moreover, Rama III may have been planning to extend Thai and Sino-Thai commercial interests and to profit directly from trade between

Saigon/Cholon and southern China, for Chinese merchants in Vietnam had supported the rebellion and had informed their counterparts in Bangkok. Finally, the Thai king may have been impressed by reports reaching him from Cambodia that many *okya* would now welcome the return of Chan's two brothers, Im and Duang (the third had died in Bangkok in 1825). The time was ripe, in Rama III's own words, "to restore the kingdom of Cambodia and to punish the insolence of Vietnam."[14]

In the short run, the campaign was a success. The Vietnamese quickly abandoned Phnom Penh and took Chan into exile in Vietnam. The Thai commander, Chaophraya (roughly, "Lord") Bodin, then occupied the capital, but soon poor communications with the naval forces attached to the expedition, which were supposed to attack the Vietnamese coast, combined with Vietnamese attacks, forced him to withdraw in early 1834.[15]

The Thai political strategy of placing Im and Duang in power also failed, because the two were unable to attract support. One chronicle, in fact, describes people's confusion early in the war, as Bodin's forces entered the kingdom:

> The people were surprised to see such a large army, and they shook with fear. The head of the army shouted at them: "Don't be afraid! His royal highness the king [sic] has arrived to rule over you." The people murmured about this, and sent messengers off to inform the king [i.e., Chan] in Phnom Penh.[16]

In Bodin's retreat from Phnom Penh approximately four thousand local people were carried off. Of these, perhaps a thousand managed to escape as the overburdened Thai column reached Udong. These people then "wandered trembling and afraid in the deep woods."[17] As the Thai columns moved north and west, they disintegrated, and at about this time, the rebellion in Saigon was finally suppressed.

THE VIETNAMIZATION OF CAMBODIA, 1835–1840

When Chan returned to his battered, abandoned capital early in 1834, he found himself under more stringent Vietnamese control. Thai successes in their overland offensive had shown Minh Mang that he could not rely on the Khmer to provide a "fence" for his southern and western borders, and with the defeat of the rebellion, he now moved to intensify and consolidate his control. To head this civilizing mission, he named the general who had crushed the rebellion in Saigon, Truong Minh Giang.

Giang needed Chan and his officials to provide the Vietnamese with labor, rice, and soldiers. Chan seems to have needed the Vietnamese somewhat less in material terms, but probably counted on them to protect him from assassination and revolt. Like later outsiders operating in Cambodia, Giang probably expected too much from the king and *okya*. Before 1834 was over, he had reported pessimistically to Hué that

> we have tried to punish and reward the Cambodian officials according to their merits and demerits. We have asked the king to help us, but he has hesitated to do so. After studying the situation, we have decided that Cambodian officials only know how to bribe and be bribed. Offices are sold; nobody carries out orders; everyone works for his own account. When we tried to recruit soldiers, the king was perfectly willing, but the officials concealed great numbers of people. When we wanted to compile a list of meritorious officials, [the officials were willing, but] the king was unwilling, because he was jealous. For the last four months, nothing has been accomplished.[18]

Giang's impatience was understandable, for Cambodian politics at the time was characterized by a diffusion of power, a shortage of resources, and a negotiability of position that effectively kept anyone from becoming powerful for very long. That Cambodians should hesitate to accomplish tasks for the Vietnamese struck Giang as insulting, even treacherous, but Minh Mang urged him to do the best he could with the human materials at hand.

Bodin, in the meantime, had settled his forces in the northwest. As the 1830s wore on, the Thai increased their military presence in Battambang and Siem Reap, placing Im and Duang in ambiguous administrative control, presumably to attract indigenous support against the Vietnamese. This program was matched to the south and east by an intensive program of Vietnamization, which affected many aspects of Cambodian life. The program was set in motion in 1834 and played itself out under the threat of Thai invasions for the rest of the 1830s, the last years of Minh Mang's reign.

An early victim of Vietnamization was Chan himself. Toward the end of 1834, according to the Vietnamese annals, he came under the influence of "magicians" who allegedly encouraged him to accept bribes and "let criminals out of jail."[19] In a sense, the "magicians" were merely asking Chan to act like a traditional king, but their influence distressed Truong Minh Giang, who had them arrested and shot. For Chan himself, the end of his struggle to stay alive and to provide for himself and his people a measure of independence had arrived. In early 1835, after a month's illness, he died aboard his royal barge, moored opposite his ruined palace in Phnom Penh. He was forty-four years old, and he had reigned, in one way or another, for nearly forty years.

Chan's death posed problems for the Vietnamese, for he had no sons and his eldest daughter, Princess Baen, was suspected of being pro-Thai. Soon after his death, the *okya* agreed to a Vietnamese suggestion that Chan's second daughter, Princess Mei, be named as queen. To officiate at her investiture, Minh Mang sent a Vietnamese official from Saigon, and in a hall built specially for the purpose, Mei and her sisters faced north, toward the emperor's letter authorizing her to reign, while the Vietnamese delegate and other officials faced south, as the emperor always did in his palace in Hué.[20]

The ceremony bore no resemblance to a traditional Cambodian coronation, but from the Cambodians' point of view, the queen's ability to grant titles and bestow official seals (as well as to officiate at royal ceremonies) meant that she *was* their queen. To the Vietnamese, who treated her as the ceremonial leader of a protectorate, these aspects of the question were unimportant when compared to the administrative reforms that Truong Minh Giang, at the emperor's request, was now ready to impose. Whereas previously the Vietnamese fort at Phnom Penh had been called Annam, or pacified south, the city itself and the surrounding countryside were now renamed Tran Tay, or western commandery, and Sino-Vietnamese names were given to all of Cambodia's *sruk*. Day-to-day administrative decisions, including personnel postings, salaries, military affairs, and the control of rice surpluses, were placed in Vietnamese hands, and some sixteen officials, seventy clerks, and ten schoolmasters were sent to Phnom Penh to form the core of an infrastructure for the administration. Until 1839–1840, however, the administration of the *sruk*— including the all-important matter of labor mobilization—was left to the *okya*, who operated with royal seals even though their appointments were cleared through the Vietnamese.

Minh Mang's policy of Vietnamizing Cambodia had several facets. He sought to mobilize and arm the Khmer, to colonize the region with Vietnamese, and to reform the habits of the people. He also tried to standardize patterns of measurement, mobilization, and food supply for military reasons. Control—that is, control of the adult male population and the formation of a standing army, if possible, to resist the Thai—was the essential ingredient of all the Vietnamese programs. Problems of recruitment arose because many of the *okya* were unwilling to relinquish control over their followers. The Vietnamese soon found, in fact, that Cham mercenaries were the only troops they could recruit.

Because ethnic Khmer caused so many problems, Minh Mang sought to colonize the region with Vietnamese. He justified this policy on the grounds that "military convicts and ordinary prisoners, if kept in jail, would prove useless. Therefore, it would be better for them to be sent to Cambodia and live among the people there, who would benefit from their teaching."[21]

Ironically, Vietnamese policies toward Cambodia in the 1830s fore-shadowed the French *mission civilisatrice* ("civilizing mission") that was, during the colonial era, to weaken and dismantle so many Vietnamese institutions. In a lengthy memorial to Truong Minh Giang, the emperor outlined his policy:

> The barbarians [in Cambodia] have become my children now, and you should help them, and teach them our customs. . . . I have heard, for example, that the land is plentiful and fertile, and that there are plenty of oxen [for plowing] . . . but the people have no knowledge of [advanced] agriculture, using picks and hoes, rather than oxen. They grow enough rice for two meals a day, but they don't store any surplus. Daily necessities like cloth, silk, ducks and pork are very expensive. . . . Now all these shortcomings stem from the laziness of the Cambodians . . . and my instructions to you are these; teach them to use oxen, teach them to grow more rice, teach them to raise mulberry trees, pigs and ducks. . . . As for language, they should be taught to speak Vietnamese. [Our habits of] dress and table manners must also be followed. If there is any out-dated or barbarous custom that can be simplified, or repressed, then do so.[22]

The emperor closed by advising Giang to move cautiously in engineering social change: "Let the good ideas seep in," he wrote, "turning the barbarians into civilized people."[23] Speed was not essential: "As for winning the hearts of the people, and teaching them, we plan to do this rather slowly."[24] In a subsequent memorial, the emperor recognized that even this slow process might never succeed, because "the customs of the barbarians are so different from our own that even if we were to capture all their territory, it would not be certain we could change them."[25]

There is no record of Vietnamese success in altering Cambodian agricultural techniques, although the need to do so was a recurrent theme in their correspondence of the 1830s. Likewise, Vietnamese efforts to quantify and systematize landholdings, tax payments, and irrigation works came to little. What impressed the Khmer about the Vietnamese, it seems, were their persistent demands for corvée labor and their cultural reforms, which struck at the root of Khmer notions of their own identity. One of these was the order that Khmer put on trousers instead of skirts and wear their hair long rather than close-cropped. Other "barbarous" Cambodian customs, according to a Vietnamese writer, included wearing robes without slits up the sides, using loincloths, eating with the fingers, and greeting from a kneeling position rather than from an upright one.[26]

The two peoples lived on different sides of a deep cultural divide, perhaps the most sharply defined of those in effect in nineteenth-century Southeast Asia; this divide was to be savagely exploited in the 1970s, first by Lon Nol and later by Pol Pot.[27]

Within his own ideological framework, however, Minh Mang tried hard to be informed about Cambodia, to be fair to its people, and to improve their way of life. There are several references to rewards given Cambodian officials at his behest for meritorious service. On one occasion, he asked that a history of the country be sent to him, because, among other things, the Khmer "have been a nation for over 1,200 years, but we do not know precisely what year they began, in terms of the Vietnamese and Chinese dynasties that were then reigning."[28] Earlier, the emperor had asked Truong Minh Giang to send him detailed information about Cambodia's

> customs, people, and agricultural produce. I want to know whether the people are prosperous, and whether or not the Cambodian militia has been trained. [I also want to know] if the barbarian people have learned Vietnamese ways, and if they are happy.[29]

In another memorial, Minh Mang outlined plans for replacing Cambodian *chaovay sruk* with Vietnamese, beginning with *sruk* close to Phnom Penh. In 1839, he was annoyed to hear that the *okya* continued to use Cambodian rather than Vietnamese official titles:

> At Tran Tay [the emperor said] Cambodian officials have all been given titles from my court. However, I understand that in correspondence and conversation they still use Cambodian titles. . . . The Cambodians should be told that it is an honor to have titles bestowed on them by this court. In conversation, therefore, they should use our titles, rather than theirs.[30]

Chan's brother Duang had been living in Battambang for several years, under Thai protection, and an obscure sequence of events in 1837 culminated in his arrest by the Thai and his return in chains to Bangkok. The sources suggest that Vietnamese emissaries from Phnom Penh had tried to lure him down to the capital with promises that he would be given the throne. Duang's replies to them were so ambiguous as to convince both the Thai and the Vietnamese that he intended to betray them, using *okya* in the capital region to gather supporters in an effort to regain Chan's somewhat dubious independence.[31]

In the meantime, the growing apprehension of the Vietnamese about Thai mobilization, and the slow progress of their own reforms, led them to tighten their administrative machinery. Anti-Vietnamese uprisings in

1837–1839 were both a cause and an effect of these reforms. According to the Vietnamese annals, there were four parts to their revised strategy. The most innovative one was to redraw the *sruk* and to replace indigenous *chaovay* throughout the country with Vietnamese. In making selections for these posts (never actually filled, it seems), the Vietnamese ministries were urged to find "about twenty" low-ranking officials, whose educational attainments were less important than their agricultural experience and their talent as military leaders. The second element of the policy was to open more plantations, to train more indigenous soldiers, and to store more rice in an attempt to free the Vietnamese and mercenary garrisons from dependence on southern Vietnam. Third, the Cambodians were to be taught Vietnamese so as to "improve communications." Finally, the Vietnamese were to encourage further colonization of Cambodia by Chinese immigrants and Vietnamese convicts, even though Truong Minh Giang had pointed out the dangers of this policy at great length in a memorial to Minh Mang earlier in the year.

These reforms led the Thai chronicles to refer to Minh Mang's naming the Khmer "new Vietnamese."[32] The Vietnamese saw nothing harmful in this, any more than they did in changing Cambodian weights, measures, fashions, and coiffures. Of the innovations, the one aimed at replacing the *chaovay sruk* probably had the most to do with the rebellion that broke out against the Vietnamese in 1840–1841. It is significant that the *okya*, when attacked in this fashion, could easily rally followers to defend the status quo rather than what might well have been a more equitable and forward-looking Vietnamese administration. There are interesting parallels here, moreover, with the opposition to the People's Republic of Kampuchea (PRK) administration in the 1980s.[33]

In December 1839, Prince Im, favored by the Thai since his brother's imprisonment, defected to Phnom Penh with several thousand men, mistakenly convinced that the Vietnamese intended to place him on the Cambodian throne. When he reached the capital, he was arrested by Truong Minh Giang and taken off to Saigon and Hué, thus removing from the scene yet another contender for the throne.[34]

One Thai response to these events, when they heard of them in early 1840, was to install a military garrison in Battambang. When Chaophraya Bodin reached the city to investigate Im's defection, he found that of three hundred Cambodians with some sort of official standing in the *sruk*, nearly two hundred had fled. His plans for a full-scale invasion of Cambodia were temporarily postponed because he was uncertain of local support.[35]

The rebellion against the Vietnamese that broke out in September and October 1840 had reached the planning stage in May. Intermittent uprisings, in fact, had broken out every year since 1836, and deteriorating conditions in Cambodia, as we have seen, had led Minh Mang to tighten his administration. One of his steps was to improve the collection of taxes. Traditionally, these had been collected through the *okya*; however, the amount of tax, paid in rice and cloth, had never been sufficient to support the Vietnamese. In an 1840 decree, Minh Mang ordered that Cambodia's arable land be remeasured and that records be maintained concerning rainfall, granaries, and irrigation works, so that Vietnamese operations in Cambodia could pay for themselves. He had been making similar demands for six years, he said, but little had been achieved.[36]

By June 1840, Minh Mang's patience was exhausted. He demoted Mei and her two sisters, giving them low ranks in the Vietnamese civil service. Following the demotion, the six highest-ranking *okya*, including the *ta-la-ha*, were placed under arrest and taken off to Saigon, accused of falsifying census records and "hiding" some fifteen thousand people otherwise liable for militia duty and corvée.[37] This was done in secret, and their followers assumed that they were dead. Their disappearance was one of the most significant causes of the revolt.

Indeed, the failure of the Vietnamese to impose a workable pattern of administration in Cambodia was connected with their willingness, in the early years at least, to work through the *okya*, whose loyalty to them was intermittent at best and whose operating styles—based on such things as fear, arrogance, patronage, local ties, and loyalties to relatives and other officials—were neither sympathetic nor conducive to a Vietnamese administration. Most of the *okya* were happy enough, it seems, to accept rewards occasionally from the Vietnamese. They showed no eagerness to become Confucian civil servants. By working with them, the Vietnamese accomplished few of their objectives; but as Vietnamese measures added up to a policy of laissez-faire, most of the *okya* had no reason to take up arms against them.

When they took over the administration of the *sruk* themselves in 1840, however, the Vietnamese reached the point at which they could impose their will at the same time that their actions perhaps inevitably ignited a revolt. With a Thai invasion imminent, however, and the failure of the *okya* to perceive that Vietnamese economic and military interests in Cambodia overlapped their own, the Vietnamese had little choice, unless they were to abandon Cambodia altogether. Minh Mang's policies failed because he was unable to understand the intransigence or ingratitude of the "barbarians" in the face of paternally administered social change. In a decree to the Cambodian people in 1838, he had stressed the irrationality of this ingratitude:

> Thanks to . . . my generosity, imperial troops were despatched to Cambodia, costing millions of coins, and brought you security by destroying the Thai.

Troops were stationed [among you] to bring peace. This action was like bringing the Cambodian people out of the mud onto a warm feather bed, and was well-known by everyone. . . . Anyone who can think for himself should be grateful to the court; why are there people who hate us and believe the rebels?[38]

The situation became worse in September 1840, when a wide-ranging rebellion broke out. The uprising, which was centered in the eastern and southern *sruk,* is a rare example in prerevolutionary Cambodia of sustained and coordinated political action; the only others that spring to mind are the anti-French rebellion of 1885–1886 and the so-called 1916 Affair (see Chapters 8 and 9). Smarting under Vietnam's *mission civilisatrice,* the *okya* had discussed the idea of rebellion for several months, in letters known today by their dates, addresses, and general contents; the letters themselves do not seem to have survived.[39] What set the rebellion in motion was an interlocking set of provocations by the Vietnamese together with Cambodian expectations of a Thai invasion and Thai support. The uprising collapsed in the early months of 1841, when a new emperor in Vietnam and the Thai invasion the insurgents had hoped for coincided with Vietnamese military successes and the rebels' shortage of supplies. The rest of the early 1840s was filled with seesawing warfare and negotiations between the Thai and the Vietnamese and by a gradual shift in the balance of power in Cambodia in favor of the Thai.

The immediate cause of the rebellion, from the standpoint of the *okya,* was a sequence of Vietnamese actions that seemed to the *okya* to be aimed at extinguishing kingship, Buddhism, and the official class in Cambodia. The sequence began with the demotion of the princesses and the reshuffling of Vietnamese officials in Phnom Penh. It continued in June 1840 when Minh Mang instituted a Vietnamese taxation system. This made new demands on the *okya* by taxing additional products, such as fruit and vegetables, and by calling for a new census, cadastral surveys, and reports on water resources.

Another part of the Vietnamese program was to call in Cambodian seals of office in at least some of the *sruk,* replacing them with Vietnamese ones that carried no indication of rank. At least one rural official was dismissed at this time for corruption, and rumors spread among the *okya* that all officials would soon be arrested by the Vietnamese.

The climax came in August, when the Vietnamese arrested Mei and her sisters in Phnom Penh. The women were lured aboard a barge after their immediate entourage had been softened up with liquor and a performance of Vietnamese opera; at this point all of them, according to an eyewitness, "laughed whenever they talked."[40] The princesses were taken off to Vietnam, and Cambodia's regalia, which Mei had inherited from her father, accompanied them. At this time, the *okya* in Phnom Penh and the *sruk*, with rumors and the Vietnamese record toward Cambodians to rely on, assumed that *Ta-la-ha* Lung, his associates, and the four princesses had been killed, and they thought that they were next.

To many Cambodians, the disappearance of their monarch, however restricted her authority might have been, signified the disappearance of the state. The absence of regalia with which to legitimize someone else made the situation worse. For the *okya*, the disappearance of their high-ranking patrons at court, the reformed tax system, the devaluation of seals of office, and the Vietnamese assault on their freedom of action were precipitants of revolt. Vietnamese "rational" actions, supposedly beneficial to the Khmer, struck at the roots of the identity of the *okya* and at their concepts of society as a whole. Vietnamese contempt for Buddhism and for Cambodia's language, culture, and institutions also hastened the decision of the *okya* to revolt.

The uprising was concentrated at first along the east bank of the Mekong but soon spread to Vietnamese settlements along the coast, like Ream and Kampot, to parts of southern Vietnam inhabited by Khmer, and to fortified villages inland. The news of the princesses' disappearance seems to have triggered the revolt, and the rebels' goal at this stage was the restoration of the status quo ante, personified by Mei and the exiled officials. Another objective, apparently, was the killing of Vietnamese. As one rebel wrote, "We are happy killing Vietnamese. We no longer fear them; in all our battles we are mindful of the three jewels [of Buddhism]: the Buddha, the law, and the monastic community."[41]

The Vietnamese were surprised by the level of coordination among the *okya* and blamed it on Thai influences, which Thai sources fail to confirm. They were also baffled by the absence of a single leader. Their estimate of rebel strength ran to thirty thousand men operating throughout the kingdom in "hundreds of" small bands and occasionally larger ones, usually in territory familiar to them and commanded by people they could trust. The formidable problems of counterguerrilla warfare were summed up in one Vietnamese report in 1841:

> The rebels have established posts along the river banks at strategic points. They appear and disappear at will. If our troops look to the east, the rebels escape to the west. . . . They concentrate their forces where the jungle is thick, and in swampy areas where our troops cannot manoeuver. Other regions have tall grass at eye-level and are very hot and dusty. One can march all day without finding potable water. Moreover, we have no intelligence about the enemy, and no guides.[42]

The Vietnamese also had problems moving troops and supplies against the river currents prevalent at that time of year, and the report adds that "not even one" rebel had surrendered, despite the "tolerant" policies of the Vietnamese court and even though the record is full of references to the Khmer fleeing like "rats and mice," or attacking like "swarms of mosquitoes." At the start of the rebellion, Minh Mang (who was to die following an accident at the beginning of 1841) thought that an adequate application of force, combined with rewards to loyal troops and local officials, would be enough to put down the rebellion, which angered him, he wrote, so much that his "hair stood on end."[43] He ordered *Ta-la-ha* Lung and others to write letters asking their relatives and clients in Cambodia to surrender, thus misreading Cambodian loyalty to unavailable and devalued patrons, and he also approved sending "monks and magicians" into Phnom Penh to undermine morale. In the last months of his reign, he demanded weekly reports from the front and suggested that Cambodian crops and orchards be burned down as a preemptive measure. "The Cambodians are so stupid," he declared, "that we must frighten them. Ordinary moral suasion has no effect."[44]

It is impossible to say what Minh Mang would have done had he survived the next seven years, but it is clear that the rebellion had begun to lose momentum before his death and also that his successor, Thieu Tri, was less committed than he had been to a victory in Cambodia.[45] The new emperor began his reign looking for a solution that would be acceptable to his court and to the Cambodians, if not necessarily to the Thai; at one stage, he brushed aside a suggestion that he negotiate directly with the Thai as being "wrong and foolish." Distance, distrust, and the momentum of the war, however, as well as the ambiguity of Thieu Tri's objectives in Cambodia, kept the conflict going until 1847.

Despite Vietnamese reports to the contrary, Cambodian troops were often poorly supplied. At the end of 1840, a rebel *okya* complained to the Thai that "we are unable to continue fighting the Vietnamese. We lack the troops to do so, the rifles, the ammunition, and the supplies. For weapons we have only knives, cross-bows, and clubs; we cannot continue to fight."[46]

THE RESTORATION OF CAMBODIAN INDEPENDENCE

As the Vietnamese court and its officials in Cambodia sought a solution to what they saw as an internal Vietnamese problem, Chaophraya Bodin's expeditionary force, numbering thirty-five thousand men, assembled near Battambang and then attacked and defeated the Vietnamese garrison at Pursat. Bodin was prepared to attack the capital but hesitated because he was short of supplies and lacked confidence in his troops. Instead he withdrew to Battambang, where he sought to consolidate his political position. During the siege of Pursat, eighteen rebellious *okya* had written him pleading for Thai support and for Duang's return from Bangkok.[47] The *okya* pledged allegiance to Rama III, complained about shortages of supplies, and asserted that Cambodians would be happy only if the political conditions of the early nineteenth century, before the Vietnamese had arrived, were reestablished.

Bodin transmitted the letter to Bangkok and added a recommendation for Duang's release from custody and his return to political power. In January 1841, Duang reached Battambang, accompanied by Thai and Cambodian advisers and carrying gifts for his supporters, including insignia of rank and royal accoutrements provided for him by Rama III.[48] According to one source, Bodin had urged Duang's release because "if there are no superior people to look after a population, the common people have no security."[49] The records also suggest that Bodin's motives included winning over the *okya* (he was eager that local Khmer, rather than his own inexperienced troops, should engage the Vietnamese) by promising them that Duang would rule over Cambodia. For the rest of the 1840s, Duang was to be closely watched and manipulated by Bodin. Duang's return to Cambodia and Rama III's solicitude for him opened an era in Thai-Cambodian relations that lasted until French intervention in 1863.

While Duang was conferring with potential courtiers and Bodin was complaining that the newcomers were consuming Thai supplies, Thieu Tri was attempting to understand and control Vietnamese policy toward Cambodia, with a view to thwarting a Thai invasion, pacifying rebellious provinces of southern Vietnam, and maintaining Vietnamese prestige. In late 1841, Truong Minh Giang attempted once again to bring Prince Im to power, but edicts issued in his name attracted no support. It was at this point, perhaps, that Truong Minh Giang realized that he had almost no chance of restoring a favorable political balance in Cambodia. He withdrew to Vietnam, taking Im, the princesses, and the population of the city, numbering some six thousand people, with him. When he arrived in Vietnam, he sent a letter to Hué in which he took the blame for "losing" Cambodia, to which he referred as the emperor's "rightful property." He then took poison and died.[50]

The Vietnamese failure did not mean that the Thai had succeeded, and by 1843 Cambodia had become a quagmire for Chaophraya Bodin. As he wrote Bangkok: "We have been in Cambodia for three years without accomplishing anything. We are short of supplies; people are going off into the forest to live on leaves and roots; and nearly a thousand men in our army have died from lack of food."[51] In 1844, he had to abandon Phnom Penh, where the Vietnamese soon reinstalled Princess Mei as Cambodia's "legitimate queen" while Thai forces congregated near Udong. The Vietnamese maneuver infuriated Bodin, who saw that many *okya* might now be unwilling to support the Thai. He complained to Bangkok that "all the Khmer leaders and nobles, all the district chiefs and all the common people are ignorant, stupid, foolish and gullible. They have no idea what is true and what is false."[52]

In spite of these difficulties, Vietnamese attempts to dislodge the Thai forces around Udong throughout 1845 were fruitless; by the end of the year, the Thai and Vietnamese had opened negotiations for a cease-fire. The talks moved forward, for they were grounded in Thieu Tri's willingness to abandon his military positions in Cambodia and, by implication, his father's policies there. They moved slowly, however, in a context of military stalemate, even though in political terms conditions were favorable to the Thai. In Prince Duang they had a seasoned, popular ruler, loyal to Bangkok and able to work through a well-established network of loyal officials in the *sruk*. But the Vietnamese still occupied a strong bargaining position, particularly as they retained Cambodia's regalia, without which Duang could not legitimately ascend the throne.

In a face-saving gesture, they demanded that a tributary mission headed by a Cambodian official travel to Hué in March 1846 and declare Cambodia's pro forma subservience to Vietnam.[53] When the embassy returned to Phnom Penh in June 1847, the Vietnamese handed over the Cambodian regalia and released several members of the royal family who had been in their custody, in some cases for many years. Soon afterward, they withdrew their forces from Cambodia; for the first time since 1811, there were no Vietnamese officials on Cambodian soil.

Over the next few months, in a series of ceremonial gestures, Duang reenacted the restoration of Thai-sponsored kingship that had been eclipsed for so many years. It would be a mistake to dismiss these ceremonial actions as mere protocol, because Duang, like most Southeast Asian rulers at the time, did not disentangle what we would call the religious and political strands of his thinking, duties, and behavior. Kingly behavior, in other words, was thought to have political results, and political actions were thought to enhance or diminish a monarch's fund of merit.[54]

Many of these ceremonies had to do with the restoration of Theravada Buddhism as the state religion. One account relates that Duang

> levelled the [Vietnamese] fortifications at Phnom Penh, and hauled away the bricks to build and restore ... [seven] Buddhist monasteries near Udong. Broken Buddha-images were recast, and new ones were carved. Monks were encouraged to live in monasteries again, and people were encouraged to respect them.[55]

To his subjects, Duang's return to Cambodia and the restoration of Buddhism there were ex post facto proofs of his kingliness, legitimacy, and merit. An inscription from 1851 describes the electric effect of this restoration in the 1840s:

> There was a mighty ruler, whose name was Duang. He came from the royal city [Bangkok] to Cambodia, and lived in the fortified city of Udong. With merit, skill, and masterly intelligence, the king scattered his enemies in terror; and soon the three warring states were friends again.[56]

On an auspicious day in April 1848, Duang was anointed by Thai and Cambodian brahmans in Udong and ascended the Cambodian throne. He was fifty-two years old, and his reign, which lasted twelve years, can be seen as something of a renaissance. For most of these years, the kingdom was at peace, and although Thai political advisers and some Thai troops lingered at Udong, Duang was relatively free to make political decisions, such as those connected with awarding titles to *okya*. The chronicles of his reign place much emphasis on its restorative aspects. A wide range of institutions and relationships was involved. The chronicle points to linguistic reforms, public works, sumptuary laws, and new sets of royal titles. From other sources, we know that Duang was an accomplished poet and presided over the promulgation of a new law code and the compilation of new chronicle histories.[57]

Chroniclers in the 1880s and the 1930s, looking back to those few years of Cambodian independence prior to French control, may have considered Duang's reign to be a kind of golden age. The king himself was relatively cautious after so many years of semicaptivity in Bangkok. His relations with Rama III and Rama IV (King Mongkut) were subservient, as his letters to these monarchs show.[58] He made no attempt to improve relations with Vietnam in the hope of gaining some freedom of maneuver, perhaps because he was frightened by the precedent of the 1830s and because from the Vietnamese point of view any improvement in relations would only have intensified his dependency on them. Instead, in 1853 he somewhat clumsily sought French protection by sending gifts and offering his "humble homage" to the emperor of France, Napoleon III, via the French consulate in Singapore. Duang was probably put up to this by French missionaries who were active near Udong. His gifts included four elephant tusks, two rhinoceros horns, and sizable quantities of sugar and white pepper. A French diplomatic mission to his court, bearing a draft treaty of friendship (see Chapter 8), was not allowed to proceed to Udong by the Thai, who had swiftly brought their client monarch to heel.

Duang seems to have sought French help not so much to escape Thai protection, which would have been impossible to manage, as to defend himself against the Vietnamese. In letters to the French, he referred to them, as Pol Pot was to do in the 1970s, as Cambodia's "traditional enemies." Ironically, in the 1860s France took over Vietnam's patronage of Cambodia, eliminated Vietnamese influence, and then proceeded to encourage Vietnamese immigration into Cambodia. After his attempt to make friends with France had failed, Duang explained himself to a French missionary, saying, "What would you have me do? I have two masters who always have an eye fixed on me. They are my neighbors, and France is far away."[59] Clearly, many conditions had to change before Cambodia could emerge from this dual dependency, which had lasted with brief interludes for more than fifty years.

CHAPTER 8

The Early Stages of the French Protectorate

There are several ways of looking at the years of French hegemony over Cambodia. One is to break them into phases and to trace the extension and decline of French control. Another would be to examine the period and its ideology and practice—political, economic, educational, and so forth—from a French point of view; a third would be to treat the period as part of Cambodian history, connected to the times before and after French control. Now that the French are gone, the third perspective seems the most attractive. Although there are serious gaps in the sources, and useful primary material in Cambodian, aside from royal chronicles, is very scarce, in this chapter I attempt to see the French as often as possible through Cambodian eyes.

In the meantime, if we look at the colonial era in terms of the waxing and waning of *French* control (the first of the three perspectives), the years break fairly easily into phases. The first phase lasted from the establishment of the protectorate in 1863 to the outbreak of a national rebellion in 1884. The second phase would extend from the suppression of the rebellion in 1886 to King Norodom's death in 1904, when a more cooperative monarch, Norodom's half-brother, Sisowath, came to the throne. The third phase lasted until Norodom Sihanouk's coronation in 1941 and spans the reigns of Sisowath (r. 1904–1927) and his eldest son, Monivong (r. 1927–1941). This period, it can be argued, was the only systematically *colonial* one in Cambodian history, for in the remainder of the colonial era (1941–1953) the French were concerned more with holding on than with systematizing their control.

From a Cambodian perspective, however, it is possible to take the view that the colonial era falls into two periods rather than four, with the break

Prince Sisowath and his entourage, 1866.

occurring at Sisowath's coronation in 1906. From that point on, Cambodians stopped governing themselves and the westernization of Cambodian life intensified. What would have been recognizable in a *sruk* in 1904
to a Cambodian official of the 1840s had been modified sharply by 1920,
when French government, particularly at the local level, had been organized as part of a total effort in Indochina.

But until the late 1940s, I suspect, few Cambodians would have considered these mechanical changes, or the French presence as a whole, as
having a deleterious effect on their lives or on their durable institutions
of subsistence farming, Buddhism, and kingship. The political stability
that characterized most of the colonial era can be traced in part to French
patronage of the king and the king's patronage of the *sangha*, which
tended to keep these two institutions aligned (politically, at least) with
French objectives—partly because kings, monks, and officials had no tradition of innovation and partly because popular methods of questioning
their authority, heresy and rebellion, had been effectively smothered by
the French since the 1880s. In terms of economic transformations, the significant developments that occurred in the technology of rice farming
tended to be limited to the northwestern part of the kingdom, where
huge rice plantations had come into being. In the rest of the country, as
Jean Delvert has shown, the expanding population tended to cultivate
rice in small, family-oriented plots.[1]

Because of this stability, perhaps, the French in many of their writings tended to romanticize and favor the Cambodians at the expense of the Vietnamese. At the same time, because in their terms so little was going on, they tended to look down on the Cambodians as "lazy" or "obedient." An ambiguous and not very thoughtful romanticism suffuses many French-language sources composed on the colonial era, especially in the twentieth century, when clichés about the people were passed along as heirlooms from one official (or one issue of a newspaper) to the next. At the same time, until the early 1940s, no Cambodian-language sources questioned the efficacy of French rule or Cambodia's traditional institutions.

For these reasons, it is tempting to join some French authors and skip over an era when "nothing happened." But to do so would be a mistake, because what was happening, especially after the economic boom of the 1920s, was that independent, prerevolutionary Cambodia (with all its shortcomings) was being built or foreshadowed despite large areas of life that remained, as many French writers would say, part of the "timeless" and "mysterious" Cambodia of Angkor.

It is tempting also to divide French behavior in Cambodia into such categories as "political," "economic," and "social," terms that give the false impression that they are separable segments of reality. What the French meant by them in the context of the colonial situation tended to be idiosyncratic. "Politics," for example, meant dissidence and manipulation rather than participation in a political process. Ideally, in a colony there should be no *politics* at all. "Economics" meant budgets, taxes, and revenues—in other words, the economics of bureaucratic control. On the rare occasions when French writers looked at Cambodia's economy, they related it to the rest of Indochina, particularly in terms of export crops and colonial initiatives, like public works, rather than to Cambodian needs and capabilities. By the 1920s, in the eyes of French officials, Cambodia had become a rice-making machine, producing revenue as well in exchange for "guidance." This meant that the essence of government—*rajakar*, or royal work—remained what it had always been, the extraction of revenue from the peasants. As for "social," the word as the French used it did not refer to solidarity among people or relationships that added up to political cohesion. Instead, "society" meant a conglomeration of families, obediently at work.

The chronological perspective and the analytical ones just dealt with may be helpful in examining the period 1863–1953, for looking at these years in terms of *Cambodian* history means looking at them in terms of continuity and change. From this angle, the alterations to Cambodian society and the thinking of the Cambodian elite are as important as the apparently timeless life in the villages, which was also changing.

THE ESTABLISHMENT OF THE
FRENCH PROTECTORATE

The beginnings of French involvement in Cambodia are to be found in the eighteenth century, when missionaries took up residence in the kingdom, especially in the vicinity of Udong. Involvement did not become political, however, before the 1850s, coincidentally with French involvement in Vietnam. In the mid-1850s, King Duang sought French support in an attempt to play off the Thai against the Vietnamese, but a French diplomatic mission to Cambodia in 1856, armed with a draft treaty of cooperation, failed to reach the Cambodian court, which was frightened away from welcoming it by Thai political advisers. The draft treaty, incidentally, contained several clauses that passed into the operative one concluded in 1863: The French wanted teak for shipbuilding, for example, as well as freedom to move about the country and freedom to proselytize for the Roman Catholic faith.[2]

French interest in Cambodia deepened with its involvement in Vietnam and also after a French naturalist, Henri Mouhot (1826–1861), visited Duang's court and then proceeded to Siem Reap, where he "discovered" the ruins of Angkor. Mouhot suggested in a book about his travels that Cambodia was exceptionally rich and that its rulers were neglecting their patrimony.[3] Duang's openness to Mouhot and to other European visitors in this period stemmed in part from his friendship with a French missionary, Monseigneur Jean Claude Miche, whose mission headquarters was located near Udong and who had actively supported the 1856 diplomatic mission. Miche persuaded the king that there could be advantages in being free from Thai control and Vietnamese threats. In the last two years of his reign, moreover, Duang saw French expansion into Vietnam as an opportunity for him to regain territory that Cambodia had lost to the Vietnamese over the preceding two hundred years.[4]

Bogged down in guerrilla warfare in Vietnam, and unsure of support from Paris, the French administrators in Saigon were slow to respond to Cambodia's assertions of friendship. The matter lapsed when Duang died in 1860 and Cambodia was plunged into a series of civil wars. Duang's designated heir, Norodom, was unpopular in the eastern *sruk* and among Cham dissidents, who had almost captured Udong while Duang was alive. Norodom had spent much of his youth as a hostage at the Thai court. Unable to rule, he fled Cambodia in 1861, returning with Thai support at the end of the following year. But he returned on a probationary basis, for his regalia remained in Bangkok. Angered by Thai interference, and attracted by French promises of gifts, Norodom reopened negotiations with the French. According to a contemporary, the French admiral in charge of southern Vietnam, "having no immediate war to fight, looked for a peaceful conquest and began dreaming about Cambodia."[5]

The colonial era began without a shot and in a very tentative way. A delegation of French naval officers concluded a treaty with Norodom in Udong in August 1863, offering him protection at the hands of a French resident in exchange for timber concessions and mineral exploration rights. Norodom managed to keep the treaty secret from his Thai advisers for several months. When they found out about it and notified Bangkok, he quickly reasserted his dependence on the Thai king, declaring to his advisers that "I desire to remain [the Thai king's] servant, for his glory, until the end of my life. No change ever occurs in my heart." The Thai, in turn, kept Norodom's change of heart a secret from the French, who learned of it only after his earlier declaration of faith had been ratified in Paris in early 1864.[6]

What Norodom wanted from the French vis-à-vis the Thai is unclear. He seems to have been playing for time, and the method he chose resembled that of his uncle, King Chan, with the French in the role of the Vietnamese. He wanted to be crowned, and by the middle of 1864, the Thai and the French had agreed to cosponsor his coronation. The unintentionally comical aspects of the ceremony are recounted by several French sources. Thai and French officials quarreled about precedent, protocol, and regalia while Norodom, using time-honored filial imagery, proclaimed his dependence on both courts. For the last time, the Cambodian king's titles were chosen and transmitted by Bangkok; for the last time, too, the Cambodian king claimed to draw legitimacy from two foreign courts. For the first time, a Cambodian king accepted his crown from a European. The next three Cambodian monarchs followed suit. From this point on, Thai influence in Cambodia began to wane, fading even more sharply and more or less for good after King Mongkut's death in 1867.[7]

The imposition of French protection over Cambodia did not end the dynastic and millenarian rebellions that had plagued the beginning of Norodom's reign, although French military forces were helpful in quelling these rebellions by 1867. The most important of these was led by Pou Kombo, an ex-monk who claimed that he had a better right than Norodom to be king. A year before, Norodom had shifted his palace to Phnom Penh. He had been urged to do so by the French, just as Chan had been encouraged to move by the Vietnamese earlier in the century, and for similar tactical reasons. In the French case, commercial motives were also at work, for Phnom Penh was more accessible from Saigon than an inland capital would have been, and it was hoped that the exploration of the Mekong River under Commandant E. Doudart de Lagrée (1823–1868) would result in data about the river's northern reaches that would justify French pipe dreams of Phnom Penh as an important commercial city.[8]

For the French, the 1860s and 1870s were a heroic period, partly because government remained in the hands of young naval officers hungry for glory, eager for promotion, and entranced by the exotic setting in which they found themselves. By and large, these pioneers of colonialism—Doudart de Lagrée, Francis Garnier, Jean Moura, and Etienne Aymonier—possessed great energy, sympathy for the Cambodians, and intellectual integrity. They explored the Mekong, translated Cambodian chronicles, deciphered inscriptions, and arranged for the shipment of tons of Cambodian sculpture to museums in Paris, Saigon, and eventually Phnom Penh. The grandeur of their exploits and of Cambodia's distant past formed a sharp contrast in their minds with the "decay" of the Cambodian court and the "helplessness" of the Cambodian people.

And yet there was probably little difference between the way Cambodia was governed in the 1860s and the way Angkor had been governed almost a thousand years before. In both cases, perhaps, and certainly for most of the years between, government meant a network of status relationships whereby peasants paid in rice, forest products, or labor to support their officials. The officials, in turn, paid the king, using some of the rice, forest products, and peasant labor with which they had been paid. The number of peasants one could exploit in this way depended on the position one was granted by the throne; positions themselves were for sale, and this tended to limit officeholders to members of the elite with enough money or goods on hand to purchase their positions.

In the nineteenth century, the destabilization of rural society pummeled the infrastructure of these arrangements, but they persisted into the colonial era when the king's personal demands on the system were taken care of increasingly by French and Chinese entrepreneurs, who frequently tempted him into unwise investments.

THE TIGHTENING OF FRENCH CONTROL

Within the palace, Norodom governed in what the French considered to be an arbitrary, authoritarian way. The French, however, offered him no alternative style, and throughout his reign, Norodom was drawn less by the idea of a sound administration than by the imperatives of personal survival. Revolts against his rule (and implicitly against his acquiescence to the French) broke out in 1866 and in the 1870s. Both attracted considerable support, and both were put down with difficulty by the French. Unwilling to blame themselves for this state of affairs, the French blamed Norodom and were increasingly drawn to support his half-brother, Sisowath, who had led troops alongside the French in both rebellions.

Under French pressure, while another half-brother, Siwotha, was in revolt against him, Norodom agreed in 1877 to promulgate a series of reforms. Although these were never carried out, they are worth noting as precursors of more extensive French control and as indications of areas of French concern. The reforms sought to dismantle royal involvement in landownership, to reduce the number of *okya*, to rationalize tax collection, and to abolish slavery. Had they been enacted, they would have worn away the power bases of the Cambodian elite. Like Minh Mang in the 1830s, the French disliked the Cambodian way of doing things, which interfered with their ideas of rational, centralized control. Institutions like slavery and absolute monarchy, moreover, went down poorly with officials of the Third Republic, less charmed by the romantic operetta aspects of Cambodia than Napoleon III and his entourage had been.

In the early 1880s, as the French tightened their grip on Vietnam, it was only a matter of time before they solved Cambodia's "problems" and imposed their will on the Cambodian court. The comedy in Phnom Penh had gone on too long and had cost too much. The Cambodians had not seen the importance of paying for French protection. The French became impatient and assumed for this reason that time was running out. The "riches" of Cambodia remained untapped. What had seemed exotic and quaint in Cambodian society in the 1860s and 1870s was now seen by a new generation of officials as oppressive; it was time for protection to become control.

In 1884, the French succeeded in getting Norodom to agree to siphon off customs duties, especially on exports, to pay for French administrative costs. Norodom sent a cable to the president of France protesting against French pressure and was chided for doing so by the governor-general of Cochin China, Charles Thomson, who had been negotiating secretly with Sisowath to arrange a transfer of power should Norodom prove resistant to the reforms.[9]

The blow fell a few months later when Thomson sailed from Saigon to Phnom Penh and confronted Norodom with a wide-ranging set of reforms encased in a treaty that went much further than previous documents had done to establish de jure French control. Thomson arrived at the palace with the treaty, traveling aboard a gunboat that was anchored within sight. As Norodom reviewed the document, Thomson's armed bodyguards stood nearby. Aided by a complaisant interpreter, Son Diep, who rose to bureaucratic heights after Norodom's death, the king signed it because he saw that doing so was the only way to stay on the throne; he undoubtedly knew of Sisowath's machinations. Perhaps he thought that the document's provisions would dissolve when the French encountered opposition to the provisions among the Cambodian elite. This is, in fact, what happened almost at once, but Article 2 of the treaty neverthe-

less marked a substantial intensification of French control: "His Majesty
the King of Cambodia [it read] accepts all the administrative, judicial, financial, and commercial reforms which the French government shall
judge, in future, useful to make their protectorate successful."[10]

It was not this provision, however, that enraged the Cambodian elite,
who by that time probably viewed Norodom as a French puppet in any
case. The features that they saw as revolutionary (and that the French
saw as crucial to their program of reforms) were those that placed French
résidents in provincial cities, abolished "slavery," and institutionalized
the ownership of land. These provisions, of course, struck at the heart of
traditional Cambodian politics, which were built up out of entourages,
exploitation of labor, and the taxation of harvests (rather than land) for
the benefit of the elite, who were now to become paid civil servants of the
French, administering rather than "consuming" the people under their
control.

Although few French officials had troubled themselves with studying
the nuances of slavery in Cambodia, and although their motives for abolishing it may have included a cynical attempt to disarm political opposition in France to their other reforms, it is clear that the deinstitutionaliza-
tion of servitude was a more crucial reform, in Cambodian terms, than
the placement of a few French officials in the countryside to oversee the
Cambodian elite. Without this reform, the French could not claim to be
acting on behalf of ordinary people, and more important, they could do
nothing to curb the power of the elite, which sprang from control over
personnel. Without abolishing slavery, moreover, the French could not
proceed with their vision—however misguided it may have been—of a
liberated Cambodian yeomanry responding rationally to market pressures.

By cutting the ties that bound masters and servants—or more precisely,
by saying that this was what they *hoped* to do—the French were able to
justify their interference at every level of Cambodian life. Their proposal
effectively cut the king off from his entourage and this entourage, in turn,
from its followers. The French wanted Cambodia to be an extension of
Vietnam, with communal officials responding directly to the French,
even though government of this sort and at this level was foreign to
Cambodia, where no communal traditions—had they ever existed—survived into the nineteenth century.

In the short run, the Cambodian reaction to the treaty was intense and
costly to the French. In early 1885, a nationwide rebellion, under several
leaders, broke out at various points.[11] It lasted a year and a half, tying
down some four thousand French and Vietnamese troops at a time when
French resources were stretched thin in Indochina. Unwilling to work
through Norodom, whom they suspected of supporting the rebellion, the

French relied increasingly on Sisowath, allowing him a free hand in appointing pro-French officials in the *sruk* and thereby further undermining Norodom's authority. It seems likely that Sisowath expected to be rewarded with the throne while Norodom was still alive, but as the revolt wore on, the French found that they had to turn back to Norodom to pacify the rebels. In July 1886, the king proclaimed that if the rebels laid down their arms, the French would continue to respect Cambodian customs and laws—in other words, the mixture as before. The rebellion taught the French to be cautious, but their goals remained the same—namely, the rationalization of Cambodian government and control over the economy of the kingdom. It was at this stage that the French began to surround Norodom with Cambodian advisers who were loyal to them rather than to the throne. These were drawn, in large part, from the small corps of interpreters trained under the French in the 1870s; the most notable of them, a Sino-Khmer named Tiounn, was to play an important role in Cambodian politics until the 1940s.

The issue at stake in the rebellion, as Norodom's chronicle points out, was that the "Cambodian people [were] fond of their own leaders," especially because alternatives to them were so uncertain. A French writer in the 1930s blamed the French for their hastiness in trying to impose "equality, property, and [an] electorate,"[12] for Cambodians were supposed to choose their own village leaders under an article of the treaty. He added that, in fact, "the masters wanted to keep their slaves and the slaves their masters"; people clung to the status quo.

Faced with the possibility of a drawn-out war, the French stepped back from their proposed reforms, and although the treaty was ratified in 1886, most of its provisions did not come into effect for nearly twenty years, after Norodom was dead.

At the same time, it would be wrong to exaggerate the Cambodian "victory" or to agree with some recent Cambodian writers who have seen the rebellion as a watershed of Cambodian nationalism, with Norodom cast as a courageous patriot cleverly opposing French control. The evidence for these assertions is ambiguous. Norodom, after all, accepted French protection in a general way but attacked it when he thought his own interests—especially financial ones—were at stake. There is little evidence that he viewed his people as anything other than objects to consume, and certainly the French distrusted him more than ever after 1886; they spent the rest of his reign reducing his privileges and independence. But it would be incorrect to endow Norodom or the rebellious *okya* with systematic ideas about the Cambodian nation (as opposed to particular, personal relationships).

With hindsight, we can perceive two important lessons of the rebellion. One was that the regional elite, despite French intervention in Cambodia, was still able to organize sizable and efficient guerrilla forces, as it had done against the Thai in 1834 and the Vietnamese in 1841; it was to do so again in the more peaceable "1916 Affair" discussed in Chapter 9. The second lesson was that guerrilla troops, especially when supported by much of the population, could hold a colonial army at bay.

The next ten years of Norodom's reign saw an inexorable increase in French control, with policies changing "from [ones] of sentiment . . . to a more egotistic, more personal policy of colonial expansion."[13] All that stood in the way of the French was the fact that Norodom still made the laws, appointed the officials, and controlled the national economy by farming out sources of revenue (such as the opium monopoly and gambling concessions), by demanding gifts from his officials, and by refusing to pay his bills. By 1892, however, the collection of direct taxes had come under French control; two years later, there were ten French *résidences* in the *sruk*. The 1890s, in fact, saw increasing French consolidation throughout Indochina, culminating in the governor-generalship of Paul Doumer (1897–1902).

In Cambodia, this consolidation involved tinkering with fiscal procedures and favoring Sisowath rather than any of Norodom's children as the successor to the throne. French officials were eager for Norodom to relinquish control but were frightened by the independent-mindedness of many of his sons, one of whom was exiled to Algeria in 1893 for anticolonial agitation. The king's health was poor in any case and was made worse by his addiction to opium, which the French provided him, in ornamental boxes, free of charge. As French officials grew more impatient with Norodom and as he weakened, they became abusive. After all, there were fortunes to be made by colonists in Cambodia, or so they thought, and Norodom barred the way. The climax came in 1897, when the *résident supérieur*, Huynh de Verneville, cabled Paris that the king was incapable of ruling the country; de Verneville asked to be granted executive authority instead. Paris concurred; the *résident* was now free to issue royal decrees, appoint officials, and collect indirect taxes. As Milton Osborne has pointed out, high-ranking Cambodian officials, previously dependent on Norodom's approval, were quick to sense a shift in the balance of power.[14] By the end of the year, the king's advice—even though he had now regained his seals and de Verneville had been dismissed—was heeded only as a matter of form; the new *résident supérieur* was in command, answerable to authorities in Saigon, Paris, and Hanoi.

In the meantime, long-postponed royal decrees—such as one allowing French citizens to purchase land—had produced a real estate boom in Phnom Penh. The effect of the reforms in the *sruk*, as far as we can tell, was less far-reaching. Throughout the 1890s, French *résidents* complained officially about torpor, corruption, and timidity among local officials, although one of the latter, sensing the tune he was now expected to play, reported to his French superiors that "the population of all the villages in my province is happy; [the people] have not even the slightest complaint about the measures that have been taken."¹⁵ The Cambodian countryside, however, as many French officials complained, remained a *terra incognita*. No one knew how many people it contained, what they thought, or who held titles to land. Although slavery had been abolished, servitude for debts—often lasting a lifetime—remained widespread. Millenarian leaders occasionally gathered credulous followers and led them into revolt; gangs of bandits roamed the countryside at will. At the village level, in fact, conditions were hardly more secure than they had ever been.

And yet high-ranking French officials still saw their role in the country in terms of a "civilizing mission" and of rationalizing their relationships with the court. In the countryside, ironically, Sisowath was more popular than Norodom, partly because the people had seen him more often, on ceremonial occasions, and partly because Norodom's rule had been so rapacious and unjust. Sisowath, in fact, looked on approvingly at developments in the 1890s, and by 1897 or so he had been formally promised the throne by French officials.

Norodom took seven more years to die. The last years of his reign were marked by a scandal involving his favorite son, Prince Yukanthor, who sought to publicize French injustice in Cambodia when he was in France by hiring a French journalist to press his case with French officialdom. Officials paid slight attention, except to take offense. Yukanthor's accusations were largely true, if perhaps too zealous and wide-ranging, as when he declared to the people of France, "You have created property [in Cambodia], and thus you have created the poor."¹⁶

Officials in Paris persuaded Norodom by cable to demand an apology from his son. It never came, for Yukanthor preferred to remain in exile. He died in Bangkok in 1934 and until then was viewed by French colonial officials with slight, but unjustified, apprehension.

The two last prerogatives that Norodom surrendered to the French were the authority to select his close advisers and the right to farm out gambling concessions to Chinese businessmen in Phnom Penh. Little by little, the French encroached on his freedom of action. Osborne has recorded the battles that Norodom lost, but the last pages of the royal chronicle (compiled during the reign of Sisowath's son, King Monivong, in the 1930s) say almost nothing about the confrontation, leaving the impression that the reign was moving peacefully toward its close.

SISOWATH'S EARLY YEARS

Norodom, like millions of people of his generation, was born in a village and died in a semimodern city, graced at the time of his death with electricity and running water. The modernization of the edges and surfaces of his kingdom, however, spread very slowly, partly because communications inside Cambodia remained so poor, partly because monks, royalty, and officials—i.e., the people held in most respect—resisted institutional change, and partly because the "modernizing" segment of the society was dominated by the French, aided by immigrants from China and Vietnam. The "modernizers," interestingly, thought in Indochinese terms, or perhaps in capitalist ones, while members of the traditional elite saw no reason to widen their intellectual horizons or to tinker with their beliefs.

Norodom's death, nonetheless, was a watershed in French involvement and in Cambodian kingship as an institution, as the next three kings of the country were handpicked by the French. Until 1953, except for a few months in the summer of 1945, Cambodian officials of high rank played a subordinate, ceremonial role, and those at lower levels of the administration were underpaid servants of a colonial power. At no point in the chain of command was initiative rewarded. While Norodom lived, the French encountered obstacles to their plans. After 1904, with some exceptions, Cambodia became a relatively efficient revenue-producing machine.

The change over the long term, easy to see from our perspective, was not immediately perceptible in the *sruk*, where French officials found old habits of patronage, dependence, violence, fatalism, and corruption largely unchanged from year to year. Offices were still for sale, tax rolls were falsified, rice harvests were underestimated. Credulous people were still ready to follow sorcerers and mountebanks. As late as 1923, in Stung Treng, an ex-monk gathered a following by claiming to possess a "golden frog with a human voice";[17] banditry was widespread; and there were frequent famines and epidemics of malaria and cholera. The contrast between the capital and the *sruk*, therefore, sharpened in the early twentieth century, without apparently producing audible resentment in the *sruk*, even though peasants in the long run paid with their labor and their rice for all the improvements in Phnom Penh and for the high salaries enjoyed by French officials, fueling the resentment of anti-French guerrillas in the early 1950s and Communist cadres later on.

When Sisowath succeeded his brother in 1904, he was sixty-four years old. Ever since the 1870s he had been an almost fawning collaborator with the French. He seems to have been a somewhat more fervent Buddhist than Norodom and more popular among ordinary people, some of whom associated him with the ceremonies that he had sponsored (and that they had paid for) rather than the taxes charged by his brother or by the French. According to one French writer, he was so frightened of his brother, even in death, that he refused to attend his cremation. The first two years of his reign, according to the chronicle, were devoted largely to ceremonial observances and to bureaucratic innovations (such as appointing an electrician for the palace and enjoining officials to wear stockings and shoes in Western style).[18] On another occasion, Sisowath harangued visiting officials—probably at French insistence—about the persistence of slavery in the *sruk*;[19] throughout the year, like all Cambodian kings, he sponsored ceremonies meant to ensure good harvests and rainfall. Each year, for the rest of his reign, the French provided Sisowath (as they had Norodom) with an allowance of high-grade opium, totaling 113 kilograms (249 pounds) per year.[20]

This early stage of his reign culminated in Norodom's cremation in 1906, which was followed almost immediately by Sisowath's coronation. For the first time in Cambodian history, the ceremony is described in detail in the chronicle (as well as by French sources). It lasted for several days. One of its interesting features was that the French governor-general of Indochina was entrusted with giving Sisowath his titles and handing him his regalia; another was that *chaovay sruk*, summoned to the palace for the occasion, solemnly pledged to the king "all rice lands, vegetable fields, water, earth, forest and mountains, and the sacred boundaries of the great city, the kingdom of Kampuchea."[21]

Almost immediately after being crowned, Sisowath left Cambodia to visit the Colonial Exhibition at Marseilles, in the company of the royal ballet troupe.[22] His voyage is scrupulously recorded in the chronicle, which makes it sound like an episode in a Cambodian poem. The king's progress through Singapore, Ceylon, and the Indian Ocean is reverently set down, and so are gnomic comments about the sights farther on (three-story buildings in Italy; the coastline of the Red Sea consisting of "nothing but sand and rock"). At Port Said, people eagerly came to pay homage to "the lord of life and master of lives in the south." In Marseilles, when the king made a speech, "All the French people who were present clapped their hands—men and women alike." The chronicle gives the impression that the king *decided* to visit France; in fact, his visit was forced on him by the requirement of the exposition officials that the royal ballet perform.[23] From the French point of view, unofficially at least, this visit by an aged potentate and his harem told them what they already "knew" about his exotic, faintly comic little country.[24]

After exchanging visits and dinners with the president of the Republic, and a trip to Nancy to observe "the 14th of July in a European way," the king returned to Cambodia. Although the chronicle makes no mention of discussion of substantive matters, Sisowath's visit to Paris coincided with Franco-Thai negotiations there that culminated, a few months later, in Siam's retrocession to Cambodia of the *sruk* of Battambang and Siem Reap.[25] The trip received little publicity at home and is mentioned in French reports from the *sruk* only in connection with a rumor that

Sisowath had gone to France to plead with the French to legalize gambling in Cambodia.

The number of pages in Sisowath's chronicle devoted to the return of Battambang and Siem Reap suggests that the compilers, like the French, considered this to be the most important event of the reign, even though the king had little to do with it beyond providing the *résident supérieur*, in 1906, with a "history" of Thai occupation. The importance of the retrocession was probably connected with the importance that Angkor, and especially Angkor Wat, retained for the Cambodian monarchy throughout Cambodia's dark ages.[26] In 1909, a copy of the Cambodian translation of sacred Buddhist writings, the *Tripitaka*, was deposited in a monastery on the grounds of Angkor Wat, and for another sixty years Cambodian monarchs frequently visited the site and sponsored religious ceremonies there.

The retrocession apparently was less painful to the Thai than the loss of the Lao states, which occurred at roughly the same time. As we have seen, the northwestern *sruk* had come under Thai control in 1794 in exchange for Thai permission for Eng to rule at Udong. Over the next hundred years, except for a brief period in the 1830s, the Thai had made little effort to colonize (or depopulate) the region, choosing to govern it at most levels with ethnic Khmer. Although they did nothing to restore the temples at Angkor, they left them intact; revenue from the two *sruk*—in stipulated amounts of cardamom and other forest products—was not especially high; and the region was more defensible by water from Phnom Penh than overland from Bangkok.[27]

For these reasons, but primarily to avoid further friction along its border, the Thai decided in 1906 to cede the *sruk* to France. The final agreement was signed by the French and the Thai in April 1907, and the *sruk* came under French control toward the end of the year. Sisowath was not encouraged to visit the area, however, until 1909, for reasons that the chronicle fails to make clear.

And yet the king and his subjects were overjoyed at the restoration of Angkor. In the *tang tok* ceremonies of October 1907, when officials traditionally offered gifts to the monarch, widely attended celebrations occurred throughout the kingdom to "thank the angels" (*thevoda*) for the return of the *sruk*, and local officials assigned to the region came to Phnom Penh to pay homage to the king.

Over the next half century, French scholars and Cambodian workers restored the temples at Angkor. In the long run, the restoration was probably France's most valuable legacy to Cambodia. Battambang, especially in the 1920s, developed into the country's most prosperous *sruk*, providing the bulk of Cambodia's rice exports and sheltering, idiosyncratically, by far the greatest number of landlords in the country as well as the high-

Entrance to the Royal Palace in Phnom Penh. Photo by Roger Smith.

est number of immigrants from elsewhere in Cambodia and from the Cambodian-speaking portions of Cochin China.[28]

By 1909, typewriters had been installed in all the *résidences;* automobiles came into use on a national scale at about the same time. These two "improvements" in French administration had several unintentional effects. For one thing, the volume of reports required by *résidents,* and consumed by their superiors in Phnom Penh, Saigon, Hanoi, and Paris, increased dramatically. *Résidents,* more than ever, were tied down to their offices, presiding over a two-way flow of paper; they were seldom in contact, socially or professionally, with the people they were intended to protect. In automobiles, tours of inspection became speedier and more superficial, for *résidents* and their aides were confined to passable roads. In fact, the intensification of French economic and political controls over Cambodia, noticeable throughout the 1920s and after, was accompanied, ironically, by the withdrawal of French officials from many levels of Cambodian life. The "government" that a Cambodian peasant might encounter in these years was composed of a minority of Cambodians and of a great many Vietnamese, brought into the protectorate because they could prepare reports in French, and this interplay between Cambodians and Vietnamese had important effects on the development of Cambodian nationalism, especially after World War II.

CHAPTER 9

Cambodia's Response to France, 1916–1945

Two events of political importance stand out from the last ten years or so of Sisowath's reign. These are the so-called 1916 Affair and the murder of a French *résident*, Félix Louis Bardez, in rural Kompong Chhnang in 1925. The first of these revealed how little the French knew about communications and social organization in Cambodia after more than fifty years of being in control. The second, perhaps because it was the only incident of its kind in the colonial era, shocked the regime and was blown out of proportion in postcolonial times by Cambodian nationalist writers.

THE 1916 AFFAIR

To understand the 1916 Affair, we must remember that the French financed almost all of their activities in Cambodia, including public works and the salaries of French officials, by a complex and onerous network of taxes on salt, alcohol, opium, rice and other crops, and exported and imported goods and by levying extensive fees for all government services. Of those too poor to pay their way out, the French could require ninety days per year of corvée, but people who paid their way out were still liable in many cases to other labor requirements. The cash to pay rice taxes came only when peasant householders had sold their harvests for cash or had been able to earn enough cash to pay the taxes by hiring themselves out in the off-season. There was a certain amount of flexibility in the system, because tax records were poorly kept and local leaders tended to underestimate the number of people they controlled in order to spread the tax burden more evenly through the population and to increase their own opportunities for profit.

During World War I, the French increased this burden throughout In-dochina by floating war loans to which local people, especially "the leisure classes" (presumably Chinese merchants), were forcefully urged to subscribe; by levying additional taxes; and by recruiting volunteers for military service abroad. In late November 1915, some three hundred peasants from the area northeast of Phnom Penh arrived in the capital with a petition to Sisowath asking him to reduce taxes, which, although levied by the French, were collected by Cambodian officials. The king met the delegation and ordered its members to go home, promising vaguely that some adjustments would be made.[1]

News of the confrontation apparently spread in the *sruk* to the east of Phnom Penh—long a hotbed of antidynastic sentiment in any case—and larger and larger delegations, sometimes numbering as many as three thousand peasants, began walking into the capital and assembling out-side the palace to place their grievances before the king. French *résidents*, reporting on these movements, registered their surprise not only at the magnitude of the delegations but also, as one wrote, at the fact that they had "been set in motion with such disconcerting speed." Another men-tioned that no one had predicted the affair, although "the entire popula-tion was involved." French police estimated that some forty thousand peasants passed through Phnom Penh in the early months of 1916 before being ordered back to their villages by the king. Other estimates run as high as a hundred thousand. Scattered incidents in the *sruk* later in the year claimed half a dozen Cambodian lives, and at the same time, Sisowath toured the eastern *sruk* by automobile, exhorting peasants to re-main peacefully in their homes and canceling any further corvée for 1916.

In the long run, the 1916 Affair had little effect on the way the French ran Cambodia or on Cambodian responses to the French. In fact, it is unclear that the demonstrations were against the French at all; French administra-tors were sidestepped by the petitioners, who sought justice directly from the king. What is extraordinary about the demonstrations is the speed and efficiency with which they were organized by leaders whose identity and motives remain obscure. The incident undermined French mythology about "lazy" and "individualistic" Cambodians, supposedly impervious to leadership or ideology. Some French officials, panicked by the size of the delegations, blamed the affair on "German agents"; still others saw evi-dence of deep-seated antimonarchic feeling, citing in evidence a manifesto that had circulated earlier in 1915, which stated: "The French have made us very unhappy for many years by keeping bad people as the king and as of-ficials while treating good people as bad."[2]

Interestingly, the 1916 Affair coincided with serious anti-French demonstrations in Cochin China. The possibility of links between the two was noted by some French officials, but the speed with which Cambodian disaffection died down suggests that people there had been demonstrating to relieve local wrongs.

In the nine years that passed before the assassination of *résident* Bardez, the French so tightened and rationalized their control over Cambodia—and especially over the organization of revenue collection and day-to-day administration—that some "aged" Cambodian officials complained to them that "too many changes" were taking place. In 1920, for example, the French arranged for rice taxes to be collected by local officials rather than by officials sent to the *sruk* from Phnom Penh. A year later, the French experimented with a "communal" reorganization of Cambodia along Vietnamese lines, only to drop the idea after a year or so. The French extended their supervisory role to cover local justice in 1923; expanded *wat* education from 1924 onward; and used corvée to build an impressive array of public works, particularly roads and a mountain resort at Bokor, favored by the king, which was built by prisoners (with a tremendous loss of life) and opened in 1925. The first rice mills had opened in Cambodia in 1917—previously, unmilled rice had been shipped to Saigon—and the period 1916–1925 (with the noticeable exception of 1918–1919, a year of very poor harvests and, in some *sruk*, famine conditions) was one of increasing prosperity in Cambodia, especially for local Chinese merchants and the French.[3]

The gap in income between the French and the Cambodians—with the rare exceptions of a few favored officials and the royal family—was very wide. A French official could earn as much as 12,000 piastres a year; with exemptions for his wife and two children, such an official would pay only 30 piastres in tax. Cambodian officials were paid less for similar jobs and were the first to have their wages cut during the depression of the 1930s. A Cambodian farmer, on the other hand, with no salary other than what he could earn (at 30 cents per day, or 90 piastres a year) or what he could sell his crops for (seldom more than 40 piastres a year), was saddled with a range of taxes that totaled in the 1920s as much as 12 piastres per year. He was taxed individually and in cash payment in lieu of corvée; his rice was taxed at a fixed percentage; he paid high prices for salt, opium, and alcohol and paid abattoir taxes when his livestock went to slaughter.

What did the peasant receive in exchange? Very little, despite French rhetoric to the contrary. Monthly reports from French *résidents* show widespread rural violence and disorder, which, because it made no direct challenge to French control, seldom rose into the "political" portions of the reports. It is clear, however, that to most villagers the perpetual harassment of bandit gangs, especially in the dry season, was far more real than any benefits brought to them by the French.[4]

Before the 1930s, moreover, the French spent almost nothing on education. A French official in 1922 accurately characterized efforts in this field as a mere facade; medical services were also derisory, and electricity and running water were almost unknown outside Phnom Penh. Cambodia's money, in other words, went to finance French officials and the things they wanted to build. In exchange, Cambodia was protected from control by anyone else, as well as from the perils of independence. The French succeeded in keeping the nineteenth century from repeating itself while keeping the twentieth century at bay. The fear of "modernity" runs through a good deal of French writing about colonial Cambodia, even though the French in another context perceived their role as one of transmitting modernity to the Khmer. Because what they were supposed to be doing was not allowed to take place, the French took refuge in beliefs about the "innate" characteristics of the Cambodians, which supposedly kept them immune from modern ideas or inherently hostile to them.

These beliefs were based on less and less direct experience with the Cambodians themselves. The most articulate critic of French colonialism at this time, André Pannetier, remarked that competence among Frenchmen in the Khmer language declined steadily as the twentieth century wore on.[5] Ironically, as the adventure and romance of serving in Cambodia wore thin, the clichés with which French bureaucrats described the Cambodian people became increasingly fuzzy and romantic. The process came to a climax of sorts in 1927, when former Governor-General Paul Doumer, by then president of France, unveiled a group of statues on the staircase that links the railroad station in Marseilles with the city below. One of these, entitled "Our Possessions in Asia," depicts a half-naked teenaged girl, decked out in approximately Angkorean garb, lying on a divan being waited on by smaller, half-clad girls representing Laos and Vietnam. As the "easiest" and oldest of French protectorates in Indochina, Cambodia was rewarded by being portrayed as the oldest child and as receiving tribute of a kind from the other two. The notion that Cambodians lay around receiving tidbits, of course, may also have been at the back of the sculptor's mind.[6]

THE ASSASSINATION OF *RÉSIDENT* BARDEZ

In late 1923, the acting French *résident* in Prey Veng, a vigorous and ambitious official named Félix Louis Bardez, reported his belief that there were three reasons why tax receipts were so low: "the complete inactivity of Cambodian officials, the lack of supervision [over the officers expected to collect the taxes], and shortcomings in collection procedures."[7] In the course of 1924, Bardez improved the procedures for tax collection in the *sruk* to the extent that all eighteen categories of tax yielded more revenues than in 1923. He showed that the system could be made more productive by working harder himself. Indeed, the two categories of tax in which revenues rose the most—rice taxes and Chinese head taxes— were precisely those that could be increased by a vigorous *résident* on the spot, eager to expose the compromises, doctored books, and exaggerations of local officials.

Bardez's success in Prey Veng attracted the attention of his superiors, and in late 1924 he was transferred ahead of many more senior officials to be *résident* in Kompong Chhnang, long bedeviled by banditry and low tax revenues. Bardez's arrival coincided roughly with the promulgation of a supplementary tax to pay for the mountain resort of Bokor, but money was hard to come by, as Bardez admitted to a friend, and receipts were slow in coming. One Cambodian official trying to collect them was severely beaten by villagers in the district in early 1925.

On April 18, angered by reports that another village, Krang Laav, was delinquent in its payments, Bardez visited the village himself, accompanied by an interpreter and a Cambodian militiaman.[8] Summoning delinquent taxpayers to the village hall, or *sala*, he had several of them handcuffed and threatened to take them to prison, even though they would not be subject to fines for their delinquency for three months. His refusal to let the prisoners have lunch while he himself was eating destroyed the patience of the large crowd of people looking on, who lacked food or shelter. In a confused melee, Bardez and his companions were set upon by twenty or thirty people. Within half an hour, Bardez, the interpreter, and the militiaman had been beaten to death with chairs, fence palings, ax handles, and the militiaman's rifle butt. The corpses were then mutilated, and according to some witnesses, the murderers danced around them. Soon afterward, incited by local leaders who were never brought to trial, seven hundred Cambodians—the crowd that had gathered to listen to Bardez—began marching on Kompong Chhnang to demand remission of their taxes. After a few hours, however, their fervor died down, and the marchers broke up or were dispersed by armed militia before they reached their destination.

The news of Bardez's murder shocked the French community in Phnom Penh, largely because it was the first case in which villagers had killed a high-ranking French official on duty; other officials had been killed by bandits or by their servants, but none while collecting taxes. The precedent obviously was a dramatic one. Moving swiftly through their puppets in the royal family, the French saw to it that Sisowath sent his eldest son, Prince Monivong, to the area with a French political counselor to communicate his discontent. This took the form of a royal ordinance changing the name of the village from Krang Laav to Direchan ("Bestiality").[9] The ordinance forced the villagers to conduct expiatory services for Bardez on the anniversary of his murder for the next ten years. The most interesting feature of the ordinance was its insistence on collective guilt. This was the line pursued by the defense in the trial of the eighteen men arrested for Bardez's murder, but it was dismissed by the prosecution, which saw danger in linking the murder with any kind of political discontent. Interestingly, one of the men arrested for the murder was still alive in 1980, when he told an interviewer that "everyone in the village" had beaten Bardez and his companions.[10]

The trial of the men accused of the murders opened in Phnom Penh in December 1925 and was widely reported in the press, in which it was fitted into a pattern of increasing anticolonial feeling elsewhere in Indochina. At the trial, the prosecution tried to prove that the defendants were "pirates" from outside the village and that robbery had been their motive. In fact, although the taxes collected by Bardez disappeared in the melee, his own billfold was untouched. More to the point, his diary was confiscated by the prosecution and classified as confidential because of the "political" material it contained. Testimony by several of Bardez's friends suggested that the diary may have recorded his pessimism about collecting any extra taxes; to one of them, he had remarked shortly before his death that there was simply not enough money in the *sruk* to meet the newly imposed demands. High-ranking French officials interfered with witnesses for the defense; at one point, the defense attorney's tea was apparently poisoned by unknown hands, and a stenographer hired by the defense was forced by her former employers to return to her job in Saigon. What the French wanted to keep quiet, it seems, was the fact that emerged at the trial—namely, that on a per capita basis the Cambodian peasants paid the highest taxes in Indochina as a price for their "docility."

The Bardez incident resembles the 1916 Affair and the 1942 monks' demonstration, discussed below, in that nothing like it had happened previously in the colonial era. It exposed the mechanics of colonial rule and the unreality of French mythology about the peaceable "Cambodian character." One aspect of the widening distance between the French and the Cambodians was the fact that Bardez, after fifteen years of conscientious service in Cambodia, was still incapable of speaking Khmer. Without knowing the language, how accurate could his assessments be of what ordinary people were thinking? It is as if a great deal of Cambodian life in the colonial period was carried out behind a screen, invisible and inaudible to the French. Another French *résident*, writing at about this time, made a perceptive comment in this regard: "It's permissible to ask if the unvarying calm which the [Cambodian] people continue to exhibit is not merely an external appearance, covering up vague, *unexpressed feelings* [emphasis added] . . . whose exact nature we cannot perceive."[11]

Résidents might justify their conduct by saying that they were paid to administer the population, not to understand it. Every month, they were required to complete mountains of paperwork, to sit for days as referees in often inconclusive legal cases, and to supervise the extensive programs of public works—primarily roads—which the French used to perpetuate corvée and to justify their presence in the kingdom.

COLONIAL RULE AND THE BEGINNINGS OF NATIONALISM

The Bardez incident also offers us a glimpse of Cambodian peasants entering the historical record. Before 1927, in fact, there were no Khmer-language newspapers or journals in the kingdom, and Cambodian literature, when it was printed at all, consisted almost entirely of Buddhist texts and nineteenth-century verse epics. The first novel in Khmer, *Tonle Sap*, was published in 1938, two years after the appearance of the first Khmer newspaper, *Nagara Vatta* ("Angkor Wat").[12] Although these facts are not especially surprising in view of French inactivity in Cambodian education, they contrast sharply with the quantity of printed material produced in the Vietnamese components of Indochina. Literacy in Cambodia had been linked since Angkorean times with the study and promulgation of religious texts, and in the colonial era, literacy in Khmer was almost entirely in the hands of the Buddhist monkhood. Before 1936, in fact, the only Khmer-language periodical, *Kambuja Surya* ("Cambodian Sun"), had been published on a monthly basis under the auspices of the French-funded Institut Bouddhique. With rare exceptions, the journal limited itself to printing folklore, Buddhist texts, and material concerned with the royal family. Even Cambodian chronicle histories in Khmer were not yet available in print.[13]

Because of these conditions, the picture that emerges from the 1930s is a peculiarly unbalanced one. The reading of French novels, official reports, and newspapers allows us to reconstruct Cambodian history with much of the population left out or merely acted upon by events. The manuscript chronicles of King Sisowath and his son, King Sisowath Monivong (r. 1927–1941), are not especially helpful, for they limit themselves to a formulaic narration of events in which the king himself was involved, although Monivong's chronicle "opens up" a little to cover such events as the 1932 coup d'état in Siam, the Italo-Ethiopian war, and the French surrender to Germany in 1940. The requirements of the genre removed individual voices from the texts; even the kings are rarely quoted.[14] Because archival sources from the *sruk* themselves for the colonial era are not available for study, it is difficult to gauge the style and extent of social change and intellectual upheaval, the extent to which they can be traced to French initiatives, and Cambodian responses to them in the period before World War II. Arguably, change in Cambodia did not filter into the villages until the 1950s; yet the face of Cambodia was already very different in the 1930s from what it had been when the French arrived or even at the beginning of the century.

Overland communications had changed dramatically. From 1900 to 1930, some 9,000 kilometers (5,400 miles) of paved and graveled roads had been built by corvée throughout the kingdom. Between 1928 and 1932, moreover, a 500-kilometer (300-mile) stretch of railroad was built between Phnom Penh and Battambang; it was later extended to the Thai border. These changes meant that thousands of rural Cambodians were now able to move rapidly about the country by bus, and visits to Phnom Penh and district capitals became easier and more frequent. These developments also favored French penetration and Chinese exploitation of the rural economy. The commercial development of Cambodia—especially in terms of rice exports and rubber plantations—benefited primarily the French and the Chinese entrepreneurs, who monopolized the export trade. In fact, as William E. Willmott has shown, Chinese immigration into Cambodia, which remained steady at around two thousand a year until the 1920s, rose to five thousand a year during the boom years.[15] The Chinese population of the kingdom rose accordingly—from perhaps one hundred seventy thousand in 1905 to three hundred thousand at the beginning of World War II. Almost invariably, these immigrants went into petty commerce, already dominated by Chinese and Sino-Cambodians. Because many Vietnamese immigrants to Cambodia, aside from those recruited to work in the rubber plantations, also preferred urban employment, cities in Cambodia, as so often in colonial Southeast Asia, were enclaves dominated by foreign bureaucrats and entrepreneurs. This fact was not lost on the Cambodian elite, but the elite was unable or unwilling to do much about it.

And the elite itself, although relatively small, was gradually increasing in importance. An interesting coincidence occurred in 1930. As the first stretch of track on the railroad went into service, the first Cambodian students—including two princes and four men destined to be ministers in the 1940s and 1950s—graduated from a French lycée in Saigon. Cambodia had to wait until 1936 for a lycée of its own, named after Sisowath and occupying the site of his former palace. Primary education, for the most part, remained in the hands of the *sangha,* and the French sponsored, at very little cost, a network of some five thousand extant *wat* schools, in which students learned traditional subjects in time-honored ways.[16]

These developments were played out against the economic boom that affected most of Indochina in the 1920s. In Cambodia, the greatest beneficiaries were the firms engaged in the export of rice and in the newly opened rubber plantations near Kompong Cham. The rubber plantations, staffed largely by Vietnamese, had little economic impact on the Cambodian countryside, but rice production rose sharply to meet international demands, and new funds generated by the widening tax base were diverted into even more extensive public works, including the beautification of Phnom Penh, the electrification of provincial towns, the road-building mentioned above, and the construction of seaside resorts and mountain hotels, which benefited the French and the embryonic tourist industry. The Bardez incident, in other words, barely ruffled the surface of French complacency.

The world depression of the 1930s, however, reversed or suspended many of these trends, as the local price of rice plummeted from 3 piastres to 1 piastre a *picul* (about 68 kilograms, or 150 pounds). The Cambodian peasants' reaction, insofar as it can be gauged from *résidents'* reports, was to reduce rice hectarage (which dropped by a third throughout the country from 1928 to 1933), to seek postponement or remission of taxes, and to find solace, in some areas in millenarian religious cults, such as the recently inaugurated syncretic cult of Cao Dai in neighboring Cochin China.[17]

The period was marked by several uprisings against the French in the Vietnamese components of Indochina, but Cambodia remained quiet. In their reports, French *résidents* frequently complimented the Cambodian peasants for the "stoicism" with which they continued to react to the highest and most variegated tax burden in Indochina; one of them traced this obedience to the Cambodians' "reverence for authority." Nonetheless, the level of rural violence—with Khmer victimizing Khmer—appears to have risen slightly, only to decline when the economic crisis faded in the mid-1930s. Tax delinquency in rural areas reached 45 percent in 1931 and more than 60 percent in the following year, when remissions were granted by the *résident supérieur*. As most Cambodians reverted to subsistence farming, Phnom Penh's population, unsurprisingly, rose only slightly—from 96,000 in 1931 to barely 100,000 in 1936. Throughout this period, and indeed until the 1970s, the capital was informally divided into three residential zones, with Vietnamese and Cham to the north, Chinese and French in the commercial center, and Cambodians to the south and west of the royal palace, which faced the Mekong River.

In an effort to increase tax revenue, in 1931 the French encouraged King Monivong to tour the *sruk*, where he admonished audiences supplied by local officials on the virtues of frugality and hard work. The king himself continued to live well, and his grandson, Norodom Sihanouk, later recalled that Monivong spent very little of his time attending to official business, preferring the company of his numerous wives and concubines.[18] One of his favorites was an elder sister of Saloth Sar, who was to emerge in the 1970s as Pol Pot, the secretary of the Cambodian Communist party. In the midst of the depression, new palace buildings were built for Monivong by the French. In 1932 he entertained the French minister of colonies, Paul Reynaud, who had come to Indochina to investigate the aftermath of the Vietnamese uprisings of the previous year. In Cambodia, the visit was entirely ceremonial and stage-managed by the powerful Cambodian official, Tiounn, who by now held the portfolios of finance, palace affairs, and fine arts. He had governed the country under the French since the beginning of Sisowath's reign, and several of his grandsons were to become prominent members of the Cambodian Communist party.

When the economy of Indochina recovered slowly in the mid-1930s, rice exports, particularly from Battambang, reached 100,000 metric tons a year, and new crops—especially maize—were grown in large quantities for export. Administratively, the last part of the decade saw increased Cambodian participation in administration, especially in the *sruk*, where many who became officials of independent Cambodia—including Nhek Tioulong, Lon Nol, and Sisowath Sirik Matak—were beginning their careers. In political terms, the French were pleased to notice that disturbances in Cochin China, arising in part from conflicts between Trotskyite and Communist supporters of the Popular Front government in France, aroused no echoes in Cambodia, whose late but well-mannered "awakening" was the subject of a tendentious French brochure published on the occasion of a governor-general's visit in 1935.[19] By "awakening," the French meant economic advances and administrative participation by the Khmer rather than any increased awareness of the colonial situation. The roots of postwar Cambodian nationalism, nonetheless, can be found in the 1930s, at first in a cooperative and well-mannered guise, while the French were looking for the sorts of "revolutionary" politics they had encountered in Vietnam. Confidential French political reports throughout the decade registered "none" under the obligatory rubric "revolutionary activities," and latter-day Cambodian historians, looking for the roots of the Cambodian Communist movement, cannot find them in this period.[20]

And yet an awakening of a sort *was* taking place, primarily among the newly formed Cambodian elite in Phnom Penh and especially among those educated at the kingdom's first high school, the Collège (and after 1936, the Lycée) Sisowath. Earlier in the decade, students at the college had appealed to the king against the favoritism allegedly shown to students of Vietnamese extraction. By 1937, an association of graduates had more than five hundred members.

This association was the first of its kind in Cambodia, where voluntary associations along professional lines had always been slow to develop and had been discouraged by the French. For years, the French had lamented the Cambodian aversion to solidarity while opposing any Cambodian attempts—by veterans of World War I, for example, or by adherents of the Cao Dai—to form associations. The fear of solidarity, in fact, appears to have dominated the French reaction to the Bardez affair, as we have seen. For administrative purposes, the French preferred to deal with a society that was, theoretically at least, arranged vertically rather than horizontally. A similarly bureaucratic turn of mind, perhaps, made many French officials suspicious of new developments in the countryside—whether they were sponsored by Protestant missionaries, the Cao Dai, or any other external agent—while doing little themselves to change the status quo, characterized by widespread poverty, poor health, and no modern education.

The three key channels for Cambodian self-awareness in the 1930s, in fact, were the Lycée Sisowath, the Institut Bouddhique, and the newspaper *Nagara Vatta*, founded in 1936 by Pach Chhoeun and Sim Var; both men, in their thirties, were soon joined by a young Cambodian judge, born in Vietnam and educated in France, named Son Ngoc Thanh.[21] The three, in turn, were closely associated with the Institut Bouddhique, to which Son Ngoc Thanh was later assigned as a librarian. This brought them into contact with the leaders of the Cambodian *sangha*, with Cambodian intellectuals, and also with a small group of French scholars and officials led by the secretary of the institute, Suzanne Karpelès, who were eager to help with Cambodia's intellectual renaissance.

The editorial stand of *Nagara Vatta* was pro-Cambodian without, for the moment, being anti-French. It objected to Vietnamese domination of the Cambodian civil service, Chinese domination of commerce, and the shortage of suitable employment for educated Khmer. Editorials also condemned the usury of Chinese rural merchants, French delays in modernizing the educational system, the shortage of credit for Cambodian farmers, and the low pay of Cambodian civil servants. More important, the paper sought to increase the distance between Cambodian history and aspirations on the one hand and those of the Vietnamese on the other. One editorial even went so far as to compare Hitler's territorial aggrandizement in Europe to that of Vietnam in nineteenth-century Cambodia. A thread of anti-Vietnamese feeling gradually emerged in the paper, a feeling that was to run through the ideology of every Cambodian government after independence until the Vietnamese invasion of 1978–1979.

But in terms of its own historical context, what was important about *Nagara Vatta* was that for the first time since 1863 a conversation had opened up between the French and their allegedly "dormant" clientele as well as among the Cambodian elite. The paper's circulation, as early as

1937, rose to more than five thousand copies per issue, and readership was undoubtedly far higher.

Who were its readers? Who were the new elite? Primarily, they seem to have been young Cambodian men in the lower ranks of the civil service, educated at least partially in the French educational system. Undoubtedly, they were concentrated in Phnom Penh. In his memoirs of this period, Bunchhan Muul, by that time a high official in the Khmer Republic, stated that the paper saw as its mission the awakening of the Cambodian people—an image that persisted into the 1950s, when Son Ngoc Thanh returned from exile and founded another nationalist paper entitled *Khmer Krok* ("Cambodians awake"). The *Nagara Vatta* was important because it gave thousands of Cambodians a chance for the first time to read about events in the outside world in their own language.

Nevertheless, the emerging Cambodian elite, defined in terms of educational qualifications, was very small. By 1939, the number of *bacheliers* graduated from the Lycée Sisowath was barely half a dozen, and perhaps a dozen Cambodians had been trained in tertiary institutions abroad. The gap between political awareness and technical proficiency, which persisted into the postcolonial period, can be blamed initially on French inertia in the field of indigenous education, itself traceable to French unwillingness to pay the bills.

Before the fall of France in the summer of 1940, none of the officials in Indochina had openly voiced doubts about the permanence of the French presence in Asia. There were no moves in Cambodia, for example, to widen the electorate, to introduce representative government on anything other than a consultative basis, or to train Cambodians to replace Frenchmen in the administration. In the *sruk,* however, some devolution took place in the 1930s whereby experienced and senior local officials, rather than Frenchmen, were allowed to prepare local budgets and write periodic reports.[22] The sense of irony among French officials, it seems, was not highly developed; in 1939, elaborate ceremonies were sponsored in Phnom Penh to honor the hundred-and-fiftieth anniversary of the French Revolution, and the venue was the Place de la République.[23]

THE IMPACT OF WORLD WAR II

World War II—or, more precisely, the period between June 1940 and October 1945—must be seen as a watershed in the history of Indochina. This is particularly true of Vietnam, but French policies in Cambodia, springing from weakness, and Cambodian responses to them differed sharply from what had gone before. By the end of 1945, Cambodian independence, impracticable and almost unthought of in 1939, had become primarily a matter of time.

Much the same state of affairs applied throughout Southeast Asia, and particularly in Burma and the Dutch East Indies (now Indonesia): The development of nationalism in Indochina differed in that France was the only colonial power in the region to retain day-to-day control of its possessions for the greater part of World War II. The French managed to do so by making substantial concessions to the Japanese. Elsewhere in Southeast Asia, between 1942 and 1945, the Japanese jailed colonial officials and ruled through local leaders, usually recruited from the ranks of opponents of colonial rule. In Indochina, on the other hand, the French sought to defuse nationalist thinking and activity by maintaining secret police surveillance, by opening up their administration to local people, and by liberalizing some of their policies. In the Cambodian case, it can be argued that this liberalization, and several events associated with it, gave birth to elite Cambodian nationalism in the form it assumed until the 1970s.[24]

Five of these events are worth examining in detail: the Franco-Siamese war of 1940–1941; the coronation of Monivong's grandson, Norodom Sihanouk, in 1941; the so-called monks' demonstration of July 1942; the romanization crisis of the following year; and finally, the Japanese *coup de force* of March 9, 1945, which dismantled French control throughout Indochina.

These events were played out against the background of Vichy rule in Indochina, from July 1940 to March 1945 in the hands of Vice-Admiral Jean Decoux.[25] Vichy rule in some ways was more flexible, in others more repressive and certainly more ideological than the governments provided by the Third Republic had ever been. This was partly because officials, to appease the Japanese, and following ideological preferences of their own, tended to follow a pro-Axis, anti-British line and partly because, perceiving their vulnerability in Southeast Asia, they sought to retain control while using very little of their depleted military forces.

Examples of their flexibility in Cambodia included raising the salaries and widening the responsibilities of indigenous officials; encouraging an enhanced sense of national identity, linked to an idealization of the Angkorean era and of Jayavarman VII in particular; and the organization of paramilitary youth groups along Vichy lines. These groups gave thousands of young Cambodians their first taste, outside the *sangha*, of membership in an extrafamilial group.

The regime was repressive as well. In late 1940, elected bodies (of some importance in southern Vietnam especially) were abolished throughout Indochina; after the monks' demonstration, *Nagara Vatta* was suppressed in 1942; and more than thirty Cambodians were imprisoned for long terms following that demonstration. These moves had their greatest impact on the people who were to lead Cambodia's nationalist movement in the 1940s and 1950s; they had little effect in the countryside as far as we can tell.

What the French were trying to do in France and in Indochina was to endure the war, hoping to reemerge even after an Axis victory with some identity and much of the French empire intact. In Cambodia and Vietnam, part of the process involved harking back to better days and to warlike heroes and heroines like Joan of Arc, the Trung sisters, and Jayavarman VII. In Cambodia, the French chose to work through the institutions of the monarchy, whereas those who opposed them became in the course of the war increasingly antimonarchic, setting the stage for factions that have endured in Cambodian politics ever since.

The Franco-Siamese war broke out in late 1940 because the pro-Japanese government of Phibul Songgram, aware of French military weakness, seized the opportunity to regain territories in Cambodia and Laos that the Thai had ceded earlier in the century to the French. These actions fitted into their irredentist nationalism of the period. On land, poorly equipped French forces suffered a series of defeats. At sea, however, French aircraft and warships scored a major victory over the Thai fleet in January 1941. Frightened by the possibility of further embarrassments to the Thai, the Japanese forced the French to negotiate in Tokyo; the upshot of these negotiations was that Battambang, most of Siem Reap, and parts of Laos—a total of slightly more than 65,000 square kilometers (25,000 square miles)—were ceded to the Thai for the derisory sum of six million piastres.[26] The French managed to retain Angkor for their Cambodian protégés, but the humiliating loss of territory so embittered King Monivong that for the remaining few months of his life (he died in April 1941), he refused to meet with French officials or to converse with anyone in French.

Monivong's death posed a problem for French officials concerned with the possibility, however faint, of dynastic squabbling so soon after their military defeat.[27] Throughout the 1930s, Monivong's son, Prince Monireth (1909–1975), had been favored for the throne, although French officials had also proposed the candidacy of Prince Norodom Suramarit, a grandson of Norodom's who was married to Monivong's daughter. Rivalry between Norodom's and Sisowath's descendants had surfaced occasionally in the colonial era, largely because many members of the royal family had little to do besides quarrel with each other. In the aftermath of the war with Thailand, the French governor-general, Decoux, favored the selection of Suramarit's son, Norodom Sihanouk (b. 1922), then a student at a French lycée in Saigon. His ostensible rationale for preferring Sihanouk to Monireth was the need to heal the rift between the Norodom and Sisowath branches of the family; it is also likely that, of the two candidates, Sihanouk seemed more malleable and less independent-minded.

The shy young man who came to the throne in April 1941 and was crowned in October seemed an unlikely candidate to dominate Cambodian politics for so much of the next half century. He was an only child whose parents were estranged; in *L'Indochine vue de Pékin*, as well as in his memoirs, he has recalled his lonely, introverted childhood.[28] Although an excellent student and a good musician, he had received no training for the throne and for the first few years of his reign worked closely with his French advisers.

In the first months of his reign, Sihanouk made modest efforts at reform to bolster his image with the Cambodian people and to compensate for the reclusiveness of his grandfather's last months. The annual gift of opium from the French was canceled, Palace Minister Tiounn was encouraged to retire, and the prince became active in Vichy-oriented youth groups.[29] His freedom of action was limited not only by French advisers but also by the fact that by August 1941, eight thousand Japanese troops had been posted to Cambodia. No one knew what the Japanese intended to do.

French military weakness and Japanese sympathy for certain anticolonial movements—evident throughout Southeast Asia by 1942—had not passed unnoticed among the intellectuals—many of the members of the *sangha*—who were associated with *Nagara Vatta* and the Institut Bouddhique. Between 1940 and 1942, the paper took an increasingly pro-Japanese and anticolonial line. During these years, at least thirty-two issues of the paper were censored and in ten issues, the lead editorial was suppressed. Perhaps in some cases the censorship involved overreaction on the part of the French. Nothing has yet been published about Japanese financial support for the Cambodian nationalists at this early stage, but some collaboration can be assumed and was actively sought by Son Ngoc Thanh and his associates. The climax of the confrontation between this group of Cambodians and the French occurred in July 1942, in the monks' demonstration.[30]

Throughout the twentieth century, the French had looked somewhat warily at the Buddhist *sangha* in both Cambodia and Laos, noticing that it offered the Lao and Khmer an alternative value system to the colonial one. In Cambodia, as in Thailand, the *sangha* was made up of two sects, the larger known as the Mahanikay and the smaller, which enjoyed royal patronage, as the Thammayut. Jurisdictional quarrels between the two, which differed on no doctrinal matters but on several procedural ones, were frequent, and because of the Thammayut's palace connections, monks with antimonarchic ideas tended to gravitate to the Mahanikay.

One of these monks, Hem Chieu (1898–1943), a teacher at the advanced Pali school in Phnom Penh, was implicated in an anti-French plot when he proposed to several members of the Cambodian militia vague plans for a coup. A pro-French militiaman apparently informed on him, and he was arrested with a fellow monk on July 17, 1942. Hem Chieu was an important member of the *sangha,* and the manner of his arrest—by civil authorities who failed to allow him the ritual of leaving the monastic order—affronted his religious colleagues while giving nationalists of the *Nagara Vatta* clique a cause célèbre. Over the next three days, the nationalists engaged in secret conversations with the Japanese, seeking their cooperation in sponsoring an anti-French demonstration in support of the arrested monks. According to Son Ngoc Thanh, Japanese authorities in Saigon (who had jurisdiction over their colleagues in Phnom Penh) agreed in some fashion to sponsor the Cambodian rally, now planned for July 20.[31]

On that morning, more than a thousand people, perhaps half of them monks, marched along Phnom Penh's principal boulevard to the office of the French *résident supérieur,* Jean de Lens, demanding Hem Chieu's release. The demonstrators were trailed by French, Cambodian, and Vietnamese police agents, who took photographs of them. The editor of *Nagara Vatta,* Pach Chhoeun, enthusiastically led the march and was arrested as he presented a petition to a French official inside the *résidence.* Along with other civilian demonstrators rounded up over the next few days, Chhoeun was quickly tried. The sentence of death imposed on him was commuted to life imprisonment by the Vichy government—the same sentence meted out to the murderers of Bardez seventeen years before. Son Ngoc Thanh, who later admitted his involvement in planning the demonstration, apparently hid in Phnom Penh for several days before escaping to the Thai-controlled city of Battambang. By early 1943, he had been offered asylum in Tokyo, where he remained for the next two years, writing forlorn, infrequent letters to nationalist colleagues in Battambang, pleading that they keep the nationalist flame alive and assuring them of continued discreet Japanese cooperation.

The collapse of the demonstration suggests that Thanh and his colleagues overestimated Japanese support and underestimated French severity. The French, in any case, were eager to demonstrate that they remained in charge. The march and Hem Chieu's name, like the 1916 Affair and the Bardez incident, passed into Cambodian anticolonial folklore, resurfacing in 1945 during the anti-French resistance and again, among different groups, following the anti-Sihanouk coup of 1970. In 1979, after the Vietnamese invasion, a boulevard in Phnom Penh, formerly named after Sisowath Monivong, was renamed in Hem Chieu's honor. The ex-monk had died of illness on the French penal island of Poulo Condore in 1943.[32] In the short term, the demonstration accomplished nothing, and Sihanouk in his memoirs dismissed it as "tragicomic." At the time, he apparently accepted the view of his French advisers that it was foolish and unjustified.

THE GROWTH OF NATIONALISM AND THE RETURN OF THE FRENCH

The remaining three years of World War II are important for Cambodian history, but they are difficult to study. French archives for the period remain closed for the most part, and the French-controlled press for the period, like Sihanouk's unpublished chronicle, is largely ceremonial and bureaucratic in emphasis. Nationalists fell silent, fled to Battambang, or spent the years in prison. For these reasons, the so-called romanization crisis of 1943 is difficult to assess.

In 1943, the new French *résident*, Georges Gautier, announced his intention to replace Cambodia's forty-seven-letter alphabet, derived from medieval Indian models, with the roman one. The transliteration was worked out by George Coedes; available samples show that the system retained the phonetics of spoken Khmer quite well. Gautier and his colleagues viewed the reform as a step toward "modernization," which in turn was seen unequivocally as a good thing. In a pamphlet devoted to explaining the reform, Gautier attacked the "Cambodian attitude to the world" as "out of date" (*démodée*) and compared the Cambodian language to a "badly tailored suit."[33] The addition of a "rational" French vocabulary to romanized Khmer, Gautier thought, would somehow improve Cambodian thought processes. Citing the example of romanization in Turkey, while remaining diplomatically silent about the romanization of Vietnamese, Gautier seems to have believed that the virtues of the reform were as self-evident as the primitiveness of the "Cambodian mind."

Many Cambodians, however, and especially the *sangha*, saw the reform as an attack on traditional learning and on the high status enjoyed by traditional educators in Cambodian society. Cambodians in civil life were less affronted by the reform, although Sihanouk has claimed that he was on the point of abdicating over the issue. Despite these objections, the reform was pushed vigorously by the French in 1944–1945, especially in government publications and in schools; the romanization decree did not apply to religious texts. Nonetheless, when the French were pushed aside by the Japanese, one of the first actions of the newly independent Cambodian government was to rescind romanization; since then, no attempt has been made by any Cambodian government to romanize the language.[34] Once again, as so often in Cambodian history, what the French saw as a self-evident improvement in the status quo was seen by the Cambodians as an attack on the essential character of their civilization, defined in part as what had been passed down from Angkorean times. Indeed, the decree abrogating the reform mentioned that for Cambodia to adopt the roman alphabet would mean the society would become "a

society without history, without value, without mores, and without traditions."[35]

On March 9, 1945, romanization became, literally, a dead letter when
the Japanese throughout Indochina disarmed French forces and removed
French officials from their posts. The move was intended to forestall
French armed resistance; it also fitted into Japanese plans to equip local
forces throughout Southeast Asia to resist Allied landings expected later
in the year. On March 13, in response to a formal Japanese request, King
Sihanouk declared that Cambodia was independent and changed its
name in French from "Cambodge" to "Kampuchea," the Khmer pronun-
ciation of the word.[36] Sihanouk's decree invalidated Franco-Cambodian
agreements, declared Cambodia's independence, and pledged Cambodia's cooperation with the Japanese.

Two weeks after this declaration, Vietnamese residents of the city ri-
oted against the French, on the basis of a rumor that the French intended
to kill—or at least imprison—all Vietnamese residents in France. Dis-
turbed by the violence of these demonstrations, the Japanese intervened
on the side of the French, whom they herded into protective custody for
the remainder of the war. In early April, speaking to the newly reinforced
Cambodian militia, Sihanouk condemned French forces, which had been
unwilling to help Japan defend Cambodia against an unspecified
"enemy"; he urged Cambodians to "awaken" also. It is likely that the
speech reflected the views of a Japanese political adviser, Lieutenant
Tadakame, assigned to the palace at about this time.[37]

Other steps toward independence taken in this period included rein-
stituting the Buddhist lunar calendar at the expense of the Gregorian one
and using Khmer instead of French to identify government ministries.
"Independence," of course, was a relative thing; the Japanese remained
in Cambodia in force. At the same time, the summer of 1945—like the
months of March 1970 and April 1975 in certain ways—allowed a clique
of Cambodian intellectuals to interpose themselves between the monarchy and the colonial or neocolonial power.

The period March–October 1945 represented the first time that Cambodian patriotic ideas could receive an open airing, as well as the first time
Cambodians were encouraged to form politically oriented groups. On
July 20, Sihanouk presided over a rally commemorating the monks'
demonstration of 1942; he was joined on this occasion by Pach Chhoeun,
just released from jail, and Son Ngoc Thanh, who had returned to Cambodia from Tokyo in April.[38] A speaker at the rally—not the king—re-
galed the crowd with a litany of Cambodian patriotism, citing antimonarchic rebellions in the 1860s, the 1884–1886 revolt, the 1916 Affair,
the Bardez incident, and the 1942 monks' demonstration. The speaker
failed to mention that on only one of these occasions—in 1884–1886—had

the Cambodian monarch chosen the "right side," but the message was not lost upon Sihanouk, and these examples of nationalism—suppressed for the rest of his reign—in the late 1940s and 1950s passed into the folklore of the Cambodian Communists and the antimonarchic wing of the Democratic party.

Another strand of postwar Cambodian nationalism consisted of officially sponsored antipathy to the Vietnamese, and clashes apparently took place, in this stirring, disorderly summer, between Khmer and Vietnamese inhabitants of southern Vietnam. At the same time, few steps were taken by Sihanouk, other than that of forming a paper alliance with the Vietnamese regime in Saigon, to formulate a joint strategy to resist the French when they returned. Sihanouk's mind at this time is difficult to read. It is likely, however, that the obscure antiroyalist coup of August 9–10, 1945, sponsored by some hotheaded members of Cambodian youth groups, deepened the king's hostility toward such figures as Pach Chhoeun and Son Ngoc Thanh.

Of seven participants later arrested by the French, five soon became active in the anti-French guerrilla movement, and three of them joined the forerunner of the Cambodian Communist party. At the end of August, after the Japanese surrender, Sihanouk's chronicle reports that a nationalist demonstration attracted thirty thousand people, including armed members of the militia and members of various youth groups. Four days later, a referendum engineered by Son Ngoc Thanh allegedly drew 541,470 votes in favor of independence, with only two opposed. There is no evidence that a full-scale referendum ever took place, although a proposal for one apparently circulated as a memorandum to officials for their approval. The figures represent an attempt by Son Ngoc Thanh to bolster his bargaining position vis-à-vis the French, who had begun to filter back into southern Indochina, under British auspices at first. Throughout September, Thanh urged his colleagues to join him in an alliance with the Vietnamese to resist the French. Many of these men disagreed with Thanh and sought to gain Cambodia's independence separate from Vietnam's. Some even preferred the return of the French to Thanh's continuing in power. For these reasons, when French officials arrested Thanh on October 12, 1945, in Phnom Penh, no one objected. Thanh himself seems to have been surprised; that very morning, he had presided, as the prime minister of Kampuchea, at the reopening of the Lycée Sisowath. He had lunch in the Saigon Central Prison.[39]

With Thanh removed from the scene (he was to spend most of the next six years in comparatively comfortable exile in Poitiers), King Sihanouk opened negotiations with the French, who appeared to many to have been ready to reimpose their control, as in 1940–1941. The modus vivendi signed by French and Cambodian delegates in early 1946, however, was a vaguely promising document, diluting French control and offering Cambodia membership in two nonexistent confederations. One of these, the Indochinese Federation, seems to have been little more than "Indochina" with somewhat increased indigenous participation at the top. The other, the French Union, was an even vaguer brotherhood of peoples who had been colonized by France, based on the shared experience of French civilization. The agreement promised Cambodia a constitution and the right to form political parties, but French control remained in such fields as finance, defense, and foreign affairs. In other words, the French of early 1946 had replaced the Japanese of the summer of 1945. They had not, however, reconstituted the previous status quo.

CHAPTER 10

Gaining Independence

It is easy with hindsight to argue that French rule in Indochina effectively came to an end in the summer of 1945. This did not appear to be the case, however, to the new breed of French officials sent out by General de Gaulle's government to replace the people who had looked after the region up to 1945. De Gaulle, in fact, had made the recovery of the French empire, and Indochina in particular, an important goal of his government in exile.

In Cambodia, the French were forced in October 1945 to make conciliatory gestures to the members of the indigenous elite whom they needed to run the kingdom's day-to-day affairs. These were the people whose "awakening" the French had celebrated in the 1930s. They had become patriots in the meantime and, from the French point of view, intellectually belligerent. Many of them interpreted the summer of 1945 less as a humiliation of the French that had to be avenged than as a victory for the Cambodians themselves. Cambodia, they argued, needed to *regain* its independence. A leading convert to the cause, although he was quieter than most, was King Sihanouk.

Once the modus vivendi had been signed in early 1946, the French began to tidy up their colony; for example, in Phnom Penh they restored the street names honoring French colonial heroes and French events that had been changed to Cambodian ones in 1945.[1] Another step was to abolish the newly instituted national holidays that honored Sihanouk's declaration of independence in 1945 and the monks' demonstration of 1942. A third was to place Son Ngoc Thanh on trial for treason, charging him with collaboration with the Japanese (against whom, incidentally, the French only belatedly declared war).

THE DEVELOPMENT OF POLITICAL PARTIES

In this atmosphere of business as usual, the electoral act that came into effect in the summer of 1946 opened up deep and unexpected fissures in the Cambodian elite. For the first time in their history, Cambodians were allowed to form political parties, and three sprang rapidly to life. As V. M. Reddi has pointed out, all of these "were led by princes, all of them shared the fear of neighboring countries, and all professed loyalty to the monarchy."[2] The first and third of these characteristics should come as no surprise, but the phrase "fear of neighboring countries" may need an explanation.

In 1946–1947, Thailand was still governed by the relatively radical civilian regime that had been financing anti-Japanese, and subsequently anti-French, guerrillas along the Cambodian frontier since the fall of the Phibul government in the summer of 1944. In 1945, these groups formed into the Khmer Issarak (Free Khmer), and a government in exile was hastily assembled in Bangkok. Throughout this period, moreover, the Thai retained control of the *sruk* that they had taken over in 1941. These regions offered sanctuary to four of the twelve persons implicated in the August 1945 coup, as well as to others, such as Bunchhan Muul, who had participated in the monks' demonstration and were now unhappy with the return of the French. The new political parties in Phnom Penh were fearful of Thai intrusions into Cambodian politics. They were probably even more frightened, however, by developments inside Vietnam, where Communist guerrillas in the south were threatening French rule and a Communist government in the north enjoyed de facto independence.[3]

There were, all the same, significant differences between the two leading parties, the Democratic party (Krom Pracheathipodei), led by Prince Sisowath Yuthevong, and the so-called Liberal party (Kanaq Sereipheap; literally, "Freedom Group"), led by Prince Norodom Norindeth. The difference between these princes encapsulated the differences between two wings of Cambodian opinion. Prince Yuthevong (1912–1947) had just returned from higher education in France, his wife was French, and he wanted Cambodia to practice the kind of democracy he had admired there. His party's program called for negotiating Cambodia's independence as quickly as possible. Prince Norindeth, on the other hand, was a conservative. As one of Cambodia's largest landowners, he believed that Cambodian politics should involve educating the people—rather slowly—and maintaining a dependent relationship with France. This was a view shared, understandably enough, by many members of the royal family. The Liberals were clandestinely funded by the French, who were fearful of the Democrats' popularity. The third party, the Progressive Democrats, led by Prince Norodom Montana, was insignificant and quickly faded from the scene, but it was certainly as conservative as the Liberal party, and it may have enjoyed a measure of support from the king and his advisers.[4]

The Democratic party attracted people who had been drawn in the early 1940s to *Nagara Vatta* and the ideas of Pach Chhoeun and Son Ngoc Thanh. Its strength came in large part from the Mahanikay sect of the *sangha*, from younger members of the bureaucracy, from supporters of the Issarak movement, and from Cambodia's "intellectual" class. Some elements within the party favored violent action, an alliance with Issarak guerrillas, and perhaps, at this early stage, with the Communist Viet Minh as well.[5]

The Liberal party, on the other hand, was dedicated to the maintenance of the status quo, and its policies appear to have been less articulate. The party drew its strength from elderly members of the government, wealthy landowners, the Cham ethnic minority, and the Sino-Cambodian commercial elite. The party had strong provincial roots, it seems, among *chamkar* (riverbank plantation) owners near Kompong Cham. Its strength could be traced in large part to patronage networks in particular regions.

Sihanouk in his memoirs related that he was drawn to neither of these groups, and neither sought him out. Many Democrats, indeed, seem to have seen Sihanouk as a puppet of the French, and much of his conduct in the 1946–1949 period appears to bear this out. At the very least, Sihanouk seems to have felt that the only way to regain his country's independence was to seek it peacefully, by negotiating with the French in a friendly, diplomatic way. The king's distrust of the Democrats probably sprang from his generalized suspicion of ideology, his traumatic experiences in the summer of 1945, and, perhaps, the feeling that he was being disrespectfully upstaged.

In September 1946, soon after the parties had been formed, elections for the Consultative Assembly were held to form a group to advise the king about a constitution for the country. More than 60 percent of the newly enfranchised voters went to the polls (a far higher percentage than did so in elections in Thailand). The Democrats won fifty of the sixty-seven seats; the Liberals, fourteen; and independent candidates, three.

These results revealed the popularity of the Democratic party among Cambodian authority figures who were in a position to "deliver the vote." In this election, as in others over the next twenty years or so, many peasants voted as they were told to vote by people whom they habitually obeyed.[6] As in the 1916 Affair, moreover, Cambodians—in this case, the Democrats—showed a disconcerting ability to organize their followers. In the case of the Democrats, these patrons would be local officials, teachers, and members of the *sangha*; those who voted for Liberal candidates were often, in fact, endorsing their traditional economic patrons. At the same time, the sub rosa connections between some Democrats and the Issarak, and the connections that others made between the party and Cambodian patriots, such as Hem Chieu, probably appealed to many voters more strongly than the Liberals' "program" of supporting the landowning elite. Indeed, the effects in the countryside of the disappearance of French control between March and October 1945 have never been examined. It would seem likely that bandit gangs, the principal target of the French-controlled Cambodian police in the colonial era, grew in number and importance. Many of these by early 1946 were referring to themselves as "Issarak," and many peasants, especially at a distance, probably thought of the bands as patriotic.[7]

Sihanouk appears to have been distressed by the Democrats' overwhelming victory, which he interpreted as a rebuff although he had no party of his own. In his memoirs, he is scathing about the party and particularly about Prince Yuthevong, suggesting that his own unformed political ideas were preferable, even in 1946, to Yuthevong's. After more than thirty years, he was still unable to respect Yuthevong, referring to him and his followers dismissively as "demos."

Because the Democrats now assumed that they had a mandate to impose a constitution on the kingdom, rather than merely to advise the king about one, and because the constitution they drafted in 1946–1947 reduced the powers of the king, Sihanouk soon became even more estranged from the constitutional process. Indeed, the 1947 Constitution was modeled closely on the Constitution of the Fourth Republic in France. In this document, real power devolved to the National Assembly and thus to the Democrats, who held the majority of Assembly seats.

But what did "power" amount to? The Democrats, like everyone else in the kingdom, were handicapped because independence could no longer be *declared*, as it had been in the summer of 1945. It had to be *granted* by the French. Before the middle of 1949, however, the French made few concessions to anyone in Indochina. Unable to deliver independence, the Democrats began to squabble among themselves. This trend was exacerbated by the death of Prince Yuthevong from tuberculosis in July 1947, the arrest of several high-ranking Democrats on spurious charges later in the year (the so-called Black Star affair), and the assassination of Yuthevong's successor, Ieu Koeuss, in 1950.[8] Even after the so-called treaty of 1949, discussed below, French police arrested a dozen leaders of the party on charges, later dropped, that they were conspiring with Issarak forces. The Democrats could do nothing about it; Cambodia's "independence," as many of them had maintained since 1946, was a façade.

The Issarak armed struggle against the French, which had caused serious disruptions to the Cambodian economy in 1946–1947, slowed down after Battambang and Siem Reap were returned to Cambodian control in 1947, and a regime unsympathetic to Issarak aspirations soon assumed power in Bangkok. In 1949, moreover, several thousand Issarak, particularly those opposed to the Viet Minh, took advantage of an amnesty offered them by Prime Minister Yem Sambaur. As non-communist resistance to the French decreased, moreover, the Democrats were in less of a position to reply to spurious French charges that they supported the Viet Minh.

Another factor that handicapped the Democrats was that the people who held economic power in the kingdom—the French, members of the royal family, Chinese, and Sino-Cambodians—opposed the kinds of disorder that a real struggle for independence would have entailed. Most of them were doing well. If they were in politics at all, they supported the Liberal party; so did the French administration. This meant that the Democrats were short of funds with which to influence officials, win elections, or finance an armed insurrection. The Democrats, forming the majority of the National Assembly (and thus theoretically enjoying political power), were in fact powerless to impose their will on the elite, the French, or their electorate—whose views, in fact, were rarely sought.

Ensconced in the National Assembly and hampered by a constitution that encouraged factional splits, the Democrats were cut off intellectually, economically, and physically from Cambodia's ordinary people. The only weapon available to them was to try to impede the orderly procedures of government by refusing to pass bills or to ratify agreements. As cabinet followed cabinet through a series of revolving doors—for unlike in the British system, no elections followed these parliamentary crises—Cambodia's government ironically came more and more to resemble the government of the Fourth Republic from which its members were so eager to liberate themselves. Moreover, governments in Paris often held power so tenuously and for such short periods that Cambodians of any political persuasion, as Sihanouk was to discover in 1953, seldom encountered coherent French policies to oppose or experienced ministers qualified to negotiate. In fact, for reasons that are not entirely clear (although financial motives were important), no French governments before 1953–1954 showed any willingness to take France out of Indochina.

By the end of 1949, all the same, the French appeared to have caved in. A treaty signed at that time granted what Sihanouk was later to call "50 percent independence."[9] The treaty allowed Cambodia some freedom of maneuver in foreign affairs as well as an autonomous military zone embracing Battambang and Siem Reap. Control over finance, defense, customs, and political resistance remained in French hands, but as Sihanouk has asserted, a process had begun that would be difficult to reverse. The Democrats opposed the treaty as inadequate, but it came into force all the same.

The French had several reasons for compromising at this point with Cambodia. The war throughout Indochina had intensified, and the Communist victory in China now provided the Viet Minh with an arsenal, a sanctuary, and an ally. The Soviet acquisition of nuclear arms in 1949 was to be followed in early 1950 by the conclusion of a thirty-year pact with the People's Republic of China. Beginning in 1948–1949, the French sought increased military aid from the United States on the grounds that they were no longer engaged in a colonial war in Indochina but were fighting a crusade against communism. To many in the United States and France, the outbreak of the Korean War in June 1950 "proved" this line of argument. U.S. aid, in any case, flowed into Indochina in ever-increasing amounts beginning in early 1950, shortly after the United States had extended recognition to the "independent" regimes of Laos, Cambodia, and non-Communist Vietnam.

THE GROWTH OF THE LEFT

The history of the next four years is crucial to an understanding of what has happened to Cambodia since. Three trends need to be discussed. The first is the waning of the Democratic party and the eclipse of the National Assembly. The second, related to this, is the flowering of comparatively right-wing political groupings and anti-Communist military forces, which often enjoyed the favor of the king. In fact, officials concerned with these groupings (e.g., Nhek Tioulong and Lon Nol) reappeared in several of Sihanouk's cabinets in the independence period. More important, perhaps, the consolidation of left-wing resistance to the French inside Cambodia, a process that began in 1950 and concluded in 1951 with the foundation of a recognizably Cambodian Communist party, also dates from this period. In a sense, these three pieces remained on the board throughout Sihanouk's rule.

The fading of the Democrats can be traced to French reluctance to negotiate with them, the king's growing hostility, and a shift by some opportunistic members of the party to a more royalist stance in order to gain preferment. Moreover, even their traditional disruptive role in the Assembly was curtailed for much of the period because Sihanouk saw to it that the Assembly was almost never in session.

Nonetheless, in 1951 he yielded to pressure to elect a new Assembly in accordance with the constitution. The Democrats, perhaps sensing a trap, said that they were unwilling to go to the polls because of increasing insecurity in the countryside. When the Liberals and several hastily formed right-wing parties (one of them led by a middle-echelon bureaucrat, Lon

Nol) threatened to contest the elections with them, the Democrats changed their minds. In the ensuing campaign, the Democrats were aided by Pach Chhouen, recently released from nearly five years of house arrest.

The results resembled those of 1947, at least on the surface, for the Democrats captured fifty-five of the seventy-eight contested seats. Ominously, from the Democrats' point of view, some 498 different candidates had presented themselves for these seats, with little hope of winning, and had siphoned off tens of thousands of votes. For this reason, as well as the persistent strength of Liberal candidates, the Democrats attracted less than half of the total vote, polling 148,000 while the Liberals attracted 82,000 voters and the various new parties attracted nearly 100,000. It was clear, as Michael Vickery has pointed out, that "any movement which could unify the right could immediately cut the ground from under the Democrats."[10]

Soon after the victory, Sihanouk asked the French to allow Son Ngoc Thanh to return from exile in France. The French concurred. In his memoirs, Sihanouk explains the action by referring to Thanh's friendship with his father, Prince Suramarit, but he may have thought, along with his French advisers, that bringing Thanh back might divide the Democrats while neutralizing Thanh himself as political threat. In any case, Thanh's return to Cambodia on October 29, 1951, was melodramatic. Thousands of people greeted him when he arrived at Phnom Penh airport, and thousands more lined the route into the city. It took the 300-car cortege almost an hour to cover the 10 kilometers (6 miles) involved. French intelligence officials estimated the crowds at more than half a million—an almost incredible indication of the organizational capacities of the Democrats and of the extent of popular support, partly for Son Ngoc Thanh himself and partly for an early solution to the problem of continuing dependence.

On the very day of Thanh's return, the French commissioner, Jean de Raymond, was murdered by his Vietnamese houseboy. The two events have never been publicly linked by scholars of the period, although the coincidence is remarkable. A clandestine Communist broadcast, two weeks later, managed to touch all the bases by asserting:

> For the French, the death of Raymond means the loss of a precious collaborator. For the puppets, it means the loss of a generous master. For the Cambodian people, Raymond's death means the end of a great enemy. For Buddhism, his death means that a devil, who can no longer harm religion, has been killed.[11]

Thanh was politically inactive for the remainder of 1951, even refusing several cabinet posts. In January and February 1952, however, he tested the water by touring the provinces with his old friend, Pach Chhoeun, recently named minister of information by the Democrats. This tour, which played down Sihanouk's importance, infuriated the king and convinced the French that Thanh was being encouraged by the Americans, who had provided public address systems for Pach Chhoeun. Soon after returning to Phnom Penh, Thanh founded a newspaper called *Khmer Krok* ("Cambodians awake"), explaining the title in his first issue: "We know that the Cambodian people, who have been anaesthetized for a long time, are now awake. . . . No obstacle can now stop this awakening from moving ahead."[12]

Soon afterward, on March 9, 1952, the seventh anniversary of the Japanese *coup de force*, Son Ngoc Thanh fled the capital with a radio transmitter and a handful of followers, the most eminent being a leftist intellectual named Ea Sichau. Within a month, Thanh had set up his headquarters along the Thai border in the northern part of Siem Reap, joining forces with an Issarak band under the leadership of Kao Tak. Between 1952 and the Geneva Conference in 1954, Thanh and his supporters were aided to an extent by Thai intelligence agencies. Within his own "zone," he experimented with a loosely regimented ideology that he labeled "national socialism," traceable in part to his admiration for the Japanese political institutions he had observed in exile during World War II.[13] It is unclear whether he believed that by going into exile in the Cambodian mountains he could remain in command of the independence movement, as he had seemed to be on his triumphal return to Phnom Penh, but his efforts to win over pro-Communist guerrillas were unsuccessful, and only a few hundred people—most of them idealistic high school students—followed him into the maquis. After independence, Thanh's importance faded, and his following decreased. In the late 1950s and 1960s, he eked out a shadowy existence working for the Thai and the Vietnamese in their efforts to destabilize Sihanouk's regime. His nationalism through 1957 or so is difficult to question, but his motives for abandoning Phnom Penh in 1952 are difficult to figure out. Perhaps he overestimated the extent of his support among the non-Communist Issarak (or, conversely, underestimated Communist support among the guerrillas). French intelligence reports assert that he still enjoyed the support of some of the older Democrats in Phnom Penh; perhaps he hoped for international support as well. After his exile, however, he was no longer a force to be reckoned with, either by Sihanouk or by the French.[14]

At this point it is appropriate to consider the growth of left-wing radicalism in Cambodia. By 1952, Communist-controlled guerrilla bands, operating in cooperation with the Viet Minh, were able to control perhaps a sixth of Cambodia's territory and to tie down several thousand French

troops. Two years later, at the time of the Geneva Conference, some estimates suggested that they controlled more than half of the kingdom.

Where had they come from? When the Indochinese Communist party
(ICP) was founded in Hong Kong in 1930, it included no Cambodian
members, and indeed only a handful of ethnic Khmer had joined the
party before the end of World War II.[15] In 1945–1947, however, Viet Minh
forces made an effort to support "liberation struggles" in Laos and Cambodia; at the same time, as we have seen, the Thai government had a policy of aiding all anti-French guerrillas in Indochina, and the Khmer Issarak, operating along the Thai frontier and in the Thai-controlled *sruk* of
Battambang and Siem Reap, included men who later formed right-wing
and left-wing factions. Left-wingers included the pseudonymous Son
Ngoc Minh (in fact a former monk, Achar Mean), Sieu Heng, and Tou
Samouth. On April 17, 1950, twenty-five years to the day before the Communist "liberation" of Phnom Penh, the First National Congress of the
Khmer Resistance was held in the southwestern part of the kingdom
under the leadership of Son Ngoc Minh. The congress, in turn, established the Unified Issarak Front, dominated by ethnic Cambodian members of the ICP. According to a subsequent history of the Cambodian
Communist party, prepared in 1973, there were only forty of these at the
time; as Ben Kiernan has pointed out, however, hundreds more had already been trained in Communist political schools set up under Vietnamese auspices as early as 1947; the most famous of these, founded in
1950, was named after the dissident monk Hem Chieu.[16]

The ICP dissolved itself in early 1951, and separate Communist parties
were soon formed in Laos, Cambodia, and Vietnam. The Khmer People's
Revolutionary party (KPRP) was founded in September 1951. Its statutes,
unsurprisingly, were drawn from those of the "newly constituted" party
in Vietnam. According to party records, the KPRP at this stage had as
many as a thousand members; French intelligence in 1952 estimated
Communist-controlled Issarak forces as numbering about five thousand.[17] This latter figure, like many from the period, is probably an underestimate, because the French appear to have been unable to infiltrate
the party and because it was in their interests, and in those of their client,
King Sihanouk, to play down estimates of Communist popularity, especially in public statements. As impatience with French control increased
among many segments of the population and as Vietnamese guerrillas
elsewhere in Indochina moved from strength to strength, these pro-
Vietnamese forces in Cambodia grew in numbers, efficiency, and cohesion. So did the KPRP. By July 1954, eight months after independence, the
party had an estimated two thousand members, nearly all of whom were
to seek refuge in Vietnam following the Geneva Accords. Another index
of the party's growth was the fact that French authorities in 1952 believed

that taxes and contributions levied by revolutionaries among the population amounted to the equivalent of half the national budget.

Although the Vietnamese cadres in these guerrilla units gradually relinquished their positions to ethnic Khmer, who were always in control of the KPRP, it is clear that these leaders in the anti-French resistance differed in several ways from their counterparts in the Democratic party and elsewhere along the political spectrum. For one thing, they saw their struggle as part of an international movement, connected with Marxist-Leninist laws of history. At another level, the liberation of Cambodia from the French did not mean, for them, the continuation of the status quo among Cambodians or the intensification of a supposedly "traditional animosity" between Cambodians and Vietnamese. Liberation from the French, in other words, was a stage in the Cambodian revolution rather than a goal. Moreover, without being puppets of the Vietnamese, these radical leaders in the early 1950s accepted Vietnam's leadership in the struggle to liberate Indochina from the French and in the formation of socialist parties throughout the region. In terms of relative power, such a policy made sense. Seen from another perspective, both the French and Sihanouk tried hard to equate anti-French resistance (as opposed to a policy of negotiated independence) with a pro-Vietnamese, pro-Communist, and therefore un-Cambodian betrayal. What was betrayed, of course, were the hierarchical social arrangements that had characterized Cambodia throughout its history. In 1952–1953, in fact, Sihanouk and his entourage frequently and absurdly labeled Son Ngoc Thanh a Communist. A decade later, he reached for the fascist label to describe his former prime minister, then allegedly in the pay of the United States.

The interplay between nationalism and internationalism inside the Cambodian Communist movement, as in many others elsewhere in the world, plagued the party throughout its history. Should "Cambodian" interests (whatever they were) come first? What was "Cambodian" socialism? And how did this, in turn, fit into the history and the alignments of the Vietnamese? By denying any socialist or internationalist component in Cambodian nationalism, one could proclaim Cambodia's *intrinsic* greatness, refer repeatedly to Angkor, and make racist slurs against the Vietnamese. This was the route that Sihanouk chose to follow in the later 1960s, and it was also followed by Lon Nol and at several points by the Pol Pot regime. It was also employed occasionally by radicals in the early 1950s. In a speech delivered in November 1951, for example, a Communist spokesman asserted that

> the Cambodian race is of noble origin. It is not afraid of death, when it is a
> question of fighting the enemy, of saving its religion, and of liberating its fa-
> therland. The entire race follows the Buddhist doctrine [sic] which places

death above slavery and religious persecution. King Yasovarman is a remarkable example.[18]

By seeking legitimacy in the Cambodian past, in antimonarchic heroes,
and in aspects of the Buddhist religion, radicals cast a wider net than the
people around King Sihanouk, who saw independence as a goal in itself,
having little effect on the structure of Cambodian society or on their own
place inside it. After all, these men saw little value in mobilizing the Cambodian people or in destabilizing the regime. For these reasons, heroes like
Siwotha, Hem Chieu, and Pou Kombo—favored by the Issaraks, by some
of the Democrats, and by Communist propaganda at this early stage—
quickly disappeared from textbooks and ideology. The fate of these heroes
under successive regimes forms an interesting leitmotif in Cambodian history. After years of neglect, they reemerged under the Khmer Republic,
alongside many former Democrats, only to vanish again under Pol Pot,
whose official ideology, while retaining a pro-Angkorean slant, also
stressed the impersonality of the regime's organization. Heroes, it was
thought, were ephemeral; the organization (*angkar*) endured. To complete
the cycle, some of the discredited heroes reemerged in 1979 under the
Heng Samrin regime, providing new names for Phnom Penh streets—
names that were altered yet again when Sihanouk became king in 1993.[19] It
was also in 1979 that a five-towered depiction of Angkor Wat on the Cambodian flag, favored by the Issarak in the 1950s, replaced the three-towered
one favored by previous regimes and reinstated in 1993.

Cambodian university students in France were another important
source of recruits for Cambodia's Communist movement. Between 1945
and 1960, several hundred of these young men and women were exposed
to an intoxicating mixture of radical politics, personal freedom, and anticolonial solidarity. Some were recruited into the French Communist
party; many more perceived a wide gap between French ideals, life in
France, and French colonial performance. Others, going further, saw
clear connections between prerevolutionary France, prerevolutionary
Russia, and twentieth-century Cambodia, ruled by a "feudal," "reactionary" elite. The suppression of the Democratic party, discussed below,
accelerated the radicalization of many young Khmers—including such
future leaders of DK as Saloth Sar (Pol Pot), Ieng Sary, Son Sen, and
Khieu Samphan.

SIHANOUK AND THE
ACHIEVEMENT OF INDEPENDENCE

Throughout the first few months of 1952, the Democrats in the National
Assembly continued as best they could to thwart Sihanouk's policies;

Son Ngoc Thanh remained a threat, although at a distance. French intelligence sources estimated that almost two-thirds of the kingdom was no longer under the day-to-day control of the Phnom Penh government. To Sihanouk and his conservative advisers, the time had come for a dramatic series of gestures to gain the country's independence forcibly from France and to maintain themselves in power.

In a scathing speech to the Assembly in early June 1952, Sihanouk declared: "All is in disorder. Hierarchy no longer exists. There is no rational employment of talent. . . . If it is right to be dissident, this means that all the best patriots will seek refuge in the forest."[20] Subsequently, with the connivance of the French, Sihanouk staged a coup against his own government. Moroccan troops secretly brought up from Saigon for the purpose surrounded the National Assembly, and the king dismissed the Democrats from office. No shots were fired. Soon afterward, Sihanouk assumed power as prime minister, appointing his own cabinet and leaving the Democratic-controlled Assembly to wither on the vine. At this point, he demanded a mandate from his people, promising to deliver complete independence within three years—i.e., before June 1955. Although no referendum was carried out at this time, Sihanouk acted as if his mandate had been granted and began what he was later to call his crusade for independence.

Although the coup had been peaceful, demonstrations against it broke out in Cambodia's lycées, where antimonarchic, pro-Democrat sentiment was strong, and radical Cambodian students in France referred to Sihanouk as a "traitor to the nation." In a vituperative manifesto issued to the king on July 6, 1952, the students called on him to abdicate, blaming him for recent French military attacks, for dissolving the Assembly, and for negotiating with the French instead of fighting them.[21] The manifesto went on to accuse Sihanouk's ancestors Sisowath and Norodom of collaborating with the French against "national heroes." The remainder of 1952, it seems, was a trying time for Sihanouk, as the French in effect decided to call his bluff.

He was aided by the Democrats' intransigence. The Assembly refused to approve his government's budget in January 1953. Declaring the nation to be in danger, Sihanouk dissolved the Assembly, promulgated martial law, and ordered the arrest of several Democratic assemblymen, who were now deprived of parliamentary immunity. As V. M. Reddi asserted, Sihanouk showed no hesitation in acting out what was obviously a well-planned scenario and justified it informally by telling a French correspondent: "I am the natural ruler of the country . . . and my authority has never been questioned."[22] He was appealing to the people over the heads of the elected officials, just as he now planned (without saying so at the time) to appeal directly to the French.

The king's newly acquired political energy and his insistence upon independence shocked many Frenchmen and members of the royal family. Some journalists came to terms with the king's awakening by labeling him "insane," because he had been "comical" and "exotic" (i.e., cooperative) for so long.

In February 1953, Sihanouk announced that he was traveling to France for his health—a tactic he was often to employ during the remaining years of his reign. In fact, as he revealed in his memoirs, he departed with meticulously prepared dossiers listing outstanding matters to be discussed and negotiated with the French. His illness was "political," but the stakes were high. When he arrived in France, he wrote immediately to the aged and constitutionally powerless French president, Vincent Auriol, warning him that "I have based my future as king and that of my dynasty on the policy of adhesion to the French Union and collaboration with France, to which I am and shall be loyal."[23] He added that if the Communists invaded Cambodia, he could not guarantee that his subjects would act to defend French interests.

Auriol's advisers apparently thought that Sihanouk's long letter, and another that arrived soon afterward, were alarmist, and Auriol waited two weeks to answer them. When he did, he said only that he had studied the letters with care and asked Sihanouk to lunch. At that point, officials in the French government concerned with Indochina respectfully told the king to return home, hinting that he might even be replaced as king.[24]

For the next month or so, Sihanouk traveled slowly homeward, pausing to give press and radio interviews in Canada, the United States, and Japan in which he publicized Cambodia's plight and the intransigence of the French. He has used this tactic of publicizing supposedly confidential discussions ever since, when it has been in his own interest to do so. In 1953, however, it was a bold course to follow, for he was gambling not only with the French and potential foreign allies but also with the opposition at home, with the Vietnamese, and with the KPRP.

He arrived back in Phnom Penh in May and dramatically offered his life in exchange for Cambodia's independence. Negotiations in Paris proceeded slowly, so in June the king went into voluntary exile, first to Thailand, where he was not welcomed, and then to the autonomous military region of Siem Reap, where he took up residence at his villa near Angkor and refused to speak with French officials in Phnom Penh. In Vietnam, the war was going badly for the French, and it had become increasingly unpopular at home. Sihanouk's increasing resistance to the French and the prospect of increased fighting in Cambodia caused them to consider his demands more seriously than they had planned.

In October 1953, the French caved in and granted the king authority over Cambodia's armed forces and judiciary and foreign affairs. Their economic hold on the kingdom, however—particularly in the import-export sphere and in the highly profitable rubber plantations—remained intact. Despite these remnants of colonial rule, Sihanouk is correct, on balance, in interpreting the French collapse at this point as a personal victory. Using the same communications network that, in 1916 and again in 1951, had frightened French authorities, Sihanouk now ordered officials in the *sruk* between Siem Reap and Phnom Penh to organize demonstrations in his favor. As he drove back to his capital, on the second anniversary of Son Ngoc Thanh's return from exile, hundreds of thousands of people lined the road, uncertain perhaps what independence would mean but at this stage happy enough to applaud their king and what they hoped would be an end to fighting. Soon afterward, he was officially proclaimed a national hero.[25]

In the short term, France's departure from the scene had three effects. In the first place, Cambodia's independence and the relatively low level of fighting in the kingdom between November 1953 and the middle of 1954 strengthened the hand of Sihanouk's delegation to the Geneva Conference in the summer of 1954. The delegation, led by Nhek Tioulong, took a stubborn view of indigenous Communists, who were allowed no part in the deliberations and were also frozen out by Vietnamese Communist delegates eager to earn concessions for Vietnam and, to a lesser degree, for pro-Vietnamese Pathet Lao forces in Laos.[26] Surprisingly, perhaps, many Cambodian radicals continued to accept leadership from Vietnam throughout the 1950s and 1960s. For over a thousand of them, 1954 marked the beginning of a "Long March" that would take them to exile in Hanoi, not to return to Cambodia until the early 1970s when most of them were killed by U.S. bombing, Lon Nol's army, or internal Communist purges at the instigation of Pol Pot, by then the leader of the Cambodian Communist party. A few hardy survivors of this group were given cabinet positions in the post-1979 government of Cambodia, established by the Vietnamese in the wake of their invasion.[27]

Another consequence of Sihanouk's so-called crusade was that the Democratic party and Son Ngoc Thanh, who had failed to deliver independence, lost much of their appeal. At the same time, figures further to the right who had remained loyal to the king, such as Lt. Col. Lon Nol, Nhek Tioulong, and Penn Nouth, now gained in stature and were favored for government posts.

Perhaps the most lasting consequence of independence in 1953 was that Sihanouk felt he had obtained a mandate to govern Cambodia as he saw fit. The subsequent decimation of the KPRP and the eclipse of the Democrats by 1955 gave him the impression (encouraged by many foreign visitors and by his entourage) that his crusade had been not only successful but also astute and that the suffusion of Cambodia the state by

Sihanouk the man was a salutary political development. A consequence of this, especially visible after 1960 or so, was that Sihanouk felt under no obligation to be at peace with Thailand and South Vietnam, or to grant much freedom of action to people he disliked. Just as he had "gone it alone" in 1953 and won, so Cambodia could be "independent" by courting the friendship of faraway powers such as China, France, and Yugoslavia.

While this was going on, the forces that had been unleashed in the summer of 1945 fell into disrepute. Sihanouk and his advisers, never partial to social change, correctly saw that these forces endangered the stability of the country. And, as we have seen, the "inherent" stability of Cambodia, often the subject of absurd romanticism among colonial writers, has rested throughout nearly all of Cambodian history on the acceptance of the status quo as defined by those in power.

What, then, did "independence" mean? The removal of the French probably meant little to most Cambodians, who continued to pay taxes to finance an unresponsive government in Phnom Penh (or Udong or Angkor) whose "royal work," almost by definition, removed it from contact with the people and made officials, for the most part, self-centered, concerned with status, and ill at ease with anyone else's aspirations. It was certainly just, in other words, to remove the Cambodian elite and the comparatively small intellectual class from French control. The removal left these people free not to govern themselves so much as to govern others without seeking their consent. Because the people in the countryside had never been asked to play a part in any government, they saw few short-term rewards in resisting those in power, who were now at least Cambodians rather than French or Vietnamese.[28] Although Cambodia celebrated its independence at the end of 1953 and gained military autonomy after the Geneva Conference in 1954, when Viet Minh troops and their Cambodian sympathizers took refuge in North Vietnam, it can be argued that the elections of 1955, and the emergence of Sihanouk as Cambodia's major political actor, marked a sharper turning point in Cambodia's political history than either of those events.

The elections had been stipulated by the Geneva Conference as part of a healing process for the non-Communist segments of Indochina. The Democrats were weakened by factional quarrels and by nearly three years away from power, but they were still the best organized political party, and their leaders looked forward to winning the elections. Many younger Democrats opposed the apparently pro-U.S. policies Sihanouk had been following since Geneva and argued that Cambodia should be neutral in its alignments. They shared this line with a pro-Communist party that had just taken shape in Cambodia, known as the Krom Pracheachon, or People's Group. Cambodia's hard-core Communist party, founded in 1951, remained concealed from view. Younger Democrats moved their own party to the left in late 1954, pushing such stalwarts as Sim Var and Son Sann aside and replacing them with antimonarchic neutralists like Keng Vannsak and Svay So and with even more radical figures, including Tiounn Mumm, then a member of the French Communist party. Mumm cooperated with Saloth Sar, who had spent some months in the Vietnamese maquis in 1953–1954, to coordinate the Democrats' tactics with those of the Pracheachon. Many observers in Cambodia at the beginning of 1955 expected the two parties to win a majority of seats in the Assembly.

The revival of the Democrats and the popularity of the Pracheachon distressed conservative politicians in Phnom Penh and enraged the king, who, as the self-proclaimed "father of Cambodian independence," had hoped to call the country's political shots. Outside of the capital and intellectual circles his own popularity remained high. A referendum in February 1955 had approved his crusade for independence by over 98 percent—people having been asked to choose between a white ballot with his picture on it and a black one inscribed with the Cambodian word for "no." The vote was enhanced by the fact that discarding the king's picture was seen as disrespectful and grounds for arrest. Then and later, Sihanouk was adept at reinforcing his genuine popularity with bullying tactics so as to gain almost 100 percent approval.

Gambling that he was now more popular than the political parties, Sihanouk abdicated the throne in early March without warning and entered political life as a private citizen, after designating his father, Prince Suramarit, as the new king. Soon afterward, Sihanouk founded a national political movement, the Sangkum Reastr Niyum, usually translated as People's Socialist Community. To be a member of the movement, one had to abjure membership in any other political group, as Sihanouk's intention was to smash the existing political parties. Several of these folded in the course of 1955, and their leaders rallied to the Sangkum. This left the Liberals, the Democrats, and the Pracheachon to contest the elections. The leader of the Liberals, Prince Norodom Norindeth, was offered a diplomatic post in Paris, and he quickly accepted it, leaving his party in disarray. Shortly after founding the Sangkum, Prince Sihanouk, as he was now called, went to Bandung in Indonesia to attend a conference of African and Asian political leaders. Before he left, he declared that he had abdicated so as to defeat the "politicians, the rich, and the educated, who are accustomed to using . . . their knowledge to deceive others and to place innumerable obstacles in the path over which I must lead the people."[29] In his absence, civil servants were bullied into joining the Sangkum in large numbers, which deprived the Democrats of several hundred registered members.

Sihanouk's tactics took the Democrats and Pracheachon by surprise, and so did his decision at Bandung to co-opt their neutralist foreign policy while holding onto U.S. military and economic aid. At the conference, Sihanouk was lionized by many anti-Western heads of state, including Indonesia's Sukarno and China's Zhou Enlai, and when he returned to Cambodia, he hastened to garnish his new importance with electoral approval.

The 1955 elections, the last before the 1990s to be freely contested by a range of political parties, also marked the first attempt of many to mobilize the security apparatus of the state in favor of one particular group. Between May and September 1955, several opposition newspapers were shut down, and their editors were imprisoned without trial. Democrat and Pracheachon candidates were harassed, and some campaign workers were killed in a rough-and-tumble campaign waged against vaguely defined "special interests" on behalf of Cambodia's so-called little people. Voters were intimidated on polling day as well, and several ballot boxes, thought to contain Democrat ballots, conveniently disappeared. When the votes were counted, Sangkum candidates had won all the seats in the Assembly and over three-quarters of the vote. The understaffed International Control Commission, set up by the Geneva Conference to oversee the elections, was unable or unwilling to sort out campaign offenses, perhaps because the generally pro-Western Indian and Canadian representatives outvoted the pro-Communist Poles on the commission.[30]

A new kind of politics had overtaken and replaced the less robust constitutional variety that had endured by fits and starts since 1947. Politics in Cambodia after 1955 were characterized for many years by Sihanouk's monopoly of political power and the emergence of Cambodia onto the international stage. Sihanouk's style was widely popular, and the kingdom prospered. As in the past, however, this prosperity was to a large extent dependent on the behavior of Cambodia's neighbors and on the policies of larger, more distant powers. Cambodia was neutral and at peace, in other words, for as long as its neutrality served the interests of other states. Sihanouk's formidable political skills may have postponed the apocalypse that overtook his country in the 1970s, but they did not prevent it. In terms of what happened then and later, many Cambodians in the 1990s saw his years in power as constituting a golden age. Others have come to perceive his ruling style as totalitarian and absurd, closing off any possibility of pluralism, political maturity, sound planning, or rational debate. By treating Cambodia as a personal fief, his subjects as children, and his opponents as traitors, Sihanouk did much to set the agenda, unwittingly, for the lackadaisical chaos of the Khmer Republic, the horrors of Democratic Kampuchea, and the single-party politics of the postrevolutionary era.

CHAPTER 11

From Independence to Civil War

For fifteen years, Prince Sihanouk and the Sangkum Reastr Niyum over-shadowed Cambodian life. Because Sihanouk was removed from office by his own National Assembly in 1970, it is convenient, but misleading, to interpret this period in terms of his "decline," a process that few observers noted at the time. Nonetheless, by 1966, Sihanouk had reached a turning point in his political career, and his grip on the political process had begun to weaken, along with his self-confidence. These changes can be linked to the intensification of the Vietnam War as well as to indigenous political factors. In any case, the Assembly elected in 1966, although allegedly made up of loyal Sangkum members, was the first since 1951 whose members the prince had not handpicked himself. In 1970, this Assembly voted Sihanouk out of office.

THE ASSEMBLY ELECTIONS

Sihanouk's principal opponents in 1955, the Democrats, were driven from politics before the 1958 elections took place. Sihanouk's vindictiveness toward this group is curious because by 1956, the party had virtually ceased to exist and nearly all its members had joined the Sangkum. Nonetheless, in September 1957, claiming that the Democrats were endangering his policies, Sihanouk summoned five leaders of the party to a debate on the grounds of the royal palace in Phnom Penh. Large crowds were assembled nearby, and the proceedings were broadcast over loudspeakers. Intimidated by the crowds, the Democrats were unable to voice any clear opinions, and after three hours of bullying by Sihanouk and his associates, they were allowed to leave. On their way out of the palace enclosure they were beaten by soldiers and police, and one of them was hospitalized. Over the next few days, thirty or forty people suspected of Democrat leanings were beaten in Phnom Penh, and before going overseas for a vacation, Sihanouk secretly decorated some of the soldiers involved in the palace beatings.[1] Soon afterward, the Democratic party dissolved itself and disappeared from the political scene.

In 1958, therefore, the only opposition to the Sangkum was the Pracheachon, which had gathered over twenty thousand votes in 1955. In a foolhardy gesture, the group nominated a handful of candidates, but all but one withdrew before election day in the face of police repression. The remaining candidate, Keo Meas, earned 350 votes out of several thousand cast in his electoral district. After the election he went underground to avoid arrest, and his candidacy marked the end of pluralistic electoral politics in Cambodia until the 1990s aside from a brief interlude under Lon Nol.

Over the next two years, Sihanouk's government survived a series of plots against it that were hatched in Saigon and Bangkok with the knowledge of the United States.[2] The plots made the prince more suspicious than ever of his neighbors and their U.S. patrons, whose cool behavior toward him contrasted sharply with the courtesy he was shown in France, Indonesia, and the Communist bloc. In the Cold War atmosphere of the time, Sihanouk was labeled "pro-Communist" by the United States. For his part, the plots enabled Sihanouk to label his opponents un-Cambodian, a tactic followed by the next two governments in Phnom Penh.

By the early 1960s, Sihanouk had forged a tactical alliance with elements of the Cambodian left as well as with Communist China. These alignments had four short-term effects. The first was a drift to the left of Cambodia's print media, which were mostly overseen by the prince himself. Related to this was a tolerance on the part of the government toward left-wing teachers in Cambodia's schools. Many of these men and women, in turn, were recruited into Cambodia's clandestine Communist movement and drew some of their students along with them. The second effect was the election to the Assembly in 1962 of several leftists educated in France, such as Khieu Samphan, Hou Yuon, and Hu Nim. Without admitting their Communist leanings, these men joined the Sangkum and were rewarded by the prince, as their colleagues in the Pracheachon were not.

A third effect was Sihanouk's decision in 1963 to cut off U.S. economic and military assistance. In a related move, he nationalized Cambodia's banks and the country's export-import trade. The circumstances surrounding these decisions, which followed the assassination of Ngo Dinh Diem in Vietnam, are still unclear. It is possible that Sihanouk expected France and China to pick up where the Americans left off, but those two powers, although remaining friendly to Cambodia, were unwilling to make that kind of financial commitment. Nationalization, like many Cambodian policies, seems to have been decided on by Sihanouk on the spur of the moment, with the intention of making Cambodia a genuinely socialist state. The fourth effect of Sihanouk's tolerance of the left was that nearly all of Cambodia's radicals were able to survive the 1950s and early 1960s without being shot or going to jail. Right-wing opponents of the prince, whom he perceived as working for foreign powers, were less fortunate.

In 1960, Sihanouk's father, King Suramarit, died, and after a series of maneuvers, Sihanouk had himself named Cambodia's chief of state, with his mother continuing to serve as a monarch for ceremonial purposes. This decision severely weakened the monarchy by which Cambodia had been governed for over a thousand years.

For the 1962 Assembly, Sihanouk sought out candidates who were younger and better educated than those they replaced. Naturally distrustful of intellectuals, the prince was convinced that he could manipulate, cajole, and outmaneuver them once they were in the Assembly or elsewhere in the government, as he viewed the Assembly as a personal possession and a rubber stamp. The 1962 elections, which occurred soon after war broke out in South Vietnam between Vietnamese loyal to the pro-U.S. government of Ngo Dinh Diem and others who sought to unify the country under the Communist leadership in Hanoi, marked a high point of Sihanouk's years in power.

As so often in Cambodia's history, the country soon became a hostage to Vietnamese events. Sihanouk's efforts to play both sides against each other, and to keep Cambodia out of the war, are reminiscent of King Chan's maneuvers in the nineteenth century. Between 1961 and 1970, Sihanouk's policies saved thousands of Cambodian lives. When he was overthrown, however, he broadcast an appeal to his "brothers and sisters" asking them to wage a civil war. Whether the three hundred thousand deaths that occurred after that—inflicted by North and South Vietnamese, U.S., and contending Cambodian forces—could have been avoided had he stepped aside is impossible to say.

The Vietnam War destabilized the Cambodian economy and drove Sihanouk from office. Had it never occurred, he would probably not have been overthrown, and Cambodia's Communists would not have come to power. The Cold War tensions that were being played out in Vietnam, at such enormous human cost, had little relevance in Cambodia, but this did not stop Cambodia from becoming engulfed in the conflict. In a sense, Cambodian history between 1965 and 1993, if not beyond, was orchestrated from the east, and from such faraway cities as Hanoi, Washington, and Beijing.

By 1965, over two hundred thousand U.S. troops had swarmed into South Vietnam to prop up the Saigon government and to prevent a Communist victory. Within a year, the United States was exploding hundreds of thousands of tons of ordnance in Vietnam and absorbing and inflicting tens of thousands of casualties. In the meantime, North Vietnamese troops had moved into position in the south to reinforce locally recruited guerrillas. As the war intensified, it threatened to spill over into Cambodia, as it had already spilled over into Laos.

Throughout 1965, Sihanouk repeatedly proclaimed Cambodia's neutrality and sought guarantees from outside powers for his country's frontiers. He broke off diplomatic relations with the United States and sought to convene an international conference that would lead to the neutralization of Southeast Asia and the withdrawal of U.S. troops. By 1966, he had also allied himself secretly with the North Vietnamese, a decision, probably impossible to avoid, that was a major reason for his deposition four years later. Sihanouk felt certain that the Vietnamese Communists would win the war. He wanted to remain in power and to keep Cambodia independent; in the meantime, he wanted to keep Cambodians from being killed. An alliance with the North Vietnamese, so long as it was kept secret, seemed a good way of accomplishing these objectives.

Under the terms of the alliance, the North Vietnamese were allowed to station troops in Cambodian territory and to receive arms and supplies funneled to them from North Vietnam and China via the Cambodian port of Sihanoukville. In exchange, they recognized Cambodia's frontiers, promised to leave Cambodian civilians alone, and avoided contact with the Cambodian army. South Vietnamese and U.S. officials soon knew about the presence of North Vietnamese troops in Cambodia, and the movements of weapons and supplies, without knowing the details of the agreement Sihanouk had reached. Sihanouk denied for several years that any Vietnamese troops were in Cambodia, which angered the United States and South Vietnam but enhanced the image of injured innocence that the prince projected to the outside world.

In September 1966, Sihanouk's political idol, Charles de Gaulle, then president of France and a supporter of neutralization, agreed to make a three-day visit to Cambodia, shortly before Assembly elections were to take place. The prince had little time or energy to stage-manage both occasions, and he felt sure that de Gaulle's visit was the more important of the two. Positions in the Assembly, however, were coveted by many middle-class Cambodians, partly because holding office offered them informal opportunities for making money, and while making plans for de Gaulle's visit, Sihanouk was besieged with petitions for endorsement from hundreds of prospective candidates. Reluctant to antagonize some of his supporters, he threw the balloting open, and over 425 Sangkum candidates competed with each other for 82 Assembly seats.

President de Gaulle's visit came to a climax with a floodlit performance by the Cambodian royal ballet on the terraces of Angkor Wat. The

French president made a warm speech in which he praised his host and urged the neutralization of Southeast Asia. Sihanouk had worked hard to make the visit a success—it cost the equivalent of several million dollars, and the foreign media coverage was favorable and extensive—and it may have been the high-water mark of Sihanouk's years in power. When the general flew off, however, Sihanouk was faced with a national election in which, for the first time since 1951, the candidates owed him nothing.

In the elections, candidates favoring local interests triumphed over those whose main credentials were based on their loyalty to Sihanouk. Some writers (including Sihanouk at the time) have called the results a triumph for reactionary forces, and certainly the elections were the first since 1951 in which candidates had to relate to the voters. To gain support, candidates made unrealistic promises, like their counterparts in other countries, and many of them spent large sums of money. Many were ideologically conservative, but so were most Cambodians, particularly in rural areas. Interestingly, however, the three leftist candidates who had paid close attention to their constituents over the years were reelected in 1966 with increased majorities.

The new prime minister, General Lon Nol, the commander of Cambodia's army, was known for his loyalty to the prince, his aloofness, and the army's loyalty to him. He also attracted the support of middle-aged conservatives, particularly among the Sino-Cambodian commercial elite. These men thought Sihanouk's style embarrassing and his economic policies disastrous. Many of them, like most of the army officer corps, regretted Cambodia's rupture with the United States and objected to the fact that the nationalization of imports and exports had moved this profitable sector of the economy into the hands of government officials. As many members of the new Assembly shared these feelings of impatience, the stage was set for a confrontation between Sihanouk on the one hand and the Assembly and the commercial elite on the other.

SIHANOUK'S POLICIES

In the 1960s, an American correspondent wrote that "Cambodia Is Sihanouk," and this view was echoed by a French writer, who entitled a chapter of a book about Cambodia "He Is the State," echoing the adage "I am the state" attributed to the seventeenth-century French monarch, Louis XIV.[3] Both assertions were true up to a point. The prince's insistence that he was the embodiment of Cambodia, and that Cambodians were his "children," made it difficult for visitors, journalists, or diplomats to disentangle national interests, problems, and priorities from those that Sihanouk proclaimed on a daily basis.

Given that situation, and knowing what happened afterward, it is difficult to reconstruct Cambodian politics and society during the Sihanouk era without considering Sihanouk or lowering the volume of his voice. The prince's speeches, the journals he controlled, and the approving words of foreign writers often drown out other documents and speakers. So did his censorship at the time. On the other hand, looking at the 1960s largely in terms of the prince's "decline" may encourage one to exaggerate the importance of his opposition (particularly among the Communists), to minimize his real accomplishments, and to blame the prince for the chaos that beset his country after he was overthrown.

To be fair to him, and to the choices he faced in the 1960s, we should note that his foreign policies now seem more defensible than his domestic ones. The key elements of these policies were his friendship with China, his search for as many foreign patrons as possible, and his secret alliance with North Vietnam. A corollary of these policies was his distrust of the United States, Thailand, and South Vietnam.

A formal alliance with North Vietnam was probably impossible to avoid. Had he forbidden the Vietnamese Communist forces to move across Cambodia, they would have done so anyway and would have decimated any Cambodian forces sent against them. They did just that in 1970–1971, when the post-Sihanouk government tried to drive them out of the country. Had the prince allied himself with South Vietnam, the Vietnamese civil war would have spilled over into Cambodia, as it did in 1970 when thousands of Cambodians died or were wounded. Nor would an alliance with Thailand have protected his country against the North Vietnamese. Neither Thailand nor South Vietnam was prepared to make the promises to Cambodia that Sihanouk extracted from Hanoi. His friendship with China was an attempt to find a counterweight to Thailand and South Vietnam, as well as a power capable of restraining the North Vietnamese in Cambodia. It was also a response to what Sihanouk interpreted as the genuine friendship and support offered him by the Chinese premier, Zhou Enlai.

Sihanouk's efforts to keep Cambodia independent and to avoid the Vietnam War were probably unrealistic, and his expectations of friendship from Communist powers were naive. But what choices did he have? In the late 1950s, the United States had made it clear that its own policies, as far as Cambodia was concerned, would always favor Thailand and South Vietnam, a favoritism that included a tolerant attitude toward the anti-Cambodian policies of the two regimes. Sihanouk believed he was surrounded by hostile powers and that the United States was unprepared to take him seriously. He was also motivated by a genuine patriotism and saw no future for his country if it were swept into the Vietnam War.[4]

The two most consistent aspects of Sihanouk's domestic policy were his intolerance of dissent and his tendency to identify his opponents with foreign powers. To be a Cambodian, in his view, meant being pro-Sihanouk, just as Sihanouk himself, the father of the Cambodian family, was pro-Cambodian. There was no real tradition of pluralist politics in the country, and throughout the Sihanouk era, dissent was viewed as a mixture of treason and *lèse majesté*.

Sihanouk was fond of keeping his opponents off-balance by seeming to favor first one and then another. Campaigns launched against the "right" were followed by others targeting the "left," and rivals' suggestions were occasionally appropriated as his own—for example, the choice of a neutralist foreign policy has already been mentioned. Placing himself in the middle of the Cambodian political spectrum—envisaged as a tricolor, with radical "red Khmer" on one side and conservative "blue Khmer" on the other—Sihanouk, the "white Khmer," refused to make formal alliances with any group. Technically neutral, he was totally in charge.

OPPOSITION TO SIHANOUK

Between 1955 and the late 1960s, opposition to Sihanouk's rule was poorly organized and ineffective. Except among a handful of radicals, segments of the elite, and the monastic order, the prince was almost as popular as he claimed to be. His advisers told him, and came to believe, that there was no basis for dissent in Cambodia. The visible alternatives, once the Democrats had been brushed aside, were the Pracheachon and the Khmer Serei, or Free Khmer, and neither was a formidable force.

The Khmer Serei comprised paramilitary units made up of ethnic Khmer who were recruited, paid, and armed by the Thai and the South Vietnamese and were more or less under the command of the discredited exile, Son Ngoc Thanh. Physically on foreign soil and patronized by foreign powers, they were easy targets for Sihanouk's vituperation. When members of the movement were caught inside Cambodia, they were tried in secret and then executed by firing squads. Films of the executions were shown publicly for several weeks.

As for the Pracheachon, its members were often under surveillance, and its newspapers, even though they toed a pro-Sihanouk, anti-U.S. line, were frequently shut down. Several of its members were killed or put in prison between 1957 and 1963. The clandestine components of the Communist movement, led by Tou Samouth until his assassination in 1962 and thereafter by Saloth Sar, had little success in maintaining the pre-1954 momentum they had commanded among rural people. In the cities, however, Sar and his colleagues, as well as the Communists in the

Assembly, were popular with intellectuals, monks, and students in their last years of school. To these people, Communist teachers like Saloth Sar and his wife, who never spoke of their party affiliations, offered an inspiring contrast in terms of their firm ideology and correct behavior to the lackadaisical and corrupt Cambodian elite. As teachers, they were dedicated and strict, but it was their moral fervor, expressed primarily as a hatred of privilege, corruption, and injustice, that endeared them to their students and to many in the Buddhist monastic order.

In early 1963, Sihanouk launched an antileft campaign by broadcasting the names of thirty-four people who he claimed were plotting to overthrow his government. The list included many left-wing schoolteachers in Phnom Penh (including Saloth Sar and Ieng Sary), leftists in the Assembly, and some intellectuals recently favored by the prince. Melodramatically, Sihanouk summoned all of them to an audience and offered to turn the government over to them. When they refused the offer and pledged loyalty to him, he allowed most of them to resume their former jobs.[5]

Saloth Sar and Ieng Sary, however, were also members of the clandestine Communist party's Central Committee, which until then had been safe from Sihanouk's police. It seems likely that Sihanouk knew nothing of their party affiliations, but they feared that he did, and they fled to the Vietnamese border where they sought protection from Vietnamese troops in an encampment they referred to as Office 100. Left-wing teachers who remained behind became cautious about expressing their views, and so did the members of the underground party in Phnom Penh, now headed by Nuon Chea and Von Vet. For the next three years, left-wing opposition to Sihanouk's rule made little headway.

A stronger restraint on Cambodia's Communists was imposed by the North Vietnamese, whose alliance with Sihanouk would have been threatened by indigenous resistance to his rule. They advised their Cambodian colleagues to wait for a Vietnamese victory and to wage a political, as opposed to an armed, struggle. This patronizing guidance gave the Cambodians the options of doing nothing or getting caught by the police, and unsurprisingly, resentment began to build up among many of them. Some felt, perhaps naively, that they had as much of a right to a national revolution as the Vietnamese. Their resentment, however, had a long fuse and exploded only after Communist military victories in 1975.

SIHANOUK'S RULE: A BALANCE SHEET

Between 1955 and 1970, Sihanouk's most positive contribution was to keep Cambodia from being swept into the firestorm in Vietnam. Doing so required skillful footwork, and he paid a price in the resulting animosity of the pro-U.S. regimes in Saigon and Bangkok, whose leaders would have been contemptuous of any Cambodian claims to genuine autonomy.

With hindsight, we can conclude that Sihanouk's domestic record is mixed. Perhaps the most positive aspect of the ramshackle ideology he called "Buddhist socialism" was his insistence on large expenditures for education (amounting in some years to over 20 percent of the national budget). Unfortunately, the prince could not foresee the discontent that would affect tens of thousands of high school graduates and hundreds of university graduates in the late 1960s when they found it hard to obtain well-paid employment. Some of these young men and women drifted into the Communist movement, and many more blamed Sihanouk for their plight.

On the psychological plane, Sihanouk's identification with Cambodia's poor, however sentimentally based, did much to increase those people's feelings of self-worth and their own identification with the Cambodian state. Ironically, by raising their political consciousness and their awareness of injustice, Sihanouk probably hastened his own demise. His repeated references to Cambodia's grandeur may have misled some younger Cambodians into thinking that they could successfully resist the Vietnamese and others, and that Cambodia's Communist revolution, when it occurred, would be purer and more far-reaching than any that had occurred so far.

Sihanouk also encouraged a certain amount of political participation and debate by means of so-called National Congresses, held twice a year outside the royal palace. In theory, any member of the Sangkum was welcome to attend these meetings and express his or her political views. The Congresses dealt with uncontroversial issues, and like so much else in Cambodian life, they were stage-managed by the prince, whose policies were voted on by a show of hands. After 1963, the caliber of the debates deteriorated, and Sihanouk used the meetings to abuse his enemies, to defend himself (and Cambodia) against criticism, and to assert that Cambodia was superior to its neighbors and, in ethical terms at least, to most larger powers.

Another positive aspect of Sihanouk's style was his capacity for hard work. He often spent eighteen hours a day reading government papers, and his energetic tours of the countryside put him in touch with literally hundreds of thousands of ordinary Khmer. These contacts almost satisfied his hunger for approval. His hyperactivity was a disadvantage, however, because he preferred talking to listening and was unwilling or unable to delegate authority, even on subjects he knew little about. He also perceived ordinary Cambodians as his children—a view inherited from the French—rather than as people capable of making choices or handling their own affairs.

Phnom Penh in the 1960s was the prettiest capital in Southeast Asia, and many Western journalists taking a break from the Vietnam War were intoxicated by Cambodia's charm. They wrote glowingly about Sihanouk's "island of peace," the contented, peaceable Khmer, and Sihanouk's "charisma." Many of them were granted interviews by the prince, which made excellent copy, but unsurprisingly, they said little about the despotic aspects of his rule or the economic problems the country faced. Had they done so, their visas would not have been renewed. Indeed, for several months in 1967–1968, on Sihanouk's order, no foreign journalists were allowed into the country.

Aligned with these more positive aspects of Sihanouk's ruling style, and affecting everything he did, were his vanity, his impatience with advice, and his unwillingness to face Cambodia's economic, infrastructural, and social problems. He rode roughshod over any opposition. Hundreds of dissidents disappeared—and are presumed to have been assassinated—during his years in power, and several thousand peasants were killed in the aftermath of a Communist-led uprising in the northwest in 1967. Like many of his ancestors, Sihanouk saw Cambodia as a personal possession, a family, or a theatrical troupe. Many of his subjects, particularly older people, agreed to play supporting roles and endowed him with supernatural powers. So did the courtesans who surrounded him. Sihanouk's genuine patriotism and his capacity for hard work were marred by his narcissism and willfulness. Chosen by the French as an instrument for their policies, he was unable to withstand the pressures that built up against him and his country in the late 1960s, when his patrons and enemies overseas conspired to dismantle his neutral stance and when the people he had generously seen through school and college refused to be treated as his children forever.

SIHANOUK'S DECLINE

The first of several turning points in Sihanouk's rule probably came in November 1963 when he broke off the U.S. military aid program that had provided the pay for his armed forces and, in effect, a 15 percent subvention to the national budget. No similar patron stepped forward, although over the next few years China provided some military equipment, and the Cambodian army declined as an effective combat force. In related decisions, Sihanouk nationalized the import-export sector of the economy and closed Cambodia's privately owned banks. His motives in cutting off U.S. aid were related to his desire to stay out of the Vietnam War and to maintain good relations with members of the Communist bloc. The other decisions were parts of an effort to gain control over the economy and to cripple the Chinese and Sino-Khmer business elite in Phnom Penh.[6]

The two decisions had unforeseen effects. Sihanouk's break with the United States made him vulnerable to pressures from the left and lowered military morale. The nationalization of foreign trade soon encouraged the commercial elite to trade clandestinely with Communist insurgents in Vietnam, and by 1967, over a quarter of Cambodia's rice harvest was being smuggled to these forces, who paid higher prices than the Cambodian government could afford. At the same time, the government lost revenue from the export taxes it normally charged on rice. Foreign trade was also hampered by the loss of entrepreneurial skills and government ineptitude.

To stem the outflow of rice, a decision was made in early 1967 that army units should gather the rice surplus in several areas, pay government prices for it, and transport it to government warehouses. In western Battambang, near Samlaut, resentment against this decision flared into armed conflict. Tens of thousands of farmers fled or were herded into the forest, where they were pursued and wiped out by government forces and hastily assembled vigilante groups. Years later, Sihanouk remarked offhandedly that he had "read somewhere that ten thousand" people had been killed in this repression, and other sources confirm the figure. The killings, of course, had been carried out under his orders.[7]

The uprising unnerved the prince, because one purpose of the alliance with North Vietnam, in his view, had been to bring Cambodian Communists under stricter Vietnamese control. Sihanouk found it inconceivable that his "children" could move against him because of genuine grievances connected with his policies—in this case, the forced collection of rice. He suspected the Vietnamese of double-crossing him but was in no position to do anything about it.

Increasingly suspicious of the left, Sihanouk was too proud to make overtures to Cambodia's conservatives, whom he had vilified so often. His tactics after Samlaut were to maintain his attacks on the left, to attempt to hold onto the middle ground, and to seek to renew diplomatic relations with the United States in the hope of reinstating economic and military aid. By then, however, most U.S. policymakers perceived Cambodia as a side issue to their country's involvement in Vietnam and wanted relations with Sihanouk only on their terms.

Because of losses of revenue as a result of clandestine trading, mismanagement of state-controlled industry, and extravagant expenditures, Cambodia's economy in 1967–1968 was faltering. Agricultural problems had never attracted Sihanouk's sustained attention. They included low yields, poor irrigation, and excessive interest charged on loans to farmers and were being exacerbated by a rapidly increasing population and fluctuations in world prices. By 1967, these problems had become severe, and Sihanouk's reaction was still to ignore them. Increasingly, he turned over political power to Lon Nol and Sirik Matak. He hoped that something would turn up to save the country's economy, or that the people in charge would perform so badly as to again enhance his power, but sensing his vulnerability, his enemies gathered strength.

Between 1963 and the end of 1966, Cambodia's leading Communists were camped along the Vietnamese border under Vietnamese protection. Communists later took credit for Sihanouk's break with the United States, but in fact, their influence on events in these years was close to zero, and Saloth Sar, the party's leader, spent more than twelve months in 1965–1966 outside the country.

In 1965 Sar was summoned to North Vietnam for consultations. Walking north along the Ho Chi Minh Trail, he took two months to reach Hanoi, where he was taken to task for his party's nationalist agenda. The secretary of the Vietnamese Communist party, Le Duan, told him to subordinate Cambodia's interests to Vietnam's, to help Vietnam defeat the United States, and to postpone armed struggle until the time was ripe.

Bruised by these attacks, Sar said nothing to antagonize his patrons. Soon afterward, however, he traveled to China and was warmly welcomed by radical officials. Inspired by the early phases of the Cultural Revolution, Sar transferred his loyalties to a new set of patrons and a more vibrant revolutionary model. With hindsight, it is interesting to speculate about the effect of events in China at the time on the members of the Cambodian delegation. How did they react to Mao Zedong's flight to Shanghai, his swim in the Yangtze, and his inauguration of the Cultural Revolution? And how did they interpret Defense Minister Lin Biao's widely publicized speech emphasizing the importance of self-reliance in Communist revolutions? The speech must have worried the Vietnamese, for whom Chinese military aid was crucial in the war with the United States; on the other hand, it may have secretly pleased those Khmer who saw Vietnamese assistance as a form of suffocation.[8]

In any event, the visit to China was a turning point in Sar's career. Prudently, however, he said nothing to the Vietnamese about his change of heart. Back home, he established his headquarters in a remote, heavily wooded section of the country. For the next four years, with a group of like-minded colleagues, he lost touch with everyday Cambodian life, polished his Utopian ideas, nourished his hatreds, and thought about seizing power.

Over a year later, just before the Vietnamese Communists launched the Tet Offensive, the Communist party of Kampuchea (CPK), as it now styled itself, inaugurated an "armed struggle" against Sihanouk, striking out from its bases in the northeast and the northwest. The struggle, insignificant at first, gathered momentum over the next two years, and by early 1970, insurgent forces had occupied, or rendered unsafe for others to occupy, nearly a fifth of Cambodia's territory. In the cities, meanwhile, many students and teachers who had been alienated by Sihanouk's narcissistic rule found themselves enthralled by the possibilities of the Cultural Revolution in China and the May 1968 uprisings in France. For many young Cambodians, these movements seemed to offer viable alternatives to the perennial corruption and conservatism of Cambodian politics.

During this volatile time, Sihanouk busied himself with making feature films over which he exercised total control as writer, director, producer, and leading actor. Making them offered relief from a political game that had become too complex for him to win and too dangerous to play. The prince also scrambled to realign himself with the United States while reasserting his friendship with that country's enemies in Vietnam. These contradictory moves discredited him even further with his enemies inside the country, and by late 1969, high-ranking conservative officials had begun plotting against him. Whether or not they received encouragement from officers in the newly reopened U.S. Embassy is a matter for speculation.[9]

The most prominent of the plotters was Sihanouk's cousin, Sisowath Sirik Matak, a career civil servant who had become deputy prime minister under Lon Nol. Matak had grown impatient with Sihanouk's mismanagement of the economy, and he was dismayed by the presence of Vietnamese bases on Cambodian soil and by his cousin's impulsive, contradictory foreign policy. Pro-Western himself, and with links to Phnom Penh's commercial elite, Matak was tired of playing a supporting role in Sihanouk's never-ending opera.

Lon Nol, the prime minister, was a more enigmatic figure. He is not known to have objected to the prince about the cutoff of U.S. aid, the alliance with the Communists, or the shipments of arms through Cambodian territory. Indeed, many of his officers became rich by dealing in arms, medicines, and supplies, for which the Vietnamese paid generously. By 1969, however, Cambodian troops were under fire from Communist insurgents, and the Vietnamese administration of many base areas had drawn complaints from local people. Lon Nol was also under pressure from some of his officers who saw Cambodia's isolation from U.S. aid and, by implication, from the Vietnam War as impediments to their financial ambitions. Moreover, Lon Nol was not immune to flattery, and he came to see himself as uniquely capable of saving Cambodia from the *thmil*, or "unbelievers," as he called the Vietnamese hammering at his country's gates.

While pressures were mounting, Sihanouk's interest in governing declined. Years of overwork had worn him down, and his inability or unwillingness to attract and keep young, competent advisers had begun to tell. For instance, his decision to open a casino in Phnom Penh to raise revenue had disastrous results. In the last six months of 1969, thousands of Cambodians lost millions of dollars at its tables; several prominent people, and dozens of impoverished ones, committed suicide after sustaining losses; and hundreds of families went bankrupt. Sihanouk, no gambler himself, was indifferent to the chaos he had caused, and his own expenditures continued to mount. A climax of sorts occurred in November, when an international film festival, stage-managed by the prince, ended with one of his own films, "Twilight," being awarded a solid-gold statue sculpted from ingots donated for the purpose by Cambodia's national bank. When Sihanouk left the country for his annual holiday in January 1970, many people who remained behind interpreted his departure as a "flight."

THE COUP OF 1970

Over the next two months, Sisowath Sirik Matak and his colleagues struggled to put Cambodia's house in order, shutting down the casino and privatizing the banks. Matak traveled secretly to Hanoi to see what could be done to remove Vietnamese troops from Cambodian soil. He was infuriated when he was shown documents signed by Sihanouk agreeing to the Vietnamese bases. Soon afterward, deliveries of supplies to Vietnamese forces inside the country were halted, and the stage was set for a full-scale confrontation with Vietnam—a scenario Sihanouk had struggled to avoid for fifteen years.

In early March, riots broke out in Phnom Penh against the embassies of North Vietnam and its surrogate in South Vietnam, the National Liberation Front. The riots got out of hand, and both buildings were badly damaged. From Paris, Sihanouk condemned the violence, although the riots had occurred with his permission. Conditions were ripening for the coup d'état Matak had been considering for several months, and the timetable was accelerated because it was feared that Sihanouk might soon return. On the night of March 17, Matak and three army officers visited Lon Nol at his house, threatened him with a pistol, and made him sign a declaration supporting a vote against the prince scheduled for the following day in the National Assembly. When he signed the document, as if aware of the long-term consequences of his action, Lon Nol burst into tears.[10]

The coup itself was an anticlimax, in sharp contrast to the operatic style of Sihanouk's politics. The National Assembly, as it was entitled to do, voted 86–3 to remove its confidence from the prince and to replace him as chief of state, pending elections, with the relatively colorless president of the Assembly, Cheng Heng. Lon Nol remained as prime minister, with Matak as his assistant. The coup was popular among educated peo-

Sihanouk dismissed from office; graffito in Phnom Penh, 1970. Author's photo.

ple in Phnom Penh and in the army, but rural Cambodians were unprepared for it. Many of the plotters wanted to declare Cambodia a republic but delayed doing so after pro-Sihanouk riots broke out in several provinces.

Meanwhile, the prince, who learned of the coup while traveling home via Moscow, was in Beijing. His first thought was to seek political asylum in France, but after talks with Zhou Enlai and the Vietnamese premier, Pham Van Dong, he agreed to take command of a united front government, allied to North Vietnam, whose Cambodian forces would consist largely of the Communists his army had been struggling to destroy only a month before. At the end of March, the prince broadcast an appeal to his "brothers and sisters" (they were no longer his "children," apparently) to take up arms against Lon Nol. Pro-Sihanouk riots broke out almost immediately in the eastern part of the country, and soon afterward, fueled by panic, arrogance, and racism, Cambodian army units massacred hundreds of unarmed Vietnamese civilians near Phnom Penh on the dubious grounds that they were allied with the Communists. They were certainly easier to locate than the North Vietnamese armed forces, and easier to kill, but the viciousness of the massacre, and Lon Nol's failure to express regret, evaporated the goodwill the regime had earned overseas.

For most Cambodians, moreover, the idea that Vietnamese forces should leave Cambodia was more popular than the coup itself. When Lon Nol gave the Vietnamese Communists forty-eight hours to leave the country—probably the most unrealistic command in modern Cambodian history—many Cambodians were enraged to learn that the Vietnamese ignored him, and tens of thousands poured into the armed forces to drive the "invaders" from the country. Thousands were killed or wounded over the next few weeks, picked off by Vietnamese soldiers who had been in combat in some cases for over twenty years. In May 1970, a joint U.S.–South Vietnamese invasion of eastern Cambodia drove the North Vietnamese forces further west. The invasion protected the U.S. withdrawal from Vietnam, but it probably spelled the end of Cambodia as a sovereign state.[11]

THE KHMER REPUBLIC'S LONG DECLINE

Lon Nol's two offensives against the Vietnamese in late 1970 and 1971 were named after the pre-Angkorean "kingdom" of Chenla. They were encouraged by the United States, but Lon Nol's troops were badly trained, poorly equipped, and often badly led. Experienced North Vietnamese forces cut them to pieces, and after 1971, Lon Nol's troops mounted no major offensive actions. After becoming a republic in October 1970, the government survived for four more years, largely because of U.S. military assistance and heavy bombing and because the Vietnamese Communists were unwilling to help their Cambodian colleagues take Phnom Penh before they managed to liberate South Vietnam.

The story of the last four years of the Khmer Republic is violent and melancholy; so is the corresponding story of the CPK's gaining control of the resistance. Lon Nol suffered a stroke in early 1971, and although he recovered rapidly, he never regained full political control. Without strong leadership, many politicians in Phnom Penh busied themselves with forming factions and amassing wealth, and a leading actor was Lon Nol's younger brother, Lon Non, whose efforts were concentrated on keeping Sisowath Sirik Matak—or anyone else—from gaining power from Lon Nol.

In the countryside, republican army officers often falsified the numbers of soldiers under their command so as to pocket the salaries provided by U.S. military aid. Some officers also sold military equipment to the Communists; few were prepared to take offensive action. Lon Nol was reluc-

Young girls in revolutionary costume, 1972. Photo by Serge Thion.

tant to punish officers who were loyal to him for malfeasance or corruption. Instead, he spent much of his time writing letters to President Nixon, asking for more U.S. aid, and listening to Buddhist mystics who promised magical solutions to the war. By the end of 1972, the Khmer Republic controlled Phnom Penh, a few provincial capitals, and much of Battambang. The rest of the country was either in Communist hands or unsafe for anyone to administer.

In the first half of 1973, the United States postponed a Communist victory by conducting a bombing campaign on Cambodia that, in its intensity, was as brutal as any conducted during World War II. Over a hundred thousand tons of bombs fell on the Cambodian countryside before the U.S. Congress prohibited further bombing. No estimate of casualties has ever been made, but the campaign probably halted the Communist forces encircling Phnom Penh, even though some people have argued that it hardened the will of the surviving Communist forces. The war dragged on for another year and a half, but President Nixon's reaction to the end of the bombing was to declare to an aide that as a result, the United States had "lost" Southeast Asia—a section of the world it had never "owned."[12]

The Communists' response to over twenty years of Vietnamese assistance to their movement was to massacre most of the Cambodians sent down from North Vietnam as soon as North Vietnamese troops withdrew from Cambodia at the end of 1972, following the cease-fire agreed upon by Vietnam and the United States. These killings occurred in secret. The Communists also experimented with programs of collectivization in the zones under their control, and in early 1973, during the U.S. bombing campaign, the CPK introduced compulsory cooperatives in some areas. By then, rumors were reaching Phnom Penh about the uncompromising conduct of the insurgents, who took no prisoners and who herded inhabitants into the forest whenever they captured a town or village. Many people in Phnom Penh dismissed these rumors as propaganda and continued to believe that the CPK was a puppet of the Vietnamese. At the same time, they were exhausted by the war and ready for almost any alternative to the corrupt and inefficient Khmer Republic.

The end came in early 1975 when the Communists mined the riverine approaches to Phnom Penh and thus prevented shipments of rice and ammunition from reaching the capital. Airlifts arranged by the United States were unable to bring in enough rice to feed Phnom Penh or enough ammunition to defend it. For three months, the Cambodian Communists tightened their noose around the city, which was now swollen with perhaps two million refugees. In early March, Lon Nol flew out of the country, taking along a million dollars awarded him by his government. Last-minute attempts to negotiate with Sihanouk, set in motion by the United States, came to nothing. At this point, or shortly beforehand, and without waiting for approval from his Vietnamese allies, Saloth Sar decided to take Phnom Penh.

On the morning of April 17, 1975, columns of Communist troops, dressed in peasant clothes or simple khaki uniforms, ominously silent and heavily armed, converged on the capital. Many of them were under fifteen years of age. Walking slowly down the capital's broad avenues, emptied of other traffic, they responded coldly to the people's welcome. Their arrival coincided roughly with the Cambodian new year and came two weeks before the Communist victory in South Vietnam. The coincidences were deliberate, for the Communists probably intended that the year to come, like Year 1 of the French Revolution, would usher in an entirely new phase of Cambodian history, without any connections to the revolution in Vietnam.[13]

CHAPTER 12

Revolution in Cambodia

It is uncertain that historians of Cambodia a hundred years from now will devote as much space to the country's brief revolutionary period as to the much longer, more complex, and more mysterious Angkorean era. For nearly all mature Cambodians in the 1990s, however, the three and a half years that followed the capture of Phnom Penh in April 1975 were a traumatic period in their lives. Because of the ferocity with which Cambodia's revolution was waged and the way it contrasted with many people's ideas about prerevolutionary Cambodia, it has also fascinated outside observers.

The Communist regime that controlled Cambodia between April 1975 and January 1979 was known as Democratic Kampuchea (DK). The revolution it sponsored swept through the country like a forest fire or a typhoon, and its spokesmen claimed that "over two thousand years of Cambodian history" had ended. So had money, markets, formal education, Buddhism, books, private property, diverse clothing styles, and freedom of movement. No Cambodian government had ever tried to change so many things so rapidly; none had been so relentlessly oriented toward the future or so biased in favor of the poor.

The leaders of DK, who were members of Cambodia's Communist party, called themselves the "revolutionary organization" (*angkar padevat*). They sought to transform Cambodia by replacing what they saw as impediments to national autonomy and social justice with revolutionary energy and incentives. Family life, individualism, and an ingrained fondness for what they called "feudal" institutions, as well as the institutions themselves, stood in the way of the revolution. Cambodia's poor, they said, had always been exploited and enslaved. Liberated by the revolution and empowered by military victory, they would now become the masters of their lives and collective masters of their country.

The Communist party of Kampuchea (CPK), which monitored every step of the revolution, concealed its existence from outsiders, did not reveal its socialist agenda or the names of its leaders, and said nothing of its long-standing alliance with Vietnam. For several months, the CPK's leaders even allowed foreigners to think that Sihanouk, who had served as a figurehead leader for the anti–Lon Nol resistance, was still Cambodia's chief of state. By concealing its alliances and agendas, the new government gave the impression that the country was truly independent. In 1978, Pol Pot boasted to Yugoslavian visitors that Cambodia was "building socialism without a model." That process began in April 1975 and continued for the lifetime of DK, but by acknowledging no precedents for what they were doing, Pol Pot and his colleagues had embarked on a perilous course.[1]

To transform the country thoroughly and at once, Communist cadres ordered everyone out of the cities and towns. In the week after April 17, 1975, over two million Cambodians were pushed into the countryside toward an uncertain fate, and only the families of top CPK officials and a few hundred factory workers were allowed to stay behind. This brutal order, never thoroughly explained, added several thousand deaths to the approximately five hundred thousand in the civil war. Reports reaching the West spoke of hospital patients driven from their beds, random executions, and sick and elderly people, as well as small children, dead or abandoned along the roads. The evacuation shocked its victims as well as observers in other countries, who had hoped that the new regime would try to govern through reconciliation—these men and women may have forgotten the ferocity with which the civil war had been fought by both sides. Still other observers, more sympathetic to the idea of revolution, saw the evacuation of the cities as the only way in which Cambodia could grow enough food to survive, break down entrenched social hierarchies, and set its Utopian strategies in motion.[2]

The decision to evacuate the cities was made by the CPK's leaders shortly before the liberation of Phnom Penh, but it was a closely kept secret and took even some Communist commanders by surprise. One reason for the decision was that the capital was genuinely short of food. Another was the difficulty of administering several million people who had, in effect, opposed the revolution. A third was that the CPK's leaders were fearful for their own security. Perhaps the overriding reason, however, was the desire to assert the victory of the CPK, the dominance of the countryside over the cities, and the privileged position of the poor. Saloth Sar and his colleagues had not spent seven years in the forest and five years fighting a civil war to take office as city councilors. They saw the cities as breeding grounds for counterrevolution, and their economic priorities were based on the transformation of Cambodian agriculture, especially on increasing the national production of rice. By exporting the surplus, it was hoped, the government would earn hard currency with which to pay for imports and, eventually, to finance industrialization. To achieve such a surplus, the CPK needed all the agricultural workers it could find.

For the next six months, the people who had been driven out of the cities—known as "new people" or "April 17 people"—busied themselves with growing rice and other crops under the supervision of soldiers and Communist cadres. Conditions were severe, particularly for those unaccustomed to physical labor, but because in most districts there was enough to eat, many survivors of DK came to look back on these months as a relatively golden age. For the first time in many years, Cambodia was not at war, and many "new people" were eager to reconstruct their battered country. Perhaps Cambodia's problems were so severe, after all, as to require revolutionary solutions. A former engineer has said, "At first, the ideas of the revolution were good." He added, however, that "they didn't work in practice."[3]

For many rural Cambodians, and especially those between fifteen and twenty, fighting against "feudalism" and the "Americans" in the early 1970s had provided beguiling glimpses of freedom, self-respect, and power—as well as access to weapons—that were unimaginable to their parents or to most Cambodians. These young people, to borrow a phrase from Mao Zedong, were "poor and blank" pages on which it was easy to inscribe the teachings of the revolution. Owing everything to the revolutionary organization, which they referred to as their "mother and father," and nothing to the past, it was thought that these young people would lead the way in transforming Cambodia into a socialist state and in moving the people toward "independence, mastery, and self-reliance." To the alarm and confusion of many people, these young Cambodians became the revolution's cutting edge.

DK TAKES POWER, 1975–1976

The revolutionary period in Cambodia was characterized by regional and temporal variations, and by and large, those parts of the country that had been under CPK control the longest tended to be the best equipped to deal with the programs set out by the party and the most accommodating to the "new people." Cadres were better disciplined in the east, northeast, and southwest than they were in the northwest. Unfortunately for "new people," the northwest, centered on the province of Battambang, had been the most productive area in prerevolutionary times, so the regime's demands for crop surpluses were heavier there than in other regions, and so were the sufferings that ensued.[4]

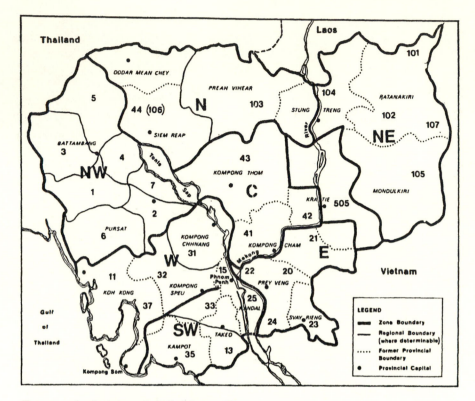

Zones and administrative divisions of Democratic Kampuchea.

The CPK divided Cambodia into seven zones (*phumipheak*), which, in turn, were broken down into thirty-two administrative regions (*dombon*). In general, conditions were tolerable, through 1976 or so, in the northeastern and eastern zones, somewhat worse in the southwest and west, and worst of all in the northern and northwestern zones. Within the zones, there was also considerable variation, reflecting differences in leadership, resources, and external factors such as the fighting with Vietnam that broke out in the east and the southwest in the middle of 1977.[5]

Life was hard everywhere. On a national scale, it is estimated that between April 1975 and January 1979, nearly two million people—or one person in five—died as a direct result of DK policies and actions. These included overworking people, neglecting or mistreating the sick, and giving everyone less food than they needed to survive. Perhaps as many as one hundred thousand others were killed outright as enemies of the revolution.[6]

The DK period can be divided into four phases. The first lasted from the capture of Phnom Penh until the beginning of 1976, when a constitution was proclaimed and a new wave of migration was set in motion from the southwest, which was heavily populated but relatively unproductive, to the rich rice-growing areas in the northwest. The southwest had been liberated early and contained many revolutionary bases. It was also crowded with refugees from Phnom Penh. Most of the northwest on the other hand had remained under republican control until April 1975. The regime was counting on this area to lead the way in expanding Cambodia's rice production, and "new people" were the instruments chosen to achieve this goal. The fact that they were socially unredeemable was seen as an advantage. In a chilling adage recalled by many survivors, they were often told: "Keeping you is no profit; losing you is no loss."

During this period, Phnom Penh Radio enjoined its listeners via anonymous speakers and revolutionary songs to "build and defend" Cambodia against unnamed enemies (*khmang*) outside and within the country. In view of the regime's collapse in 1979, there was a poignant optimism built into these pronouncements, but in the early stages of the revolution, many Cambodians believed that the revolution would succeed. Moreover, from the perspective of the party's leaders, genuine or imagined enemies had not yet surfaced.

DK's second phase lasted until the end of September 1976, and in a sense, this phase marked the apogee of the regime, although conditions in the countryside, and especially the northwest, deteriorated as the year progressed. It is uncertain why the leaders of the CPK waited so long to proclaim a government of their own, but they controlled the population without identifying themselves for nearly a year and a half. Perhaps this anonymity made them feel secure, and the Chinese patronage of Sihanouk might also have been a factor in the CPK's delay in its open seizure of power. When the Chinese prime minister, Zhou Enlai, Prince Sihanouk's important patron, died in January 1976, the leaders of the CPK prepared to brush the prince aside by forcing him to retire as chief of state. A confidential party document of March 1976 stated that "[Sihanouk] has run out of breath. He cannot go forward. Therefore we have decided to retire him."[7] Sihanouk resigned three days later. He was offered a pension that was never paid and a monument in his honor that was never erected. By April 1976, he was living under guard in a small villa on the grounds of the royal palace, and he stayed there, in relative comfort but in fear of his life, until he was sent by DK on a diplomatic mission in January 1979. The DK document also noted that the new government "must be purely a party organization" and stated that "Comrade Pol" (a pseudonym for Saloth Sar) would be prime minister. In an earlier confidential document, compiled in October 1975, Saloth Sar had assumed responsibility for the economy and defense.

The constitution of Democratic Kampuchea, promulgated in January 1976, guaranteed no human rights, defined few organs of government, and, in effect, abolished private property, organized religion, and family-oriented agricultural production. The document acknowledged no foreign models, denied any foreign alliances or assistance, and said nothing about the CPK or Marxist-Leninist ideas. Instead, it made the revolution sound like a uniquely Cambodian affair with no connection to the outside world.[8]

When National Assembly elections were held in March, the CPK's candidates were elected unopposed. They included members of the CPK Central Committee, elected as "peasants," "rubber workers," and so on, as well as others harder to identify. Pol Pot, not otherwise identified, represented "rubber workers in the eastern zone." The candidates had no territorial constituencies, being seen instead as representatives of certain classes of Khmer. "New people" were not nominated or eligible to vote. The Assembly met only once, to approve the constitution, and never played a significant role in DK. Like the elections themselves, the Assembly seems to have been formed to placate foreign opinion.

The people who achieved a prominent place in the new government were a mixture of intellectuals who had studied in France (Pol Pot, Ieng Sary, Sary's wife Ieng Thirith, Hu Nim, Tiounn Thioenn, and Son Sen), older members of the Indochinese Communist party (Nuon Chea, Nhem Ros, Chou Chet, Non Suon, and Sao Phim), and younger militants who had never left Cambodia (Von Vet, Khek Pen, and Chhim Samauk). Those in charge of the seven zones did not include any ex-students from France; they were concentrated in the newly established ministries of Phnom Penh.[9]

THE FOUR-YEAR PLAN

Over the next few months, Pol Pot and his colleagues drafted a four-year economic plan "to build socialism in all fields." The plan was to go into effect in September 1976, but it was never formally launched. It called for the collectivization of all Cambodian property and proposed ever-increasing levels of rice production throughout the country, with the aim of achieving an average national yield of 3 metric tons per hectare (1.4 tons per acre). The prerevolutionary average, harvested under less stringent conditions and with monetary incentives, had been less than a ton per hectare, one of the lowest in Southeast Asia. The goal of tripling the average was to be achieved by extensive irrigation, double and triple cropping, longer working hours, and the release of revolutionary fervor connected with people's liberation from exploitation and individual concerns. The plan had been hastily written. There was no time to conduct studies to see if its proposals were appropriate to soil and water conditions in particular areas or if the infrastructure needed for other programs was in place. Instead, the plan called for an "all out, storming offensive" by all the people. Some writers have drawn parallels between the CPK's program and the so-called war communism of the Soviet Union in the early 1920s; others compare DK's policies to those known as the Great Leap Forward in China in the 1950s. No material incentives were offered the Cambodian people except the bizarre promise that everyone would enjoy dessert on a daily basis—by 1980! Cambodia's newfound independence, the empowerment of the poor, and the end of exploitation were thought to be sufficient incentives and rewards.[10]

Under the Four-Year Plan, crops such as cotton, jute, rubber, coconuts, sugar, and kapok were to be cultivated for export. With the money earned from exports, light industry was to be established and eventually heavy industry as well. Plans for the latter were particularly Utopian, for they were dependent on raw materials like iron, steel, and petroleum, which did not exist in DK. In explaining the plan to high-ranking members of the party, an unnamed spokesman, presumably Pol Pot, stated that the plan could be accomplished swiftly. The DK revolution, after all, was "a new experience, and an important one for the whole world, because we don't perform like others. We leap [directly to] a socialist revolution, and swiftly build socialism. We don't need a long period of time for transformation."[11]

The plan said nothing about leisure, religion, formal education, or family life. Although it was deemed crucial to "abolish illiteracy among the population," nothing was said about what people would be allowed to read. Some primary schools existed in base areas by 1976, but education was not extended to "new people" or their children until 1977 or 1978, and education above the primary level did not exist before 1978, when a belated attempt was made to establish a technical college in Phnom Penh. In part, DK officials were making a virtue of necessity, since most men and women known to be experienced schoolteachers, and hostile to the CPK, were suspected of treasonous intentions and were often killed as "class enemies." Former teachers who were members of the party now had more rewarding tasks to perform.

Most Cambodians had to work ten to twelve hours a day, twelve months a year, to accomplish the objectives of the plan. Many of those who were unaccustomed to physical labor soon died of malnutrition and overwork, but even those who had been farmers in prerevolutionary times often found themselves working much harder than they had before 1975, with no material rewards, limited access to their spouses and children, and very little free time. By early 1976, food was already scarce, since the surpluses from the first harvests had been gathered up to feed the army, to be stored, or even to be exported. The situation deteriorated in 1977 and 1978, when many parts of the country were stricken with famine. Many survivors recall months of eating rice gruel without much else. One of them, now living in Australia, has recalled: "We looked like the Africans you see on television. Our legs were like sticks; we could barely walk."[12]

A similar famine had swept through China in the early 1960s in the wake of the disastrous Great Leap Forward. In Cambodia, news of the famine was concealed from the leaders in Phnom Penh; starvation was seen as evidence of treachery by those cadres charged with distribution of food. The DK's leaders seem to have believed that the forces they had mobilized to defeat "the Americans"—two weeks earlier than a similar victory in Vietnam—were sufficient for any task set by the "clear-sighted" CPK.[13]

During this second stage of the DK era, inexperienced cadres, in order to meet the targets imposed from the center, placed unbearable pressures on the "April 17 people" and everyone else under their command. One way of achieving surpluses was to cut down the amount of rice used for seed and what had been set aside to feed the people. In the plan itself, rations were sufficient for survival, and in several parts of the country people had enough to eat for most of 1976. In much of the northwest, however, rations diminished as the center's priorities came into force. Several hundred thousand more "new people" had been brought into the area in early 1976, and many of them were set to work hacking clearings out of the jungle. No Western-style medicines were available, and thousands soon died from malaria, overwork, and malnutrition. The few hundred men and women who managed to escape to Thailand reported executions, Spartan conditions, and insufficient food.

CRISIS IN THE PARTY

In early September 1976, the death of Mao Zedong occurred shortly before the CPK was to celebrate its twenty-fifth anniversary. It seems likely that the party had hoped to use this occasion to announce its existence to outsiders and to launch its Four-Year Plan, but as the month wore on, a split developed inside the CPK between those who favored the 1951 date for the foundation of the party and those who preferred 1960, when a special congress convened in Phnom Penh, probably at the behest of the Vietnamese, and had named Pol Pot and Ieng Sary, among others, to the party's Central Committee. To those who preferred the 1960 date, the earlier one was suggestive of Vietnamese domination of the party. They viewed those who favored 1951 as counterrevolutionaries whose primary loyalties were to Vietnam. What Pol Pot later described as the putting down of a potential coup d'état against his rule was more likely a preemptive purge of several party members whose loyalties to the party (or Vietnam) seemed to be greater than their loyalties to Pol Pot.[14]

Two prominent members of the CPK, Keo Meas and Non Suon, who both had ties to the Pracheachon—and thus to the Vietnamese-dominated phase of the party's history—were arrested and accused of treason. Their confessions, parts of which have survived, show that they supported a 1951 founding date for the CPK.[15] Overall, several thousand typed and handwritten confessions have survived from the DK interrogation center in the Phnom Penh suburb of Tuol Sleng. At least fourteen thousand men and women were questioned, tortured, and executed there between the end of 1975 and the first few days of 1979, and over four thousand of their dossiers survive. Although the confessions are invaluable for historians, it is impossible to say whether a genuine conspiracy to dethrone Pol Pot and his associates had gathered much momentum by September 1976. Like Sihanouk and Lon Nol, Pol Pot considered disagreements over policy to be tantamount to treason, and arguments over the party's founding date suggested to him that certain people wanted him removed from power. He was suspicious of the links that the people who argued for 1951 maintained with Cambodian Communists in Hanoi and with those Cambodians sent down from North Vietnam to assist the Cambodian revolution.[16]

At the end of the month, barely four days before the twenty-fifth anniversary of the party was to be celebrated, Pol Pot resigned as prime minister "for reasons of health" and was replaced by the second-ranking man in the CPK, Nuon Chea. Pol Pot's health had often broken down in the preceding year and a half, but he probably announced his resignation at this point to throw his enemies off balance, and perhaps to seek shelter outside Phnom Penh while the people he believed were plotting against him were rooted out. By mid-October, in any case, he was back in office. By then, a special issue of the CPK's theoretical journal, *Revolutionary Flags*, had celebrated the party's *sixteenth* anniversary, and Keo Meas, among others, had been executed as a traitor.

There was still no announcement of the party's existence, however, as its leaders had decided to keep the matter secret for the time being, to postpone a formal announcement of the Four-Year Plan, and to intensify the search for "enemies" inside the party. The regime's interrogation center at Tuol Sleng expanded its operations. Only 200 prisoners had entered the facility in 1975, but more than ten times that many (2,250) were brought there in 1976, and more than two-thirds of them were imprisoned between September and November. Another 5,000

Democratic Kampuchean cadre, Thai-Cambodian border, 1979. Photo by Brian L. Stevens.

prisoners were taken there in 1977, and approximately the same number were imprisoned in 1978. Factory workers in Phnom Penh, who knew about the center's existence but not about what went on inside its barbed-wire walls, called it the "place of entering, no leaving" (*konlanh choul ot cenh*). Only seven of the prisoners taken there for interrogation survived.[17]

In December 1976, as the purges intensified, Pol Pot presided over a "study session," restricted to high-ranking members of the party, that was called to examine the progress of the Cambodian revolution. One document that has survived from this meeting is darker and more pessimistic than those produced earlier in the year. In a vivid passage, Pol Pot spoke of a "sickness in the party" that had developed during 1976:

> We cannot locate it precisely. The illness must emerge to be examined. Because the heat of [previous stages of the revolution] was insufficient at the level of people's struggle and class struggle . . . we searched for the microbes within the party without success. They are buried. As our socialist revolution advances, however, seeping more strongly into every corner of the party, the army and among the people, we can locate the evil microbes. . . . Those who defend us must be truly adept. They should have practice in observing. They must observe everything, but not so that those being observed are aware of it.[18]

Who were the observers, and who were the observed? People opposed to the revolution, or counterrevolutionaries, were moving targets depending on the evolving policies and priorities of the party's leadership. At different stages of DK's short history, the "evil microbes" were those with middle-class backgrounds or soldiers who had fought for Lon Nol; those who had joined the Communist movement when it was guided by Vietnam or those who had been exposed to foreign countries. By 1978, victims included high-ranking members of the party, military commanders, and officials associated with the eastern zone. To be suspected, a person had only to be mentioned in the confessions of three other people, those accused would name the people they knew, and so on. Hundreds, probably thousands of those who were taken to Tuol Sleng were completely innocent of the charges brought against them, but everyone who was interrogated was considered guilty, and all those who were interrogated were killed. News of people's "disappearances" was used to keep their colleagues in the party in line, but the deaths themselves were not made public. The regime never expressed regret for anyone it had executed by mistake. For Pol Pot and his colleagues, too much hung in the balance for them to hesitate in attacking enemies of the party: the success of the revolution, the execution of policy, the survival of the leaders themselves. At the end of his December 1976 speech, Pol Pot remarked that such enemies "have been entering the party continuously. . . . They remain—perhaps only one person, or two people. They remain."[19]

The effect of these brutal, ambiguous threats on the people listening to them is impossible to gauge. Within a year, many of these men and women had been arrested, interrogated, tortured, and put to death. In most cases, they were forced to admit that they had joined the "CIA" (a blanket term for counterrevolutionary activity) early in their careers. Others claimed to have worked for Soviet or Vietnamese intelligence agencies. It is unclear whether Pol Pot and the cadres associated with Tuol Sleng believed in these interconnected conspiracies or merely in the efficacy of executing anyone who was suspected by those in power.[20]

CONFLICT WITH VIETNAM

The third phase of the DK era, between the political crisis of September 1976 and a speech by Pol Pot twelve months later in which he announced the existence of the CPK, was marked by waves of purges and by a shift toward blaming Cambodia's difficulties and counterrevolutionary activity on Vietnam. Open conflict with Vietnam had been a possibility since April 1975, when Cambodian forces had attacked several Vietnamese-held islands in the Gulf of Siam with the hope of making territorial gains in the confusing final stages of the Vietnamese civil war. The Cambodian forces had been driven back, and differences between the two Communist regimes, after May 1975, had been papered over, but DK's distrust of Vietnamese territorial intentions was still very deep. So were Pol Pot's suspicions of the Vietnamese Communist party, whose leaders had been patronizing toward their Cambodian counterparts for many years and had allowed Cambodia's revolution to flourish only in the shadow of Vietnam's. Pol Pot's suspicions deepened in July 1977 when Vietnam signed a treaty of cooperation with Laos, a move Pol Pot interpreted as part of Vietnam's plan to encircle Cambodia and to reconstitute and control what had once been French Indochina.[21]

Realizing the relative strengths of the two countries, however, Pol Pot tried at first to maintain correct relations and was unwilling to expand DK's armed forces to defend the eastern part of Cambodia against possible Vietnamese incursions. The Vietnamese were also cautious. After nearly thirty years of fighting, they were reluctant to wage war against anyone, least of all their neighbor. In 1975–1976, however, their attempts to open negotiations about the frontier were rebuffed by the Cambodians, who demanded that the Vietnamese honor the verbal agreements they had reached with Sihanouk in the 1960s. Cambodians claimed parts of the Gulf of Siam, where they hoped to profit from offshore oil deposits, but these claims were rejected by the Vietnamese, who harbored similar hopes. Skirmishes along the border between heavily armed, poorly disciplined troops in 1976 led Vietnamese and Cambodian leaders to doubt each other's sincerity. The Cambodian raids were much more brutal, but the evidence for centralized control or approval for attacks on either side, before the middle of 1977, is contradictory.[22]

The situation was complicated further by the fact that Pol Pot and his colleagues believed the Cambodian minorities in southern Vietnam were ready to overthrow Vietnamese rule and wanted to attach themselves to Phnom Penh. This dream of a "greater Cambodia" had also been held by Sihanouk and Lon Nol. In fact, whatever the views of the Khmer in Vietnam, they were insufficiently armed and too poorly organized to revolt against that country. When no uprising occurred, Pol Pot suspected treachery on the part of the agents he had dispatched to foment it. His troops were also merciless when, on their cross-border raids, they encountered and massacred hapless Khmer.

As so often in Cambodian history, what Cambodians interpreted as an internal affair, or a quarrel between neighbors, had unforeseen international dimensions. For several months after the death of Mao Zedong and the arrest of his radical subordinates, known as the Gang of Four, the Chinese regime was in disarray. Although the radicals were swiftly discredited, the new ruler, Hua Guofeng, tried to maintain Mao's momentum by opposing the Soviet Union, praising Mao's ideas indiscriminately, and supporting Third World revolutions like DK's. Many Chinese officials perceived Vietnam as a pro-Soviet threat along their southern border—much as the United States saw Cuba—and for the Chinese, Cambodia made a convenient and conveniently radical ally. By early 1977, large quantities of arms, ammunition, and military equipment were coming into DK from China. Ironically, the Chinese were asking DK to play a role similar to the one played by the regime DK had overthrown, when the Khmer Republic had been "groomed" to serve the interests of the United States.[23]

This phase of the DK era ended in September 1977 when Pol Pot, in a five-hour speech delivered over Phnom Penh Radio, announced the existence of the CPK on the occasion of the seventeenth anniversary of its foundation.[24] The speech failed to explain why the party's existence had been kept a secret for so long, and the announcement may have been made as a result of pressure from China in exchange for that country's military assistance. In any case, the day after giving the speech, Pol Pot flew off to Beijing where he was feted by Mao's successor, Hua Guofeng. The Chinese offered extensive help to DK in its confrontation with Vietnam. More realistic than DK's leaders, they did not support a full-scale war, knowing that Cambodia would lose, until they were pushed by Pol Pot, and Vietnamese intransigence, toward that position in 1978.

Pol Pot's speech about the CPK, read with hindsight, contained warnings to Vietnam, but his main intention was to trace the triumphant trajectory of the CPK. The format was chronological, divided into a discussion of events before 1960, between 1960 and 1975, and developments in DK itself. The 1960 congress, he asserted, marked the establishment of a "correct line" for the CPK, but since armed struggle was postponed for eight more years, and the party's leaders had to flee Phnom Penh in 1963, he found few benefits to mention that flowed from the party's line in terms of revolutionary practice. Benefits flowed after the anti-Sihanouk coup, to be sure, but Pol Pot failed to mention the most significant of them, Vietnamese military assistance. Similarly, Sihanouk's name was never mentioned.

In closing, he noted that "with complete confidence, we rely on the powerful revolutionary spirit, experience, and creative ingenuity of our people"—he failed to mention Chinese military aid. Optimistically, he predicted that Cambodia would soon have twenty million people ("Our aim is to increase the population as quickly as possible") and claimed that the average food intake was over 300 kilos (660 pounds) of rice per person per year. Many refugees later took issue with the latter statement, pointing out that by the middle of 1977, in much of the country and for the first time in Cambodian history, rice had virtually disappeared from the diet.

DK CLOSES DOWN

The DK-Beijing alliance, strengthened during Pol Pot's visit to China, was seen by the Vietnamese as a provocation, and in late 1977, they mounted a military offensive against Cambodia. Fourteen divisions were involved, and Vietnamese troops penetrated up to 32 kilometers (20 miles) into Cambodia in some areas. In the first week of 1978, after DK had broken off diplomatic relations with Vietnam, most of the Vietnamese troops went home, taking along thousands of Cambodian villagers as hostages. The Vietnamese soon began grooming some of these hostages as a government in exile; others were given military training. One of the exiles, a young DK regimental commander, Hun Sen, who had fled Cambodia in 1977, emerged as the premier of the People's Republic of Kampuchea (PRK) in the mid-1980s.

Pol Pot's response to the Vietnamese retreat was to claim a "total victory" while secretly purging military officers and CPK cadres in the eastern zone, where the Vietnamese penetration had been the deepest. These men and women were said to have "Cambodian bodies and Vietnamese minds." Several hundred of them were executed at Tuol Sleng; hundreds of others were executed on the spot. In the confusion, many DK soldiers from the eastern zone sought refuge in Vietnam—one of them, Heng Samrin, later became the chief of state of the PRK. In addition, thousands of people living in the east were forcibly transferred toward the west in early 1978, and local troops were massacred and replaced by troops from the southwest. The man in charge of the eastern zone, an ICP veteran named Sao Phim, committed suicide in June 1978 when summoned to Phnom Penh for "consultation," which he knew meant execution.[25]

At this time, the DK regime belatedly tried to open itself to the outside world and to improve its image with the Cambodian people; the fighting with Vietnam, the leaders reasoned, called for a united front strategy. Gestures included a general amnesty offered to the population, the establishment of a technical high school in Phnom Penh, welcoming visits from sympathetic journalists and foreign radicals, and establishing diplomatic relations with several non-Communist countries such as Burma and Malaysia. These actions had mixed results. For example, a Yugoslavian television crew visited DK in 1978, and the footage broadcast later in the year gave the outside world the first glimpse of life in DK, and of Pol Pot. One of the cameramen later told an Australian journalist that the only person the crew had seen smiling in Cambodia was Pol Pot, who had informed the crew of his visit to their country as a student in 1950. Other visitors, like the radical Swedish journalist Jan Myrdal, praised everything they saw. They were taken to see places the regime was proud of, and what they saw fitted their preconceptions. Most survivors of the regime, interviewed in the 1980s, remember 1978 as the harshest year of DK, when communal dining halls were introduced in many areas and rations fell below the starvation levels of 1977.

By this time also, Vietnamese attempts to reopen negotiations had failed, and both sides were building up their forces. Nearly a hundred thousand Vietnamese troops were massed along the Cambodian border by April 1978, just before Pol Pot's suppression of "enemies" in the eastern zone. Vietnam also signed a twenty-five-year treaty of friendship with the Soviet Union, to balance the threat from China, and in early December announced that a Kampuchean Front for National Salvation had been set up in "liberated Cambodian territory" to overthrow the Cambodian regime. In China, meanwhile, these Vietnamese actions were seen as provocative, and Deng Xiaoping referred to the Vietnamese at this time as "the hooligans of the East." Contingency plans were set in motion to attack Vietnam.[26]

Vietnam and DK were now embarked on a costly struggle that played into the hands of larger powers. These powers, in turn, were not prepared to take any risks. There is evidence, for example, that Pol Pot requested that the Chinese provide a force of "volunteers" to help DK combat Vietnam, but the request was turned down. DK would have to face the Vietnamese (and serve Chinese interests) on its own. The parallels between the last days of DK and the last days of Lon Nol's regime in 1975 are striking, and ironic.

In early December 1978, two American journalists and a Scottish Marxist academic, Malcolm Caldwell, visited Cambodia. The journalists, Elizabeth Becker and Richard Dudman, had worked in Cambodia in the early 1970s, and they were the first nonsocialist writers to visit DK. Caldwell, who had written sympathetically about the regime, was invited as a friend, but Becker and Dudman were thought by DK officials to be working for the CIA, and the movements of all three were closely monitored. Nonetheless, their lucid observations, published separately at the end of the year, provide a valuable record. On their last night in the country, December 22, Caldwell was killed in his hotel room by unknown assailants, perhaps connected with an anti–Pol Pot faction anxious to destabilize the regime.[27]

On Christmas Day 1978, Vietnamese forces, numbering over one hundred thousand, mounted a major offensive on several fronts. Because DK forces were crowded into the eastern and southwestern zones, Vietnamese attacks in the northeast encountered little resistance, and by the end of the year, several major roads to Phnom Penh were in Vietnamese hands. At this point, the Vietnamese altered their strategy, which had been to occupy the eastern half of the country, and decided to capture the capital itself.

224

Democratic Kampuchean killing ground near Phnom Penh, exhumed in 1979.
Photo by Kelvin Rowley.

The city, by then containing perhaps fifty thousand bureaucrats and factory workers, was abandoned on January 7, 1979. Up to the last, DK officials had confidently claimed victory. Pol Pot, like the U.S. ambassador in 1975, escaped at the last moment in a helicopter; other high officials and foreign diplomats left by train. They were followed several months later by the half-starved, poorly equipped remnants of their armed forces.

It was a humiliating end for the DK leaders and for their Utopian vision of Cambodia. The "revolutionary organization" never expressed regret for the appalling loss of life that had occurred since "liberation," and even after DK's demise, well into the 1990s, tens of thousands of Khmer, particularly young people, were still prepared to give their lives to the first organization that had given them power and self-respect. Some of these people stayed on in the ranks of the organization, forming the backbone of its guerrilla army in the 1980s. Moreover, once the purges had burnt themselves out, the leaders of the CPK (despite or perhaps because of the party's official dissolution in 1981) remained in place, and in command of the resistance, throughout the 1980s.

Nearly everyone else welcomed the Vietnamese invasion and accepted the puppet government swiftly put in place by the invaders as preferable to what had gone before. The new government called itself the People's Republic of Kampuchea (PRK) and was staffed at its upper levels by former CPK members who had defected to Vietnam in 1977–1978, as well as by some Khmer who had remained in exile in Vietnam throughout the DK period. Most Cambodians rejoiced at the disappearance of *a-Pot* ("the contemptible Pot"), as they now called the deposed prime minister. For nearly everyone, the DK era had been one of unmitigated suffering, violence, and confusion. With luck, in exile or in the PRK, most Cambodians now thought they could resume their prerevolutionary lives, which DK had held in such contempt.[28] The revolution had failed for the people who had been unwilling to change their points of view and ways of living to serve a supposedly higher cause. For them, what had happened in the 1970s made as little sense as an earthquake, a prairie fire, or a typhoon, and for most of them, the memories, damage, and effects of the DK era were to persist, like the memory of a natural disaster, for the remainder of their lives. For others, their brief period of empowerment, and their vision of Utopia, would make it difficult for them to resume their prerevolutionary careers.

CHAPTER 13

Cambodia Since 1979

Any attempt to make sense of Cambodia's history since 1979 suffers because the period is open-ended. The closing pages of this chapter, in other words, will coincide arbitrarily with the time when they were composed rather than with a crisis or a sequence of events that might separate the period from later history.

Another problem with analyzing this period in Cambodia stems from the narrow range of primary sources. For most of the period, the government in Phnom Penh—known until 1989 as the People's Republic of Kampuchea (PRK), later as the State of Cambodia (SOC), and since 1993 as the Kingdom of Cambodia—conducted its business in private. Debates among the leaders of the People's Revolutionary party of Kampuchea (PRPK) or among their Vietnamese advisers are not accessible; primary sources, in other words, consist largely of faits accomplis. In the 1990s, foreign media coverage of Cambodia expanded, but the process of decisionmaking in party circles, and in the entourage of Hun Sen, remained impenetrable to outsiders.

A third difficulty facing the historian stems from changes in the geographical definition of Cambodia itself. Although the SOC claims jurisdiction over the same territory as previous regimes, large tracts of the country were often controlled, at least at night, by resistance factions, much as they were during the civil war of 1970–1975 and the earlier conflict with France. In the 1980s over three hundred thousand Cambodian refugees, encamped since the early 1980s along the Thai-Cambodian border, provided recruits for the resistance. Three factions of the resistance—claiming to be loyal to Sihanouk, to a former prime minister named Son Sann, and to DK—were recognized as a coalition government in exile by the United Nations in 1982. These factions shared a desire to seize power in Phnom Penh and a distrust of the Vietnamese; they were also hostile to each other.

Despite these problems, it is easy to characterize the political history of the 1980s at least in general terms. Inside Cambodia, the decade witnessed a gradual decline of Vietnamese military and political influence on the one hand (particularly after 1987) and a corresponding increase in the autonomy of the Cambodian government on the other. These processes occurred in the context of continuing international isolation and civil war, and they accelerated after the withdrawal of the last Vietnamese military units from Cambodia in September 1989. Along the border, the history of the coalition can be seen in terms of the contradictions between the forces binding its components together and those that, under other circumstances, would have driven them apart.

Finally, Cambodia's foreign relations in 1979–1990 can be seen as a series of repeated attempts—sincere, misguided, or frankly mischievous—to find a diplomatic solution to the civil war, to establish some form of consensual, legitimate government in Phnom Penh, and to end Cambodia's isolation from the rest of the world.[1] These efforts culminated in the Paris Agreements of 1991, and the next nine years were marked by continued foreign interest and interference in Cambodian affairs. International interest waned at the end of the 1990s, and Cambodia found itself, for better or worse, a member of ASEAN and more or less on its own.

THE PRK: EARLY PHASES

In early 1979, for the first time since the 1950s, Cambodia was controlled by a foreign power. The situation was reminiscent of the 1830s insofar as the power was Vietnam, but closer parallels existed with the final years of the French protectorate, when the French took responsibility for Cambodia's defense, internal security, and foreign affairs, leaving less crucial areas (from their point of view) in Cambodian hands.[2]

Almost immediately after capturing Phnom Penh, the Vietnamese set up what purported to be an independent government in Cambodia, styling itself the People's Republic of Kampuchea (PRK). Its leading officials were DK military officers who had defected to Vietnam in 1978, Cambodians who had lived in Vietnam since the 1950s, and members of ethnic minorities untainted by service to the previous regime. Several figures in this original group—including Heng Samrin, Chea Sim, and Hun Sen—remained powerful through the 1980s, although Hun Sen gradually assumed more and more power on his own and, by the mid-1990s, was in command of the country.[3]

The new government promised to respect human rights, including freedom of opinion and association, but it treated political opponents severely, as all earlier regimes had done. No elections were held until 1981—and even those were not contested by opposing parties.

Barely a month after declaring its existence, the PRK signed a treaty of friendship and cooperation with Vietnam. This gesture, combined with the Vietnamese occupation and the severe hardships affecting all Cambodians, convinced many Cambodians that they would be better off outside the country and persuaded many who stayed behind that the Vietnamese planned to annex Cambodia, or at least dominate its politics for an indefinite period of time. During the first few months, the Vietnamese kept foreign observers away from Cambodia and denied their own military presence there.[4]

Vietnam's occupation of Cambodia and its alliance with the Soviet Union angered the Chinese, who launched a military attack on northern Vietnam in February 1979, with the tacit support of the United States. The campaign involved two hundred thousand Chinese troops and lasted for two weeks. Thousands of people were killed on both sides, and several Vietnamese cities along the border were laid to waste; but when the Chinese withdrew, supposedly after "teaching Vietnam a lesson," Vietnamese policies toward Cambodia (and Chinese policies, for that matter) were unchanged. The main effects of the attack were to encourage tens of thousands of Sino-Vietnamese to flee Vietnam and to strengthen the informal U.S.-Chinese alliance. Thailand's similar alliance with China, encouraged by the United States, was beneficial to the DK remnants filtering into Thailand and made the Vietnamese even more reluctant to withdraw from Cambodia. Like those of DK in 1978, Vietnam's leaders believed themselves surrounded by enemies.[5]

Nearly all Cambodians welcomed the Vietnamese at first, not because they preferred being invaded to being autonomous, but because the invasion signaled the end of DK. Almost at once, nearly everyone began moving. Throughout 1979 and the first few months of 1980, hundreds of thousands of Cambodians crisscrossed the country looking for relatives, returning to their homes, trading, or seeking refuge overseas. Although Vietnamese forces pursued DK armed units into the northwest, the civil authorities did nothing to prevent this less organized movement of people or the informal revival of trade. As the PRK struggled to its feet, many prerevolutionary institutions came back to life, including markets, Buddhism, and family farming. The PRK's laissez-faire policy did not extend to political activity, however; that was monopolized by the government and the People's Revolutionary party of Kampuchea (PRPK), a Communist grouping that shared its pre-1975 history with the discredited CPK.

Amid so much disorder, most of the 1979 rice crop went untended, and by the middle of the year a famine had broken out. Very few Cambodians stayed put long enough to plant the 1979–1980 rice crop, and when grain stored under the previous regime had been consumed, or appropriated by Vietnamese forces, hundreds of thousands of Khmer had little or nothing to eat. Famine conditions were exacerbated by a drought, and it was at this point that Cambodia gained attention in the West, where television audiences, already vaguely aware of the horrors perpetrated in DK, were shocked to see skeletal Khmers stumbling into Thailand or dying of starvation beside Cambodia's roads. The sufferings provoked a massive charitable response, but the delivery of food and medicine from foreign countries was often delayed by bureaucratic rivalries, by constraints imposed by Thailand and its allies, and to a lesser extent by the Vietnamese themselves, who understandably used some of the food and medicine to support their own hard-pressed military and administrative personnel.[6]

Conditions stabilized in 1980 when the rice harvest doubled in size. In rural areas, most Vietnamese forces withdrew from villages into garrisons, and local people were once again put in control of their own affairs. Rural society, however, was a shambles. Villages had been abandoned or torn down; tools, seed, and fertilizer were nonexistent; hundreds of thousands of people had emigrated or been killed; and in most areas the survivors suffered from malaria, shock, or malnutrition. So many men had died or disappeared in DK that in some districts, more than 60 percent of the families were headed by widows; thousands of widows, whose children had died, lived alone. In response to these conditions, as well as to collectivist ideas, the PRK instituted "solidarity groups" (*krom sammaki*), composed of several family groups, as collective units to cultivate the land. Private ownership was not recognized, but collectives and communes, so despised in DK, were not reintroduced. At the district and provincial levels, PRK officials endeavored to exert a degree of centralized control but made no effort to collect taxes or to conscript young men for military service. Schools reopened throughout Cambodia in 1979, and currency was reintroduced in 1980. By and large, if we ignore the regime's treatment of its political opponents, evidence from the time, combined with hindsight, tends to confirm Michael Vickery's 1983 assessment that "the policies of the PRK regime and its Vietnamese backers [were] humane, pragmatic and unoppressive."[7]

For most Cambodians, the reappearance of a certain amount of personal freedom, and the PRK's unrevolutionary caution, contrasted sharply with their experiences during the DK years. At the same time, however, they knew that the PRK owed its existence to a foreign invasion and that it depended on Vietnamese and Soviet-bloc support. Many high-ranking officials and regional cadres had served happily enough in DK, and some educated Cambodians sensed an unwholesome continuity between the successive socialist regimes. PRK officials, moreover, refused to distance themselves from Marxism-Leninism or one-party rule. Instead, they preferred to demonize the "genocidal Pol Pot–Ieng Sary clique," blaming the 1975–1979 catastrophes on individuals rather than on the extreme but recognizably socialist policies of the CPK. The two villains were tried in absentia in Phnom Penh in August 1979. No evidence was offered in their defense, and they were condemned to death. Soon afterward, the DK interrogation center at Tuol Sleng was inaugurated by the Vietnamese as a "genocidal museum." The use of the word "genocide," and comparisons of Pol Pot to Hitler (comparisons to Stalin or Romania's Ceaucescu would have been more fruitful), suggested that as far as the PRK was concerned, DK had had a fascist rather than a Communist government.[8]

OPPOSITION TO THE PRK

The PRK was unable to engender widespread trust among what remained of Cambodia's educated elite. Most of these men and women, after the trauma of DK, were not prepared to entrust Cambodia to foreigners or to endure more socialism. In 1979–1980, tens of thousands of them walked into exile in Thailand, eventually finding residence abroad or in the refugee camps that sprang up along the border. The loss of so many educated people, on top of the tens of thousands who had perished in DK, was a serious blow to the country.

By the end of 1979, the refugee camps sheltered several anti-Vietnamese resistance factions. One of the largest of these, led by former prime minister Son Sann, sought foreign support to remove the Vietnamese occupation forces and to reimpose prerevolutionary institutions—except for Sihanouk, whom Son Sann had come to distrust. This faction drew many supporters from Cambodians living overseas, nostalgic for the past, and from recent arrivals at the border, enraged by the destruction of the 1970s and by what they saw as open-ended Vietnamese control. Son Sann was unable to establish an effective military force, however, and obtained little material support from Vietnam's principal antagonists—China, Thailand, and the United States. In military terms, these powers preferred DK.

In the meantime, DK's leadership in exile remained complacent and unchanged. The CPK continued its shadowy existence, and a DK delegation held onto Cambodia's seat at the United Nations. It was clear that China and the United States were willing to support this state of affairs as punishment for Vietnam's invading Cambodia, standing up to China, and defeating the United States. They were joined by Singapore and Thailand, both of which pursued anti-Communist, pro-Chinese policies. Supporting DK was a small price for these powers to pay to keep their more important alliances intact. In 1979 and 1980, the Thai military gov-

Democratic Kampuchean soldiers, Thai frontier, 1980. Photo by James Gerrand.

ernment fed, clothed, and restored to health several thousand DK soldiers who straggled across the border, and these soldiers also received arms, ammunition, and military supplies from China, ferried through Thai ports. By 1982, these remnants had become an effective, well-equipped military force. Their dependents, who were treated as political refugees, were fed and housed by United Nations agencies. Because of the PRK's pariah status, however, UN development agencies were prohibited from operating in Cambodia itself.[9] The PRK, for its part, had to be content with diplomatic recognition—and economic aid—from India, a few small anti-American states, and what remained of the Soviet bloc.

In 1980 and 1981, more and more information emerged about the horrors of DK. Evidence from the Pol Pot–Ieng Sary trial was confirmed and amplified by refugee testimony, written memoirs, and confessions found in the archives at Tuol Sleng. DK spokesmen, for their part, admitted only a few "mistakes" and blamed the Vietnamese for executing over two million Khmer. Although Vietnamese anti-DK propaganda was often heavy-handed and inaccurate, even cautious estimates of DK-related deaths caused by overwork, starvation, mistreated diseases, purges, and executions came close to two million Cambodians, or one in five.[10]

Faced with the task of improving DK's image while continuing to punish Vietnam, China and other foreign powers began pressuring Prince Sihanouk, who was living in exile in Beijing, to return to political life. The prince was reluctant to do so except on his own terms. He did not want to renew his alliance with DK; he feared the Vietnamese; and he knew that Son Sann's faction opposed his coming back into power. At the same time, it was difficult for him to resist Chinese pressure and to remain inactive, for he still identified himself with the destiny of his country.

Maneuvers to form a coalition involving Sihanouk, Son Sann, and the DK occupied much of 1981 and 1982, and the PRK and its Vietnamese advisers worked hard, without much success, to improve their image overseas. In June 1981, a constitution modeled to a large extent on Vietnam's was introduced in the PRK. The document bestowed a range of human rights on Cambodia's people but also enjoined them to carry out the "state's political line." This document was followed by the establishment of several new ministries, the emergence from concealment of the PRPK, and elections for a National Assembly, which approved the constitution. The policies of the PRK, if not dictated by Vietnam, certainly fitted closely with Vietnamese priorities, although positions of responsibility, as the government expanded, increasingly fell to men and women without any socialist credentials. Little by little, the PRK became a responsive, functional government, whose military, police, and foreign affairs were subject to Vietnamese control. Over one hundred thousand Vietnamese troops remained on Cambodian soil, and rumors circulated that hundreds of thousands of Vietnamese emigrants, rather than the sixty thousand admitted by the PRK, had settled in the country. Rumors led resistance figures to suggest that the Cambodian "race" was being drowned by the Vietnamese, but evidence to support this claim was scrappy and ambiguous.[11]

Developments in the PRK combined with DK's squalid reputation added urgency to efforts to form a coalition government. In early 1981, Sihanouk met with Khieu Samphan, representing DK, to discuss how a coalition might be formed. Son Sann was reluctant to join the talks, but in September 1981, the three factions concealed their differences long enough to announce that they would form a coalition. Soon afterward, as evidence of its good faith, the CPK's Central Committee announced the dissolution of the party and that faction's conversion to capitalist ideas. Ieng Thirith remarked that DK had "changed completely" and had, among other things, "restored religious beliefs." Her husband, Ieng Sary, added that Cambodia would not be subjected to socialism for "many generations." The "dissolution" of the CPK was a farcical gesture that convinced no one, but it did enable the Coalition Government of Democratic Kampuchea (CGDK) to claim it was a capitalist formation. All the party's high officials, including Pol Pot and Ieng Sary, remained in place in the CGDK, and no non-Communists were given responsible positions. Despite their conversion to free-market economics, DK-controlled camps remained much stricter than camps controlled by other factions. Those inside them were not allowed to leave, military commanders attended annual "study sessions" as they had done in the 1970s, and military aid continued to flow to the faction from China.[12]

The CGDK was unveiled in the middle of 1982, and to display its territorial base, some of its followers and armed units were moved a few miles across the border into Cambodia. DK representatives assumed control of the CGDK's foreign affairs (the only viable portfolio for a government in exile) and stayed on at the United Nations, and its military forces were the best trained, most numerous, and most active of the three factions. Sihanouk remained under Chinese control, and Son Sann lost even his limited freedom of maneuver. For the next ten years, the three factions continued to distrust each other, and their spokesmen made no promises about what Cambodians might expect if the coalition came to power. Militarily, the coalition's forces consisted of forty thousand men and women, more than half mobilized by DK. The Son Sann faction, known as the Khmer People's National Liberation Front (KPNLF), was racked with factional squabbles, and Sihanouk's troops numbered only about five thousand. The CGDK attracted little support inside Cambodia, although from time to time, one faction or another, using information provided by troops making incursions into the country, reported that farmers thought the PRK was corrupt and were angry at the Vietnamese.

In 1983–1985, Vietnamese and PRK troops, in a series of sharp offensives, drove the coalition's forces and their dependents back into Thailand and destroyed their encampments. The PRK then conscripted tens of thousands of workers to lay mines along the border and to block the approaches from Thailand into Cambodia. Thousands died of disease while this work was going on. In the meantime, the Vietnamese had raised and trained a PRK army, thirty thousand strong, to defend the country when they eventually withdrew. As in the past, conscription was often at random, and privileged Cambodians, particularly the children of PRPK cadres, often seemed immune from it. They were favored for scholarships to study overseas, however, and by 1988, some five thousand Cambodians had undergone technical or academic training abroad, principally in the Soviet Union and Eastern Europe.[13]

For the rest of the 1980s, a military stalemate prevailed, but following the withdrawal of Vietnamese troops in 1989, coalition forces consolidated their hold on bases inside the country, and DK troops captured the gem-producing area near Pailin, slightly south and west of Battambang. In early 1991, DK artillery shelled the Battambang market, killing seventeen civilians. Their forces were unable or unwilling to follow this action up, and the resistance never controlled any major Cambodian towns.[14]

In the early 1990s, nonetheless, DK forces still posed a serious menace to the government in Phnom Penh. By 1990, DK troops had occupied the sparsely populated mountainous regions of Cambodia's northwest and southwest and threatened the deep-water port of Kompong Som, the provincial capital of Kampot, and Cambodia's second-largest city, Battambang. At night, these forces were able to raid villages and plant antipersonnel mines along paths and in rice fields, which sooner or later killed unwary people or blew off their arms or legs. Eighty or ninety casualties caused by these mines came into Cambodia's hospitals and clinics every week, and presumably, hundreds of other victims were untreated or had been killed. The warfare waged allegedly against the Vietnamese, like Lon Nol's war in the 1970s, was now killing only Khmer.

THE VIETNAMESE WITHDRAWAL

Several factors encouraged the Vietnamese to withdraw the last of their troops—some twenty-six thousand men—from Cambodia in September 1989. One was the growing self-sufficiency of the PRK, which earlier in the year had renamed itself the State of Cambodia (SOC). Another reason was that Soviet aid, and aid from the Soviet bloc, were sharply reduced in 1989 following crises in the USSR and Eastern Europe. Given these conditions, the Vietnamese occupation had become too expensive to maintain. A third factor was the example provided by the USSR itself, which had withdrawn its troops from Afghanistan.

Prior to the withdrawal, but clearly associated with it, the Cambodian government announced a series of reforms that were to be widely popular, especially in Phnom Penh. The reforms, which were partly intended to improve the PRK's image overseas, included revising the national anthem, changing the flag, amending the constitution to make Buddhism Cambodia's state religion, and abolishing the statute that had limited monkhood to middle-aged Khmer. New laws also allowed farmers to pass title to land on to their children and householders elsewhere to buy and sell real estate. The death penalty was also abolished, in response to criticism of Cambodia's human rights record. Although the PRPK remained in charge of Cambodia's political life, free markets and black markets flourished, and collectivism was dead.

The new laws regarding Buddhism led to heavy expenditures on Buddhist temples and memorial constructions, with much of the cost paid for by émigré Khmers. Lifting the restrictions on real estate produced a mini-boom in speculation, restoration, and rebuilding in Cambodia as families squatting in once-prosperous villas, with government permission, endeavored to put them on the growing rental market, inspired by rumors of peace and the hopes of renewed foreign aid that would presumably follow. During the boom, visitors to Phnom Penh noted the reemergence of a small elite, perceptible because of the cars they drove, the villas they lived in, and their often obnoxious behavior in restaurants and bars. The level of corruption in the SOC did not reach that in effect under Sihanouk or Lon Nol, probably because there was so much less money circulating in the SOC and a less effective entrepreneurial class. A quiet extraction of privileges had characterized PRPK cadres and high-ranking government officials over the years, and many of them had been able to shoulder their way into business enterprises, including clandestine trading operations between Thailand and the northwest; others were assured comfortable houses, cars, and perquisites. In 1990, at a time when hospitals and schools were woefully short of equipment, a lavish PRPK political school was built on the outskirts of Phnom Penh, only to be abandoned by the party two years later.

Outside Phnom Penh, the picture that emerges from this period—and from the rest of the 1990s—was of a rural population that was poorer, less healthy, and more poorly served than at any time since the 1920s. The rate of infant mortality was one of the highest in the world; so was the birthrate. Malaria and other fevers were endemic; so was malnutrition. By the late 1990s, the incidence of HIV-AIDS in Cambodia was the highest in per capita terms in Southeast Asia. The frequency of mental illness,

Traffic in downtown Phnom Penh, 1998. Photo by Stephen Randall.

traceable in part to the traumas of the 1970s and in part to the absence of appropriate medication, was high but impossible to calculate. Schools and hospitals were poorly equipped, and education, school attendance, and medical care lagged far behind prerevolutionary levels. Conditions in most of rural Cambodia were comparable to those in some of the poorer African nations.

Political changes in Eastern Europe in 1989–1990 and the economic boom elsewhere in Southeast Asia, which lasted until 1997, gave the SOC and successor regimes in Cambodia some freedom of maneuver but also threatened their existence. Changes in Europe cut off the aid coming from Communist powers, and the boom encouraged entrepreneurs to seek short-term returns from construction and the sale of raw materials. The boom also produced a "black economy" in much of the country. Timber, gems, dried fish, and other products were exported illicitly to Thailand and Vietnam, earning profits for the entrepreneurs, and in some cases for SOC officials, but little or no revenue for the SOC itself. The frontier zones of the country, such as Koh Kong in the southwest and Ratanakiri in the northeast, where fortunes were made overnight, were comparable to the nineteenth-century "wild West" in the United States. In Battambang, trade sprang up between producers inside Cambodia and countrymen strung out along the border. In all areas, raw materials, especially timber, were being removed at a breakneck pace, with unpredictable but presumably disastrous environmental effects.

In sharp contrast to this black economy, the SOC itself was almost without funds. Oil to fuel electric generators, cars, and thousands of small motorcycles—to say nothing of the war machine—was in short supply. On the other hand, the resistance factions, whose subsistence needs were met by the United Nations and foreign aid and who had few bureaucrats to pay and no services to provide, enjoyed the advantages of all guerrilla movements. In the aftermath of the Vietnamese withdrawal, all the factions concentrated on winning Cambodians' hearts and minds. The non-Communist factions did so by inaugurating model villages in the areas under their control; the DK faction worked harder at indoctrination and "gathering forces" among the poorest of the poor.

After a decade of confronting economic, military, and political problems, the SOC failed to solve most of them. To some extent, the ruling party and its Vietnamese mentors were to blame. Attempts by some officials to loosen the country's alliance with Vietnam had been thwarted by hard-liners in the PRPK. In June 1990, the SOC imprisoned a handful of these officials without trial, accusing them of counterrevolutionary activities. Such gestures and other human rights abuses (trivial when compared to DK's record) alienated foreign supporters of the SOC and for a time endangered the ongoing negotiations—spearheaded by France and Indonesia, among others—to bring an end to Cambodia's civil war. On the SOC side, the negotiations were ably handled by Cambodia's young, articulate prime minister, Hun Sen, whose activities were closely scrutinized by his mentors in the PRPK, including Heng Samrin and Chea Sim. The influence of these figures eventually diminished, except in party circles, and Hun Sen soon enjoyed a free rein in running the country.

Many of Cambodia's problems in the early 1990s were imposed from outside the country. Perhaps this has always been the case. At the end of the 1980s most observers agreed that without drastic changes in the foreign support the SOC and the government in exile were receiving, their problems would remain unsolved. In July 1990, however, U.S. Secretary of State James Baker signaled the possibility of change when he announced that the United States would cease backing the CGDK's representative at the United Nations. Baker made this move partly to deflect criticism in the United States about the country's support of the resistance, seen by many people as tantamount to condoning the excesses of Pol Pot. The new policy was also related to a lessening of the Cold War tensions that had governed U.S. policies toward the region since the 1950s.

Baker's move encouraged China to diminish its patronage of DK, and many observers soon became optimistic about the possibility of a diplo-

matic breakthrough regarding Cambodia. Some hoped that the breakthrough would involve the massive intervention of the United Nations,
which might establish a caretaker regime pending national elections.

THE UNTAC PERIOD AND AFTER

These hopes were fulfilled by decisions made at the international conference on Cambodia that convened in Paris in October 1991. Under the
terms of agreements reached in Paris, a temporary government was established in Phnom Penh comprising representatives of the incumbent
regime and delegates from the factions that had been opposing it since
1981. The four factions joined to form a Supreme National Council (SNC)
presided over by Prince Sihanouk, who returned briefly to Cambodia in
November 1991 after twelve years of exile. The SNC's decisions were to
be monitored by UN representatives on the spot.

The Paris agreements coincided with the end of the Cold War, in which
Cambodia had participated in one way or another since gaining its independence from France. The agreements withdrew the patronage of larger
powers from the contending Cambodian factions, reinserting the factions, in theory, into a nonaligned Cambodia where they would be free to
compete for political advantage.

Vietnam, to be sure, had all but ended its patronage of the incumbent
regime in Phnom Penh. In Paris, the United States and its allies ended
their support for the so-called non-Communist resistance, while China
withdrew its patronage from the Khmer Rouge. Pol Pot's faction reen-
tered Cambodian life not as a component of a government in exile with
powerful friends but as an indigenous, discredited political group. The
change in status as well as its squalid history was to prove fatal to the
movement. For several more years, however, the Khmer Rouge continued to enjoy clandestine support from military factions in Bangkok. Its
demise was not a foregone conclusion.

The arrangements envisaged in Paris were to be monitored in Cambodia by UN personnel, pending disarmament and cantonment of the factional troops, the repatriation of over three hundred thousand refugees
from camps in Thailand, and national elections for a constituent assembly. To achieve these ambitious goals, the United Nations established a
short-term, multinational protectorate over Cambodia. During 1992,
some thirteen thousand soldiers and over seven thousand civilians, including detachments of police, took up residence in the country. Recruitment and deployment were delayed by sluggish UN administrative procedures. The United Nations Transitional Authority in Cambodia
(UNTAC) arrived too late and moved too slowly to gain the respect it
needed from the Cambodian factions.[15] In May 1992, the Khmer Rouge

expanded the territory under their control, refused to be monitored by the UN, and refused to disarm their forces. For these actions, they were neither punished nor chastised. The Phnom Penh regime, in response, also refused to disarm and refused to allow the United Nations to oversee its daily operations or its powerful national police, even though such oversight was a feature of the Paris agreements.

UNTAC embarked on its Utopian, multifaceted mission sluggishly and with foreboding. Its mandate was ambiguous, its time was limited, and most of its personnel knew nothing about Cambodia. By the time the mission ended in October 1993, UNTAC had spent over US$2 billion, making it the most costly operation to date in UN history. Much of the money had gone into inflated salaries. The extravagance and insensitivity of many UN personnel were widely criticized. Phnom Penh grew more crowded and more prosperous, but the rural economy declined, the country's infrastructure remained abysmal, and security was marred by a spate of politically motivated killings. Khmer Rouge forces, claiming that Vietnam remained secretly in control of the country, massacred over a hundred Vietnamese civilians in the UNTAC era. The Phnom Penh regime's police, in turn, targeted activists from other political parties. In 1992–1993, over two hundred unarmed people were victims of politically motivated assassinations. None of the offenders were ever arrested or brought to trial.

On a more positive note, the Cambodian media enjoyed unaccustomed freedom in the UNTAC period. Local human rights organizations, unthinkable in earlier times, also flourished. These organizations received Sihanouk's support and backing from the human rights component of UNTAC, which trained hundreds of Khmer human rights workers and investigated hundreds of complaints.

Other positive developments in this period, from UNTAC's point of view, were the peaceful repatriation of over three hundred thousand Cambodian refugees from Thailand and the national elections themselves, which took place on schedule in July 1993, following a massive voter-registration campaign conducted by UN workers. Contrary to many people's fears, the elections, although boycotted by the Khmer Rouge, were peaceful. Over 90 percent of the registered voters—at least four million people—went to the polls in Cambodia's freest, fairest, and most secret election since the colonial era. The message that they delivered was ambiguous. A royalist party, using the acronym FUNCINPEC, was led by Prince Sihanouk's eldest son, Norodom Rannaridh, and won seven more seats for a constituent assembly than did the party formed by the incumbent government to contest the elections. An anti-Communist, anti-Vietnamese party won ten of the remaining eleven seats. For the first time in their history, a majority of Cambodians had voted against an armed, incumbent government. Unlike most Cambodian voters in the past, they had courageously rejected the status quo. What they were voting *for*, aside from peace, was much less clear.

The SOC refused to accept defeat. By the end of 1993, a fragile compromise was reached whereby FUNCINPEC and the regime's party, the Cambodian People's party (CPP), formed a coalition government with two prime ministers—Prince Rannaridh and Hun Sen. Cabinet posts were divided among the three parties represented in the assembly. Day-to-day political power in the form of provincial governorships, police, defense, and the national police, to say nothing of the entire civil service, remained in the hands of the CPP. Over the next few years the royalist party lost its voice in decisionmaking and its derisory freedom of maneuver.

The constitution drafted in 1993 restored the monarchy and placed Sihanouk on the throne he had abandoned in 1955 but gave him very little power. Becoming a king again pleased the seventy-one-year-old monarch and his wife, who were eager to erase a personally humiliating period of Cambodian history and to reestablish themselves as Cambodia's legitimate rulers. Because the king had no access to armed force, he was unwilling or unable to influence events. Throughout the rest of the 1990s, pleading poor health, he spent long periods of each year outside the country.

The losers in 1993, aside from the people who had voted against the government, were the Khmer Rouge. After halfhearted efforts by Sihanouk to bring the movement into the Cambodian "family," it was outlawed in 1994, and thousands of its followers defected to the government. The Khmer Rouge leaders remained unrepentant, in hiding, and in good health. In the mid-1990s the Khmer Rouge still had over five thousand men and women under arms. Military efforts to dislodge them were inept. The Khmer Rouge forces controlled perhaps a fifth of Cambodia's territory, mostly in the inhospitable north and northwest, where they concluded profitable deals with Thai entrepreneurs to exploit timber and gem deposits and sallied forth from time to time to attack government outposts. Their entrepreneurial activities had disastrous ecological effects. As Thai government support for the Khmer Rouge faded in 1994–1995, however, and as defections from the movement increased, the Khmer Rouge became more violent, massacring timber workers, kidnapping and killing half a dozen foreigners, and mounting sporadic military attacks. Scattered evidence at the time, confirmed later, suggested that the leadership had fragmented after the elections, and that the movement was split between those willing to effect a modus vivendi with the Phnom Penh authorities and those wanting to rekindle a full-scale revolutionary conflict.

Pol Pot is denounced as a murderer of his countrymen at a
trial in the Cambodian jungle in July 1997. Copyright 1997
Nate Thayer, and Tom Keller & Associates LLC.

THE END OF THE KHMER ROUGE

In August 1996, Ieng Sary, the former DK foreign minister, defected to
Phnom Penh. He received a royal pardon and was allowed to remain,
with thousands of adherents, in the relatively prosperous northwestern
enclave of Pailin. Over the next few months, hundreds of Khmer Rouge
soldiers from other factions were absorbed into the national army. Efforts
in 1996–1997 to bring the Khmer Rouge leaders to trial for crimes against
humanity, despite or perhaps because of foreign pressure, came to nothing.

During this time, the remnants of the Khmer Rouge came apart. The effective leader was Ta Mok, a brutal military commander. Pol Pot, suffer-

ing from poor health, was sidelined. In June 1997, in an effort to regain control, the former dictator ordered the assassination of Son Sen, a high-ranking cadre and close associate whom he accused of treason. The assassination, which also involved the killing of Son Sen's children and grandchildren, shocked middle-ranking Khmer Rouge cadres, who assumed they might be next. Fearing arrest, Pol Pot fled his headquarters, but was captured a few days later and put on trial in a bizarre proceeding filmed by the American journalist Nate Thayer, whom the Khmer Rouge invited to attend. Pol Pot was given no defense and was not allowed to speak. He was accused only of killing Son Sen and trying to restart the Cambodian civil war, not of committing the crimes he had perpetrated during his years in power. Subjected to the winners' justice that had sent hundreds of thousands of Cambodians to their deaths in the DK era, Pol Pot was condemned to life imprisonment and led away, under guard, to his two-room house. Ten months later, he died in bed.

THE *COUP DE FORCE* OF 1997

In the meantime, the Phnom Penh regime had encountered serious difficulties. Tensions between the CPP and FUNCINPEC, which had heated up throughout 1996, were exacerbated by Hun Sen's acceptance of Khmer Rouge defectors into the National Army and, in effect, into his entourage. Generals loyal to FUNCINPEC sought, without success, to negotiate with hard-line Khmer Rouge elements, led by Ta Mok; but their efforts angered Hun Sen who, in early July 1997, launched a preemptive *coup de force* against FUNCINPEC. In the surprise attack, over a hundred FUNCINPEC supporters were killed, many of them executed after being arrested and tortured. CPP casualties were minimal. Widespread looting accompanied the coup.

Although the violence of the coup was not surprising, its timing, from an international perspective, was inept. Several donor nations, appalled by the event, suspended aid. Foreign investment dried up. Cambodia's membership in ASEAN was delayed. After consolidating his power in a manner that had seemed appropriate, Hun Sen found himself being treated as a pariah. Donor nations urged him to sponsor "free and fair" elections in 1998, as scheduled, for the National Assembly.

Neither the CPP nor FUNCINPEC wanted to repeat the experience of 1993. The CPP feared another defeat, while FUNCINPEC and smaller parties feared a renewal of CPP-sponsored violence. Nonetheless, as negotiations for elections crept forward, many observers believed that the CPP would gain an overwhelming victory.

The runup to the election seemed to confirm these suspicions. Opposition parties were given no access to the electronic media and were not allowed to campaign in the countryside. Party workers were harassed. Several of them died under suspicious circumstances. None of the perpetrators of violence in the coup was brought to justice. Prince Rannaridh returned to the country in March 1998, less than four months before the elections, and campaigned with surprising vigor. So did Sam Rainsy, who headed another opposition party and courageously attacked the CPP, drawing widespread support.

The elections themselves, probably because Hun Sen was able to control the nation's security system so effectively, were free and fair, in the view of both local and foreign electoral observers. Parties opposed to the CPP garnered 60 percent of the votes, but as they were unwilling to form an alliance, arrangements were made between FUNCINPEC and the CPP to govern the country in a genuine coalition. By the end of 1998, the new government had gotten off to a relatively good start. In April 1999, Cambodia was welcomed into ASEAN, the last country in the region to be admitted.

In many respects, conditions in Cambodia at the end of the 1990s were worse than ever. The country suffered from the highest infant mortality rates in Southeast Asia. The educational system, starved of funds, was functioning so poorly that illiteracy was higher than it had been in the 1960s. Violent crimes, rare in prerevolutionary times, were now frequent, and sexually transmitted diseases, including HIV-AIDS, had reached epidemic proportions. Unrestrained logging was having disastrous ecological effects, including increased erosion, changes in rainfall patterns, and laterization. And because of the economic slump elsewhere in the region, foreign investment was at a standstill.

Yet the end of the twentieth century also saw Cambodia at peace. For the first time in decades, the Cambodian government was not dependent on a predominant foreign patron. Instead, Cambodia was participating as fully as it could in the affairs of Southeast Asia, from which it had been placed at arm's length since independence. Despite Hun Sen's authoritarian style, the print media in Cambodia were relatively unrestrained, and human rights organizations—both foreign and domestic—were free to operate in the country. The 1998 elections revealed the enduring sophistication of the voting public, and as the bloated, underpaid army demobilized, there were signs that the government might make a serious effort to direct its revenues and attention toward the social sector neglected for so long. The future of the monarchy remained uncertain, but Cambodia was no longer subjected to the one-party rule that had been such a feature of its earlier history. At the millennium, there were perhaps as many grounds for optimism (of a cautious kind) as for pessimism. The grounds for pessimism, unfortunately, were encouraged by the repetitive patterns of Cambodian history depicted in this book.

CONCLUSION

Cambodian history since World War II, and probably for a much longer period, can be characterized in part as a chronic failure of contending groups of patrons and their clients to compromise, cooperate, or share power. These hegemonic tendencies, familiar in other Southeast Asian countries, have deep roots in Cambodia's past.

In the 1950s and 1960s, Prince Sihanouk's narcissistic style encouraged his enemies, when they replaced him, to be equally high-handed, uncompromising, and self-absorbed. Alternative traditions of pluralism or a peaceful transfer of power did not exist. After 1970, Sihanouk, Lon Nol, and Pol Pot sought absolute power for themselves. Under Pol Pot, this took the form of a national vendetta. The Leninist politics he favored and the purges he carried out—far worse than anything else in Cambodia's recent history—can be seen in part as reflecting time-honored ideas of political behavior. Under the Vietnamese protectorate, Cambodian politicians were more cautious (as Sihanouk had been when the French were in control), but in the post-UNTAC era, those in power reverted to form and became thin-skinned, vengeful, and abrupt.

In S-21, Pol Pot's secret prison for counterrevolutionaries in Phnom Penh, the phrase "doing politics" was used by interrogators to describe the ritual of indoctrination, questioning, and torture. To many Cambodians before and since, "politics" has been synonymous with exploitation alternating with neglect. The 1993 elections, for many Khmer, were an attempt to liberate themselves from the politics that had dominated the country for so long.

Although it is fruitful to study Cambodian political history from a Cambodian perspective, the country's location, topography, and demographic weakness have meant that its fate for over two hundred years has often been entangled with Thailand and Vietnam. These countries, in turn, because of their size, have consistently tried to patronize or absorb their neighbor. Having Vietnam next door in the 1820s and 1830s led to a Vietnamese protectorate; in the 1860s, the French loosened what had become Thai control over the Cambodian court and effectively removed Cambodia from Southeast Asia by making it part of "Indochina," which is to say a surrogate of Vietnam. In the 1940s and 1950s, Cambodian resistance to the French was dominated by the Vietnamese and served their interests. Later still, the fighting in Vietnam, exacerbated by U.S. intervention, reduced Cambodia's capacity to remain neutral or to control its frontier with Vietnam. The loss of sovereignty embittered many Khmer. Sihanouk knew that his country would be swept into the fighting and could never emerge a victor. Unlike Lon Nol or Pol Pot, the prince had no illusions about Cambodia's military strength.

Before 1979, it was difficult for any Cambodian government to con-template an alliance with Vietnam. The uneasy friendship cobbled to-gether by Sihanouk and the Vietnamese Communists favored the Viet-namese and collapsed as soon as Sihanouk was overthrown. Spurred on by their resentments, Lon Nol and Pol Pot conducted vicious and doomed campaigns against Vietnam. To put an end to this, Vietnam in-vaded the country and established a protectorate over Cambodia dis-guised as an alliance between sovereign states. For all intents and pur-poses, "Indochina" was reborn. Imitating France, Vietnam embarked on a "civilizing mission."

Relations with Thailand have been somewhat different. Despite, or perhaps because of, cultural affinities, relations have never been marked by a sincere effort on the part of Bangkok regimes to treat Cambodia as a sovereign nation. In the 1830s, in World War II, and again in the 1950s and 1960s, the Thai worked to subvert what they perceived to be hostile governments in Phnom Penh. They also were indifferent to Cambodian sovereignty. Faced with the imposition of a Vietnamese protectorate over Cambodia in the 1980s, Thailand dusted off its nineteenth-century re-sponse and gave support to dissident Cambodian factions, including the Khmer Rouge. In the mid-1990s, licenses for Thai timber companies to exploit Cambodian resources were still being granted by the Thai min-istry of the interior. However, as the Bangkok government, following China's lead, backed away from its patronage of Pol Pot, there were signs that relations between the two countries were beginning to mature.

The Paris agreements, UNTAC, the elections of 1993 and 1998, and membership in ASEAN all thrust Cambodia into the world of Southeast Asia from which it had been isolated, by accident or design, since the eighteenth century. No longer an isolated player, a protectorate, or a com-ponent of Indochina, Cambodia became part of a region about which its people knew little and for whose rapacity they were unprepared. Becom-ing part of the region, however, offered ordinary Cambodians some pro-tection against what they perceived, accurately or not, as the perennial ambitions of its neighbors.

Cambodia's past greatness, as reconstructed and presented to the Cam-bodians by the French, is another aspect of its history that has weighed heavily on its leaders and enhanced their self-confidence. In the 1950s and 1960s Sihanouk allowed himself to be compared favorably to Jayavarman VII and other Angkorean kings. Similarly, Lon Nol claimed that he had a divine mission to rescue Cambodia from "unbelievers" (thmil). Pol Pot, believing that his forces had single-handedly defeated the United States, was similarly misled. In his marathon 1977 speech, he remarked: "If our people can build Angkor, they are capable of anything."

The combination of personalistic, domineering political habits, proximity to Vietnam, and unrealistic notions of innate greatness has blended into Cambodia's volatile form of nationalism. Sihanouk considered himself a world statesman of major proportions, and Cambodia a model for other developing countries. Under Lon Nol and Pol Pot, Cambodians hurled their poorly equipped armies against Vietnam, expecting Cambodian "superiority" to overcome material obstacles. All three leaders drew on Cambodian xenophobia to maintain themselves in power and in part to preserve the Cambodian "race."

Intense and widely shared conservatism, perhaps, and the tempestuous changes in the country since 1970 have made many Cambodians reluctant to resist or even consider changing the social arrangements and political leadership that have given them so much suffering and injustice. Traditions of deference and hegemony enshrined in these arrangements form much of the substance of Cambodia's "two thousand years of history" and provide insights into the country's politics and culture that are less apt when applied to Thailand or Vietnam.

Much of Cambodia's uniqueness appears to spring from deep continuities or refusals, rather than from calculated or prudent responses to the rapid and largely destructive influences of modern times. Pol Pot's revolution failed in part because so many Cambodians, finding its premises painful and irrelevant, were unwilling and unable to carry it out. Similarly, a decade of Vietnamese occupation and experiments with a less demanding form of socialism seems to have left few lasting marks. In the 1993 elections, millions of Cambodians voted for change but chose to look backward rather than ahead. In more recent times, as the country has opened up, Cambodians seem to have been less willing than outside investors have been to join the scramble for "development" that has mesmerized their Southeast Asian neighbors. In the process, a few Cambodians have become rich, many are poorer than ever, and foreign investors have made enormous profits by depleting Cambodia's natural resources.

The so-called timelessness of Cambodia, made up to a large extent of its own perennial and self-absorbed terms of reference, has been part of its appeal to visitors and scholars for many years. In the Pol Pot period, this conservatism was a source of enormous strength, and in the end it was the conservatism that, at enormous human cost, defeated the Pol Pot regime. But as the country opens up, willingly or not, to the wider world, and without the promise of anyone's sustained protection, it is uncertain whether its inward-looking, family-oriented conservatism, so helpful in surviving the impact of the past and the incursions of foreign powers and ideas, will be of much help if Cambodia hopes to remain intact and flourish as a twenty-first-century state.

Notes

CHAPTER 1

1. Adhémard Leclère, *Histoire du Cambodge* (Paris, 1914). See also George Coedes's critical review in *Bulletin de l'Ecole Française d'Extrême Orient (BEFEO)*, Vol. 14 (1914):47–54.

2. These subsequent surveys include Martin Herz, *A Short History of Cambodia* (New York, 1958), and A. Dauphin Meunier, *Histoire du Cambodge* (Paris, 1968). David P. Chandler, *The Land and People of Cambodia* (New York, 1991), is an even briefer account, geared to secondary schools. See also Ian Mabbett and David Chandler, *The Khmers* (Oxford, 1995).

3. See Lucien Hanks, "Merit and Power in the Thai Social Order," *American Anthropologist*, Vol. 64 (1962):1247–1261; David P. Chandler, "The Tragedy of Cambodian History," *Pacific Affairs (PA)*, Vol. 52, No. 3 (Fall 1979):410–419; and Chandler, "The Tragedy of Cambodian History Revisited," in Chandler, *Facing the Cambodian Past: Selected Essays, 1971–1994* (Sydney and Chiangmai, 1996), pp. 310–325.

4. See Centre d'Études et de Recherches Marxistes (comp.), *Sur le "mode de production asiatique"* (Paris, 1969). For a more recent discussion of the Asiatic Mode of Production (AMP), see Michael Vickery, *Society, Economics, and Politics in Pre-Angkor Cambodia: The 7th–8th Centuries* (Tokyo, 1998), ch. 1.

5. See David Joel Steinberg et al. (eds.), *In Search of Southeast Asia* (Honolulu, 1987), pp. 177–244, for a discussion of the notion of "frameworks for nations."

6. On Cambodian demography, see J. Migozzi, *Cambodge: Faits et problèmes de population* (Paris, 1973).

7. See David Chandler, *Voices from S-21: Terror and History in Pol Pot's Secret Prison* (Berkeley and Los Angeles, 1999).

8. For a discussion of this problem, see David P. Chandler, "Seeing Red: Perceptions of Cambodian History in Democratic Kampuchea," in David P. Chandler and Ben Kiernan (eds.), *Revolution and Its Aftermath in Kampuchea: Eight Essays* (New Haven, 1983). See also Claude Jacques's perceptive article, "Nouvelles orientations pour l'étude de l'histoire du pays khmer," *Asie du sudest et monde insulindien*, Vol. 14 (1982):39–57. Under the subsequent regime, historical continuities were reestablished. In this connection, see Viviane Frings, "Rewriting Cambodian History to "Adapt" It to a New Political Context: The KPRP's Historiography," *Modern Asian Studies* (1997):807–846.

CHAPTER 2

1. C. Mourer, "The Prehistoric Industry of Laang Spean," *Archaeology and Physical Anthropology of Oceanea*, Vol. 5, No. 2 (1970):128–146; updated in Mourer, "Contribution à l'étude de la préhistoire du Cambodge," *BEFEO*, Vol. 80 (1993):143–187. See also J. P. Carbonnel, "Recent Data on the Cambodian Neolithic," in R. B. Smith and W. Watson (eds.), *Early Southeast Asia* (Oxford, 1979), pp. 223–226; Donn Bayard, "The Roots of Indo-Chinese Civilization: Recent Developments in the Pre-history of Southeast Asia," *PA*, Vol. 53, No. 1 (Spring 1980):89–114; Charles Higham, *The Archaeology of Mainland Southeast Asia* (Cambridge, 1989), especially pp. 239–320; and Maud Girard-Geslan, "Cambodia from Its Beginnings," in Helen Ibbitson Jessup and Thierry Zephir (eds.), *Sculpture of Angkor and Ancient Cambodia* (New York, 1997), pp. 3–12.

2. For a recent study of this phenomenon, see Yashushi Kojo and Sytha Preng, "A Preliminary Investigation of a Circular Earthwork at Krek, Southeastern Cambodia," *Anthropological Science*, Vol. 106 (1998):229–244. I am grateful to Professor Miriam Stark for directing me to this intriguing paper.

3. See I. W. Mabbett, "The Indianization of Southeast Asia," *Journal of Southeast Asian Studies (JSEAS)*, Vol. 8, No. 1 (March 1977):1–14, and Vol. 8, No. 2 (September 1977):143–161; Paul Mus, *India Seen from the East*, trans. by I. W. Mabbett and D. P. Chandler (Clayton, Australia, 1975); and Michael Vickery, *Society, Economics, and Politics in Pre-Angkor Cambodia: The 7th–8th Centuries* (Tokyo, 1998), pp. 51–58, which emphasizes social factors. See also Humansi Prabha Ray, "Early Maritime Contacts Between South and Southeast Asia," *JSEAS*, Vol. 20, No. 1 (March 1989):42–54. For linguistic evidence, see Judith M. Jacob, "Sanskrit Loanwords in Pre-Angkor Khmer," *Mon-Khmer Studies*, Vol. 4 (Honolulu, 1977), pp. 151–168.

4. G. Coedes, *The Making of Southeast Asia* (London, 1966), pp. 54–55. Questions that will probably never be resolved are when, where, and how ancient south Indian Calukya-Pallava script arrived in Cambodia or was adapted to written Khmer. Is it possible that missionaries of some sort were involved? An interesting parallel would be to the romanization of Vietnamese, which was carried out by European missionaries in the seventeenth century.

5. See Paul Mus, *L'Angle de l'Asie*, ed. S. Thion (Paris, 1977), especially pp. 109–121.

6. I. W. Mabbett, "*Varnas* in Angkor and the Indian Caste System," *Journal of Asian Studies (JAS)*, Vol. 36, No. 3 (May 1977):429–442.

7. L. Finot, "Sur quelques traditions indochinoises," *Bulletin de la Commission Archéologique de l'Indochine* (1911), pp. 20–37. See also Evéline Porée-Maspero, "Nouvelle étude sur le nagi Soma," *Journal Asiatique (JA)*, Vol. 238 (1955):257–267, and R. Gaudes, "Kaundinya Preah Thaong and the 'Nagi Soma': Some Aspects of a Cambodian Legend," *Asian Folklore*, Vol. 52 (1993):333–358.

8. K. Bhattacharya, *Les Religions brahmaniques dans l'ancien Cambodge* (Paris, 1961), p. 11n.

9. See Miriam T. Stark, "The Transition to History in the Mekong Delta: A View from Cambodia," *International Journal of Historical Archaeology*, Vol. 2, No. 3 (1998):175–203, which summarizes the ongoing excavations and multidisciplinary research being carried out at Angkor Borei. Her article and the research it

describes make it clear that Angkor Borei was an important urban center before, during, and after the "Funan" period, which is not to say, of course, that it was the "capital" of "Funan." Vickery, *Society, Economics, and Politics*, p. 19, confirms her suggestion.

10. Louis Malleret, *L'Archéologie du delta du Mekong*, 4 vols. (Paris, 1959–1963), especially Vols. 1 and 2. See also G. Coedes, "Fouilles en Cochinchine," *Artibus Asiae (AA)*, Vol. 10 (1947):190–199, and Girard-Geslan, "Cambodia from Its Beginnings," notes 6 and 36, where the author points to ongoing Vietnamese research at Oc-Eo and other sites. This research has not yet been translated from Vietnamese or synthesized by Western scholarship.

11. See O. W. Wolters, *Early Indonesian Commerce: A Study of the Origins of Srivijaya* (Ithaca, N.Y., 1967), and Wang Gungwu, "The Nanhai Trade: A Study of the Early History of Chinese Trade in the South China Sea," *Journal of the Malay Branch of the Royal Asiatic Society (JMBRAS)*, Vol. 31, No. 2 (June 1958):31–45. If we read "Vietnam" for "China," it seems as if more or less the current land area of Cambodia—with the addition of southern Laos—was involved.

12. Cited by G. Coedes, *The Indianization of Southeast Asia* (Honolulu, 1968), p. 61. The capital of "Funan," however, was probably Angkor Borei. (See Note 9 above.)

13. Paul Wheatley, "The Mount of the Immortals: A Note on Tamil Cultural Influence in Fifth Century Indo-China," *Oriens Extremus*, Vol. 21, No. 1 (June 1974):97–109.

14. C. Jacques, "'Funan,' 'Zhenla': The Reality Concealed by These Chinese Views of Indo-China," in Smith and Watson, *Early Southeast Asia*, pp. 371–379. See also O. W. Wolters, "Northwestern Cambodia in the 7th Century," *Bulletin of the School of Oriental and African Studies (BSOAS)*, Vol. 37, No. 2 (1974):355–384.

15. Cited by L. P. Briggs, *The Ancient Khmer Empire* (Philadelphia, 1951), p. 29.

16. Ibid., p. 28.

17. See P. Paris, "Anciens canaux réconnus sur photographes aeriennes dans les provinces de Takeo et Chaudoc," *BEFEO*, Vol. 31 (1931):221–224, and Paris, "Anciens canaux réconnus sur photographes aeriennes dans les provinces de Takeo, Chaudoc et Rach Gia," *BEFEO*, Vol. 41 (1941):365–370.

18. J.D.M. Derrett, "Rajadharma," *JAS*, Vol. 35, No. 4 (August 1976):605. The full quotation reads: "The agricultural population is fascinated with power, which is essential to its very life. The soil cannot be tilled without *protection* and *rain*." On the subject of prowess, see O. W. Wolters, "A 'Hindu' Man of Prowess," in Wolters, *History, Culture and Region in Southeast Asian Perspectives* (Ithaca, N.Y., 1999), pp. 226–228. See also Vickery, *Society, Economics, and Politics*, pp. 190–196.

19. K. Bhattacharya, "La Secte des Pacupata dans l'ancien Cambodge," *JA*, Vol. 243 (1955):479–487. These arguments have been overtaken to a large extent by those in Vickery, *Society, Economics, and Politics*, pp. 321–417, which draw on and expand the arguments in Vickery, "Some Remarks on Early State Formation in Cambodia," in David G. Marr and A. C. Milner (eds.), *Southeast Asia in the 9th to 14th Centuries* (Singapore, 1986), pp. 95–115, and Vickery, "Studying the State in Ancient Cambodia," paper presented to the International Conference on Khmer Studies, Phnom Penh, 1996.

20. O. W. Wolters, "Khmer 'Hinduism' in the Seventh Century," in Smith and Watson, *Early Southeast Asia*, pp. 427–442.

21. See David P. Chandler, "Royally Sponsored Human Sacrifices in Nineteenth Century Cambodia: The Cult of *Me Sa* (Uma Mahisasuramardini) at Ba Phnom," *Journal of the Siam Society (JSS)*, Vol. 62, No. 2 (1974):207–221.

22. See Evéline Porée-Maspero, *Etude sur les rites agraires des cambodgiens*, 3 vols. (Paris, 1962–1969).

23. See Institut Bouddhique (comp.), *Prachum ruong preng phak ti 8* [Collected folktales, volume 8] (Phnom Penh, 1971), which is concerned with *nak ta*, and my review in *JSS*, Vol. 61, No. 2 (July 1973):219–221. See also Ang Choulean, "Le Sol et l'ancêtre: L'Amorphe et l'anthromorphe," *JA*, Vol. 283 (1995):213–238, and Alain Forest, *La Culte des génies protecteurs au Cambodge* (Paris, 1993), which includes some valuable translations.

24. W. Solheim, "Regional Reports: Cambodia, Laos and Vietnam," *Asian Perspectives (AP)*, Vol. 3 (1960):25.

25. Mus, *India Seen from the East*, pp. 13ff.

26. C. Jacques, "Etudes d'épigraphie cambodgienne IX: La Stèle du Baphuon," *BEFEO*, Vol. 63 (1976):351–368, and K. 441, Sambor Prei Kuk inscription, *Inscriptions du Cambodge (IC)*, Vol. 4, p. 14. ("K." preceding a number places the inscription in the inventory of the Ecole Française d'Extrême Orient.) See also David J. Welch, "Archaeology of Northeast Thailand in Relation to the Pre-Khmer and Khmer Historical Records," *International Journal of Historical Archaeology*, Vol. 2, No. 3 (1998):205–234. I am grateful to Louise Cort for drawing this paper to my attention.

27. See P. N. Jenner, *A Chronological Inventory of the Inscriptions of Cambodia* (Honolulu, 1980). The earliest datable inscription found in Cambodia, K. 600, was discovered at the site of Angkor Borei by French scholars in 1935.

28. J. Jacob, "Pre-Angkor Cambodia," in Smith and Watson, *Early Southeast Asia*, pp. 406–426. For a stimulating discussion of state formation in early Southeast Asia from a Marxist perspective, see Jonathan Friedman, *System, Structure, and Contradiction in the Evolution of "Asiatic" Social Formations* (Ann Arbor, Mich., 1975), especially pp. 373ff. See also Michael Vickery, "Some Remarks on Early State Formation in Cambodia," in Marr and Milner (eds.), *Southeast Asia in the 9th to 14th Centuries*, pp. 95–116, which draws on Friedman's work, and Claude Jacques, *Angkor* (Paris, 1990), pp. 35ff. And for a nuanced discussion that cautions against use of the word "slave" to deal with pre-Angkorean Cambodia, see Vickery, *Society, Economics, and Politics*, pp. 225ff.

29. See Briggs, *Ancient Khmer Empire*, pp. 38–57, for a summary of the evidence. For more recent discussions, see Michael Vickery, "Where and What Was Chenla?" in François Bizot (ed.), *Recherches nouvelles sur le Cambodge* (Paris, 1994), pp. 197–212, and Vickery, *Society, Economics, and Politics*, pp. 33–35.

30. Jacques, "'Funan,' 'Zhenla,'" p. 376. But cf., in the same volume, Ronald C. Ng, "The Geographical Habitat of Historical Settlement in Mainland Southeast Asia," p. 271, which mentions "the rise and fall of . . . important civilizations and centers of power, such as Funan, Chenla, Champa and finally Angkor."

31. Friedman, *System, Structure*, pp. 341–344. This discussion also draws on Michael Vickery, "Angkor and the Asiatic Mode of Production" (unpublished seminar paper, Monash University, November 27, 1981).

CHAPTER 3

1. See B. P. Groslier, *Angkor et le Cambodge au XVIe siècle* (Paris, 1958).

2. L. P. Briggs, *The Ancient Khmer Empire* (Philadelphia, 1952), and G. Coedes, *The Indianized States of Southeast Asia* (Honolulu, 1968). For syntheses of more recent research, see Claude Jacques, *Angkor* (Paris, 1990), and Bruno Dagens, *Angkor: La Forêt de pierre* (Paris, 1989).

3. G. Coedes, "L'Avenir des études khmères," *Bulletin de la Société des Etudes Indochinoises (BSEI)*, Vol. 40 (1965):205–213. The rest of this chapter, like all scholarship on Cambodia, owes a great deal to Coedes's work and that of his colleagues and pupils at the Ecole Française d'Extrême Orient.

4. J. Boisselier, *Le Cambodge* (Paris, 1966), synthesizes the work of previous scholars.

5. G. Coedes and P. Dupont, "L'Inscription de Sdok Kak Thom," *BEFEO*, Vol. 43 (1942–1943):57–134. See also I. W. Mabbett, "Devaraja," *JSEAH*, Vol. 10, No. 2 (1969):202–223; I. W. Mabbett and David Chandler, *The Khmers* (Oxford, 1995), pp. 88–90; and Nidhi Aeusrivognse, "The *Devaraja* Cult and Khmer Kingship at Angkor," in K. R. Hall and J. K. Whitmore (eds.), *Explorations in Early Southeast Asian History* (Ann Arbor, Mich., 1976), pp. 107–148.

6. K. 956, from Wat Samrong, *IC*, Vol. 7, pp. 128–129.

7. C. Jacques, "La Carrière de Jayavarman II," *BEFEO*, Vol. 59 (1972):194–220.

8. Ibid.; see also O. W. Wolters, "Jayavarman II's Military Power: The Territorial Foundation of the Angkor Empire," *Journal of the Royal Asiatic Society (JRAS)*, (1973):21–30. There is an extended discussion of Jayavarman II's career in Michael Vickery, *Society, Economics, and Politics in Pre-Angkor Cambodia* (Tokyo, 1997), pp. 393–408.

9. K. 989, stele from Prasat Ben, *IC*, Vol. 7, pp. 164–189.

10. Hermann Kulke, *The Devaraja Cult*, trans. I. W. Mabbett (Ithaca, N.Y., 1978).

11. G. Coedes, "Les Capitales de Jayavarman II," *BEFEO*, Vol. 28 (1928):116.

12. P. Stern, "Diversité et rhythme des fondations royales khmères," *BEFEO*, Vol. 44, No. 2 (1951):649–685. See also Hermann Kulke, "The Early and Imperial Kingdom in Southeast Asian History," in David Marr and A. C. Milner (eds.), *Southeast Asia in the 9th to 14th Centuries* (Singapore, 1986), pp. 1–22.

13. A. Bergaigne, *Les Inscriptions sanscrites du Cambodge* (Paris, 1882), p. 127.

14. For a discussion of this style, see G. de Coral Remusat, "Influences javanaises dans l'art de Roluoh," *JA*, Vol. 223 (1933):190–192. See also Michael Vickery, "The Khmer Inscriptions of Roluos (Preah Ko and Lolei): Documents from a Transitional Period in Cambodian History," *Seksa Khmer* (new series, 1999):47–92. At p. 84, Vickery notes: "These inscriptions indicate that the polity centered at Roluos was dominant over a wide area of northern Cambodia extending from the present northwestern border to Kratie and including Kompong Cham and Kompong Thom. On the other hand, there is no sign of any authority over the heartland of pre-Angkor Cambodia, what is now the center and the south."

15. K. 713, stele from Preah Ko, *IC*, Vol. 1, pp. 18–31. On the notion of "three worlds" shared by Hinduism and Buddhism, see G. Coedes and C. Archaimbault, *Les Trois mondes* (Paris, 1973).

16. K. 809, from Prasat Kandol Dom, *IC*, Vol. 1, p. 43.

17. Cited in S. Sahai, *Institutions politiques et organisation administrative du Cambodge* (Paris, 1970), p. 42n. The small eighth-century temple of Ak Yum, in the

Angkor region, may have been a rudimentary temple-mountain. See Vickery, *Society, Economics, and Politics*, p. 391.

18. See Eleanor Mannika, *Angkor Wat: Time, Space and Kingship* (Honolulu, 1996), and R. Stencel and Eleanor Moron, "Astronomy and Cosmology at Angkor Wat," *Science*, Vol. 193 (July 23, 1978):281–287.

19. See G. Coedes, "A la recherche du Yasodharasrama," *BEFEO*, Vol. 32 (1932):84–112; and Bergaigne, *Inscriptions sanscrites*, pp. 166–211.

20. On the importance of the northeast, see P. Paris, "L'Importance rituelle du nord-est et ses applications en Indochine," *BEFEO*, Vol. 41 (1941):301–333.

21. See B. P. Groslier, *Inscriptions du Bayon* (Paris, 1973), p. 156, and David P. Chandler, "Maps for the Ancestors: Sacralized Topography and Echoes of Angkor in Two Cambodian Texts," *JSS*, Vol. 64, No. 2 (July 1976):170–187, especially note 28.

22. See V. Goloubew, "Le Phnom Bakheng et la ville de Yasovarman," *BEFEO*, Vol. 33 (1933):319–344, and V. Goloubew, "Nouvelles recherches autour de Phnom Bakheng," *BEFEO*, Vol. 34 (1934):576–600.

23. J. Filliozat, "Le Symbolisme du monument du Phnom Bakheng," *BEFEO*, Vol. 44, No. 2 (1954):527–554.

24. See John Black, *The Lofty Sanctuary of Khao Prah Vihar* (Bangkok, 1976).

25. Bergaigne, *Inscriptions sanscrites*, p. 322. For similar passages, see pp. 227, 376.

26. See G. Coedes, "Le Véritable fondateur du culte de la royauté divine au Cambodge," in H. B. Sarkar (ed.), *R. C. Majumdar Felicitation Volume* (Calcutta, 1970), pp. 56–66. See also Sahai, *Institutions*, p. 46n.

27. Kulke, *Devaraja Cult*, pp. 33ff.

28. G. Coedes, "Les Inscriptions de Bat Chum," *JA*, Vol. 10, No. 8 (1908): 213–254. See also Michael Freeman, *A Guide to Khmer Temples in Thailand and Laos* (Bangkok, 1996) pp. 58–60.

29. K. 806, Pre Rup stele, *IC*, Vol. 1, pp. 73–142.

30. See L. Finot and V. Goloubew, *Le Temple d'Içvarapura* (Paris, 1926).

31. K. 111, stele from Wat Sithor, *IC*, Vol. 6, p. 196, where Senart's comment is cited by G. Coedes.

32. "L'Inscription de Toul Komnap Ta Kin (K. 125)," *BEFEO*, Vol. 28 (1928): 140–144.

33. Michael Vickery, "The Reign of Suryavarman I and Royal Factionalism at Angkor," *JSEAS*, Vol. 16, No. 2 (1985):226–244. On the notion of the Asiatic mode of production as related to Angkor, which Vickery discussed in detail, see L. Sedov, "La Société angkorienne et le problème du mode de production asiatique," in Centre d'Études et de Recherches Marxistes (comp.), *Sur le "mode de production asiatique"* (Paris, 1969), pp. 327–344.

34. M. De Coral Remusat, "La Date de Takev," *BEFEO*, Vol. 34 (1934):425.

35. G. Coedes, "Le Serment des fonctionnaires de Suryavarman I," *BEFEO*, Vol. 13, No. 6 (1913):11–17. For a similar oath sworn by Cambodian officials in the nineteenth and twentieth centuries, see Chandler, "Maps for the Ancestors," passim.

36. H. de Mestrier du Bourg, "La Première moitié du XIe siècle au Cambodge," *JA*, Vol. 258 (1970):281–314.

37. Kenneth Hall, "Eleventh Century Commercial Development in Angkor and Champa," *JSEAS*, Vol. 10, No. 2 (September 1979):420–434, and Hall, "Khmer Commercial Development and Foreign Contacts Under Suryavarman I," *Journal of Economic and Social History of the Orient (JESHO)*, Vol. 18, No. 3 (1975):318–336. On the question of trade in early Southeast Asia, see Karl L. Hutterer (ed.), *Economic Exchange and Social Interaction in Southeast Asia: Perspectives from Prehistory, History and Ethnography* (Ann Arbor, Mich., 1977), especially the chapter by Brian Foster, "Trade, Social Conflict, and Social Integration: Rethinking Some Old Ideas on Exchange," pp. 3–22. See also Claude Jacques, "Sources on Economic Activities in Khmer and Cham Lands," in Marr and Milner, *Southeast Asia in the 9th to 14th Centuries*, pp. 327–334.

38. A. Barth, *Inscriptions sanscrites du Cambodge* (Paris, 1885), p. 139.

39. Paul Mus, "Cultes indiens et indigènes à Champa," *BEFEO*, Vol. 33 (1933): 367–450.

40. I. W. Mabbett, "Kingship at Angkor," *JSS*, Vol. 66, No. 2 (July 1978):1–58. See also Mabbett and Chandler, *The Khmers*, pp. 34–106.

41. I. W. Mabbett, "Some Remarks on the Present State of Knowledge About Slavery at Angkor," in Anthony Reid (ed.), *Slavery, Bondage, and Dependency in Southeast Asia* (St. Lucia, Australia, 1983); Y. Bongert, "Note sur l'esclavage en droit khmer ancien," in *Etudes d'histoire du droit privé offertes à Paul Pettiot* (Paris, 1959), pp. 27–44; and A. Chakravarti, "Sources of Slavery in Ancient Cambodia," in D. C. Sircar (ed.), *Social Life in Ancient India* (Calcutta, 1971), pp. 121–142. See also C. Jacques, "A propos de l'esclavage dans l'ancien Cambodge," in B. P. Lafont (ed.), *L'Asie du sud-est continentale* (Paris, 1976), Vol. 1, pp. 71–76.

42. I. W. Mabbett, "*Varnas* in Angkor and the Indian Caste System," *JAS*, Vol. 36, No. 3 (May 1977):429–442.

43. Institut Bouddhique, Phnom Penh, Commission des Moeurs et Coutumes Cambodgiennes (CMCC), Archive number 94.004. The disappearance of this important archive in the Khmer Rouge period was a serious blow, although some portions of the archive, collected before 1950, have survived on microfilm.

44. L. Finot, "L'Inscription de Ban Theat (K. 364)," *BEFEO*, Vol. 12 (1912):1–27, stanzas 33–34.

45. See Mannika, *Angkor Wat*.

46. For a summary of this debate, see G. Coedes, *Pour mieux comprendre Angkor* (Paris, 1947), pp. 68–84.

47. Eleanor Moron, "Configuration of Time and Space at Angkor Wat," *Studies in Indo-Asian Art and Culture*, Vol. 5 (1977):217–267. These findings are amplified in Mannika, *Angkor Wat*.

48. See Stencel and Moron, "Astronomy and Cosmology," pp. 281–287, and Mannika, *Angkor Wat*, pp. 42–44.

49. Groslier, *Inscriptions du Bayon*, p. 141.

50. Briggs, *Ancient Khmer Empire*, p. 206.

51. For a review of the literature, see B. P. Groslier, "La Cité hydraulique angkorienne. Exploitation ou surexploitation du sol?" *BEFEO*, Vol. 66 (1979): 161–202. See also Groslier, "Agriculture et religion dans l'empire angkorien," *Etudes rurales*, Nos. 53–56 (January–December 1974):95–117. For a contrary argument advanced by a hydraulic engineer, see W. J. Van Liere, "Traditional Water

Management in the Lower Mekong Basin," *World Archaeology*, Vol. 11, No. 3 (Fall 1980):265–280. Van Liere suggested that the artificial lakes at Angkor had no distributive function but served merely as adjuncts to the metaphysical worldview of Angkorean kings. The farming of the shores of the Tonle Sap when the lake receded, however, was quite advanced and may have been able to support the sizable populations needed to build the temples and serve in them. A perceptive essay that builds on Van Liere's arguments is Robert Acker, "New Geographical Tests of the Hydraulic Thesis at Angkor," *Southeast Asia Research*, Vol. 6, No. 1 (March 1998):5–47. See also François Grunewald, "A propos de l'agriculture dans le Cambodge medieval," *Asie du Sud-Est et Monde Insulindien*, Vol. 13 (1982): 23–38.

52. Groslier, "La Cité hydraulique angkorienne." See also Rhoads Murphey, "The Ruin of Ancient Ceylon," *JAS*, Vol. 16, No. 1 (February 1957):181–200.

53. Michael Coe, "The Khmer Settlement Pattern: A Possible Analogy with That of the Maya," *American Antiquity*, Vol. 22 (1957):409–410, and Coe, "Social Typology and Tropical Forest Civilizations," *Comparative Studies in Society and History (CSSH)*, Vol. 4 (1961–1962):65–85.

54. For discussions of the Asiatic Mode of Production (AMP) and the extent to which it might apply to pre-Angkorean Cambodia, see Vickery, *Society, Economics, and Politics*, pp. 7–16, 311–312. See also Timothy Brook (ed.), *The Asiatic Mode of Production in China* (Armonk, N.Y., 1989), and Stephen P. Dunn, *The Fall and Rise of the Asiatic Mode of Production* (London, 1982).

CHAPTER 4

1. G. Coedes, *Pour mieux comprendre Angkor* (Paris, 1947), pp. 176–210.

2. B. P. Groslier, *Inscriptions du Bayon* (Paris, 1973), p. 141.

3. This statue was discovered in 1958. See G. Coedes, "Le Portrait dans l'art khmer," *AA*, Vol. 7, No. 3 (1960):179–188.

4. See J. Boisselier, "Réflexions sur l'art du Jayavarman VII," *BSEI*, Vol. 27, No. 3 (1952):261–273; Paul Mus, "Angkor at the Time of Jayavarman VII," *Indian Arts and Letters*, Vol. 11 (1937):65–75; and Mus, "Angkor vu du Japon," *France Asie (FA)*, Nos. 175–176 (1962):521–538. Groslier, *Inscriptions du Bayon*, p. 118, makes the point that Jayavarman VII, unlike some of his predecessors, restored no temples dedicated by earlier kings. Intriguingly, Jayavarman may have been converted to Buddhism while he was in Champa, where Mahayana Buddhism was widespread in the twelfth century; see Ian Mabbett, "Buddhism in Champa," in David Marr and A. C. Milner (eds.), *Southeast Asia in the 9th to 14th Centuries* (Singapore, 1986), p. 304.

5. See Mus, "Angkor at the Time of Jayavarman VII"; Mus, "Angkor vu du Japon"; and Boisselier, "Réflexions."

6. G. Maspero, *Le Royaume de Champa* (Paris, 1928), p. 164.

7. Ibid.

8. K. 485, stele from Phimeanakas, *IC*, Vol. 2, p. 171.

9. Ibid., p. 175.

10. Coedes, "Le Portrait." (Groslier, *Inscriptions du Bayon*, p. 194, however, claims that Coedes's inventory of portrait statues is incomplete.) See also Son

Soubert, "Head of Jayavarman VII," in Helen Ibbetson Jessup and Thierry Zephir (eds.), *Sculpture of Angkor and Ancient Cambodia: Millennium of Glory* (New York, 1997), pp. 300–301.

11. L. Finot, "L'Inscription sanscrite de Say-Fong," *BEFEO*, Vol. 3, No. 2 (1903):18–33. See also G. Coedes, "Les Hôpitaux de Jayavarman VII," *BEFEO*, Vol. 40 (1940):344–347. The translation here, amending that of Louis Finot, was kindly provided by Claude Jacques (personal communication). See also Jacques, *Angkor* (Paris, 1990), pp. 156–157.

12. Boisselier, "Réflexions," p. 263.

13. P. Stern, *Les Monuments khmers du style de Bayon et Jayavarman VII* (Paris, 1965), passim. See also J. Auboyer, "Aspects de l'art bouddhique au pays khmer au temps de Jayavarman VII," in W. Watson (ed.), *Mahayanist Art After A.D. 900* (London, 1977), pp. 66–74, and H. W. Woodward, Jr., *Studies in the Art of Central Siam, 950–1350 A.D.* (Ann Arbor, Mich., 1975).

14. K. 273, Ta Prohm inscription, *BEFEO*, Vol. 6, No. 2 (1906):44–81.

15. G. Coedes, "Les Gîtes d'étape à la fin du XIIIe siècle," *BEFEO*, Vol. 40 (1940):347–349.

16. See G. Coedes, "Le Stèle de Preah Khan," *BEFEO*, Vol. 41 (1941):256–301. The passage quoted appears on p. 287.

17. Groslier, *Inscriptions du Bayon*, p. 167.

18. This passage derives in large part from arguments advanced by Hiram W. Woodward, Jr., in private communications.

19. See Ta Prohm inscription.

20. See L. Finot and V. Goloubew, "Le Symbolisme de Nak Pean," *BEFEO*, Vol. 23 (1923):401–405, and V. Goloubew, "Le Cheval Balaha," *BEFEO*, Vol. 27 (1927):223–238.

21. J. Boisselier, "Pouvoir royal et symbolisme architectural: Neak Pean et son importance pour la royauté angkorienne," *AA*, Vol. 21 (1970):91–107.

22. J. Boisselier, "Notes sur l'art du bronze dans l'ancien Cambodge," *AA*, Vol. 29 (1967):275–350.

23. See G. Groslier, *A l'ombre d'Angkor* (Paris, 1916), pp. 148–182, and Groslier, "Etude sur le temps passé à la construction d'un grand temple khmer (Banteay Chhmar)," *BEFEO*, Vol. 35 (1935):159–176.

24. See Jacques Dumarçay, *Le Bayon, histoire architectural du temple* (Paris, 1973), especially pp. 57–64. For an interesting explanation of changes in the iconography of the Bayon, see Hiram W. Woodward, Jr., "Tantric Buddhism at Angkor Thom," *Ars Orientalis*, Vol. 12 (1981):57–68. See also J. Boisselier, "The Meaning of Angkor Thom," in Jessup and Zephir, *Sculpture of Angkor and Ancient Cambodia*, pp. 117–121, and Claude Jacques, "Les Derniers siècles d'Angkor," *Comptes Rendus de l'Académie des Inscriptions et Belles-Lettres* (in press). I am grateful to M. Jacques for sending me a typescript of this important paper.

25. K. 287, stele from Prasat Chrung, *IC*, Vol. 4, p. 250.

26. See Jean Boisselier and David Snellgrove (eds.), *The Image of the Buddha* (Paris, 1978), p. 410.

27. Hiram W. Woodward, personal communication.

28. For a detailed discussion of this religious shift, see G. Coedes, "Documents sur l'histoire politique et religieuse du Laos occidental," *BEFEO*, Vol. 25

(1925):1–202. See also N. A. Jayawickrama (trans.), *The Sheaf of Garlands of the Epochs of the Conqueror* (London, 1968), and A. Leclère, *Le Bouddhisme au Cambodge* (Paris, 1989), pp. 1–34.

29. L. P. Briggs, *The Ancient Khmer Empire* (Philadelphia, 1952), pp. 242 and 259.

30. P. Pelliot (ed.), *Mémoires sur les coutumes du Cambodge de Tcheou Ta Kuan* (Paris, 1951). For an English translation of the Pelliot text, see Chou ta Kuan [Zhou Daguan], *The Customs of Cambodia* (Bangkok, 1987).

31. K. 287, stele from Prasat Chrung, *IC*, Vol. 4, p. 208.

32. Jan Myrdal and Gun Kessle, *Angkor: An Essay on Art and Imperialism* (New York, 1970), p. 140.

33. A. Thompson, "Changing Perspectives: Cambodia After Angkor," in Jessup and Zephir, *Sculpture of Angkor and Ancient Cambodia*, pp. 22–32 at 23.

34. For a summary of the evidence, see David P. Chandler, "Folk Memories of Angkor in Nineteenth Century Cambodia: The Legend of the Leper King," *JSS*, Vol. 67, No. 1 (January 1979):54–62. Following Jacques, I now think it more likely that leprosy was popularly attributed to Jayavarman VIII, the controversial Hindu king who reigned from 1243 to 1295, just before Zhou Daguan's visit. Jayavarman VIII desecrated the Buddhist monuments in Angkor Thom and destroyed or damaged many of the inscriptions of his two predecessors. His animosity toward Indravarman II may explain the absence of inscriptions praising that king. See Jacques, "Les Derniers siècles d'Angkor."

35. G. Coedes, "Une période critique dans l'Asie du Sud Est: Le XIIIe siècle," *BSEI*, Vol. 33 (1958):387–400.

36. Pelliot, *Mémoires*, pp. 411–420.

37. Interestingly, although Cambodian classical literature makes almost no mention of slaves, one of the most popular folktale cycles is concerned with the triumphs of a wily, unscrupulous slave, Tmenh Chey, who outwits everyone he meets, including the emperor of China. See Pierre Bitard (trans.), *La Merveilleuse histoire de Thmenh Chey l'astucieux* (Saigon, 1956). Tmenh Chey is also prominent in Thai folklore.

38. M. C. Ricklefs, "Land and Law in the Epigraphy of Tenth Century Cambodia," *JAS*, Vol. 26, No. 3 (May 1967):411–420.

39. L. Finot and V. Goloubew, *Le Temple d'Içvarapura* (Paris, 1926), p. 83.

40. L. Finot, "Temple de Mangalatha à Angkor Thom," *BEFEO*, Vol. 25 (1925):393–406; C. Jacques, "Les Derniers siècles d'Angkor"; and Jacques, "A propos de modifications dans quelques temples d'Angkor et leur signification pour l'histoire khmère," in Y. Manguin (ed.), *Southeast Asian Archaeology 1994* (Hull, U.K., 1997), pp. 195–205.

CHAPTER 5

1. O. W. Wolters, "The Khmer King at Basan," *Asia Major*, Vol. 12, No. 1 (1966):86. On Chinese relations, see Wang Gungwu, "China and Southeast Asia 1402–1424," in his *Community and Nation* (Singapore, 1981), pp. 58–80. And for a vigorous rebuttal of the notion of "decline" at Angkor, see Claude Jacques, "Les Derniers siècles d'Angkor," *Comptes Rendus de l'Académie des Inscriptions et Belles Lettres* (in press). Jacques suggests that it is likely that the site at Angkor was an

urban conglomeration at least until the mid-sixteenth century, and that the royal palace may even have been occupied for much of this time by figures claiming to be Cambodian kings. These men, of course, have disappeared from the largely fictional chronicles composed much later for this period.

2. Michael Vickery, "The 2/k 125 Fragment: A Lost Chronicle of Ayuthaya," *JSS*, Vol. 65, No. 1 (January 1977):1–80. See also Vickery, *Cambodia After Angkor: The Chronicular Evidence for the Fourteenth to Sixteenth Centuries* (Ann Arbor, Mich., 1977), pp. 500ff., and A. Thompson, "Changing Perspectives: Cambodia After Angkor," in Helen Ibbetson Jessup and Thierry Zephir (eds.), *Sculpture of Angkor and Ancient Cambodia: Millennium of Glory* (New York, 1997), passim.

3. See Note 1 above.

4. G. Coedes, "La Fondation du Phnom Penh," *BEFEO*, Vol. 13, No. 3 (1913): 6–11.

5. See M. M. Gullick, *Indigenous Political Systems of Western Malaya* (London, 1958), especially pp. 125–143.

6. Vickery, "The 2/k 125 Fragment," pp. 60–62.

7. See B. P. Groslier, *Le Cambodge au XVIe siècle* (Paris, 1958), pp. 142–144.

8. This and the quotation in the preceding paragraph are taken from C. R. Boxer (ed.), *South China in the Sixteenth Century* (London, 1953), p. 63.

9. Groslier, *Le Cambodge au XVIe siècle*, p. 69. See also J. Dumarçay, "Le Prasat prei près d'Angkor Wat," *BEFEO*, Vol. 59 (1970):189–192, and G. Coedes, "La Date d'exécution des deux bas-reliefs tardifs d'Angkor Wat," *JA*, Vol. 250 (1962):235–243.

10. Khin Sok, "Deux inscriptions tardifs du Phnom Bakheng," *BEFEO*, Vol. 65, No. 1 (1978):271–280.

11. Khin Sok, "L'Inscription de Vatta Romlock," *BEFEO*, Vol. 67 (1980): 125–131, and Saveros Pou, "Inscription du Vat Romlok," *BEFEO*, Vol. 70 (1981):126–130.

12. See G. Janneau, *Manuel pratique pour le cambodgien* (Saigon, 1876), pp. 87–88. See also Evéline Porée-Maspero, *Etude sur les rites agraires des cambodgiens*, 3 vols. (Paris, 1962–1969), Vol. 1, p. 11. A seven-volume version of the legend, in verse, was published in Phnom Penh in 1952. In 1971, Cambodia's chief of state, Lon Nol, related the legend to the U.S. ambassador as a way of explaining how Cambodia's superiority to its neighbors had been depleted. See David P. Chandler, *The Tragedy of Cambodian History: Politics, War, and Revolution Since 1945* (New Haven, 1991), ch. 7. A related reference is Mak Phoeun, "Les Chroniques royales du Cambodge" (doctoral thesis, University of Paris IV, 1974), p. 129. For a spirited retelling of this legend, see Ang Choulean, "Nandin and His Avatars," in Jessup and Zephir, *Sculpture of Angkor and Ancient Cambodia*, pp. 62–70.

13. Ang Choulean, "Nandin and His Avatars."

14. See A. Cabaton (ed. and trans.), *Brève et véridique relation des évènements du Cambodge par Gabriel Quiroga de San Antonio* (Paris, 1941). See also L. P. Briggs, "Spanish Intervention in Cambodia," *T'oung Pao* (1949), pp. 132–160.

15. See W.J.M. Buch, "La Compagnie des Indes et l'Indochine," *BEFEO*, Vol. 36 (1936):97–196, and Vol. 37 (1937):121–237; H.P.N. Muller, *De Oost-Indische compagnie in Camboja en Laos* (The Hague, 1917); and D. K. Basset, "The Trade of the English East India Company in Cambodia, 1651–1656," *JRAS* (1962):35–62. For a ju-

dicious survey of the European-language resources for this period, see Jean-Claude Lejosne, "Historiographie du Cambodge aux XVIe et XVIIe siècles: Les Sources portugaises et hollondaises," in Pierre L. Lamant (ed.), *Bilan et Perspectives des Etudes Khmeres (Langue et Culture)* (Paris, 1997), pp. 179–208.

16. Cabaton, *Brève et véridique relation*, p. 100.

17. Jean Delvert, *Le Paysan cambodgien* (The Hague, 1961), especially pp. 371ff. In *Cambodia After Angkor*, pp. 513–520, Vickery argues that trade and communication in the Angkor period were primarily over roads built and maintained by corvée labor. Riverine traffic, carried out by individuals, foreigners, and local entrepreneurs, on the other hand, linked the country together and Cambodia to the outside world after the shift of the government to the south.

18. Cabaton, *Brève et véridique relation*, p. 208.

19. See the nineteenth-century prose chronicle numbered P-6 in the Fonds Phnom Penh collection of the Ecole Française d'Extrême Orient in Paris. For a detailed discussion of this period, see May Ebihara, "Societal Organization in Sixteenth and Seventeenth Century Cambodia," *JSEAS*, Vol. 15, No. 2 (September 1984):280–295. For a perceptive regional overview, see Anthony Reid, *Southeast Asia in the Age of Commerce:* Vol. 1, *The Lands Below the Winds* (New Haven, 1988), and Vol. 2, *Expansion and Crisis* (New Haven, 1993).

20. S. Pou, *Etudes sur le Ramakerti* (Paris, 1977), pp. 48–49.

21. See *BEFEO*, Vol. 62 (1975):369–384; *BEFEO*, Vol. 63 (1976):313–350; and Saveros Pou, "*Subhasit* and *Cpap* in Khmer Literature," in *Ludwik Sternbach Felicitation Volume* (Lucknow, 1979), pp. 331–348. See also Saveros Pou and K. Haksrea, "Liste d'ouvrages de *Cpap*," *JA*, Vol. 269 (1981):467–483, and David P. Chandler, "Narrative Poems (*Chbap*) and Pre-Colonial Cambodian Society," *JSEAS*, Vol. 15, No. 2 (September 1984):271–279. For the Cambodian texts of these poems, and an elegant French translation, see Saveros Pou, *Guirlande de cpap*, 2 vols. (Paris, 1988).

22. Clifford Geertz, *The Religion of Java* (New York, 1960), pp. 248–260. A partly successful attempt to dismantle the hierarchy of pronouns occurred in the revolutionary era; see John Marston, "Language Reform in Democratic Kampuchea" (M.A. thesis, University of Minnesota, 1985).

23. Saveros Pou's three-volume edition and critique of the *Ramakerti* was published by *BEFEO* in Paris in 1977–1979. These volumes include a Cambodian text, a French translation, and a volume of commentary, *Etudes sur le Ramakerti*. See also Saveros Pou, "Etudes ramakertiennes," and Saveros Pou, Lan Sunnary, and K. Haksrea, "Inventaire des oeuvres sur le Ramayana khmer (Ramakerti)," *Seksa Khmer*, Vol. 3, Nos. 3–4 (December 1981):87–126; Judith Jacob (trans.), *The Reamker* (London, 1987); and Jacob, *The Traditional Literature of Cambodia* (London, 1996), a useful survey.

24. See Porée-Maspero, *Etude sur les rites*, Vol. 3, p. 528, and Pou, "Etudes ramakertiennes," p. 93, note 15.

25. F. Bizot (ed.), *Histoire de Reamker* (Phnom Penh, 1973). According to Thong Thel (personal communication), this Khmer text resembles Thai-language versions more closely than it does the seventeenth-century Cambodian text.

26. See David P. Chandler, "Songs at the Edge of the Forest: Perceptions of Order in Three Cambodian Texts," in Alexander Woodside and David K. Wyatt

(eds.), *Moral Order and the Question of Change: Essays on Southeast Asian Thought* (New Haven, 1982), pp. 53–77, and Peter Carey, *The Cultural Ecology of Early Nineteenth Century Java* (Singapore, 1974), p. 4.

27. See F. Martini, "Quelques notes sur le Reamker," *AA*, Vol. 24, Nos. 3–4 (1961):351–362, and Martini, *La Gloire de Rama* (Paris, 1978), pp. 19–30.

28. I am grateful to Barbara Hatley for this insight into *wayang*.

29. A. Leclère, *Les Codes cambodgiens*, 2 vols. (Paris, 1898), Vol. 1, pp. 123–175.

30. Phoeun, "Les Chroniques royales," p. 176.

31. On Vietnam's "march south" and early relations with Cambodia, see Michael Cotter, "Toward a Social History of the Vietnamese Southward Movement," *JSEAH*, Vol. 9, No. 1 (March 1968):12–24; Thai Van Kiem, "La Plaine aux cerfs et la princesse de jade," *BSEI*, Vol. 34 (1959):378–393; and Pham Dinh Khiem, "Une grande page d'histoire oubliée: De l'alliance des cours de Hué et d'Oudong à la première ambassade à demeure du Vietnam au Cambodge au début du XVIIe siècle," *Etudes interdisciplinaires sur le Vietnam*, Vol. 1 (1974): 145–164. See also Mak Phoeun and Po Dharma, "La Deuxième intervention militaire vietnamienne au Cambodge," *BEFEO*, Vol. 77 (1988):229–262.

32. E. Gaspardone, "Un chinois des mers du sud," *JA*, Vol. 240, No. 3 (1952):361–385. On Cambodian relations with Siam in this period, see Dhiravat na Pembejra, "Seventeenth Century Ayutthaya: A Shift to Isolation?" in Anthony Reid (ed.), *Southeast Asia in the Early Modern Era: Trade, Power and Belief* (New Haven, 1997).

33. See Saveros Pou, "Les Inscriptions modernes d'Angkor," *JA*, Vol. 260, No. 242 (1972):107–129, and David P. Chandler, "An Eighteenth Century Inscription from Angkor Wat," *JSS*, Vol. 59, No. 2 (July 1971):151–159.

34. On Taksin's reign, see C. J. Reynolds, "Religious Historical Writing and the Legitimation of the First Bangkok Reign," in Anthony Reid and David Marr (eds.), *Perceptions of the Past in Southeast Asia* (Singapore, 1979), pp. 90–107, and Lorraine Gesick, "The Rise and Fall of King Taksin: A Drama of Buddhist Kingship," in Lorraine Gesick (ed.), *Centers, Symbols, and Hierarchies: Essays on the Classical States of Southeast Asia* (New Haven, 1983), pp. 90–105.

35. Frank Huffman, "Thai and Cambodian: A Case of Syntactic Borrowing?" *JAS*, Vol. 93, No. 4 (1973):488–589, and Huffman, "Khmer Loan-Words in Thai" (unpublished paper prepared for a seminar at the Center of South and Southeast Asian Studies, University of Michigan, 1980). I am grateful to Professor Huffman for allowing me to read this paper.

36. See Clifford Geertz, *Negara: The Theater State in Nineteenth Century Bali* (Princeton, N.J., 1980), especially pp. 110–127. See also Gesick (ed.), *Centers, Symbols, and Hierarchies*. The essays in this collection were composed for seminars on Southeast Asian kingship organized by Professor Geertz in 1977 and 1978, and my ideas about Cambodian kingship benefited greatly from discussions with the other guests at these occasions.

CHAPTER 6

1. For a discussion of Asian "maps," see David P. Chandler, "Maps for the Ancestors: Sacralized Topography and Echoes of Angkor in Two Cambodian Texts,"

JSS, Vol. 64, No. 2 (July 1976): passim, and E. R. Leach, "The Frontiers of 'Burma,'" *CSSH*, Vol. 3 (1960–1961):49–68. See also Thongchai Winichakul, *Siam Mapped: A History of the Geo-Body of a Nation* (Honolulu, 1989), a penetrating study of the effects of mapping on Thai nationalism. According to Adhémard Leclère, *Recherches sur le droit publique des cambodgiens* (Paris, 1894), p. 221, the boundaries of a *sruk* in traditional Cambodia were "those of the rice fields belonging to it." These varied from year to year.

2. National Library, Bangkok, *Chotmai Het (CMH)* 1203/1 *kho* 41, mentions a Thai map of Cambodia, and Democratic Republic of Vietnam, Bureau of Historical Research (comp.), *Dai nam thuc luc chinh bien* [Primary compilation of the veritable records of imperial Vietnam] (*DNTL*), Vol. 19, p. 240, mentions a Vietnamese one; these have not survived.

3. Eng Sut, *Akkasar mahaboros khmaer* [Documents about Khmer heroes] (Phnom Penh, 1969), p. 1148.

4. *DNTL*, Vol. 15, p. 115, and Vol. 22, p. 157.

5. E. Aymonier, *Géographie du Cambodge* (Paris, 1876), pp. 31–59.

6. Ibid., p. 49.

7. *CMH* 3/1192/4/1, and 3/1204/1 *ko* /2.

8. See W. E. Willmott, "History and Sociology of the Chinese in Cambodia Prior to the French Protectorate," *JSEAH*, Vol. 7, No. 1 (March 1966):15–38.

9. C. E. Bouillevaux, *Voyage en Indochine* (Paris, 1858), p. 168. See also Alexander Hamilton, *A New Account of the East Indies* (London, 1727, reprinted 1930), p. 106: "There are about two hundred *Topasses*, or *Indian Portugeze* settled and married in *Cambodia*, and some of them have pretty good posts in the Government, and live great after the Fashion of that Country."

10. On the ethnography of nineteenth-century Cambodia, see Wolfgang Vollman, "Notes sur les relations inter-ethniques au Cambodge du XIXe siècle," *Asie du Sud-Est et Monde Insulindien*, Vol. 4, No. 2 (1973):172–207.

11. *DNTL*, Vol. 15, p. 171.

12. *DNTL*, Vol. 3, p. 385. See also C. Flood (trans.), *The Dynastic Chronicles, Bangkok Era, the Fourth Reign*, 3 vols. (Tokyo, 1965–1967), Vol. 1, p. 171, which quotes King Duang of Cambodia as writing the French in 1858: "Cambodia wanted to build ships, put masts on them and sail them in order to trade with other countries, but Vietnam would not permit Cambodia to sail in and out."

13. William Milburn, *Oriental Commerce* (London, 1813), pp. 449–450.

14. See Chapter 4.

15. Saveros Lewitz, "La Toponymie khmère," *BEFEO*, Vol. 53, No. 2 (1967): 467–500.

16. For a description of rice-growing villages, see Jean Delvert, *Le Paysan cambodgien* (Paris, 1962), pp. 322–370.

17. See Institut Bouddhique, *Brajum ruong preng bhak ti 4* [Collected folk stories, vol. 4] (Phnom Penh, 1966), pp. 1–10. Both texts are analyzed in David P. Chandler, "Songs at the Edge of the Forest: Perceptions of Order in Three Cambodian Texts," in Alexander Woodside and David K. Wyatt (eds.), *Moral Order and the Question of Change: Essays on Southeast Asian Thought* (New Haven, 1982), pp. 53–77.

18. These two texts are dealt with in detail in Chandler, "Songs at the Edge of the Forest," pp. 76–99.

19. France, Archives l'outremer, Aix-en-Provence (AOM), Fonds Indochinois A-30 (22), "Rapport confidentiel sur le Cambodge," August 1874.

20. Truong Buu Lam, "L'Autorité dans les villages vietnamiens du XIXe siècle," in G. Wijawardene (ed.), *Leadership and Authority* (Singapore 1968), pp. 65–74.

21. G. Janneau, "Le Cambodge d'autrefois," *Revue Indochinoise (RI)*, Vol. 17, No. 3 (March 1914):266.

22. See H. D. Evers (ed.), *Loosely Structured Social Systems: Thailand in Comparative Perspective* (New Haven, 1969), and Robert Textor, "The 'Loose Structure' of Thai Society: A Paradigm Under Pressure," *PA*, Vol. 50, No. 3 (Fall 1977):467–473.

23. See Eric Wolf, "Kinship, Friendship, and Patron-Client Relations," in M. Banton (ed.), *The Social Anthropology of Complex Societies* (London, 1966), pp. 1–22.

24. Louis Finot, "Proverbes cambodgiens," *RI*, Vol. 7, No. 2 (January 1904):74.

25. Tiounn, "Cérémonial cambodgien concernant la prise des fonctions des mandarins nouveaux promus," *RI*, Vol. 10, No. 1 (January 1907):75. See also P. Bitard, "Les Songes et leurs interprétations chez les cambodgiens," in *Sources orientales II: Les songes et leur interprétation* (Paris, 1959), p. 258, which reports that to dream of eating human flesh or a freshly severed head means that one will become a provincial governor.

26. See Chapter 7.

27. J. Gonda, *Ancient Indian Kingship from a Religious Point of View* (Leiden, 1966), p. 91.

28. The Thai system is discussed in A. Rabibhadana, *Organization of Thai Society in the Early Bangkok Period* (Ithaca, N.Y., 1969), pp. 98–104.

29. See Chapter 3.

30. See manuscript chronicle P-6, Fonds Phnom Penh collection, Ecole Française d'Extrême Orient, pp. 11–12.

31. Rabibhadana, *Organization of Thai Society*, p. 44.

32. See A. Leclère, "Sdach tranh," *RI*, Vol. 7 (1905):1378–1384.

33. Gonda, *Ancient Indian Kingship*, p. 36.

34. A. Leclère, *Les Codes cambodgiens* (Paris, 1898), Vol. 1, p. 216.

35. For an analysis of the Chinese system, see John K. Fairbank (ed.), *The Chinese World Order* (Cambridge, Mass., 1968), especially pp. 1–19 and 63–89.

36. See P. Boudet and A. Masson (eds.), *Iconographie historique de l'Indochine française* (Paris, 1931), plates 128–129.

37. See D. G. Deveria, *Histoire des relations de la Chine avec Annam du XVIe au XIXe siècles* (Paris, 1880), pp. 52–54.

38. See W. Vella, *Siam Under Rama III* (Locust Valley, N.Y., 1957), p. 60.

39. John Crawfurd, *Journal of an Embassy to the Courts of Siam and Cochin-China* (London, 1828), p. 146: "The Cochin-Chinese Ambassadors were yesterday presented to the King. They were received, I am told, without much ceremony, the intercourse being considered of so friendly and familiar a nature as not to call for extraordinary formalities."

40. AOM, Fonds Indochinois A-30 (6), Carton 10.

41. Institut Bouddhique, manuscript chronicle from Wat Srolauv, p. 23.

42. Rama III, *Collected Writings* [in Thai] (Bangkok, 1967), p. 140.

CHAPTER 7

1. Eng Sut, *Akkasar mahaboros khmaer* [Documents about Khmer heroes] (Phnom Penh, 1969), p. 1013.

2. AOM, Fonds Indochinois A-30 (12), Carton 11. Letter from Doudart de Lagrée to the governor of Cochin China, January 8, 1866.

3. Quoted in C. Wilson, *State and Society in the Reign of Mongkut, 1851–1867* (Ann Arbor, Mich., 1971), p. 983.

4. For a summary of Thai evidence, see David P. Chandler, *Cambodia Before the French: Politics in a Tributary Kingdom 1794–1847* (Ann Arbor, Mich., 1974), pp. 83–84.

5. *CMH* 2/1173/19 ko. See also *DNTL*, Vol. 3, pp. 146–147.

6. For a discussion of the rebellion, see David P. Chandler, "An Anti-Vietnamese Rebellion in Early Nineteenth Century Cambodia," *JSEAS*, Vol. 6, No. 1 (March 1975):16–24. See also *DNTL*, Vol. 5, pp. 85ff.; *DNTL*, Vol. 6, p. 107; and L. Malleret, *Archéologie du delta de Mekong*, 4 vols. (Paris, 1959–1963), Vol. 1, pp. 27–33.

7. Institut Bouddhique, manuscript chronicle from Wat Prek Kuy (1874), p. 27.

8. See David P. Chandler, "Royally Sponsored Human Sacrifices in Nineteenth Century Cambodia: The Cult of Me Sa (Uma Mahisasuramardini) at Ba Phnom," *JSS*, Vol. 62, No. 2 (1974):207–221.

9. See Chapter 9.

10. Manuscript chronicle from Wat Prek Kuy, p. 58.

11. A. Leclère, *Recherches sur le droit publique des cambodgiens* (Paris 1894), p. 151.

12. *DNTL*, Vol. 7, p. 79.

13. *DNTL*, Vol. 14, p. 123.

14. Rama III, *Collected Writings* (Bangkok, 1967), p. 142.

15. The campaign is discussed in Chandler, *Cambodia Before the French*, pp. 113–118.

16. Chronicle from Wat Prek Kuy, p. 61.

17. *DNTL*, Vol. 14, pp. 53–54. The practice of kidnapping urban populations was a feature of precolonial Southeast Asian wars and resurfaced with a vengeance when the Cambodian Communists drove over two million urban Cambodians into the countryside in April 1975; see Chapter 12.

18. *DNTL*, Vol. 15, p. 113.

19. Ibid., p. 232.

20. *DNTL*, Vol. 16, pp. 21–22, 106.

21. *DNTL*, Vol. 18, pp. 249–250. See also *DNTL*, Vol. 19, p. 55, which discusses some shortcomings of the system. Most convicts and military colonists were expected to spend at least three years in Cambodia.

22. *DNTL*, Vol. 17, p. 30.

23. Ibid., p. 230.

24. *DNTL*, Vol. 19, p. 238.

25. Ibid., p. 329.

26. G. Aubaret (trans.), *Gia Dinh Thung Chi* [History and description of lower Cochin China] (Paris, 1867), p. 131.

27. See Milton Osborne, *Aggression and Annexation: Kampuchea's Condemnation of Vietnam* (Canberra: Australian National University, Research School of Pacific

Studies, Working Paper No. 15, 1979). See also David P. Chandler, *The Tragedy of Cambodian History: Politics War and Revolution Since 1945* (New Haven, 1991), pp. 203–204. Although anti-Vietnamese racism seemed on the wane in the 1990s, some politicians in the 1998 election campaign stirred up anti-Vietnamese sentiment by accusing Cambodia's ruling party of being a puppet of Vietnam.

28. *DNTL*, Vol. 19, p. 310.

29. *DNTL*, Vol. 18, p. 225. In 1839, Minh Mang ordered a survey of Cambodia's raw materials: *DNTL*, Vol. 21, pp. 239–240.

30. *DNTL*, Vol. 21, pp. 173, 235.

31. *DNTL*, Vol. 19, pp. 88–89; see also *DNTL*, Vol. 16, p. 109.

32. Thipakarawong, *Phraratchapongsawadan Chaophraya* [Royal chronicle] (Bangkok, repr. 1961), Vol. 2, p. 9. In 1838, one of Minh Mang's advisers suggested that "indigenous people be allowed to rule themselves and collect taxes" so as to save the Vietnamese money. He was told by the emperor to desist from making suggestions of this sort.

33. See, for example, Nguyen Khac Vien and Françoise Corrèze, *Kampuchea 1981: Témoignages* (Hanoi, 1981). A detailed comparison of the Vietnamese tutelage of the 1830s and that of the 1980s would make an interesting study.

34. *DNTL*, Vol. 21, pp. 269–272.

35. Chandler, *Cambodia Before the French*, pp. 140–141.

36. *DNTL*, Vol. 20, p. 263.

37. *DNTL*, Vol. 22, p. 157.

38. *DNTL*, Vol. 20, p. 7.

39. See Chandler, *Cambodia Before the French*, p. 25, note 37.

40. For an eyewitness report, see *CMH, ratchakan thi 3* [Official correspondence from the third reign of the Bangkok period] 3/1202/43 *ko* 10. See also Ian Hodges, "The Testimonies of Vietnamese Prisoners in the Third Reign: An Essay in Thai Historiography" (M.A. thesis, Australian National University, 1987).

41. Thailand, Royal Institute, *Chotmaihet ruang thap yuan khrang ratchakan thi 3* [Correspondence about the Vietnamese army in the third reign] (Bangkok, 1933), p. 17.

42. *DNTL*, Vol. 23, p. 112.

43. *DNTL*, Vol. 22, p. 228.

44. *DNTL*, Vol. 23, p. 155.

45. Ibid., p. 114.

46. Thailand, Royal Institute, *Chotmaihet*, p. 38.

47. Thailand, Royal Institute, *Chotmaihet*, p. 33, and *CMH*, 3/1202/40.

48. Chandler, *Cambodia Before the French*, pp. 156–158.

49. K.S.R. Kulap (pseud.), *Sayam Anam yut* [Siam's wars with Vietnam] (Bangkok, 1906, repr. 1971), p. 916.

50. *DNTL*, Vol. 23, p. 351.

51. Chandler, *Cambodia Before the French*, p. 155.

52. *CMH*, 3/1206/6.

53. Chandler, *Cambodia Before the French*, pp. 179–181.

54. See David P. Chandler, "Going Through the Motions: Ritual Aspects of the Reign of King Duang of Cambodia," in Lorraine Gesick (ed.), *Centers, Symbols,*

and Hierarchies: Essays on the Classical States of Southeast Asia (New Haven, 1983), pp. 106–124.

55. Eng Sut, *Akkasar mahaboros*, p. 1027.

56. Inscription K. 142, from Wat Baray, translated in E. Aymonier, *Le Cambodge* (Paris, 1904), pp. 349–351.

57. For a discussion of these chronicle histories, see Chandler, "Going Through the Motions," passim. See also A. Leclère, *Histoire du Cambodge* (Paris, 1914), p. 441. For a political history of Duang's reign, see Bun Srun Theam, "Cambodia in the Mid-Nineteenth Century: A Quest for Survival, 1840–1863" (M.A. thesis, Asian Studies, Australian National University, 1981), especially pp. 104–168.

58. Many of these letters are contained in Thailand, Office of the Prime Minister (comp.), *Thai sathapana kasat khamen* [The Thai establish the Khmer kingdom] (Bangkok, 1971), especially pp. 49–65.

59. Charles Meyniard, *Le Second empire en Indochine* (Paris, 1891), p. 461. Minh Mang had noted in 1822 that "Cambodia is in the midst of powerful neighbors, and the fear of being invaded is great." Bun Srun Theam, "Cambodia in the Mid-Nineteenth Century," pp. 138–167, discusses the mission in some detail.

CHAPTER 8

1. Jean Delvert, *Le Paysan cambodgien* (The Hague, 1961), pp. 425–428.

2. Charles Meyniard, *Le Second empire en Indochine* (Paris, 1891), pp. 403–408.

3. Henri Mouhot, *Voyage dans les royaumes de Siam, du Cambodge, et de Laos* (Paris, 1972), pp. 174–176.

4. See G. Taboulet (ed.), *La Geste française en Indochine*, 2 vols. (Paris, 1955), p. 334, and Milton Osborne, *The French Presence in Cochinchina and Cambodia: Rule and Response (1859–1905)* (Ithaca, N.Y., 1969), p. 27.

5. F. Julien, *Lettres d'un précurseur* (Paris, 1885), p. 46.

6. See Taboulet, *La Geste*, pp. 621–629, and R. S. Thomson, "Establishment of the French Protectorate over Cambodia," *Far Eastern Quarterly (FEQ)*, Vol. 4 (1945):313–340.

7. Taboulet, *La Geste*, pp. 630–635. See also Eng Sut, *Akkasar mahaboros khmaer* [Documents about Khmer heroes] (Phnom Penh, 1969), p. 1113.

8. For a stirring treatment of this expedition, see Milton Osborne, *River Road to China* (London, 1975).

9. Osborne, *French Presence*, pp. 211–214, and Eng Sut, *Akkasar mahaboras*, p. 1172.

10. For the full text of the treaty, see Taboulet, *La Geste*, pp. 67–72. See also Khing Hoc Dy, "Santhor MOK, poète et chroniqueur du XIXe siècle," *Seksa Khmer*, Vol. 3, Nos. 3–4 (December 1981):142. Mok, a courtier, tried to keep Thomson from entering Norodom's quarters. Thomson kicked him out of the way, and Mok later composed a poem about the incident, beginning, "Oh Frenchman, you miserable robber, you dared to lift your foot and kick the secretary to the king."

11. For a discussion of the rebellion, see Osborne, *French Presence*, pp. 206–228. See also Ke Khi You, "L'Insurrection générale de 1885–1886 au Cambodge," *Mémoire de maîtrise* (University of Paris VII, 1971).

12. Luc Durtain, *Dieux blancs, hommes jaunes* (Paris, 1930), p. 261.

13. L. Henry, *Promenade au Cambodge et au Laos* (Paris, 1894), p. 64n.

14. Osborne, *French Presence*, p. 237.

15. AOM, 3E 3(i), report from Kandal, May 1898.

16. Jean Hess, *L'Affaire Yukanthor* (Paris, 1900), p. 77. For discussions of this crisis, see P. Doumer, *L'Indochine française* (Paris, 1905), pp. 230–231; Osborne, *French Presence*, pp. 243–246; and Alain Forest, *Le Cambodge et la colonisation française: Histoire d'une colonisation sans heurts* (Paris, 1980), pp. 59–78. See also Pierre Lamant, *L'Affaire Yukhanthor* (thesis, University of Paris III, 1979).

17. AOM, 3 E-10 (2), second trimester report from Stung Treng, 1923.

18. Manuscript chronicle of Sisowath's reign, formerly in the library of the royal palace, microfilmed by Centre for East Asian Studies, Tokyo (hereafter Sisowath chronicle), p. 1025. See also John Tully, *Cambodia Under the Tricolour: The Sisowath Years, 1904–1927* (Clayton, Australia, 1996), a penetrating study.

19. Ibid., p. 1034.

20. See Harry Franck, *East of Siam* (New York, 1926), pp. 24–25. A. Pannetier, *Notes cambodgiennes* (Paris, 1921), p. 140, asserted that opium addiction was widespread among the Cambodian militia. See also R. Meyer, *Saramani* (Paris, 1922), pp. 122–123. P. Collard, *Cambodge et cambodgiens* (Paris, 1926), p. 277, mentioned Sisowath's addiction to opium but added that the drug is "not harmful to Asiatics."

21. A. Leclère, *Cambodge: Fêtes civiles* (Paris, 1916), pp. 30–31. See also Sisowath chronicle, pp. 1068–1074.

22. See Meyer, *Saramani*, pp. 132–151; Jean Ajalbert, *Ces phénomènes, artisans de l'Empire* (Paris, 1941), pp. 189–192; and Forest, *Le Cambodge*, pp. v–vii.

23. Sisowath chronicle, pp. 1077–1086. See also Forest, *Le Cambodge*, and Jean Ajalbert, *L'Indochine en péril* (Paris, 1906), pp. 87–111.

24. Cambodian dancers participated in the colonial exhibition of 1931 and also performed at the New York World's Fair in 1939–1940. See Bruno Dagens, *Angkor: La Forêt de pierre* (Paris, 1989), pp. 110ff.

25. For a discussion of the retrocession, see L. P. Briggs, "The Treaty of March 23, 1907, Between France and Siam," *FEQ*, Vol. 5 (1946):439–454.

26. Sisowath chronicle, pp. 1107–1110.

27. See C. Wilson, "The *Nai Kong* of Battambang, 1824–1868," in C. Wilson et al. (eds.), *Royalty and Commoners, Contributions to Asian Studies*, Vol. 15 (Leiden, 1980), pp. 66–72, and *Phongsawadan muang phratabong* [Chronicle of the region of Battambang], No. 16 of series, *Prachum Phongsawadan* [Collected chronicles] (Bangkok, 1969), pp. 94–106.

28. The unusual frequency of landlordism, sharecropping, and outsiders in these two regions was extrapolated by radical theorists in the 1970s to characterize rural society throughout the country. According to Pol Pot, landlordism, which was in fact rare on a national scale, was the "major problem" facing prerevolutionary Cambodia. Communist party favoritism toward poor peasants flowed from this analysis. See William Willmott, "Analytical Errors of the Kampuchean Communist Party," *PA*, Vol. 54, No. 2 (Summer 1981):209–227.

CHAPTER 9

1. Sisowath chronicle, pp. 1166–1167. See also John Tully, *Cambodia Under the Tricolour: The Sisowath Years, 1904–1927* (Clayton, Australia, 1996).

2. AOM 3 E12 (2), report from Svay Rieng, 1915.

3. For a discussion of developments in Cambodia in the 1920s, see F. Baudouin, *Le Cambodge pendant et après la grande guerre* (Paris, 1927), and A. Silvestre, *Le Cambodge administratif* (Phnom Penh, 1924). See also Réné Morizon, *Monographie sur le Cambodge* (Paris, 1930).

4. See A. Souyris-Rolland, "Les Pirates au Cambodge," *BSEI*, Vol. 25, No. 4 (1950):307–313. The rubric *piraterie* follows immediately after *situation politique* in the format of monthly French reports from the various *résidences*, but banditry is seen in the reports in terms of security rather than ideological dissidence. AOM 3 E12(2), a report from Svay Rieng in 1921, dismissively asserts that "a life of raiding others, full of the unexpected, composed of tricks, pursuits and ambushes, all without great physical danger, is one of the sports to which Cambodians are addicted." See also Alain Forest, *Le Cambodge et la colonisation française: Histoire d'une colonisation sans heurts* (Paris, 1980), pp. 373–412. For a Thai perspective, see David Johnston, "Bandit, *Nakleng*, and Peasant in Rural Thai Society," in C. Wilson et al. (eds.), *Royalty and Commoners, Contributions to Asian Studies*, Vol. 15 (Leiden, 1980), pp. 90–101, and more generally, E. Hobsbawm, *Bandits* (London, 1969).

5. A. Pannetier, *Notes cambodgiennes* (Paris, 1921, repr. 1986), p. 75.

6. The sculpture was carved by Louis Bottinelly. For a study of the influence of Indochina on French imaginative writers, see L. Malleret, *L'Exotisme indochinois dans la littérature française depuis 1860* (Paris, 1934), especially pp. 183–192, 216–244. Novels set in Cambodia dating from this period include Charles Bellan, *Fleur de lotus* (Paris, 1924); Pierre Benoit, *Le Roi lépreux* (Paris, 1927); Jean Dorsenne, *Sous le soleil des bonzes* (Paris, 1934); André Malraux, *Le Voie royale* (Paris, 1930); and Marguerite Duras, *Un barrage contre la Pacifique* (Paris, 1952). See also "Neang," *L'Echo du Cambodge*, July 30, 1927, and Penny Edwards, *The Cultivation of "Cambodge"* (in press). In this masterful study Edwards argues that "Cambodge," the unit that became the state of Cambodia after 1954, was a cooperative, only partially conscious construction, in colonial times, by the French and members of the Cambodian elite.

7. AOM 3E 8(3), report from Prey Veng, 1924. Félix Louis Bardez, born in Paris in 1882, had served in Indochina, largely in Cambodia, since 1908.

8. For a detailed account of these incidents, see David P. Chandler, "The Assassination of *Résident* Bardez (1925)," *JSS*, Vol. 72, No. 2 (1982):35–49. See also *L'Echo du Cambodge*, especially the issues of December 1925; Walter Langlois, *André Malraux: The Indo-China Adventure* (New York, 1966), pp. 185–188; and Luc Durtain, *Dieux blancs, hommes jaunes* (Paris, 1930), pp. 264–265.

9. For the French text of this ordinance, see Dik Keam, *Phum Direchan* [Bestiality village] (Phnom Penh, 1971), pp. 154–159.

10. I am grateful to Ben Kiernan for lending me his recorded interview with one of the assailants, Sok Bith, which took place in September 1980. Bith served a fifteen-year sentence for the assault.

11. AOM 3E 7(6), annual reports from Kratie, 1925–1926.

12. This paper has at last received the attention it deserves in Edwards, *The Cultivation of "Cambodge."* See also Bunchhan Muul, *Kuk Niyobay* [Political prison] (Phnom Penh, 1971), pp. 8–14.

13. Like *Nagara Vatta*, the colonial issues of *Kambuja Surya*, which effectively *published* Cambodian-language literature for the first time, deserve detailed attention. See Jacques Nepote and Khing Hoc Dy, "Literature and Society in Modern Cambodia," in Tham Seong Che (ed.), *Essays on Literature and Society in Southeast Asia* (Singapore, 1981), pp. 56–81.

14. For a discussion of these two texts, see David P. Chandler, "Cambodian Royal Chronicles (*Rajabangsavatar*), 1927–1949: Kingship and Historiography in the Colonial Era," in Anthony Reid and David Marr (eds.), *Perceptions of the Past in Southeast Asia* (Singapore, 1979), pp. 207–217, and David P. Chandler, "Instructions for the Corps of Royal Scribes: An Undated Cambodian Manuscript from the Colonial Era," *JSS*, Vol. 63, No. 2 (July 1975):343–348.

15. William E. Willmott, *The Chinese in Cambodia* (Vancouver, 1967), and Willmott, "History and Sociology of the Chinese in Cambodia Before the French Protectorate," *JSEAH*, Vol. 7, No. 1 (March 1966):15–38. See also *L'Echo du Cambodge*, September 7, 1938, which reports on the continuing influx of Chinese immigrants.

16. On education, see Forest, *Le Cambodge*, pp. 143–165, and Jacques Nepote, "Education et développement dans le Cambodge moderne," *Mondes et développement*, No. 28 (1974):767–792. See also Jean Delvert, "L'Oeuvre française d'enseignement au Cambodge," *FA*, Nos. 125–127 (October–December 1956):309–322. On women in colonial Cambodia, see Penny Edwards, "Womanizing Indochina: Fiction, Nation and Co-Habitation in Colonial Cambodia, 1890–1930," in Judith Clancy-Smith and Frances Gouda (eds.), *Domesticating the Empire: Race, Gender and Family Life in French and Dutch Colonialism* (Charlottesville, Va., 1998), pp. 108–130. For some intriguing photographs from this period, see Michel Igout, *Phnom Penh Then and Now* (Bangkok, 1993).

17. For reports on the effects of the depression on Cambodia, see, for example, AOM 3E 15 (8), annual reports from Kampot; AOM 3 (5), from Kandal; and AOM 3E 10 (4), from Stung Treng. See also Khy Phanra, "Les Origines du caodaisme au Cambodge," *Mondes asiatiques* Vol. 3 (1975):315–348, and Khy Phanra, *La Communauté vietnamienne au Cambodge à l'époque du protectorat francais*, 2 vols. (thesis, University of Paris III, 1974). Alert to positive developments, one French administrator reported in 1933 that the crash had led to the collapse of private fortunes throughout Takeo, adding that "a powerful form of solidarity was born in shared poverty, making a *table rase* of ancient antagonisms of class and even of race"; see AOM 3E 7 (6), report from Takeo.

18. Norodom Sihanouk, *L'Indochine vue de Pékin* (Paris, 1972), pp. 27–28.

19. See H. de Grauclade, *Le Réveil du peuple khmer* (Hanoi, 1935). For a less optimistic view, see G. de Pourtales, *Nous, à qui rien n'appartient* (Paris, 1931), pp. 115ff.

20. See, for example, Ben Kiernan, "Origins of Khmer Communism," in *Southeast Asian Affairs 1981* (Singapore, 1980), pp. 161–180. See also Ben Kiernan, *How Pol Pot Came to Power* (London, 1985), pp. 8ff.

21. A description of Thanh's activities during and after World War II can be found in the present chapter.

22. See, for example, AOM 3E 8 (12), 1923, annual report of the governor of Prey Veng.

23. *L'Écho du Cambodge*, July 19, 1933.

24. A helpful study of this period, although it says very little about Cambodia, is A. W. McCoy (ed.), *Southeast Asia Under Japanese Occupation* (New Haven: Yale University Southeast Asian Studies, Monograph Series No. 22, 1980).

25. Decoux has discussed this period in his memoirs, *A la barre de l'Indochine* (Paris, 1949). See also N. Sihanouk, *Souvenirs doux et amers* (Paris, 1981), pp. 59–114.

26. Charles Robequain, *The Economic Development of French Indo-China* (Oxford, England, 1944), p. 366.

27. See Milton Osborne, "King-making in Cambodia: From Sisowath to Sihanouk," *JSEAS*, Vol. 4, No. 3 (September 1973):169–185.

28. Sihanouk, *L'Indochine vue de Pékin*, pp. 19–30, and Sihanouk, *Souvenirs doux et amers*, pp. 35–50.

29. Sihanouk chronicle, pp. 136–140.

30. See V. M. Reddi, *A History of the Cambodian Independence Movement 1863–1955* (Tirupati, 1971), pp. 82–84; Bunchhan Muul, *Kuk niyobay* [Political prison] (Phnom Penh, 1971); and Kong Somkar, *Achar Hem Chieu* [Venerable Hem Chieu] (Phnom Penh, 1971).

31. This information is drawn from unpublished correspondence between Son Ngoc Thanh, in exile in 1943, and his nationalist colleagues in Cambodia.

32. Interestingly, Sok Bith, the illiterate farmer implicated in Bardez's assassination (see Note 10 above), knew about Hem Chieu but about few other nationalist figures.

33. G. Gautier, *Jeune Cambodge* (Phnom Penh, 1943), p. 4. See also *Indochine*, No. 153 (August 5, 1943) and No. 210 (August 10, 1944). AOM E 11 (7), note from Pursat, 1944, states that romanized Khmer was being taught at that time in all Cambodian schools. Romanization had mixed, not necessarily unhappy, results (Eveline Porée-Maspero, letter of August 27, 1982).

34. Robert Ollivier, "Le Protectorat français au Cambodge" (Ph.D. dissertation, University of Paris, 1969), p. 213.

35. Sihanouk chronicle, p. 399.

36. Ollivier, "Le Protectorat français," p. 198. The French name for the kingdom became "Cambodge" again in 1946. See also David P. Chandler, "The Kingdom of Kampuchea, March–October 1945," in Chandler, *Facing the Cambodian Past* (Chiangmai and Sydney, 1996), pp. 165–188; Chandler, *The Tragedy of Cambodian History: Politics, War, and Revolution Since 1945* (New Haven, 1991), ch. 1; and Pierre Brocheux, William Duiker et al. (eds.), *L'Indochine française 1940–1945* (Paris, 1982).

37. Lt. Tadakame, attached as a political adviser to the palace, remained in Cambodia after the war and even joined an Issarak band.

38. Sihanouk chronicle, p. 493.

39. See Charles Meyer, *Derrière le sourire khmer* (Paris, 1971), pp. 115–116; Ollivier, "Le Protectorat français," p. 242; Reddi, *History of the Cambodian Independence Movement*, pp. 105–109; and *Realités cambodgiennes*, July 9 and 16, 1967.

CHAPTER 10

1. Robert Ollivier, "Le Protectorat français au Cambodge" (Ph.D. dissertation, University of Paris, 1969), p. 267. See also David P. Chandler, *The Tragedy of Cambodian History: Politics, War, and Revolution Since 1945* (New Haven, 1991), ch. 1.

2. V. M. Reddi, *A History of the Cambodian Independence Movement 1863–1955* (Tirupati, 1971), p. 124.

3. The material in this paragraph is drawn from Ben Kiernan, "Origins of Khmer Communism," in *Southeast Asian Affairs 1981* (Singapore, 1980), pp. 161–180; Bunchhan Muul, *Charet Khmer* [Khmer mores] (Phnom Penh, 1974); and Wilfred Burchett, *Mekong Upstream* (Hanoi, 1957).

4. Ollivier, "Le Protectorat français," pp. 282–290; P. Preschez, *Essai sur la démocratie au Cambodge* (Paris, 1961), pp. 17–19; Reddi, *History of the Cambodian Independence Movement*, pp. 124–126; and AOM, Cambodge, 7 F 29 (4), "Etude sur l'évolution de la politique intérieure et les partis politiques khmers" (1951), passim. This period is discussed in detail in Chandler, *The Tragedy of Cambodian History*, chs. 2 and 3. See also Michael Vickery, "Looking Back at Cambodia," in Ben Kiernan and Chanthou Boua (eds.), *Peasants and Politics in Kampuchea, 1942–1981* (London, 1982), pp. 89–113.

5. AOM, Cambodge 7F 29 (7), "Etude sur les mouvements rebelles au Cambodge, 1942–1952" (hereafter "Etude sur les mouvements"), pp. 9–10.

6. Reddi, *History of the Cambodian Independence Movement*, p. 129. There were additional elections in 1947, 1951, and 1955. Women were not allowed to vote nationally until the 1958 elections. Arguably, the 1947 and 1951 elections were the last "free and fair" elections in Cambodia until those sponsored by the United Nations in 1993. They were also, of course, the first elections of any kind in Cambodian history.

7. "Etude sur les mouvements." See also Kiernan, "Origins of Khmer Communism," pp. 163–167, and Reddi, *History of the Cambodian Independence Movement*, pp. 151–154.

8. Norodom Sihanouk, *Souvenirs doux et amers* (Paris, 1981), pp. 134–142. Yuthevong, a fascinating figure, has not been studied in detail. When he died while undergoing treatment for tuberculosis in a French hospital in Phnom Penh in 1947, rumors spread that he had been assassinated by the French. See Reddi, *History of the Cambodian Independence Movement*, p. 137n.; Burchett, *Mekong Upstream*, p. 112; and Chandler, *The Tragedy of Cambodian History*, p. 37.

9. Sihanouk, *Souvenirs*, pp. 158–168; Ollivier, "Le Protectorat français," pp. 314–320; Reddi, *History of the Cambodian Independence Movement*, pp. 165–173.

10. Vickery, "Looking Back at Cambodia," p. 97. See also Ollivier, "Le Protectorat français," pp. 323–325, and Martin Herz, *A Short History of Cambodia* (New York and London, 1958), p. 83.

11. United States, Foreign Broadcast Information Service (FBIS), *Broadcasts from the Far East*, November 7, 1951.

12. Quoted in Reddi, *History of the Cambodian Independence Movement*, p. 183.

13. Interviews with Channa Samudvanija, Chiangmai, September 1981, and Bangkok, May 1988.

14. See Chandler, *The Tragedy of Cambodian History*, pp. 59–61; Donald Lancaster, *The Emancipation of French Indo-China* (Oxford, 1961), p. 272; and Herz,

Short History of Cambodia, pp. 84–85. See also M. Laurent, *L'Armée au Cambodge et dans les pays en voie de développement en Sud Est Asiatique* (Paris, 1968), especially pp. 283–291.

15. "Etude sur les mouvements," p. 64ff, and Ollivier, "Le Protectorat français," pp. 320–322.

16. Kiernan, "Origin of Khmer Communism," p. 168.

17. See "Etude sur les mouvements," pp. 84, 87. The second citation notes that some "autarchic collective farms, like *kholkozes*, have been noted . . . in Kompong Cham" in 1952. Interestingly, this region was a stronghold of radical activity in the 1950s and the 1960s and a seedbed in the 1970s for cadres in Democratic Kampuchea.

18. FBIS, November 28, 1951.

19. FBIS, April 4, 1979.

20. Quoted in Ollivier, "Le Protectorat français," pp. 333–334. For further details, see Chandler, *The Tragedy of Cambodian History*, pp. 61–67.

21. "Lettre de l'Association des Etudiants Khmers en France à sa Majesté Norodom Sihanouk," Paris, July 6, 1952. According to Ben Kiernan, this document was the work of Hou Yuon, a Cambodian radical purged in 1975. The manifesto appeared in Khmer in *Khmer Nisut* [Khmer student], No. 14 (August 1952). In the same issue, writing as "Khmer Daom" [Original Khmer], Saloth Sar, later known as Pol Pot, contributed two essays, both strongly critical of the Cambodian monarchy. One of these ("Monarchy or Democracy?") has been translated as an appendix to Ben Kiernan and Serge Thion, *Khmers Rouges!* (Paris, 1981), pp. 357–360. The other, entitled "The Royal Trip to European Countries," closes with a short poem claiming that "royal edicts are dishonest" and seek to destroy the "solidarity of students." Interestingly, none of the articles in the periodical takes an internationalist view of the Indochina war; the antimonarchic, pro-Assembly position they all assume suggests instead that Pol Pot and his colleagues, at this stage in their careers, supported Son Ngoc Thanh's form of dissidence rather than the Vietnamese-sponsored KPRP. For a survey of Pol Pot's activities in France, see David P. Chandler, *Brother Number One: A Political Biography of Pol Pot*, 2d ed. (Boulder, Colo., 1999), pp. 31–40.

22. Reddi, *History of the Cambodian Independence Movement*, p. 205. For discussion of this period, see also Norodom Sihanouk, *La Monarchie cambodgienne et la croisade royale pour l'indépendance* (Phnom Penh, c. 1957), passim, and Chandler, *The Tragedy of Cambodian History*, pp. 67–72.

23. Norodom Sihanouk and Wilfred Burchett, *My War with the CIA* (Harmondsworth, 1973), p. 153, and Reddi, *History of the Cambodian Independence Movement*, p. 20.

24. Ollivier, "Le Protectorat français," pp. 344–346.

25. Ibid., pp. 358ff., conveys the impression of approaching anarchy in Phnom Penh; such an atmosphere may well have accelerated French willingness to negotiate with the king.

26. Sihanouk, *Souvenirs*, pp. 209–212.

27. Kiernan, "Origins of Khmer Communism," p. 179.

28. In 1981, Nhek Tioulong stated that, in the mid-1950s, when he served in Sihanouk's cabinet, it soon became almost impossible for the newly independent

Cambodian regime to collect taxes levied on land and harvests. To Cambodian peasants, it seems, "independence" meant being relieved of these particular levies (interview with Nhek Tioulong, Bangkok, August 1981).

29. *Cambodge*, April 14, 1955.

30. On the 1955 election, see Chandler, *The Tragedy of Cambodian History*, pp. 81–84. Some of the ideas that follow can be traced to my conversations over many years with Stephen Heder, Ben Kiernan, Serge Thion, and Michael Vickery. See also Serge Thion, "The Pattern of Cambodian Politics," in David Ablin and Marlowe Hood (eds.), *The Cambodia Agony* (Armonk, N.Y., 1988), pp. 149–164; Karl Jackson (ed.), *Cambodia 1975–1978: Rendez-vous with Death* (Princeton, N.J., 1989); and William E. Willmott, "Analytical Errors of the Cambodian Communist Party," *PA*, Vol. 54, No. 2 (Summer 1981):209–227.

CHAPTER 11

1. For details of this confrontation, see David P. Chandler, *The Tragedy of Cambodian History: Politics, War, and Revolution Since 1945* (New Haven, 1991), ch. 4. See also Michael Vickery, "Looking Back at Cambodia," in Ben Kiernan and Chanthou Boua (eds.), *Peasants and Politics in Kampuchea, 1942–1981* (London, 1982), pp. 89–112.

2. U.S. intelligence agencies were tangentially involved in both the Sam Sary plot of 1958–1959 and the Dap Chhuon plot of February 1959. Sam Sary, a high official formerly favored by Sihanouk, became a dissident and fled to Thailand, perhaps with U.S. encouragement, in early 1959. Hoping to overthrow Sihanouk, Thai officials unsuccessfully tried to forge an alliance between Sary and Son Ngoc Thanh. In February, Dap Chhuon, the warlord of Cambodia's northwest, threatened to revolt. He had been provided with gold bullion, arms, and radio equipment by the Saigon regime and perhaps by the Thai as well. The U.S. Central Intelligence Agency (CIA) was aware of the plot but did nothing to inform Sihanouk about it. For a detailed discussion, see Chandler, *The Tragedy of Cambodian History*, pp. 99–107. Sam Sary's son, Sam Rainsy, became a prominent Cambodian politician, opposed to the ruling party, in the 1990s.

3. Simone Lacouture, *Cambodge* (Lausanne, 1964), pp. 133–152. See also Milton Osborne, *Sihanouk: Prince of Light, Prince of Darkness* (Sydney, 1995). Julio Jeldres, formerly Sihanouk's personal secretary, is working on an analytical biography of the prince. Sihanouk's own memoirs for this period, *Souvenirs doux et amers* (Paris, 1981), make lively reading but should be used with caution.

4. Two astute analyses of Sihanouk's foreign policy are Roger Smith, *Cambodia's Foreign Policy* (Ithaca, N.Y., 1965), and Nasir Abdoul Carime, "Mise en perspective de la diplomatie sihanoukienne," *Peninsule*, Vol. 36 (1998):175–191.

5. See Ben Kiernan, *How Pol Pot Came to Power* (London, 1985), pp. 202ff. This study, based largely on interviews conducted between 1979 and 1982, provides a valuable account of Cambodian radicalism prior to 1975. See also David P. Chandler, *Brother Number One: A Political Biography of Pol Pot*, 2d ed. (Boulder, Colo., 1999), pp. 64–71.

6. See Kenton J. Clymer, "The Perils of Neutrality: The Break in US-Cambodian Relations, 1965," *Diplomatic History*, Vol. 23, No. 4 (Fall 1999):609–631.

7. For analyses of the Samlaut response, see Kiernan, *How Pol Pot Came to Power*, pp. 249ff; Elizabeth Becker, *When the War Was Over* (New York, 1986), pp. 119–122; and Chandler, *The Tragedy of Cambodian History*, ch. 5.

8. On Saloth Sar's visit to Vietnam, see Thomas Engelbert and Christopher Goscha, *Falling Out of Touch: A Study of Vietnamese Communist Policy Toward an Emerging Cambodian Communist Movement, 1930–1975* (Clayton, Australia, 1995), which draws on Vietnamese documentation, and Chandler, *Brother Number One*, pp. 69–73. For a discussion of conditions in China at this time, see David Milton and Nancy Dall Milton, *The Wind Will Not Subside: Years in Revolutionary China* (New York, 1976), a sympathetic account, and Roderick MacFarquhar, *The Origins of the Cultural Revolution*, Vol. 3: *The Coming of the Cataclysm, 1961–1966* (Oxford, 1997). See also Jin Qiu, *The Culture of Power: The Lin Biao Incident in the Cultural Revolution* (Stanford, 1999).

9. For contemporary treatments of this period, hostile to the prince, see Charles Meyer, *Derrière le sourire khmer* (Paris, 1971), and J. C. Pomonti and Serge Thion, *Des courtisans aux partisans: La Crise cambodgienne* (Paris, 1971). A more judicious account is Milton Osborne's *Before Kampuchea* (London, 1979). See also Laura Summers, "The Sources of Economic Grievance in Sihanouk's Cambodia," *Southeast Asian Journal of Social Science*, Vol. 14, No. 1 (1986), and Remy Prud'homme, *L'Économie du Cambodge* (Paris, 1969).

10. For a detailed account of the coup, based to a large extent on interviews, see Chandler, *The Tragedy of Cambodian History*, pp. 197–199. See also Pomonti and Thion, *Des courtisans aux partisans*; Justin Corfield, *Khmers Stand Up!* (Clayton, Australia, 1994); and William Shawcross, *Sideshow: Nixon, Kissinger, and the Destruction of Cambodia* (New York, 1979), a withering attack on U.S. "policies" toward Cambodia in the early 1970s.

11. For a stirring evocation of this period, see Robert Sam Anson, *War News* (New York, 1989).

12. For accounts of the U.S. bombing, see Shawcross, *Sideshow*, pp. 209–219, and Ben Kiernan, "The American Bombardment of Kampuchea, 1969–1973," *Vietnam Generation*, Vol. 1, No. 1 (Winter 1989):4–42. Lt. Gen. Sak Sutsakhan, *The Khmer Republic at War and the Final Collapse* (Washington, D.C., 1980), provides a detailed military history.

13. For accounts of the Communist entry into Phnom Penh, see, among others, François Ponchaud, *Cambodia Year Zero* (New York, 1978), pp. 1–22, and Someth May, *Cambodian Witness* (London, 1986), p. 100–105.

CHAPTER 12

1. See David P. Chandler, "Seeing Red: Perceptions of History in Democratic Kampuchea," in David P. Chandler and Ben Kiernan (eds.), *Revolution and Its Aftermath in Kampuchea: Eight Essays* (New Haven, 1983); Serge Thion, "The Pattern of Cambodian Politics," in David Ablin and Marlowe Hood (eds.), *The Cambodian Agony* (Armonk, N.Y., 1988), pp. 149–164; François Ponchaud, "Social Change in the Vortex of Revolution," in Karl Jackson (ed.), *Cambodia 1975–1978: Rendez-vous with Death* (Princeton, N.J., 1989), pp. 151–178; Ben Kiernan, *The Pol Pot Regime: Politics, Race, and Genocide Under the Khmer Rouge* (New Haven, 1995); and Steve

Heder, "Racism, Marxism, Labeling and Genocide in Ben Kiernan's *The Pol Pot Regime," Southeast Asian Research*, No. 5 (1997):101–153.

2. For vivid accounts of the evacuation, see François Ponchaud, *Cambodia Year Zero* (New York, 1978), pp. 1–51; Bernard Hamel, *De sang et de larmes* (Paris, 1977), pp. 66–115; and Pin Yathay, *L'Utopie meurtrière* (Paris, 1980), pp. 39–56. See also Kevin McIntyre, "Geography as Destiny: Cities, Villages and Khmer Rouge Orientalism," *Comparative Studies in Society and History*, Vol. 35 (1996):730–758.

3. Interview with a former civil engineer, Melbourne, April 1987. See also David P. Chandler, Muy Hong Lim, and Ben Kiernan, *The Early Phases of Liberation in Cambodia: Conversations with Peang Sophy* (Clayton, Australia, 1976).

4. See Michael Vickery, "Democratic Kampuchea: Themes and Variations," in Chandler and Kiernan, *Revolution and Its Aftermath*, pp. 99–135, and Vickery, *Cambodia 1975–1982* (Boston, 1983), pp. 64–188. Vickery's findings about temporal and spatial variations in the DK era have been corroborated by several scholars, and by my own interviews in 1986–1990; see David P. Chandler, *The Tragedy of Cambodian History: Politics, War, and Revolution Since 1945* (New Haven, 1991), chs. 7 and 8.

5. See Timothy Carney, "The Organization of Power," in Jackson, *Cambodia 1975–1978*, pp. 79–107.

6. See Michael Vickery, "How Many Died in Pol Pot's Kampuchea?" *BCAS* (1988):377–385; Stephen R. Shalom, *Deaths in China Due to Communism* (Tempe, Arizona, 1984); and Patrick Heuveline, "'Between One and Three Million': Towards the Demographic Reconstruction of a Decade of Cambodian History (1970–1979)," *Population Studies*, Vol. 52 (1998):49–65.

7. See David P. Chandler, Ben Kiernan, and Chantou Boua (eds.), *Pol Pot Plans the Future: Confidential Leadership Documents from Democratic Kampuchea, 1976–1977* (New Haven, 1988), pp. 6–7.

8. For the text of the constitution, see Ponchaud, *Cambodia Year Zero*, pp. 199–206. See also David P. Chandler, "The Constitution of Democratic Kampuchea: The Semantics of Revolutionary Change," *PA*, Vol. 49, No. 3 (Fall 1976):506–515.

9. See Ben Kiernan, "Pol Pot and the Kampuchean Communist Movement," in Ben Kiernan and Chanthou Boua (eds.), *Peasants and Politics in Kampuchea, 1942–1981* (London, 1982), pp. 27–318, and Jackson, *Cambodia 1975–1978*, pp. 100ff.

10. For the text of the Four-Year Plan, see Chandler, Kiernan, and Boua, *Pol Pot Plans the Future*, pp. 36–118. See also Charles Twining, "The Economy," in Jackson, *Cambodia 1975–1978*, pp. 109–150, and Marie Martin, *Le Mal cambodgien* (Paris, 1989), pp. 156–202.

11. Chandler, Kiernan, and Boua, *Pol Pot Plans the Future*, p. 36.

12. Author's interview with former Buddhist monk, Melbourne, March 1988.

13. DK officials called their economic plan the "great leap forward" (*maha lout ploh*), borrowing Chinese terminology without acknowledgment. Parallels with the disastrous Chinese experiment are numerous and would repay detailed study. It will probably never be known whether Pol Pot and his colleagues were aware in the 1970s that China's Great Leap had failed; see William Joseph, "A Tragedy of Good Intentions: Post-Mao Views of the Great Leap Forward," *Mod-*

ern China, Vol. 12, No. 4 (October 1986):419–457. For a magisterial treatment of the aftermath of this era in China, see Roderick MacFarquhar, *The Origins of the Cultural Revolution*, Vol. 3: *The Coming of the Cataclysm, 1961–1966* (Oxford, 1997).

14. On the 1951–1960 controversy, see Chandler, Kiernan, and Boua, *Pol Pot Plans the Future*, pp. 164–176.

15. See David Chandler, *Voices from S-21: Terror and History in Pol Pot's Secret Prison* (Berkeley, 1999), pp. 57–62.

16. See David P. Chandler, "Revising the Past in Democratic Kampuchea: When Was the Birthday of the Party?" *PA*, Vol. 56, No. 2 (Summer 1983):288–300, and Chandler, *Voices from S-21*, pp. 59–60.

17. See Anthony Barnett, Ben Kiernan, and Chanthou Boua, "Bureaucracy of Death: Documents from Inside Pol Pot's Torture Machine," *New Statesman*, May 2, 1980. See also Douglas Niven and Chris Riley (eds.), *Killing Fields* (Santa Fe, 1996), a haunting collection of photographs from the prison known as S-21.

18. See Chandler, Kiernan, and Boua, *Pol Pot Plans the Future*, p. 183.

19. Ibid., p. 185.

20. See "The Last Plan," a Tuol Sleng document from mid-1978 translated by Timothy Carney and Khem Sos, in Jackson, *Cambodia 1975–1978*, pp. 299–314. Unfortunately, the translation has been printed without any introduction or notes. The linked ideas of a postrevolutionary continuation of class warfare and the ubiquity of antiparty conspiracy were shared by DK leaders with the Cultural Revolution's leaders in China, who may in turn have been inspired by Stalinist models; see Andrew Walder, "Cultural Revolution Radicalism: Variations on a Stalinist Theme," in William Joseph et al. (eds.), *New Perspectives on the Cultural Revolution* (Cambridge, Mass., 1991), pp. 41–62. See also Chandler, *Voices from S-21*, pp. 44–76.

21. See Nayan Chanda, *Brother Enemy* (New York, 1986), pp. 94–96, 109–110.

22. On the conflict, see Chanda, *Brother Enemy*, and Grant Evans and Kelvin Rowley, *Red Brotherhood at War* (London, 1984; rev. ed., 1990).

23. See Chanda, *Brother Enemy*, pp. 255ff., and Evans and Rowley, *Red Brotherhood at War*, pp. 115ff.

24. Pol Pot, "Long Live the 17th Anniversary of the Communist Party of Kampuchea," speech delivered on September 29, 1977; FBIS, October 4, 1977.

25. See Ben Kiernan, "Wild Chickens, Farm Chickens, and Cormorants: Kampuchea's Eastern Zone Under Pol Pot," in Chandler and Kiernan, *Revolution and Its Aftermath*, pp. 136–211.

26. See Evans and Rowley, *Red Brotherhood at War*, ch. 5.

27. On this visit, see Chandler, *The Tragedy of Cambodian History*, ch. 8; Chandler, *Brother Number One: A Political Biography of Pol Pot*, 2d ed. (Boulder, Colo., 1999), pp. 153–155; Elizabeth Becker, *When the War Was Over* (New York, 1986), pp. 406–435; and Norodom Sihanouk, *Prisonnier des khmers rouges* (Paris, 1986), pp. 281ff.

28. See Kate Frieson, *The Impact of the Revolution on Khmer Peasants: 1970–1975* (Ann Arbor, Mich., 1992), which traces the indifference of most rural Cambodians to revolutionary pressures in the early 1970s. Frieson argues persuasively that this was due not to people's preference for another political party or other political ideas but to the importance they placed on such nonpolitical activities as family life, Buddhism, leisure, and freedom of movement—all denied, condemned,

or curtailed by the CPK. See also Frank Smith, *Interpretive Accounts of the Khmer Rouge Years: Personal Experience in Cambodian Peasant World View* (Madison, Wisc., 1989).

CHAPTER 13

1. The only detailed study of this period, in political terms, is Michael Vickery, *Kampuchea* (London, 1986). Evan Gottesman's work in progress, when published, will provide a sorely needed analytical history of the PRK regime.

2. See Grant Evans and Kelvin Rowley, *Red Brotherhood at War* (London, 1984; rev. ed., 1990), and William Shawcross, *The Quality of Mercy* (New York, 1984), for contrasting viewpoints on this period. See also Stephen J. Morris, *Why Vietnam Invaded Cambodia: Political Culture and the Causes of War* (Stanford, 1999).

3. For a breakdown of the affiliations of PRK officials, as well as those of the party congress, see Vickery, *Kampuchea*, pp. 44ff., 65.

4. Vivid accounts of these early months, written by two journalists sympathetic to the PRK, are John Pilger and Anthony Barnett, *Aftermath* (London, 1982), and Wilfred Burchett, *The China-Cambodia-Vietnam Triangle* (London, 1984).

5. See Evans and Rowley, *Red Brotherhood at War*, pp. 130ff., and Nayan Chanda, *Brother Enemy* (New York, 1986), pp. 360ff.

6. For contrasting accounts, see Shawcross, *The Quality of Mercy*, passim, and Michael Vickery, *Cambodia 1975–1982* (Boston, 1983), pp. 218ff. Shawcross describes the bureaucratic infighting associated with the aid program, and Vickery argues that the Vietnamese and the PRK did the best they could under the circumstances.

7. Vickery, *Cambodia 1975–1982*, p. 225. See also Chanthou Boua, "Observations of the Heng Samrin Government," in David P. Chandler and Ben Kiernan (eds.), *Revolution and Its Aftermath in Kampuchea: Eight Essays* (New Haven, 1983), pp. 259–290, and Ben Kiernan, "Kampuchea Struggles to Its Feet," in Ben Kiernan and Chanthou Boua (eds.), *Peasants and Politics in Kampuchea, 1942–1981* (London, 1982), pp. 363–385.

8. See Burchett, *The China-Cambodia-Vietnam Triangle*. Even the lawyer named by the court to defend Ieng Sary and Pol Pot called them "criminally insane monsters" and requested that they be condemned to death; see Vietnam Courier (ed.), *Kampuchea Dossier III: The Dark Years* (Hanoi, 1979), p. 212.

9. See Eva Mysliwiec's eloquent study, *Punishing the Poor: The International Isolation of Kampuchea* (Oxford, 1988).

10. See Michael Vickery, "Democratic Kampuchea: CIA to the Rescue," BCAS, Vol. 14, No. 4 (1982):42–54. The most recent attempt to assess the number of deaths under DK is P. Heuveline, "'Between One and Three Million': Towards the Demographic Reconstruction of a Decade of Cambodian History (1970–1979)," *Population Studies*, Vol. 52 (1998):49–65.

11. See Vickery, *Kampuchea*, pp. 111–113, and Timothy Carmey, "Kampuchea in 1981," *Asian Survey*, Vol. 22, No. 1 (January 1982):78–87. In the 1981 elections, the number of candidates only slightly exceeded the number of seats in the Assembly, and voters were asked to cross out the name on each slate of candidates as unsatisfactory. In all cases, the electorate "voted" overwhelmingly against the names that appeared at the bottom of each respective list. The tradition of rigged

elections, of course, extended back into the 1950s. No exact estimate of Vietnamese civilians in Cambodia has been made, but most observers agree that the number stabilized in the late 1980s around three hundred thousand, roughly similar to the size of the Vietnamese minority in Cambodia before 1970.

12. Chinese aid to the DK faction has been estimated at approximately $30 million per year, but no figures have ever been published.

13. For a hostile treatment of the PRK by a French aid worker, see L. Luccioli, *Le Mur de bambou* (Paris, 1988). For a more nuanced assessment, see Viviane Frings, *Le Paysan cambodgien et le socialisme: La Politique agricole de la Republique Populaire du Kampuchea et de l'Etat du Cambodge* (Paris, 1997). Frings's "Rewriting Cambodian History to 'Adapt' It to a New Political Context: The KPRP's Historiography," *Modern Asian Studies* (1997):807–846, is also useful.

14. For a helpful series of articles about Cambodia in 1990, see the Spring 1990 special issue of *Cultural Survival*. See also May Ebihara, Carol Mortland, and Judy Ledgerwood (eds.), *Cambodian Culture Since 1975: Homeland and Exile* (Ithaca, N.Y., 1994), and Toni Samantha Phim and Ashley Thompson, *Cambodian Dance* (New York, 1999).

15. On the UNTAC period in Cambodia, see Peter Bartu, "The 'Fifth Faction': The United Nations Intervention in Cambodia 1991–1993" (Ph.D. dissertation, Monash University, 1998); Michael Doyle et al. (eds.), *Keeping the Peace: Multi-Dimensional UN Operations in Cambodia and El Salvador* (Cambridge, 1997); Trevor Findlay, *Cambodia: The Legacy and Lessons of UNTAC* (New York, 1995); and Steve Heder and Judy Ledgerwood (eds.), *Propaganda, Politics, and Violence in Cambodia in the UNTAC Period* (Armonk, N.Y., 1996). For a valuable collection of essays on the post-UNTAC period, see Frederick Z. Brown and David G. Timberman (eds.), *Cambodia and the International Community: The Quest for Peace, Development and Democracy* (Singapore, 1998). See also Grant Curtis, *Cambodia Reborn?* (Washington, D.C., 1998).

Bibliographic Essay

Readers competent to read Thai, Cambodian, and Vietnamese sources are directed to the appropriate footnote references in the text. This brief essay will try to select and evaluate a few major primary and secondary sources for Cambodian history available in French and English. A reading knowledge of French is helpful for people interested in Cambodian history before 1954.

GENERAL WORKS

The best bibliographic introduction to Cambodia is Helen Jarvis, *Cambodia* (Santa Barbara, Calif., 1997), which provides astute commentary to its numerous citations. See also John Marston (comp.), *An Annotated Bibliography of Cambodia and Cambodian Refugees* (Minneapolis, 1987), and Charles R. Keyes's useful *Southeast Asian Research Tools: Cambodia* (Honolulu, 1979). Another helpful compilation is Russell R. Ross (ed.), *Cambodia: A Country Study* (Washington, D.C., 1990). For a brief, masterly reading of Cambodian history from a Marxist perspective, see Michael Vickery, "Cambodia (Kampuchea): History, Tragedy, and an Uncertain Future," *Bulletin of Concerned Asian Scholars*, Vol. 21, Nos. 2–4 (April–December 1989):35–58.

An early attempt to synthesize Cambodian history, relying heavily on chronicle histories, is Adhémard Leclère's *Histoire du Cambodge* (Paris, 1914; repr. 1975). Unfortunately, Leclère is cavalier in his use of sources and is difficult to verify. Martin Herz wrote *A Short History of Cambodia* (New York and London, 1958) after serving in Phnom Penh as a U.S. Foreign Service officer; the chapters on the 1940s and 1950s are better than those dealing with earlier times. A more recent synthesis, emphasizing early history, is Ian Mabbett and David Chandler, *The Khmers* (Oxford, 1995). David Chandler, *Facing the Cambodian Past: Selected Essays 1971–1994* (Chiangmai and Sydney, 1996), is a collection of essays about Cambodia, largely historical in nature. The best brief synthesis of Cambodian culture in a historical framework is still Solange Thierry's *Les Khmers* (Paris, 1964).

There are no serious studies of Cambodian urban life. Those that examine rural conditions are dominated by Jean Delvert's magisterial *Le Paysan cambodgien* (Paris and the Hague, 1961). The most thorough examination of folk beliefs and rituals in Cambodia is still E. Porée-Maspero's three-volume study, *Etude sur les rites agraires des cambodgiens* (Paris and the Hague, 1962–1969). See also Ang Choulean, *Les Etres surnaturels dans la religion populaire khmère* (Paris, 1986), and Alain Forest, *Le Culte des génies protecteurs au Cambodge* (Paris, 1992). Two good monographic studies of village life are May Ebihara, *Svay* (Ann Arbor, Mich.,

1971), and G. Martel, *Lovea* (Paris, 1975). See also Marie-A. Martin, *Les Khmer daoeum "khmers d'origine"* (Paris, 1997), a study of the Porr minority. On Cambodian Buddhism, see François Bizot, *Le Figuier a cinq branches: Recherche sur le bouddhisme khmer* (Paris, 1976). The Sihanouk-era economy is ably discussed in Rémy Prud'homme, *L'Economie du Cambodge* (Paris, 1969), and A. Migozzi approaches demographic issues in his perceptive monograph, *Cambodge: Faits et problèmes de population* (Paris, 1973). Both studies were overtaken by the catastrophe of the 1970s.

FROM PREHISTORY TO THE DECLINE OF ANGKOR

Work on prehistory is not as advanced in Cambodia as in Vietnam and Thailand. The best introduction to the subject is Donn Bayard, "The Roots of Indo-Chinese Civilization," *Pacific Affairs*, Vol. 53, No. 1 (Spring 1980):89–114. See also C. Mourer and R. Mourer, "Prehistoric Research in Cambodia During the Last Ten Years," *Asian Perspectives*, Vol. 14 (1971):35–42. For more recent developments, see Miriam T. Stark, "The Transition to History in the Mekong Delta: A View from Cambodia," *International Journal of Historical Anthropology*, Vol. 2, No. 3 (1998):175–203, which discusses ongoing excavations at Angkor Borei in southwestern Cambodia, and *Asian Perspectives* (Summer 1999), a special issue devoted to Angkor Borei. For a synthesizing account, see Charles Higham, *The Archaeology of Mainland Southeast Asia* (Cambridge, 1989). See also Peter Bellwood, "Southeast Asia Before History," in *The Cambridge History of Southeast Asia*, edited by Nicholas Tarling (Cambridge, 1992), pp. 55–136.

The historiography of the pre-Angkorean period has been revolutionized by Michael Vickery's pioneering study, *Society, Economics, and Politics in Pre-Angkor Cambodia: The 7th–8th Centuries* (Tokyo, 1998), the fruit of over twenty years of research on Khmer-language inscriptions. See also Claude Jacques, "Le Pays khmer avant Angkor," *Journal des savants* (January–September 1986):59–83. Fortunately for English readers, L. P. Briggs, *The Ancient Khmer Empire* (Philadelphia, 1951), and Christopher Pym's stylistically more accessible *The Ancient Civilization of Angkor* (New York, 1968) are both excellent, although their work on the pre-Angkorean period has been overtaken by Vickery's study. See also the English-language version of G. Coedes, *Angkor* (London, 1962).

A masterly overview is G. Coedes, *The Indianized States of Southeast Asia* (Honolulu, 1975), while a readable synthesis of writing on the period can be found in Ian Mabbett and David Chandler, *The Khmers* (Oxford, 1995), pp. 78–218. Students wishing to examine Cambodian inscriptions may consult A. Barth and A. Bergaigne, *Inscriptions sanscrites du Cambodge*, 2 vols. (Paris 1885, 1893), and G. Coedes, *Les Inscriptions du Cambodge*, 8 vols. (Hanoi and Paris, 1937–1966). The eighth volume of Coedes's compilation is an index of the entire corpus. See also Coedes's *Articles sur le pays khmer*, 2 vols. (Paris, 1989, 1992); P. N. Jenner, *A Chronological Inventory of the Inscriptions of Cambodia* (Honolulu, 1980); P. N. Jenner, *A Chrestomathy of Pre-Angkorean Khmer*, 3 vols. (Honolulu, 1980); and Michael Vickery, "The Khmer Inscriptions of Roluos (Preah Ko and Lolei)," *Seksa Khmer*, nouvelle séries (January 1999):47–92. Many inscriptions have been translated into French over the years in the *Bulletin de L'Ecole Française d'Extrême Orient* (1900–).

The *Bulletin* also contains important studies of classical Cambodia; many of these are cited in the notes to Chapters 2 and 3 of the present volume.

Monographic studies of Angkorean culture and institutions include S. Sahai, *Les Institutions politiques et l'organisation administrative du Cambodge ancien* (Paris, 1970); Jean Boisselier, *Le Cambodge* (Paris, 1966), an archaeological handbook; and B. P. Groslier and Jacques Arthaud, *Angkor: Art and Civilization* (New York, 1966). See also Bruno Dagens, *Angkor: La Forêt de pierre* (Paris, 1989), which traces the role of Angkor in later history, and Claude Jacques, *Angkor* (Paris, 1990), a beautifully illustrated text that reflects recent research and is probably the most authoritative introduction to Angkor. Travelers to Cambodia are urged to consult Dawn Rooney, *Angkor: An Introduction to the Temples* (Bangkok, 1997), as well as Helen Ibbetson Jessup and Thierry Zephir (eds.), *Sculpture of Angkor and Ancient Cambodia: Millennium of Glory* (New York, 1997), which is the catalogue for a stunning 1997 exhibition of Khmer art.

Two important studies of kingship and its relation to religion at Angkor are H. Kulke, *The Devaraja Cult* (Ithaca, N.Y., 1978), and Ian Mabbett, "Kingship in Angkor," *Journal of the Siam Society*, Vol. 66, No. 2 (July 1978):1–58. Another stimulating study is Eleanor Moron [now Eleanor Mannika], "Configuration of Time and Space at Angkor Wat," *Studies in Indo-Asian Art and Culture*, No. 5 (1977):217–267. For a more detailed argument, see Eleanor Mannika, *Angkor Wat: Time, Space, and Kingship* (Honolulu, 1996).

The most detailed study of the reign of Jayavarman VII is B. P. Groslier, *Les Inscriptions du Bayon* (Paris, 1973), which has a good bibliography. Students should also consult Phillipe Stern, *Les Monuments khmers du style du Bayon et Jayavarman VII* (Paris, 1965). The best introduction to everyday life at Angkor is Chou Takuan [now Zhou Daguan], *The Customs of Cambodia*, trans. J. Paul (Bangkok, 1990).

CAMBODIA AFTER ANGKOR

The so-called middle period of Cambodian history has not yet been studied in much detail, although it is ripe for reassessment. For a stimulating essay in this direction, see Claude Jacques, "Les Derniers siècles d'Angkor," *Comptes Rendus de l'Académie des Inscriptions et Belles-Lettres* (in press), which extends the life span of "Angkor" well into the fifteenth century, and Ashley Thompson (who prefers the terms "middle Cambodia" and "early modern Cambodia" to "post-Angkor Cambodia"), "Changing Perspectives: Cambodia After Angkor," in Jessup and Zephir, *Sculpture of Angkor*, pp. 22–33, and "Between the Lines: Writing Histories of Middle Cambodia" (in press), drawn from her unpublished doctoral dissertation, "Mémoires du Cambodge" (University of Paris VIII, 1999). One explanation for the previous neglect of this important period is that the Cambodian chronicle texts are so unreliable, as Michael Vickery has shown in his *Cambodia After Angkor: The Chronicular Evidence for the Fourteenth to Sixteenth Centuries* (Ann Arbor, Mich., 1977). Vickery's last chapter is a valiant attempt to make sense of the period as a whole. For the sixteenth century, B. P. Groslier, *Angkor et le Cambodge au XVIe siècle d'après les sources portugaises et espagnoles* (Paris, 1958), is helpful. Inscriptions from Angkor from the sixteenth century to the eighteenth have been ably edited by Saveros Pou in *Bulletin de l'Ecole Française d'Extrême Orient*,

Vol. 59 (1972) and Vol. 62 (1975); see also Pou, "Les Inscriptions modernes d'Angkor," *Journal Asiatique,* Vol. 260 (1972). In addition, Dr. Pou has edited and translated the *chef d'oeuvre* of classical Cambodian literature, the *Reamker,* 3 vols. (Paris, 1977–1979). See also François Martini (trans.), *La Gloire de Rama: Ramakerti* (Paris, 1978); Judith Jacob (trans.), *Reamker* (London, 1987); and J. Jacob, *The Traditional Literature of Cambodia* (Oxford, 1996). For an analysis of post-Angkorean artistic styles, see M. Giteau, *L'Iconographie du Cambodge post-Angkoréen* (Paris, 1975). See also Anthony Reid, *Southeast Asia in the Age of Commerce,* 2 vols. (New Haven, 1988, 1994); May Ebihara, "Societal Organization in Sixteenth and Seventeenth Century Cambodia," *Journal of Southeast Asian Studies,* Vol. 15, No. 2 (September 1984):280–295; Khin Sok (ed. and trans.), *Chroniques royales du Cambodge: De Bana Yat à la prise de Lanvek* (Paris, 1988); and Mak Phoeun (ed. and trans.), *Chroniques royales du Cambodge (de 1594 à 1677)* (Paris, 1981), pp. 179–208. On Europeans in Cambodia in the sixteenth and seventeenth centuries, see Jean-Claude Lejosne, "Historiographie du Cambodge aux XVIe et XVIIe siècles," in Pierre L. Lamant (ed.), *Bilan et perspectives des études khmères (Langue et Culture)* (Paris, 1997); and for a narrative history using Cambodian chronicle sources, see Mak Phoeun, *Histoire du Cambodge de la fin du XVIe siècle au debut du XVIIe* (Paris, 1995).

The eighteenth century in Cambodia has not yet been seriously studied, but it should be, as chronicle histories for this period appear to be factually reliable and can be checked against the comparatively voluminous Thai and Vietnamese sources.

For the first half of the nineteenth century, see David P. Chandler, *Cambodia Before the French: Politics in a Tributary Kingdom, 1794–1847* (Ann Arbor, Mich., 1974), and Khin Sok, *Le Cambodge entre le Siam et le Vietnam (de 1775 à 1860)* (Paris, 1991).

THE FRENCH PROTECTORATE, 1863–1954

For the early colonial period, G. Taboulet (ed.), *La Geste française en Indochine,* 2 vols. (Paris, 1955), is useful, and so is Milton Osborne's pioneering study, *The French Presence in Cochinchina and Cambodia: Rule and Response (1859–1905)* (Ithaca, N.Y., 1969). The early twentieth century is intelligently treated in Alain Forest, *Le Cambodge et la colonisation française: Histoire d'une colonisation sans heurts (1897–1920)* (Paris, 1980), and John Tully, *Cambodia Under the Tricolour: The Sisowath Years, 1904–1927* (Clayton, Australia, 1996). Robert Ollivier, "Le Protectorat français au Cambodge" (Ph.D. dissertation, University of Paris, 1969), is useful for the period 1940–1953; so is Philippe Preschez's monograph, *Essai sur la démocratie au Cambodge* (Paris, 1961), which is especially good on the proliferation of political parties in Cambodia after World War II. See also V. M. Reddi, *A History of the Cambodian Independence Movement 1863–1955* (Tirupati, 1971). Milton Osborne, *Politics and Power in Cambodia* (Hawthorn, Australia, 1973), also contains a good summary of politics in this period. Penny Edwards, "The Cultivation of 'Cambodge'" (Ph.D. dissertation, Monash University, 1999), is a masterly analysis of the colonial period from a sensible postmodernist perspective. For an analysis of politics in the closing years of the colonial era, see David P. Chandler, *The Tragedy of Cambodian History: Politics, War, and Revolution Since 1945* (New Haven, 1991), chs. 1 and 2.

For details on the early phases of Cambodian radicalism, see Wilfred Burchett, *Mekong Upstream* (Berlin, 1959); Ben Kiernan, *How Pol Pot Came to Power* (London, 1984); Charles Meyer, *Derrière le sourire khmer* (Paris, 1971); and J. C. Pomonti and Serge Thion, *Des courtesans aux partisans: La Crise cambodgienne* (Paris, 1971). Ben Kiernan and Chanthou Boua (eds.), *Peasants and Politics in Kampuchea, 1942–1981* (London, 1982), contains much valuable primary material, some of it translated for the first time from Khmer. For a discussion of decolonization in Cambodia, see Donald Lancaster, *The Emancipation of French Indo-China* (New York, 1961). Norodom Sihanouk's memoirs, *L'Indochine vue de Pékin* (Paris, 1972) and *Souvenirs doux et amers* (Paris, 1981), may be used with caution by historians of the period.

CAMBODIAN HISTORY, 1955–1975

For an overview of events in this period, see David P. Chandler, *The Tragedy of Cambodian History: Politics, War, and Revolution Since 1945* (New Haven, 1991), chs. 3 through 6. Ben Kiernan's *How Pol Pot Came to Power* (London, 1984) is a pathbreaking history of Cambodian radicalism up to 1975. See also Ben Kiernan and Chanthou Boua (eds.), *Peasants and Politics in Kampuchea, 1942–1981* (London, 1982). Once again, Sihanouk's own memoirs, *Souvenirs doux et amers* (Paris, 1981), should be used with caution. See also Milton Osborne's insightful *Politics and Power in Cambodia* (Hawthorn, Australia, 1973) and his *Before Kampuchea* (London, 1979). Osborne's biography of Sihanouk, *Sihanouk: Prince of Light, Prince of Darkness* (Honolulu, 1994), is perceptive but somewhat less thorough than his earlier books. For a relatively hostile treatment of the Sihanouk era that has stood up well, see Charles Meyer, *Derrière le sourire khmer* (Paris, 1971). William Shawcross, *Sideshow: Nixon, Kissinger, and the Destruction of Cambodia* (New York, 1979), is a withering attack on U.S. policies toward Cambodia in the Lon Nol era. The best political history of the period is Justin Corfield, *Khmers Stand Up!* (Clayton, Australia, 1994). See also Ros Chantrabot, *La République Khmer et l'Asie du Sud-Est après son écroulement* (Paris, 1993) and Henry Kamm, *Cambodia: Report from a Stricken Land* (New York, 1998), a useful survey of events since 1970 by a seasoned journalist. For military aspects of the early 1970s, see Sak Sutsakhan, *The Khmer Republic at War and the Final Collapse* (Washington, D.C., 1980). And for an insightful history of Cambodian-Vietnamese Communist relations, see Thomas Engelbert and Christopher Goscha, *Falling Out of Touch: A Study of Vietnamese Communist Policy Toward an Emerging Cambodian Communist Movement, 1930–1975* (Clayton, Australia, 1995).

THE POL POT ERA AND BEYOND

There are many readable accounts of the Pol Pot era, some written by survivors. An early analysis of the revolution, and still one of the best, is François Ponchaud, *Cambodia Year Zero* (New York, 1978). Two fine-grained studies are Michael Vickery's *Cambodia 1975–1982* (Boston, 1983) and R. A. Burgler, *The Eyes of the Pineapple: Revolutionary Intellectuals and Terror in Democratic Kampuchea* (Saarbrücken, 1990). Elizabeth Becker, *When the War Was Over* (New York, 1986), reviews the Pol Pot era perceptively, and two useful collections of essays on the period are David P. Chandler and Ben Kiernan (eds.), *Revolution and Its Aftermath in Kampuchea: Eight Essays* (New Haven, 1983), and Karl Jackson (ed.), *Cambodia 1975–1978: Rendezvous with Death* (Princeton, N.J., 1989). David Chandler, Ben Kiernan, and Chantou Boua (eds. and trans.), *Pol Pot Plans the Future: Confidential Leadership Documents from Democratic Kampuchea 1976–1977* (New Haven, 1988), is a useful compilation, and David Chandler, *Voices from S-21: Terror and History in Pol Pot's Secret Prison* (Berkeley, 1999), is a study of a key Khmer Rouge facility, benefiting from DK archives. For an interesting anthropological perspective on this period, see Alexander Hinton, "Cambodia's Shadow: An Examination of the Cultural Origins of Genocide" (Ph.D. dissertation, Emory University, 1997). For a powerful collection of essays written over twenty years, see Serge Thion, *Watching Cambodia* (Bangkok, 1993). The demography of the Cambodian genocide is dealt with in Marek Sliwinski, *Une analyse démographique du génocide des khmers rouges* (Paris, 1995). See also Patrick Heuveline, "'Between One and Three Million': Towards the Demographic Reconstruction of a Decade of Cambodian History (1970–1979)," *Population Studies*, Vol. 52 (1998):49–65. An often insightful study hostile to the PRK is Marie Martin, *Cambodia: A Shattered Society* (Berkeley, Calif., 1994). The best survivors' accounts are Pin Yathay, *L'Utopie meurtrière* (Paris, 1980); Someth May, *Cambodian Witness* (London, 1986); and Ung Bunheang and Martin Stuart Fox, *The Murderous Revolution* (Sydney, 1984). See also Henri Locard and Moeung Sonn, *Prisonnier de l'Angkar* (Paris, 1993), and Henri Locard, *Le "Petit livre rouge" de Pol Pot ou les paroles d'Angkar* (Paris, 1996), a collection of Khmer Rouge sayings. Laurence Picq's vivid memoir, *Beyond the Horizon* (New York, 1989), recounts the experiences of a Frenchwoman who was married to a DK official and worked in the DK Ministry of Foreign Affairs. This period is approached from a biographical angle in David Chandler, *Brother Number One: A Political Biography of Pol Pot*, 2d ed. (Boulder, Colo., 1999). Ben Kiernan's study of the regime, *The Pol Pot Regime: Politics, Race, and Genocide Under the Khmer Rouge* (New Haven, 1995), is based to a large extent on oral evidence gathered in the 1980s. Material now being collected by the Cambodian Genocide Program, sponsored by Yale University and the U.S. Department of State and housed in the Documentation Center–Cambodia in Phnom Penh, should prove invaluable for anyone interested in the DK period.

For events since 1979, see Grant Evans and Kelvin Rowley, *Red Brotherhood at War* (London, 1984; rev. ed., 1990); Nayan Chanda, *Brother Enemy* (New York, 1986); and William Shawcross, *The Quality of Mercy* (New York, 1984), which concentrates on the international response to the collapse of Democratic Kampuchea. Michael Vickery's *Kampuchea* (London, 1986) is the only scholarly overview so far of the PRK/SOC regime, but Evan Gottesman's work in progress should provide a much-needed analytical account. See also Viviane Frings, *Le Paysan cambodgien et le socialisme: La Politique agricole de la République Populaire du Kampuchea et l'Etat du Cambodge* (Paris, 1997). Martin Wright (ed.), *Cambodia: A Matter of Survival* (London, 1989), is a useful survey. See also Eva Mysliwiec, *Punishing the Poor: The International Isolation of Kampuchea* (Oxford, 1988); Robert J. Muscat and Jonathan Stromseth, *Cambodia: Post-Settlement Reconstruction and Development* (New York, 1989); Grant Curtis, *Cambodia Reborn?* (Washington, D.C., 1998), which deals with the UNTAC and post-UNTAC periods; and David Ablin and Marlowe Hood (eds.), *The Cambodian Agony* (Armonk, N.Y., 1988), a helpful collection of essays. Some worthwhile recent collections include Ben Kiernan (ed.), *Genocide and Democracy in Cambodia: The Khmer Rouge, the United Nations, and the International Community* (New Haven, 1993); Christian Lechervy and Richard Petris (eds.), *Les Cambodgiens face à eux-mêmes* (Paris, 1993); Steve Heder and Judy Ledgerwood (eds.), *Politics, Violence, and Propaganda in Cambodia in the UNTAC Period* (Armonk, N.Y., 1996); and Frederick Z. Brown and David G. Timberman (eds.), *Cambodia and the International Community* (Singapore, 1998). See also Raoul Jennar, *Chroniques cambodgiennes, 1990–1994* (Paris, 1995), and Patrick Raszelenberg and Peter Schier, *The Cambodia Conflict: Search for a Settlement, 1979–1991. An Analytical Chronology* (Hamburg, 1995).

Two more valuable studies of the UNTAC period are Michael W. Doyle, *UN Peacekeeping in Cambodia: UNTAC's Civil Mandate* (Boulder, Colo., 1995), and Trevor Findlay, *Cambodia: The Legacy and Lessons of UNTAC* (Oxford, 1995), which has a useful documentary appendix. See also Peter Bartu, "The 'Fifth Faction': The United Nations Intervention in Cambodia 1991–1993" (Ph.D. dissertation, Monash University, 1998).

On cultural matters in recent years, see May Ebihara, Judy Ledgerwood, and Carol Mortland (eds.), *Cambodian Culture Since 1975: Homeland and Exile* (Ithaca, N.Y., 1994); Ashley Thompson, "O Cambodia! Poems from the Border," *New Literary History*, Vol. 24, No. 3 (Summer 1993):519–544; and Toni Shapiro, *Dance and the Spirit of Cambodia* (Ann Arbor, Mich., 1994). See also Toni Samantha Phim and Ashley Thompson, *Cambodian Dance* (New York, 1999). Finally, Cambodian literature throughout history is treated in detail in Khing Hoc Dy, *Contribution à l'histoire de la littérature khmère*, 2 vols. (Paris, 1990, 1993).

Index